A GUIDE
TO PROSE FICTION
IN THE *TATLER*
AND THE *SPECTATOR*

GARLAND REFERENCE LIBRARY
OF THE HUMANITIES
(VOL. 71)

A GUIDE
TO PROSE FICTION
IN THE *TATLER*
AND THE *SPECTATOR*

James E. Evans
University of North Carolina at Greensboro

John N. Wall, Jr.
North Carolina State University, Raleigh

GARLAND PUBLISHING, INC. • NEW YORK & LONDON
1977

Library of Congress Cataloging in Publication Data

Evans, James E.
A guide to prose fiction in The Tatler and The Spectator.

(Garland reference library of the humanities; v. 71)

Bibliography: p.

Includes indexes.

1. English fiction—18th century—Bibliography—Catalogs.
2. The Tatler (London, 1709-11)—Indexes.   3. The Spectator
(London, 1711-14)—Indexes.   I. Wall, John N., joint
author.   II. Title.
Z2014.F5E93   [PR851]   016.823'5   76-24751
ISBN 0-8240-9926-5

PRINTED IN THE UNITED STATES OF AMERICA

CONTENTS

ACKNOWLEDGEMENTS

While preparing this guide the authors have become indebted to numbers of people whose gracious assistance and support have made possible its completion. We are thankful for the assistance of the librarians and staff of the D. H. Hill Library at North Carolina State University and the Walter C. Jackson Library of the University of North Carolina at Greensboro in locating items for the bibliography and in making available materials for the catalogue. We are grateful to the Department of English at North Carolina State University for providing funds to prepare the manuscript, and to Su Brooks and Charlene Turner for typing it in all of its various forms.

We are especially grateful to a series of students of England in the eighteenth century who, over the years, have guided the authors in this and other endeavors but chiefly have exemplified the best of our inheritance from that period in their generosity, courtesy, support, and enthusiasm. To Lodwick Hartley of North Carolina State University who supported this project with his continued interest, to Benjamin Boyce of Duke University who read this work in an earlier form and provided generous commentary, to Maurice Johnson of the University of Pennsylvania who offered insight and encouragement in the study of eighteenth-century fiction, and especially to Albrecht B. Strauss of the University of North Carolina at Chapel Hill who is more responsible than anyone else for the authors being in this profession, go our undying gratitude and appreciation. We must also thank Donald F. Bond, an editor for all time, for sharing generously with us his conclusions as to the authorship of numerous *Tatler* papers; the counsel was his, but we must take full responsibility for the actual opinions expressed in this catalogue.

Most of all, we must thank our wives and families, who have shared us with Joseph Addison and Richard Steele out of all reasonable compass, and now, we hope, will have us back. Let Mr. Spectator speak for us both:

> A Marriage of Love is pleasant; a Marriage of Interest easie; and a Marriage, where both meet, happy. A happy Marriage has in it all the Pleasures of Friendship, all the Enjoyments of Sense and Reason, and, indeed, all the Sweets of Life. Nothing is a greater Mark of a degenerate and vitious Age, than the common Ridicule which passes on this State of Life. It is, indeed, only happy in those who can look down with Scorn or Neglect on the Impieties of the Times, and tread the Paths of Life together in a constant uniform Course of Virtue.

INTRODUCTION

The *Tatler* and the *Spectator* abound with fiction.
The statement seems so obvious that one can scarcely believe the scant attention given to the miscellany of
anecdotes, sketches, tales, fables, and allegories in
these two pre-eminent periodicals of the English Augustan
age. Benjamin Boyce expresses surprise that "In view of
the fame and quality of *The Tatler* and *The Spectator* . . .
there is in print no scholarly, inclusive discussion of
the large quantity of fiction in these two delightful
publications."[1] Although two recent books have lessened
this oversight, the fictional riches of the two periodicals have yet to be fully explored. Richmond P. Bond in
The Tatler: The Making of a Literary Journal assesses the
personae and forms of the *Tatler* fiction and speculates
that "the whole *Tatler* is a grand fiction, the greatest
prose fiction of 1709-1710."[2] Donald Kay in *Short Fiction
in* The Spectator isolates one hundred pieces of fiction,
though he acknowledges much more: "By scattering innumer-
able illustrative anecdotes throughout the *Spectator*,
many so brief that they defy listing or naming as individual narratives, the authors continually emphasize the
fact that Mr. Spectator—preacher, critic, philosopher,
observer, and pedant—is first and last a story teller."[3]
These studies enable us to sample the fictional cornuco-
pia; yet the fictionality of these journals extends
beyond the bounds of types like the character or the
oriental tale because a fictional presence filters almost
every narrative, whether it be Isaac Bickerstaff, Mr.
Spectator, one of their friends or relatives, or the many
correspondents whose accounts permeate the *Tatler* and the
Spectator. "Indeed," as Henry Seidel Canby remarked many

9

years ago, "it is astonishing to learn by investigation
how much pure narrative they contain."[4]

A Guide to Prose Fiction in the Tatler and the
Spectator offers a more comprehensive analysis of the
abundant fiction in these periodicals. In this introductory essay we describe Bickerstaff and Mr. Spectator,
their positions as narrators and their fictional societies; we then evaluate the forms of this fiction. We
document its variety, extent, and artistry in catalogues
which list and detail briefly each issue of the Tatler
and the Spectator. We also index the contents of the
periodicals with a focus on characters, authors, narrative techniques, and recurrent topics in the fiction. We
conclude with an annotated bibliography of relevant
secondary sources. The parts of this Guide, considered together, confirm the pervasive and significant
place of fiction in the Tatler and the Spectator.

I.

Spectator no. 11 illustrates the uses of fiction in
these periodicals. The framework of the issue is a visit
by Mr. Spectator to Arietta's assembly, where she argues
with a male "Common-Place Talker" about constancy in love.
Mr. Spectator gives brief sketches of Arietta and the
Talker and reports that each tells a tale. In response
to the latter's "celebrated Story of the Ephesian Matron"
from the Satyricon (which portrays women unfavorably and
which Mr. Spectator does not, for rhetorical reasons,
reproduce) Arietta tells AEsop's brief "Fable of the Lion
and the Man," which implies that a female portrayal of
women would be very different; then she presents "the
History of Inkle and Yarico," the story of a virtuous
Indian maiden betrayed by a selfish Englishman. Mr.
Spectator indirectly praises Arietta through his tearful
response to the tale. This one issue thus contains character sketches, a fable, a story within the larger fiction of the persona, his club (Will Honeycomb provides

the necessary introduction to this assembly), and his new
acquaintances. Since both Mr. Spectator and Arietta serve
as narrators, the point of view is diversified. And, as
usual in the *Spectator*, the didactic point is clear--the
vindication of female integrity against libertine attacks.
Though the story of Inkle and Yarico has often been discussed separately, it is carefully enmeshed in a much
broader fictional matrix. Both the *Tatler* and the *Spectator* use fiction in this integral manner, seldom telling
stories for entertainment alone, seldom presenting fiction without a clear, usually fictional, context for it.
The peregrinations of Bickerstaff and Mr. Spectator, the
intrusions of the former's family and the latter's club,
the incessant tale-telling of the personae's acquaintances, new and old (often readers sending their epistles),
are all prominent features of these two journals.

The *Tatler* ran for 271 issues from April 12, 1709
until January 2, 1711; the *Spectator*, for 555 issues from
March 1, 1711 until December 6, 1712 and again, for 80
issues from June 18, 1714 until December 20, 1714.[5] For
these years at the end of Queen Anne's reign, primarily
under the editorship of Richard Steele and Joseph Addison,
the *Tatler* and the *Spectator* provided England with a kind
of laboratory for fictional points of view, characters,
and forms which influenced the development of short fiction and the novel during the subsequent century. Though
the *Tatler* began partly as a rival to other newspapers,
the first issue established the role of fiction in the
journal with the emergence of Isaac Bickerstaff as the
fictional commentator on the London scene and the first
installment of a serialized romance about a young gentleman, later called Cynthio. In early issues Steele discovered, too, the value of fiction for interpreting the
news, as we see in the allegory of Felicia (*T* 4e) and the
dream of a hero's death (*T* 8c). While news gradually
disappeared as a feature of the *Tatler*, the indirection

of fiction became the predominant means to evaluate people and events as well as manners and morals.[6] Even the
Tatler's most partisan essays use satiric fictions, such
as the puppet show of Martin Powell of Bath (*T* 44b) and
a letter supposedly from J. Downes, a theatrical prompter
(*T* 193), to attack a Bishop and a minister of state,
respectively. Although news and party propaganda were
never part of the *Spectator*, fiction also flourished
there. If we except the news items, theater and literary
criticism, and essays on philosophy or religion presented
with no effort to characterize the persona, we find that
more than four-fifths of the issues of the *Tatler* and the
Spectator contain some kind of fiction. Within a spectrum of narratives--from non-fiction, news,presenting
accounts of real events, to tales and sketches representing the life of the gentry and middle class, to fables
and allegories illustrating political, moral, and religious ideas--most issues use fiction in a significant way.

Historically, this achievement was important, for,
as Robert D. Mayo notes, Steele and Addison made fiction
"palatable" to many readers who objected on the basis of
principle;[7] much as Defoe and even Bunyan had to ration-
alize their narratives to a middle-class, puritan audience, wary of idle literature. The *Tatler* and the *Spectator* criticized fashionable kinds of fiction, like
French romances and scandal novels, while they printed
more acceptably moral fiction.[8] In nomenclature, the
editors avoided the terms "novel" and "romance," prefer-
ring to designate a piece of fiction primarily as a
"story," an "account," or a "history," less often as a
"narration," a "narrative," a "representation," or a
"relation," and even less frequently as a "tale," an
"illustration," or an "instance." While introducing the
story of Eudoxus and Leontine, Mr. Spectator utters this
characteristic statement: "This makes me often think on
a Story I have heard of two Friends, which I shall give

12

my Reader at large, under feigned Names. The Moral of it
may, I hope, be useful, though there are some Circumstances which make it rather appear like a Novel, than a
true Story" (*S* 123). The subtle depreciating phrase
"like a Novel" and the pretense to moralized truth recall
similar claims by Defoe, who, in the preface to *Robinson
Crusoe* calls his book "Account," "Story," and "just History of Fact" and expresses the hope that he will lead
"to the Instruction of others by this Example."[9] Steele
and Addison, too, interchange these terms. In the *Tatler*
Jenny Distaff believes that "history . . . written by a
woman" will be "an exact account of all false lovers"
(*T* 36a). Mr. Spectator proposes a pleasing "History of
the reigning Favourites" and speculates what he will do
in "such an Account" (*S* 156). A correspondent writes
him:

> The Account I have extracted from the Journal of
> this sleeping Worthy, as it has been faithfully
> kept by a Gentleman of *Lincoln's-Inn* who has
> undertaken to be his Historiographer. I have
> sent it to you, not only as it represents the
> Actions of *Nicholas Hart*, but as it seems a very
> natural Picture of the Life of many an honest
> *English* Gentleman, whose whole History very often
> consists of Yawning, Nodding, Stretching, Turning,
> Sleeping, Drinking, and the like extraordinary
> Particulars. (*S* 184)

Though the betrayal of Yarico by Inkle is designated a
"History," the merchant is called "the Hero of my Story"
(*S* 11). Pontignan's "Love-Adventure" is called both
"Story" and "Account" (*S* 90). Autobiographical narra-
tives from correspondents are labelled similarly; Thomas
Trusty sends "a short Account of my own Life" (*S* 96),
while Jeremy Lovemore presents the "History of my Life"
(*S* 596). Among non-human narrators, the shilling gives
an "account of his life and adventures" (*T* 249), but Pugg
the monkey supposedly provides his "History in Writing"
(*S* 343). Titled narratives include *"The History of
Orlando the Fair," "The History of Caelia,"* and the "first

13

Part of the History of the *Rival Mother*" (*T* 50a, 198;
S 91).

In his survey of such labels in prose fictional
titles between 1700 and 1739, William Harlin McBurney
concludes that most (including "history" and "account")
"were borrowed from purely factual types of publications
and used as authenticating devices to avoid the stigma of
'a meer Fiction, or Lye.'"[10] The term "story" in the
Tatler or the *Spectator* is often accompanied by circumstances adding credence to the narrated action. For example, "A very pleasant gentleman of my acquaintance"
tells Bickerstaff "a story of this kind of falsehood and
vanity in an author" (*T* 91). Mr. Spectator hears the
"very remarkable Story" of Constantia and Theodosius from
a French priest and finds the "very remarkable Story" of
Eginhart and Imma "recorded in an old Chronicle" (*S* 163,
181). Of the tragic events narrated by Octavia, Mr.
Spectator remarks:

> It is often said, after a Man has heard a Story
> with extraordinary Circumstances, it is a very
> good one if it be true: But as for the following
> Relation, I should be glad were I sure it were
> false. It is told with such Simplicity, and
> there are so many artless Touches of Distress in
> it, that I fear it comes too much from the Heart.
> (*S* 322)

The truth of the heart has an authenticity in the *Tatler*
and the *Spectator* equal to that provided by an acquaintance or document. In fact, the overall effect of these
labels is to suggest that, whether they are literally
true, the narratives are true to human experience and do
not falsify it like the romances which delude Sir Roger
de Coverley's friend, Leonora. Like Fielding thirty
years later in his first "History," Steele and Addison
saw themselves creating a kind of fiction superior to its
popular predecessors and rivals.

II

In our assessment of the fiction in the *Tatler* and
the *Spectator* we must turn first to Isaac Bickerstaff and
Mr. Spectator, the personae who lend coherence and credibility to the diverse materials of their periodicals. As
Richmond P. Bond points out, the *Tatler* was the first
socio-literary journal to use "in a subtle and substantial way the device of assumed author-editorship."[11] The
successful creation of a persona provides a voice that
merited readers' attention. Steele describes several advantages of such a mask in the last issue of the *Tatler*:

> I considered, that severity of manners was ab-
> solutely necessary to him who would censure
> others, and for that reason, and that only,
> chose to talk in a mask. I shall not carry my
> humility so far as to call my self a vicious man;
> but at the same time must confess, my life is at
> best but pardonable. And with no greater char-
> acter than this, a man would make but an indif-
> ferent progress in attacking prevailing and fash-
> ionable vices, which Mr. Bickerstaff has done
> with a freedom of spirit that would have lost
> both its beauty and efficacy, had it been pre-
> tended to by Mr. Steele. (*T* 271)

At the end of the *Spectator*'s first series he repeats
these claims on behalf of Mr. Spectator:

> It is much more difficult to converse with the
> World in a real than a personated Character.
> That might pass for Humour, in the *Spectator*,
> which would look like Arrogance in a Writer who
> sets his Name to his Work. The Fictitious Person
> might contemn those who disapproved him, and
> extoll his own Performances, without giving
> Offence. He might assume a mock-Authority; with-
> out being looked upon as vain and conceited.
> (*S* 555)

This aesthetic distance eased acceptance of the persona's
vision of human experience. And, while authenticating the
truth of his fictions, the persona also amused by being a
likeable eccentric whose reappearance three or six times
weekly evolved into an intimate relationship with his
reader. Though not fully rounded or consistent like

figures in novels, Bickerstaff and Mr. Spectator become
memorable characters. Occasionally Steele or Addison
seem to speak *in propria persona*, but we need only compare Bickerstaff and Mr. Spectator with Defoe's Mr. Review,
Swift's Examiner, Fielding's Hercules Vinegar, or Johnson's Rambler to appreciate how much more fully the personae are characterized in the *Tatler* and the *Spectator*.
The phrase "beauty and efficacy" in the quotation from
the *Tatler* suggests aptly the dual roles Bickerstaff and
Mr. Spectator assume--entertainers and instructors. Similar is the Spectator's aim "to make [readers'] Instruction agreeable, and their Diversion useful" (*S* 10).
Steele and Addison establish their moral authority by
using the device of a persona but artfully decrease the
distance between themselves and readers by using amiable
characters in the censorial and spectatorial chairs.

Steele derived Isaac Bickerstaff, of course, from
Swift's mock astrologer and reincarnated him "in the
character of an old man, a philosopher, a humourist, an
astrologer, and a censor" (*T* 271), roles cleverly designed
to balance teaching and delighting.[12] An old and learned
bachelor, a member of the Society for the Reformation of
Manners, Bickerstaff is sufficiently removed from fashionable London life to evaluate it without self-deception.
His modest lodgings in Sheer Lane and his small retinue
attest to Bickerstaff's moderation. His credo, expressed
in *Tatler* 111, convinces us of his gentlemanly demeanor.
For example, he resolves to avoid the faults of age: "As
I am an old man, I take particular care to avoid being
covetous, and telling long stories." Or the faults of
family pride: "As I am descended of the ancient family of
the Bickerstaffs, I never call a man of merit an upstart."
Or those of religion: "As a Protestant, I do not suffer
my zeal so far to transport me, as to name the Pope and
the devil together." The voice of good sense, attended
by humor, emerges from his amusing body--the oval,

16

spectacled face atop a tall, lean figure, supported by slender limbs. Though unmarried, he shows keen interest in the well-being of his family, especially of his half-sister and her husband. Gregarious, he frequents the prominent coffee houses of London and belongs to a club at the Trumpet. Despite some genial whims (such as his fencing lessons), Bickerstaff seems most effectively created to comment on the sociable animal under his consideration. The qualities of this good man provide an authoritative *ethos* for his position as Censor of Great Britain.

Bickerstaff is not present to the same degree in every paper attributed to him. Often he is involved in a narrative as a character, observing, participating, sometimes speaking; we get the immediacy of an eyewitness account in these issues. Often he presents fiction invented, heard, or read in which he is not personally involved but about which he may comment; in these narratives we encounter a more omniscient perspective with Bickerstaff in the role of the third-person narrator. On other occasions Bickerstaff is the recipient of letters on which he may or may not comment. In all three instances Bickerstaff usually provides some introductory or concluding remarks to point the moral. Once, following "THE HISTORY OF CAELIA" he devotes the next paper to problems arising from her dilemma (*T* 199). In a few issues Bickerstaff does not provide such guidance. But whether he directly states his attitude or implies it through his tone, Bickerstaff seldom leaves the reader in doubt what to think. Even in evaluating more open-ended fiction, the reader is so accustomed to the rhetoric of this narrator that there are few ambiguities.

Very early in the *Tatler* Steele involves Bickerstaff in the action of his narratives, sending him to visit Sappho and letting him witness the wedding party of his French tailor and Madame Depingle's maid (*T* 6a, 7b). His

17

involvement can be comic or serious. Steele presents
Bickerstaff's visits to the family of an old friend,
where he first finds domestic virtue but, then, on his
second arrival, sorrow accompanying the wife's death.
His joy in reporting his young godson's drumming and
learning (*T* 95) is replaced by the harshness of death:

> My heart was torn in pieces to see the husband
> on one side suppressing and keeping down the
> swellings of his grief, for fear of disturbing
> her in her last moments; and the wife even at
> than time concealing the pains she endured, for
> fear of increasing his affliction. She kept her
> eyes upon him for some moments after she grew
> speechless, and soon after closed them forever.
> In the moment of her departure my friend . . .
> gave a deep groan, and fell into a swoon by her
> bedside. (*T* 114)

Surely Bickerstaff's presence and his earlier participation in the family's happiness heighten the poignancy of
this description. Addison's portrayal of Bickerstaff
seldom involves such pathos and is usually witty. For
example, when Bickerstaff meets the pretentious poet Ned
Softly at Will's Coffee House, he deals expertly with a
foolish sonnet, offering criticism in the guise of faint
praise: "'Why,' says I, 'this is a little nosegay of con-
ceits, a very lump of salt" (*T* 163). The comic difficulties of Sir Harry Quickset and Sir Giles Wheelbarrow,
who march single file to a coffee house, are rendered
even more ridiculous when Bickerstaff "whips in" between
them (*T* 86a). Bickerstaff proves a flexible character
whose encounters with others, whether while being visited
at home, frequenting coffee houses, or presiding over the
Court of Honor, could be colored with humor or sentiment,
as the context demanded.

In the more limited role of tale-teller Bickerstaff
exemplifies his own observation that "as there is nothing
more ridiculous than an old trifling story-teller, so
there is nothing more venerable than one who has turned
his experience to the entertainment and advantage

of mankind" (*T* 132). Four titled tales show several variations in Bickerstaff's narrative technique. Both "*The History of Orlando the Fair*" (*T* 50a,51a) and "*Delamira resigns her Fan*" (*T* 52a) are presented without moral commentary, while "*The Civil Husband*" (*T* 53a) and "*Of the Government of Affection*" (*T* 54a) are explicitly exemplary. With less attention to "advantage" the stories of Orlando and Delamira offer more entertainment; yet we never doubt that Bickerstaff ridicules the proud lover or the powerful female weapon. One sentence in "*Orlando the Fair*" evidences the kind of clue that Bickerstaff provides: "Fortune being now propitious to the gay Orlando, he dressed, he spoke, he moved, as a man might be supposed to do in a nation of pigmies, and had an equal value for our approbation or dislike" (*T* 51a). The adjective "gay" and the analogy suggest the character's vanity, after the opening phrase hints at the impermanence of his felicity. In the first sentence of "*The Civil Husband*," on the other hand, Bickerstaff labels Osmyn "inconstant" and his wife Elmira "faithful." About halfway through their story he intrudes to generalize about the husband: "But such is man's unhappy condition, that though the weakness of the heart has a prevailing power over the strength of the head, yet the strength of the head has but small force against the weakness of the heart" (*T* 53a). He concludes by telling us how the town should rightly judge the injured Elmira. At the end of the story of Duumvir, "husband and keeper," Bickerstaff reflects: "It is melancholy to consider, that the virtue of a wife is like the merit of a poet, never justly valued till after death" (*T* 54a). Bickerstaff clearly expresses approval and disapproval in these two tales: the reader is taught to pity Osmyn and to revile Duumvir for their failures as husbands.

Most of the even shorter fiction narrated by Bickerstaff follows this latter method. He sketches Sophronius and Jack Dimple to illustrate his definition of a gentleman, by showing us both what he is and is not (T 21a). He uses the one-paragraph anecdote of a rival mother and daughter, Flavia and Lucia, to illustrate the desire to win esteem (T 206). Bickerstaff's dreams really conform to this pattern, too, because they show us little more about him than some literary or philosophical inclinations and are presented for the sake of their ideas. In his vision of the Goddess of Justice, for instance, Bickerstaff merely observes and does not participate in the satirical events (T 100, 102). When he wields Ithuriel's spear (T 237) or transports himself with a magic ring (T 243), Bickerstaff remains a satiric observer, though both events show his interest in occult phenomena. In narratives where Bickerstaff is more narrator than actor he clearly sits in the chair of the Censor, fulfilling his responsibility to review the people, by "disposing them into proper classes" and "to look into the manners of the people, and to check any growing luxury" (T 162).

When Isaac Bickerstaff ceased his Lucubrations, Mr. Spectator soon began to publish his essays, resolving "to Print my self out, if possible, before I Die." Wisely, Addison and Steele chose not to repeat their success and created a new persona, both odder and graver. Unlike Bickerstaff, Mr. Spectator begins with his "History" and devotes several later essays to his character. He even presents a sketch of himself as it might be written by a future historian of Queen Anne's reign: "We know very little of the Name or Person of this Author, except only that he was a Man of a very short Face, extreamly addicted to Silence, and so great a Lover of Knowledge that he made a Voyage to *Grand Cairo* for no other Reason but to take the Measure of a Pyramid. . . . He lived as a Lodger at a House of a Widow-Woman, and was a great Humourist in all parts of his Life" (S 101). Although details of this self-portrait are amusingly repeated in

20

other issues, the most whimsical trait is Mr. Spectator's
taciturnity. A gentleman "born to a small Hereditary
Estate," he "scarce uttered the Quantity of an hundred
Words" during his eight years at the university (*s* 1).
His silence, which once caused his beloved to reject him
for a more talkative "pretty fellow," now leads Sir Roger
de Coverley's neighbors to suspect him of being either a
murderer, a conjurer, or a Jesuit. Unlike the garrulous
Bickerstaff, Mr. Spectator prefers to be a "Looker-on,"
who becomes "a Speculative Statesman, Soldier, Merchant
and Artizan, without ever meddling with any Practical
Part in Life"; he is "very well versed in the Theory of
an Husband, or a Father, and can discover the Errors in
the Oeconomy, Business, and Diversion of others, better
than those who are engaged in them" (*s* 1). From his ludicrous reticence emerges the persona's peculiar strength,
the heightened power of observation responsible for his
vicarious involvement in the lives of characters he will
not talk to. Even more detached from fashionable life
than Bickerstaff, on account of his professed desire for
obscurity, Mr. Spectator reports, however, that "There is
no Place of general Resort, wherein I do not often make
my Appearance" (*s* 1). Roger Ramsey judges this ambiva-
lence to be an excellent characterizing stroke, which
would be called neurosis in a more rounded character.[13]
Functionally, it enables Mr. Spectator to be both aloof
from and interested in his fellow citizens. Surprisingly,
this silent man has six friends in a club, a membership
which helps us accept Mr. Spectator's concern for human
sociability. Yet, unlike Bickerstaff, he has no family
ties and needs more help from correspondents in discussing matrimonial matters. While not placing himself in a
formal role like the Censor, he reveals an *ethos* appropriate for his plan to bring "Philosophy out of Closets
and Libraries, Schools and Colleges, to dwell in Clubs
and Assemblies, at Tea-Tables, and in Coffee-Houses"
(*s* 10).

We encounter Mr. Spectator in much the same relationships in which we meet Bickerstaff--an eyewitness to
actions including himself, a tale teller, and "Dear Spec."
(so called by Will Honeycomb), the recipient of hundreds
of interesting epistles. However, because of his character, Mr. Spectator cannot really be said to act very
often in these narratives. Though he describes his visits
to Westminster Abbey and the Royal Exchange and his journey alone from Richmond through London, Mr. Spectator
remains a silent observer. He meets no one at the Abbey,
though Sir Andrew Freeport and an Egyptian merchant may
acknowledge him on the Exchange; in London he exchanges
glances with a female Vainlove and is teased by a beggar
(*s* 26, 69, 454). Some characteristics do emerge--his
pleased melancholy among the tombs, his ecstasy among the
factors, and his benevolence toward Londoners. In actions
involving him more directly with other characters, Mr.
Spectator is no more voluble. For instance, he listens
silently while his club debates the proper subjects of
his paper (*s* 34). During his lengthy stay at Sir Roger's
country estate and with him at the theatre, the Abbey, or
Spring Garden, Mr. Spectator's presence enhances our
comic appreciation of the knight because of the persona's
fondness for him, but he does not even elicit Sir Roger's
remarks on the Perverse Widow or ask for descriptions of
his family's portraits. In terms of narrative development, Mr. Spectator is no catalyst. Once, Sir Roger provokes him to comment on the squire's resemblance to the
sign above an inn: "I at first kept my usual Silence; but
upon the Knight's conjuring me to tell him whether it was
not still more like himself than a *Saracen*, I composed my
Countenance in the best Manner I could, and replied, *That*
much might be said on both Sides" (*s* 122). These words,
among Mr. Spectator's only dialogue, wittily repeat Sir
Roger's own expression. The Spectator also says "yes"
to Leonora (*s* 37) and to Sir Roger (*s* 116) according to

the design suggested later: "As a Monosyllable is my
Delight, I have made very few Excursions in the Conversations which I have related beyond a Yes or No" (s 550).
The effect of Mr. Spectator's taciturnity is almost to
collapse the distinction between the eyewitness and the
teller. So slight is his involvement in the lives of
other characters that he is essentially a detached narrator throughout. Despite the risible assertion that he
has become more talkative in the second series, Mr. Spectator continues to say little to others.

In telling anecdotes and sketching figures, like
Bickerstaff, Mr. Spectator is both a humorist and a sen-
timentalist. He appreciates "odd and uncommon Characters," calling them "the Game that I look for, and most
delight in" (s 108); but he also sheds tears for Yarico,
appreciates the sacrifices of Fidelia (s 449), and sympa-
thizes with a young prostitute (s 266). Like his prede-
cessor, Mr. Spectator often tells us the rhetorical purpose of his fiction. For example, having characterized
the Salamander as a type, he turns to "such Females only
as are made of Flesh and Blood," advises them to "avoid
as much as possible what Religion calls *Temptations*, and
the World *Opportunities*," and relates a story about a
Castilian's wife whose familiarities with another man
lead to infidelity and treachery (s 198). Often Mr.
Spectator uses fables from AEsop and the Orient to illustrate ideas in essays which otherwise include no fiction.
He also tells some stories, like those of Brunetta and
Phyllis (s 80) and of Constantia and Theodosia (s 164)
with no didactic framework; but the folly of pride in the
first and the beauty of fidelity in the second strike the
reader with force. Introducing John Enville's epistle,
Mr. Spectator states:

> It is observed, that a Man improves more by read-
> ing the Story of a Person eminent for Prudence
> and Virtue, than by the finest Rules and Precepts
> of Morality. In the same manner a Representation

of those Calamaties and Misfortunes which a weak
Man suffers from wrong Measures, and ill-concerted
Schemes of Life, is apt to make a deeper Impression
upon our Minds, than the wisest Maxims and Instructions than can be given us, for avoiding the like
Follies and Indiscretions in our own private Conduct. It is for this Reason that I lay before
my Reader the following Letter, and leave it with
him to make his own use of it, without adding any
Reflection of my own upon the Subject-Matter. (S 299)

Fielding would later begin *Joseph Andrews* with an analogous statement: "It is a trite but true Observation, that
Examples work more forcibly on the Mind than Precepts:
And if this be just in what is odious and blameable, it
is more strongly so in what is amiable and praise-
worthy."[14] When the reader knows Mr. Spectator's mind
and is familiar with this moral rationale for fiction, he
does not find his stories ambiguous. Perhaps this is
Philip Stevick's point when he argues that Mr. Spectator
is a straw man, "less a person than a shared state of
mind," and that the "I" of the *Spectator* is equivalent to
"men of taste and moderation and good will."[15] However,
Addison and Steele chose a fictional representative.
Though neither Bickerstaff nor Mr. Spectator can be consistently heard in every issue, though neither is a
wholly successful characterization, the presence of these
imaginary editors shapes our reading of the periodicals.

III.

Steele and Addison situate their fictional editors
in imagined social contexts, limning Bickerstaff's family
and club and later describing more fully the Spectator
Club. Such group identification enables more rounded
characterization of each persona and adds variety through
new characters representing differing viewpoints. In
both periodicals the social microcosm also increases narrative unity. A. R. Humphreys writes of the *Tatler* that
"the spirit and manner of domestic-social fiction . . .
begins to rise from the criss-cross of relationships and
events in the affairs of the Bickerstaffs."[16] And

Charlotte E. Morgan, overstating her case, suggests of
the framework in the *Spectator* that "all that is needed
is a plot to make a novel of manners."[17] Though the
social milieu is not well rendered like societies in the
novels of Fielding or Austen, the authors' decision to
define such relationships for their spokesmen illustrates,
by example again, their fundamental interest in man the
sociable animal. Their success in portraying the "dis-
crete unit" of family or club, as Ronald Paulson points
out, influenced the milieu of subsequent fiction, in
which the "limited society" replaced picaresque wandering.[18]

Bickerstaff's circle consists principally of his
half-sister, her husband, and his club at the Trumpet.
In addition, he is visited by nephews and receives letters from relatives, including one from D. Distaff containing the genealogy of the "-staff" family. We encounter the most prominent of these figures, Mrs. Jenny
Distaff, from two perspectives--her own, as the supposed
author of six issues, and her brother's, as the subject
of five more. Jenny describes herself as being "turned
of twenty, and being of a small fortune, some wit, and
(if I can believe my lovers and my glass) handsome" (*T*
33a). Bickerstaff complements this portrait when he
calls her a "girl of great merit, and pleasing conversation," whose "only imperfection is an admiration of her
parts" (*T* 75). He presents this humor amusingly: "Thus
my sister, instead of consulting her glass and toilet for
an hour and a half after her private devotions, sits with
her nose full of snuff, and a man's nightcap on her head,
reading plays and romances" (*T* 75). Jenny's issues provide a feminist viewpoint for Steele to assert the integrity of women. She has "not patience" with her
brother's treatise on governing wives (*T* 10a). She
bristles at the libertine treatment of Almeira: "Methinks
I feel all the woman rise in me, when I reflect upon the

nauseous rogues that pretend to deceive us. Wretches, that can never have it in their power to overreach anything living but their mistresses! In the name of goodness: if we are designed by nature as suitable companions to the other sex, why are we not treated accordingly" (*T* 247). This usually reasonable young woman proclaims the dignity and worth of all women. Jenny also recounts a personal experience with a rakish lord that illustrates the "breach of commerce between the sexes . . . by which a woman is to the last degree reproachable for being deceived, and a man suffers no loss of credit for being a deceiver" (*T* 33a). Having escaped that predicament with honor intact, Jenny accepts a match arranged by Bickerstaff, which enables him to give domestic advice, more in the role of father than brother, as their age difference dictates. He first urges Jenny to avoid disputes arising from trivial causes, helps her cope with her first marital quarrel, coaxes her to please her husband, and criticizes her vanity as Mrs. Tranquillus (*T* 79, 85a, 104, 143a). Tranquillus, "a plain, worthy, and honest man," is well suited for his spritely wife. As Bickerstaff plans to go to the theater with the couple, he muses: "It is a hard task to speak of persons so closely related to one with decency, but I may say, all who shall be at the play will allow him to have the mien of a worthy English gentleman; her, that of a notable and deserving wife" (*T* 184). As part of his plan to dignify courtship and marriage, Steele's decision to make examples of the persona's half-sister and brother-in-law reflects a skillful rhetorical strategy.

The remainder of Bickerstaff's limited society is even less fully drawn. His nephews visit their guardian twice. During a ramble they permit him to suggest "what great evils or benefits arise from putting us in our tender years to what we are fit, or unfit" (*T* 30a); later the future courtier, trader, and scholar compete for the

attention of a beautiful lady and allow their uncle to
observe that "There is not a greater pleasure to old age,
than seeing young people entertain themselves in such a
manner as that we can partake of their enjoyments" (*T*
207). The designation of some contributors as "cousins"
augments the sociability theme, implying, perhaps, the
interrelations among the larger family of readers. Bickerstaff's "kinsman," Humphry Wagstaff (really Swift) begins this family activity with a poem in *Tatler* 9a and
contributes another later. His first correspondent in
Tatler 11b is one of many relatives to write him, including his Oxford cousin Benjamin Beadlestaff, Lady Whittlestick, Biddy Twig, and Obadiah Greenhat, whose brother is
mentioned as Bickerstaff's companion (*T* 45b, 71b, 84a,
59b, 65a, 66b). Bickerstaff uses some relatives for examples, such as his great aunt, Mrs. Margery Bickerstaff,
and Samuel Bickerstaff, Esq. and his "ill-bred cubs" (*T*
151, 189). Dorothy Drumstick hints at the broader family
role: "This comes from a relation of yours, though unknown
to you, who besides the tie of consanguinity, has some
value for you on account of your lucubrations, those being designed to refine our conversation, as well as cultivate our minds" (*T* 140).

Just as his fictional relatives quietly underscore
Bickerstaff's avuncular role in society, his clubs attest
to his status as friend or companion. The *Tatler* begins
with a quasi-club framework, with news of gallantry coming from White's Chocolate-House, that of poetry, from
Will's Coffee-House, that of learning, from the Graecian,
and that of politics from St. James Coffee-House.[19] Although Steele later focuses the source of Bickerstaff's
Lucubrations more exclusively on his apartment, he does
sketch a group of poetical and critical friends at Will's
in several early issues. More important, because it
anticipates the Spectator Club, is Bickerstaff's "society
at the *Trumpet*," introduced in *Tatler* 132. This club of

27

old men includes four types: a country gentleman, Sir
Jeffrey Notch, a soldier, Major Matchlock, a "good
natured indolent man," Dick Reptile, and a witty bencher.
Though Robert J. Allen justly praises Steele's "intimacy
of portraiture" in this issue as a major contribution to
the literature of clubs,[20] our interest in these members
is not sustained. Several, particularly Reptile, recur
briefly to diversify Bickerstaff's social life. But of
all the features of Bickerstaff's milieu, only his family
is drawn in sufficient detail to be satisfactory.

None of this uncertainty continues in the *Spectator*,
which introduces "our Society" in its second issue and
integrates it thoroughly into the paper's framework. From
the first meeting with Sir Roger, the Templar, Sir Andrew
Freeport, Captain Sentry, Will Honeycomb, and the Clergyman until the deaths of the squire and the divine, the
retirement of the merchant, the inheritance of the soldier, and the marriage of the rake near the end of the
first series, Addison and Steele keep the members before
us to help Mr. Spectator, occasionally as contributors,
sometimes as actors, infrequently as links to other characters, like Arietta or Leonora. Though not so dominant
as it easily could have been, the club device of the *Spectator* is, as Allen concludes, "consistently sustained."[21]
We cannot criticize the authors for not exploiting their
club more exhaustively; the *Spectator*, though it adum-
brates the novel, in which such a fault would be more
serious, is a periodical and cannot be judged in the same
way. Even more important than the club's extent is its
function. Mr. Spectator clearly recognizes that his club,
drawn "out of the most conspicuous Classes of Mankind,"
is a social microcosm: "My Readers too have the Satisfaction to find, that there is no Rank or Degree among
them who have not their Representative in this Club, and
that there is always some Body present who will·take Care
of their respective Interests, that nothing may be

written or publish'd to the Prejudice or Infringement of their just Rights and Privileges" (*s* 34). This club, observes Jane Jack, is a rhetorical device, "a symbol for the English people as it struggled to coalesce, and a flattering portrait of the reading public that the writers had as their aim."[22] Edward A. and Lillian D. Bloom agree about the club's social significance, judging the friendship of Sir Roger and Sir Andrew to be "a genial fiction" that argues for an "*entente cordiale*" between the aristocracy and the middle class.[23] The order of introduction in *Spectator* 2 suggests the attempt to reconcile other social tensions through the use of typical characters. The country squire is followed by the town lawyer-critic; these men of leisure are succeeded by two men of action, the merchant making the nation great and the soldier responsible for keeping it so. Finally we contrast the amiable rake with the upright clergyman. Though the reader may laugh affectionately at Sir Roger, the Templar, and Will, he is expected to listen prudently to the advice of Sir Andrew, Captain Sentry, and the Clergyman.

We seldom witness the whole club together. In their first narrated meeting each member, out of self-interest, advises Mr. Spectator what social groups to treat gently in his periodical, until the Clergyman asserts that "not Quality but Innocence . . . exempted Men from Reproof" and ends the dispute amicably (*s* 34). The "constant, though friendly, Opposition of Opinion" between Sir Roger and Sir Andrew is the focus of a meeting in which, after Captain Sentry intervenes, the merchant defends trade (*s* 174). A more humorous meeting occurs when Sir Roger sits unusually pensive. Mr. Spectator narrates:

> We saw the Knight shake his Head, and heard him say to himself *A foolish Woman! I can't believe it*. Sir ANDREW gave him a gentle pat upon the Shoulder, and offer'd to lay him a Bottle of Wine that he was thinking of the Widow. My old Friend

> started, and recovering out of his brown Study,
> told Sir ANDREW, that once in his Life he had
> been in the right. (*S* 359)

Will Honeycomb lightens the occasion by telling of his
many courtships and concludes with some verses from
Paradise Lost, to which Sir Roger listens with "great
Attention." We learn that some of these figures are assembled when they receive the butler's notice of Sir
Roger's death; Mr. Spectator reports that there is "not
a dry Eye in the Club" (*S* 517). We are told more often
that the club is the setting for an issue than shown several members in action together. On these occasions the
club is the context for some other narrative. Will tells
the club about Picts, about Pugg's transmigration, and
about Sir Roger's encounter with a prostitute (*S* 41, 343,
410); Sir Roger once lectures the group (*S* 6); the Clergyman discourses against complaisance to his friends (*S*
103); Sir Andrew presents them with a citizen's journal
(*S* 317); and Captain Sentry reads aloud a letter describing a naval encounter (*S* 350). Even more often, we read
of Mr. Spectator's visits with or letters from one member.

Most of the members, especially those portrayed less
humorously, function as spokesmen rather than fully realized characters. The idealized merchant, Sir Andrew,
voices his authors' Whig economics, as in his view of
empire: "My Friend Sir ANDREW calls the Vineyards of
France our Gardens; the Spice-Islands our Hot-Beds; the
Persians our Silk-Weavers, and the *Chinese* our Potters"
(*S* 69). This exemplary representative of the trading
interest, with his "noble and generous" business practices, has never even been sued. So Mr. Spectator remarks: "No one had any Colour for the least Complaint
against his Dealings with him. This is certainly as uncommon, and in its Proportion as laudible in a Citizen,
as it is in a General never to have suffered a Disadvan-
tage in Fight" (*S* 82). Clearly, Sir Andrew is not a

wholly representative type, but a model toward which the merchant class could aspire. Despite his favorite proverb, "a Penny saved is Money got," he is benevolent (though not, for theoretical reasons, to beggars) and plans in retirement to find a "great Opportunity of being charitable in my way" by "settling my poor Neighbours to Work, and giving them a comfortable Subsistence out of their own Industry" (s 549). This conservative economic dogma merges easily with Sir Andrew's Christian intention "to ballance Accounts with my Maker." In addition, his belief that his wealth resulted from the "Favours of Providence, and Blessings upon an honest Industry" links religion suggestively with his successful mercantilism. The earthly rewards of the Protestant ethic reach the London merchant as effectively as they do Defoe's shipwrecked mariner.

Three members, the soldier, the Clergyman, and the Templar, are much less vividly presented. As the other active man in the club, Captain Sentry appears few times, but he serves, Donald F. Bond suggests, as a "vehicle" to defend the integrity of the military against Tory propaganda.[24] Sir Roger's heir, however, has quit "a Way of Life in which no Man can rise suitably to his Merit, who is not something of a Courtier as well as a Souldier" (s 2). Implied in this remark is some criticism of the institution which does not advance a man of "strict Honesty and an even regular Behavior," though we are not led into military corruption like that in Fielding's Amelia. The Captain might have had many military adventures "in the Relation of which he is very agreeable to the Company," but unfortunately he only recounts one (s 152). After his armed appearance at the theater to protect Sir Roger from Mohocks (s 335), this soldier takes his farewell in a letter to Mr. Spectator detailing his inheritance of Sir Roger's estate (s 544). The Clergyman, who likewise displays few characterizing traits, validates Mr. Spectator's

31

decision to attack vice and folly, lending Christian support to the gentle lash of this satirist. He gives his
silent friend letters from three persons with whom he has
discussed religious duties and sends him a letter-sermon
on atheism and a meditative epistle during illness (*S* 27,
186, 513). The reader feels little grief for the death
of this "Excellent Man in Holy Orders" because he is so
slightly presented. Of even less interest is the Templar,
who might have been a lively comic figure. The initial
sketch is promising: "He was plac'd there [the Inner
Temple] to study the Laws of the Land, and is the most
learned of any of the House in those of the Stage. *Aristotle* and *Longinus* are much better understood by him than
Littleton or *Cooke*" (*S* 2). Observed at a play and
glimpsed twice ridiculing Will Honeycomb, the Templar
dominates only one issue, his valedictory essay, announcing "a closer Pursuit of the Law" (*S* 541).

If we omit Mr. Spectator's celebrated visit to Sir
Roger's estate, the most prominent member of the club is
his London companion, Will Honeycomb, a comic representation of "those old-fashioned Men of Wit and Pleasure of
the Town, that shews his Parts by Raillery on Marriage"
(*S* 499). This aging fop, being "a great Admirer of the
Gallantries in King *Charles* the Second's Reign," views
his past with nostalgia and "thinks the Town grown very
dull" (*S* 301, 151). Mr. Spectator sketches Will's ridiculous obsession with fashion: "He knows the History of
every Mode, and can inform you from which of the *French*
King's Wenches our Wives and Daughters had this Manner of
curling their Hair, that Way of placing their Hoods;
whose Frailty was covered by such a Sort of Petticoat,
and whose Vanity to shew her Foot made that Part of the
Dress so short in such a Year" (*S* 2). Because such
knowledge is not easily acquired, Mr. Spectator later
adds a brief account of Will's youthful inclination toward "studying of Mankind": "He should never have been

32

the Man he is, had not he broke Windows, knocked down
Constables, disturbed honest People with his Midnight
Serenades, and beat up a Lewd Woman's Quarters" (*S* 105).
Will himself must tell his decorous friend "of several
Hags whose Bloom was given up to his Arms" or of numerous
rich widows courted for "twenty Years successively" (*S*
151, 311). Because of his knowledge of the "female World"
Will's opinions frequently complement the Spectator's in-
experience. He cites briefly Will's ideas on "*kissing
Dances*," on love rivalry, on hoods, on the "outragiously
virtuous," and on "*Valetudinarians* in Chastity" (*S* 67,
156, 265, 266, 395). In addition Will introduces Mr.
Spectator to women who "brought up the Fashion of receiving Visits in their Beds" (*S* 45). Will's role is defined
more precisely when Mr. Spectator confronts a new feminine
fashion: "I left her without a Reply, and made the best
of my Way to WILL. HONEYCOMB'S lodgings, without whose
Advice I never communicate any thing to the Public of
this Nature" (*S* 277). Nowhere do we see more clearly how
Addison and Steele use Mr. Spectator as a fictional character whose knowledge does not equal their own.

Will also serves appropriately as a major source of
anti-feminist satire. He tells of the fallen expectations of three sisters, "the most inaccessible haughty
Beauties in Town"; he gives the Spectator a letter written by a Restoration wit to his lover, an allegory of
Love, Youth, and Old-Age; he relates a story and lectures
on the "Usefulness of looking-Glasses" for women; and he
tells of a woman duped by his friend Jack Freelove into
believing that her pet monkey has been metamorphosized
(*S* 282, 301, 325, 343). Will's final satires are included in two letters to "*Dear* SPEC." The first is a dream-
vision ridiculing wives, each of whom flees London with
one valued possession, never a husband, but always a
lover, pet, cards, china, or money (*S* 499). Twelve
issues later he ridicules marriage customs by proposing

an English fair for match making and a plan to dispose of "all the unmarried women in *London* and *Westminster*" by bringing them "to Market in Sacks" (*S* 511). What follows Will's most vituperative satire is his sudden marriage to a tenant's daughter, announced in a letter Mr. Spectator calls "the Picture of a Converted Rake" (*S* 530). This reformation should not really surprise us. Throughout the *Spectator*, despite Will's faults, he has been portrayed affectionately. His sympathetic articulation of Mr. Spectator's glances or his absent-mindedness cause only amiable laughter (*S* 4, 77). When he asks Mr. Spectator whether, nearing the age of sixty, he should marry a town woman (*S* 475), we are likely being forewarned that, for all his subsequent raillery of women, this figure is ready to retire from gallantry. We may recall, too, that Will only offends in one way, as the Spectator notes in the introduction of his friend: "To conclude his Character, where women are not concerned, he is an honest worthy Man" (*S* 2). In the inclusive comic world of the *Spectator* the likeable rake *must* become a husband. Thomas Lockwood observes correctly that when Addison and Steele ridicule a character, such as Will, "the tone and the context suggest the hope of improvement"; the desired resolution is a "reunion" of the humorous character with his society, represented by Mr. Spectator.[25] The dedication of the last volume of the *Spectator* to this fictitious gentleman emphasizes his successful integration. Will's progress also exemplifies the effect Addison and Steele hope their periodical will have on readers.

One problem in discussing recurrent characters in the *Spectator* is that they are likely to be composites drawn by two or more authors and may, consequently, lack consistency. What should really surprise us is that such characters are as consistent as they are. For example, Eustace Budgell handles Will Honeycomb, enlarged by Addison from Steele's sketch, with so much skill that the character seems depicted by one hand. In similar fashion this trio of writers delineate their most famous character, Sir Roger, whose portrayal shows few misdirections, only one of which is serious. Steele introduces this archetypal country squire, noting briefly his singularity, his benevolence, and some details about his history, including relationships with a Perverse Widow, Restoration rakes, and unchaste beggars and gypsies. Mr. Spectator concludes: "He is now in his Fifty sixth Year, cheerful, gay, and hearty, keeps a good House both in Town and Country; a great Lover of Mankind; but there is such a mirthful Cast in his Behaviour, that he is rather beloved than esteemed" (*S* 2). Following this portrait, Steele uses Sir Roger to express some of his own ideas about the "publick Good" (*S* 6). Addison first turns to Sir Roger when he advises Mr. Spectator not to ridicule country squires, "the Ornaments of the *English* Nation," and when he introduces the Spectator to Leonora, who admits Sir Roger "with great Pleasure, and without Scandal" (*S* 34, 37). At first, then, Sir Roger remains a minor figure, while Will Honeycomb appears in more issues.

When Mr. Spectator goes to the country, the authors expand their initial sketches and transform Sir Roger into a major character. Mr. Spectator reemphasizes the squire's benevolence and shows more esteem for his friend's mirth:

> I have observed . . . that my Friend Sir ROGER amidst all his good Qualities, is something of an Humourist; and that his Virtues, as well as Imperfections, are as it were tinged by a certain Extravagance, which makes them particularly *his*, and distinguishes them from those of other Men. This Cast of Mind, as it is generally very innocent in itself, so it renders his Conversation highly agreeable, and more delightful than the same Degree of Sense and Virtue would appear in their common and ordinary Colours. (*S* 106)

Steele quickly adjusts his conception of the character to Addison's humorist, letting Mr. Spectator judge him "a

Man of Honour and Generosity" who enjoys the "Respect and
Love" of his dependents (*S* 107). When Addison depicts
Sir Roger in church, he has Mr. Spectator observe: "The
general good Sense and Worthiness of his Character, make
his Friends observe these little Singularities as Foils
that rather set off than blemish his good Qualities" (*S*
112). Finally, ten issues later,when the Spectator comments, "Sir ROGER is one of those who is not only at
Peace within himself, but beloved and esteemed by all
about him" (*S* 122), esteem is added to love, and Sir
Roger's improvement from Steele's sketch is complete.
Stuart M. Tave remarks that the Spectator's epithets for
Sir Roger—the "good old Knight," as well as the "good
old Man" or the "good Knight"—are positive signs that he
is an "amiable humorist" whose basic quality is "not a
particular folly but a more diffuse delightfulness and
innocence."[26] We might add two other frequent epithets—
"my Friend" and "my worthy Friend"—that signal the benevolent tendencies of this comedy. Sir Roger, Tave notes,
is "natural in the sense of unspoiled and unaffected,"
and has many important virtues, such as patriotism, religiosity, and benevolence.[27] As Samuel Johnson comments,
Sir Roger's oddities derive from "habitual rusticity."[28]

Addison authored many of the most memorable accounts
of Sir Roger in country and town. He shows him, for example, on a "Country *Sunday*" being "surprized into a
short Nap at Sermon" and "lengthening out a Verse in the
Singing-Psalms half a Minute after the rest of the Congregation have done with it" (*S* 112). Whether presenting
Sir Roger in the country (at the assizes, or with
gypsies), or in town (at Westminster Abbey, a play, or
Spring Garden), Addison generates comedy from the whims
of his character while stressing his good nature and
humanity (*S* 122, 130, 329, 335, 383). Steele's major
contribution to Sir Roger's development stems from the
hint of the Perverse Widow. Sir Roger tells of his

unrequited love for a neighbor with "the finest Hand of
any Woman in the World" (*s* 113). Although he advances to
be considered the tamest "Brute" in the country, Sir
Roger's unsuccessful courtship Mr. Spectator believes to
be "the secret Cause of all that Inconsistency which appears in some parts of my Friend's Discourse." A few
issues later Steele lets Sir Roger come as close to self-
awareness as we could expect in such a humorous character.
The following passage is not often quoted, but Sir Roger's
words to Mr. Spectator deserve our attention:

> However, when I reflect upon this Woman, I do
> not know whether in the Main I am the worse for
> having loved her: Whenever she is recalled to
> my Imagination my Youth returns, and I feel a
> forgotten Warmth in my Veins. This Affliction
> in my Life has streaked all my Conduct with a
> Softness, of which I should otherwise have been
> incapable. It is, perhaps, to this dear Image
> in my Heart owing, that I am apt to relent,
> that I easily forgive, and that many desirable
> things are grown into my Temper, which I should
> not have arrived at by better Motives than the
> Thought of being one Day hers. I am pretty well
> satisfied such a Passion as I have had is never
> well cured; and between you and me, I am often
> apt to imagine it has had some whimsical Effect
> upon my Brain; For I frequently find, that in
> my most serious Discourse I let fall some com-
> ical Familiarity of Speech or odd Phrase that
> makes the Company laugh. (*s* 118)

Sir Roger's insight into his benevolence and oddity is
suggestively represented in this speech, which juxtaposes
the softening with the distracting powers of love. Addison uses the squire's love humorously (*s* 295, 383), but
Budgell more successfully conveys Steele's tenderness
mingled with laughter in the previously discussed club
meeting (*s* 359). Budgell also develops an Addisonian
hint into the benevolent rabbit hunt during which Sir
Roger cannot "find it in his Heart to murther a Creature
that had given him so much Diversion" (*s* 115, 116).

Steele's success in according his portrayal of Sir
Roger with Addison's does not end until *Spectator* 410,

Will's account of Sir Roger's solicitous attention to
Sukey, a prostitute. Though he remains chaste, the
squire escorts this "Fair one" to a tavern and sends her
a brief invitation to the country. Tradition holds that
Addison resolved to abandon Sir Roger rather than let him
be demeaned; certainly he did not want his character to
lose the esteem so attentively added to his reader's
love. After Mr. Spectator recalls Sir Roger's observations of a lady equestrian from his country visit (*S* 435),
the squire appears no more. His death and character are
described in two letters, one from Edward Biscuit, the
butler, written by Addison (*S* 517), and a second from
Captain Sentry, written by Steele. Sir Roger's heir
attributes his response to Sukey to "the Simplicity and
Innocence of his Mind, which made him imagine it a very
easy thing to reclaim one of those Criminals, and not as
an Inclination in him to be guilty with her" (*S* 544).
Whatever Steele's intent in the encounter with the prostitute, his final gesture again is to accomodate his concept of Sir Roger with Addison's. Though these authors
may have created Sir Roger to satirize the "Tory landowner who resists all that is to make England prosperous"
and though he may be "functionless" in a society gauged
by performance,[29] they succeed in creating an affectionate
tribute to human benevolence, like Sterne's Uncle Toby.
As one of Mr. Spectator's correspondents writes: "Your
Readers are so well pleased with your Character of Sir
ROGER DE COVERLY, that there appeared a sensible Joy in
every Coffee-House, upon hearing the old Knight was come
to Town" (*S* 271). In the issue following the announcement of his death, Mr. Spectator prints a letter beginning: "It is with inexpressible Sorrow that I hear of the
Death of good Sir *Roger*, and do heartily condole with you
upon so melancholly an Occasion. I think you ought to
have blacken'd the Edges of a Paper which brought us so
ill News" (*S* 518). Such tributes from readers, whether

invented or genuine, betoken the esteem with which Addison first, then later Steele and Budgell, render their figure.

Following the dissolution of his club, Mr. Spectator speculates briefly about forming a new one but never does, not even during the periodical's second series, when his only regular assistance comes from a gentleman calling himself the Love-Casuist. Mr. Spectator recounts a prophetic dream which occurred many years earlier in Cairo foretelling his "great Comfort . . . in the Company of half a Dozen Friends," his diversion with Sir Roger and Will, and his regret about the former's death (*s* 604). However, during and after the existence of this club, other such societies are important to Mr. Spectator. Just as Isaac Bickerstaff and Jenny Distaff attracted numerous relatives to fill out the social context of the *Tatler*, the Spectator Club, with its "King of Clubs," Mr. Spectator, received information about and correspondence from numerous clubs, beginning with the Hum-Drum Club, of which Mr. Spectator was once a member (*s* 9), and concluding with the Rattling Club (*s* 630). As Allen suggests, the twenty-seven, mostly fictional, groups which appear in the *Spectator* manifest the "human gregariousness" which is the basis of Mr. Spectator's morality.[30] The persona's remark introducing the first clubs is indicative: "Man is said to be a Sociable Animal, and, as an Instance of it, we may observe, that we take all Occasions and Pretences of forming our selves into those little Nocturnal Assemblies, which are commonly known by the Name of *Clubs*" (*s* 9). Prominent among these is the Ugly Club of Oxford, first described by Alexander Carbuncle, who later depicts the election of Mr. Spectator; its history is even disputed by a Cambridge writer (*s* 17, 32, 48, 52, 78). Of real groups the Mohocks are thoroughly depicted in letters from Philanthropos and Jack Lightfoot, following a fictional adventure; after their activity

39

threatens Sir Roger at the theatre, Mr. Spectator prints
a fictitious manifesto from the supposed emperor of the
Mohocks (*S* 324, 332, 335, 347). In a lighter vein is the
rural correspondence he receives detailing the establishment by a "Set of Company" of an infirmary for the ill-
humored (*S* 424, 429, 440). The Spectator gets a humorous
account of the Widow Club, whose president writes in a
subsequent issue to vindicate their treatment of men (*S*
561, 573). More often in the *Spectator* clubs are mentioned only once. For example, Mr. Spectator describes
the Everlasting Club and coffee-house politicians, and
letters depict the Amorous Club and the club of She-Romps
(*S* 72, 403, 30, 217). Like Bickerstaff's family, these
clubs emphasize the importance of social life to self-
realization by showing many ways of belonging. By implication, the most inclusive club consists of Mr. Spectator's readers, a loosely defined social organization
gathered daily, except Sundays, for entertaining and instructive discussions of their species.

IV.

The most direct way of involving, or at least of
seeming to involve, readers in such sociable activity
proved to be letters to the editors. Both Bickerstaff,
in his seventh Lucubration, and Mr. Spectator, in his
first essay, invite readers to participate in their periodicals. And readers responded. More than 200 letters
appear in the 271 issues of the *Tatler*, while the first
555 issues of the *Spectator* contain about 500 epistles.[31]
They range in length from a sentence to an issue, in tone,
from frivolity to gravity, and in subject matter, from
fans to God. William Kinsley calls the *Spectator* a "truly
collaborative enterprise" because of Mr. Spectator's success in persuading "his readers to co-operate in his program of social reform."[32] Both the *Tatler* and the *Spectator* replace the anticipated communication from persona
to reader with the illusion of a printed dialogue. For

instance, Mr. Spectator introduces a letter about sleeping with this remark: "My Correspondents take the Hint
[for a new vein of humor] I give them, and pursue it into
Speculations which I never thought of at my first starting it. This has been the Fate of my Paper on the Match
of Grinning, which has already produced a second Paper on
parallel subjects [yawning and whistling], and brought me
the following Letter by the last Post" (*S* 184). Richmond
P. Bond, noting the similar "timeliness" of letters in the
Tatler, counts many referring to papers within two weeks
after publication but few that depend on issues more than
two months old.[33] The impression of timely collaboration
is only one advantage accruing to the *Tatler* and the
Spectator from their letters. By diversifying point of
view the periodicals drew widespread elements of their
audience into a social relationship of compelling mutual
interest. After issuing a renewed invitation for letters,
Mr. Spectator makes this point: "This Sort of Intelligence will give a lively Image of the Chain and mutual
Dependance of Humane Society, take off impertinent Prejudices, enlarge the Minds of those, whose Views are
confin'd to their own Circumstances" (*S* 428). The
reader's participation in the society of Bickerstaff or
Mr. Spectator leads, at its fullest, toward his acknowl-
edgement of human interdependence.

Although many of these letters are fictional, even
in origin, Addison and Steele do not break the illusion
of reader authorship until near the end of the *Spectator*'s first series. When Nick Doubt queries "pray tell
me, did not you write that letter in praise of the squire
and his lucubrations yourself!" Bickerstaff's answer is
negative, with the reservation that he is "as likely to
play such a trick as another" (*T* 91). In response to the
accusation that "I often write to my self, and am the
only punctual Correspondent I have," Mr. Spectator admits
that letters "furnish me with Materials for new Specula-

tions" which he sometimes uses as hints for his "Invention" and sometimes rewrites in "my own way of speaking and thinking" (*S* 271). Bickerstaff implies a similar process when he compares his "more regular and elaborate dissertations," presumably his finished essays, to "miscellaneous hints, and sudden starts of fancy," exemplified in his drawers of letters (*T* 78). Mr. Spectator proposes to present some letters "in the artless Dress in which they hastily send them" or "in their own native Dress and Colours" (*S* 268, 442). However, he finally does affirm responsibility for some specific "Letters of Mirth" and "Multitudes of the same Nature" (*S* 542). In fact, scholars now agree that we can establish the authenticity of few letters and that we must assume some alteration in almost all. Donald F. Bond believes it a "general rule . . . that letters were considerably modified if not completely rewritten before appearing in print."[34] Thus letters not invented by the periodicals' authors went through a fictionalizing process, whether in content, style, or attribution (such as the use of fictional names to characterize the writer or his problem). When Steele uses his own letters to his wife, he attributes one to Cynthio (*T* 35b), and lets Andromache submit a packet of six others as "the Images of a Worthy Passion" (*S* 142). Addison's letter from Switzerland is printed as though it were from a friend of Bickerstaff's to illustrate "the proper use of an epistolary commerce" (*T* 93a). In his confession Mr. Spectator mentions the use of fictional letters to try out new material or to enhance the paper's image. But his three most important stated purposes involve adding "a great variety of Characters into my Work, which could not have been done, had I always written in the Person of the *Spectator*," maintaing the "Dignity Spectatorial," which "would have suffered, had I published as from my self these several ludicrous Compositions," and finally, bringing in "more naturally, such

42

additional Reflections as have been placed at the End of them [essays]" (*S* 542). The use of letters to diversify narrative perspective and to amplify ideas with invented examples, while preserving some consistency for the flexible personae, reflects artful attention to the rhetoric of fiction in the *Tatler* and the *Spectator*. Bickerstaff and Mr. Spectator, supported by their fictional relatives or clubs, write for an audience whose fictional representatives reply.

Like the multiple narrators of *Clarissa* and *Humphry Clinker*, these letter writers sometimes create the impression of dramatic interaction. As in those novels, letters themselves become involved in the narrative. For example, Bickerstaff receives a letter from Alexander Landlord, successfully entreating him to print an enclosed letter to a lady: "I have a very good estate, and wish myself your husband. Let me know by this way, where you live, for I shall be miserable till we live together" (*T* 74a). Bickerstaff soon reports her reply, citing her aversion to marriage, and leaves her to discover her admirer with this observation: "Bless me! What is this age come to, that people can think to make a pimp of an astronomer?" (*T* 76b). A fortune hunter uses Bickerstaff similarly, getting him to print a letter to Mopsa (*T* 128), who was first mentioned four issues earlier. The requested printing of Antony Freeman's letter in *Spectator* 212 precipitates the events reported by A. Noewill and Tom Meggot four issues later, when Freeman's tyrannical wife is enraged to find herself ridiculed through the paper. And Mr. Spectator becomes the last resort for a jilt named Amoret, when she promises him "all Gloves and Favours" if he will help her regain Philander's favor by printing her reply to his distraught letter. Her postscript contains a final ironic twist that necessitates no response from Philander: "I must desire you, dear Mr. *Spectator*, to publish this my Letter to *Philander* as soon as possible, and to assure him that I know nothing at all of the Death of his rich Uncle in *Gloucestershire*" (*S* 401). Letters like Amoret's and Freeman's may be a form of self-satire, ridiculing the paper's expected effect on its audience.

In addition to letters involving the periodicals in their actions, we should recall Bickerstaff's letters from relatives and Mr. Spectator's from his and other clubs as further evidence of this tendency toward dramatic interplay. Bickerstaff also gets letters from characters he satirizes, like the Political Upholsterer and Tom Folio (*T* 160, 232a); and the widow of the virtuoso Nicholas Gimcrack writes with more information about him (*T* 221). Bickerstaff receives a letter of love from Maria, which he answers with parental tenderness; surprisingly this correspondent appears at his apartment seeking advice about two suitors (*T* 83a, 91). Mr. Spectator has few extended episolary relationships outside the clubs. After he exchanges letters with John Trott, giving him leave to dance, Eliz. Sweepstakes writes from York complaining of Trott's minuets and leading the Spectator to permit Trott only country dances; Trott writes again, asking but not receiving pardon (*S* 296, 308, 314). Though Trott never comes on the scene like Maria, he is mentioned again as a prospective dancing master, in a letter from Rachel Watchfull (*S* 376). Letters may also be the occasion for the action of an issue. Bickerstaff presents a letter written by Sergeant John Hall of the Footguards to a comrade for the discussion of a "cluster of critics" at Will's Coffee House (*T* 87a); Mr. Spectator rewrites a romantic epistle from a servant to his mistress as his major activity for one day (*S* 71). When Bickerstaff initiates a correspondence with King Louis XIV of France, he, unsurprisingly, receives an alleged reply three issues later (*T* 23b, 26a). Of course, many letters in the *Tatler* and the *Spectator* do not suggest such dramatic interaction, though they may be related to previous issues in other ways.

Melvin R. Watson identifies two principal kinds of
letters in these periodicals; one presents personal problems on which advice is sought, and the second portrays
the habits, actions, and foibles of individuals, types,
or society as a whole.[35] Most prevalent among personal
problems are love and marriage. A typical instance is a
letter from Sylvia, the daughter of a country gentleman,
who writes Bickerstaff about the conflict between her
lover and her father; she hopes that "Your thoughts upon
the whole may perhaps have some weight with my father,
who is one of your admirers" (*T* 185). Another Sylvia, a
wealthy country widow, asks Mr. Spectator to help her
choose between two suitors, one richer and one poorer
than herself (*S* 149). Such letters permit the personae
to comment on the importance of mutual love and esteem in
making a match. Florinda, certain that Mr. Spectator
will "not deny your Advice to a distressed Damsel, who
intends to be determined by your Judgment in a Matter of
great Importance to her," wants help in rationalizing her
affection for a gentleman of small fortune, whom, she
tells us in a postscript, she has already married (*S* 278).
This letter receives no comment, but Florinda's decision
to marry despite the "Vain World" likely merits tacit
approval. When Diana Doubtful, desirous of winning
Fabio's love from Cleora, tells Bickerstaff "You are an
astrologer, what shall I do?" he resolves to help her (*T*
98a). A forlorn virgin also asks him to "advise whether
I shall or ought to be prevailed upon by the imperti-
nencies of my own sex, to give way to the importunities
of yours" (*T* 210a). After Bickerstaff raises questions
about the true nature of virginity, she writes again two
issues later for more help: "May a woman be said to live
any more years a maid than she continues to be courted?"
(*T* 212). This foolish question gets no reply. Often
problems following marriage arise. When an unnamed writer
applies for Mr. Spectator's agreement with his "very just

Pretentions to a Divorce" from a cosmetic wife, the persona concurs (*S* 41). Later Asteria, separated from her
military husband, asks the Spectator for a "Dissertation
upon the Absence of Lovers" (*S* 241). Although many such
queries focus on relations between the sexes, both before
and after marriage, Bickerstaff and Mr. Spectator also
receive numerous letters about education, especially regarding the education of a lady or a gentleman. Jeffry
Nicknack sends a ridiculous request about his gentlemanly
progress, while Ralph and Bridget Yokefellow seek help
raising their children, asking "is it absolutely necessary that all who wear breeches must be taught to rhyme,
all in petticoats to touch an instrument?" (*T* 27c, 252).
Celimene seeks advice from Mr. Spectator about the "fine
Breeding" she has in mind for her country relative (*S* 66).
Such examples reflect, in their comic failures, the com-
mitment of these two periodicals to the "good Breeding"
demonstrated in more theoretical epistles.

From letters to the editors primarily concerned with
advice on these and many other subjects, we may turn to
those designed to describe interesting characters. For
instance, in brief letters to Bickerstaff, Josiah Couplet
depicts the "assuming and absurd" Cleontes, Jeffry Chanticleer objects to the "imprudent conduct" of Stentor,
and Scoto-Britannus presents a gentleman who repeatedly
uses the phrase "the best of any man in England" (*T* 64b,
54b, 241a). Bickerstaff transcribes a longer letter from
Epsom describing Sir Taffety Trippet, a silly fortune
hunter, while Martha Tatler writes of Lady Autumn and Lady
Springly at that resort (*T* 36a, 47a). The *Spectator* also
abounds with epistolary character sketches, often more
generalized in implication. From the country Philonus
sends his "true Account of a *British* Free-thinker";
another rural writer, Rustick Sprightly ridicules a
"Courtier, or Town-Gentleman" (*S* 234, 240). Tim. Watchwell, father of an heiress, offers "a Picture of those

46

audacious young Fellows among us, who commonly go by the
Name of *Fortune-Stealers*" (*S* 311). Charles Yellow's
lengthy epistle characterizes jilts (*S* 187). Occasionally, the personae bring together letters describing similar characters; Ralph Valet and Patience Giddy both complain of their masters (*S* 137). Both periodicals use
letters for more generalized satire, as we can see in
those from Pasquin and J. Downes in the *Tatler* and from
the Love-Casuist and Moses Greenbag in the *Spectator* (*T*
129, 187a, 193; *S* 591, 602, 605, 607, 614, 623, 625, 498,
526). Mr. Spectator, in later issues, even uses letters
as a source for dream visions, previously the province of
himself and Bickerstaff alone.

More prominent in the *Spectator* than in the *Tatler*
is the kind of descriptive epistle that Robert Adams Day
calls the "my story" letter.[36] Self-portraits, like that
of the "smart fellow" (*T* 26a), are less frequent in the
Tatler; only once does a correspondent's way of living
fill an entire issue, which is mostly about his greenhouse (*T* 179). The *Spectator* successfully extends the
advantages of the letter to particularize characters,
often letting them speak for themselves in issues as "the
Entertainment of this Day." The Valetudinarian, the
Castle-Builder, and Clarinda portray their humors briefly
enough that Mr. Spectator has space to remark about them,
but the narratives of Cleanthes and Rebecca Nettletop,
filling most of an issue, receive no comment (*S* 25, 167,
323, 272, 190). The "my story" letter achieves its fullest realization in the accounts of Thomas Trusty, John
Enville, Octavia, and Ephraim Weed. Trusty's autobiog-
raphy is a miniature picaresque tale showing his passage
from master to master as he gradually learns the way of
the world and rises in it. Though he intends to show
that servants are no worse than their masters, Trusty
writes with good humored irony of his situations, including the current one: "In the Family I am now in, I am

47

guilty of no one Sin but Lying; which I do with a grave
Face in my Gown and Staff every Day I live, and almost
all Day long, in denying my Lord to impertinent Suitors,
and my Lady to unwelcome Visitants" (*s* 96). The unfortunate effects of ambition highlight Enville's narration.
His rise from Jack Anvil, tradesman, to knighthood leads
him to wed Lady Mary Oddly, "an Indigent young Woman of
Quality" who now tyrannizes over him, ironically turning
his public success to personal failure. Enville depicts
his wife's dominion "with great Sorrow of Heart," yearn-
ing again for his earlier life (*s* 299). Octavia's story
is a small tragedy of the "piercing Affliction" of "Innocence exposed to Infamy" (*s* 322). Her clandestine marriage, a mismatch in both fortune and virtue, is undone
by the accidental burning of her certificate. As she
concludes her letter, Octavia quivers with pathos:

> I believe [my husband] means to bring me,
> through Necessity, to resign my Pretentions to
> him for some Provision for my Life; but I will
> dye first. Pray bid him remember what he said,
> and how he was charmed when he laughed at the
> heedless Discovery I often made of my self; let
> him remember how awkward I was in my dissembled
> Indifference towards him before Company; ask
> him how I, who could never conceal my Love for
> him, at his own Request, can part with him for
> ever? (*s* 322)

The classical name Octavia, that of Mark Anthony's abandoned wife, suggests the dignity Steele accords this distressed correspondent.

Weed's "plain Narrative of my own Life" (*s* 450) is a
neglected masterpiece of Augustan irony in which the
writer, like one of Swift's projectors, pleads eloquently
but exposes an ungenerous soul. While he intends to
prove that love of money is "a special Antidote against
Immorality and Vice," Weed exemplifies the debilitating
moral effects of steady devotion to gain. The letter is
skillfully organized, beginning with two paragraphs stating his general views, followed by three paragraphs

detailing his profitable family life and one showing how
money rendered him "honest, sober, and religious," and
concluding with a brief exhortation to Mr. Spectator to
"turn ready Wit into ready Money as fast as you can."
Like the economic language of "A Modest Proposal," Weed's
discourse reveals his spiritual poverty. When his wife
and two children, "all my Stock" as he calls them, died
of the plague, he found he could live "far cheaper than
before." He provides us with a financial analysis of his
next two marriages and concludes: "I had been a Gainer by
my Marriages, and the Damages granted me for the Abuses
of my Bed (all Charges deducted) Eight thousand three
hundred Pounds within a Trifle." Complementing this
strict computation are Weed's repeated assurances that
the blessings of Providence have led to his wealth. Because of money, he is devout: "On *Saturday* Nights, upon
casting up my Accounts, I always was grateful for the Sum
of my Week's Profits, and at *Christmas* for that of the
whole Year." Such smugness damns this tradesman, who
arrogantly judges the Great Fire of London to be God's
"*just Wrath and Indignation*" toward a sinful People, from
whom he profited. We do not need the more laudable example of Sir Andrew Freeport to appreciate this Browning-
like character.

In addition to letters addressed to themselves,
Bickerstaff and Mr. Spectator print correspondence between characters within issues. Some present the mental
or emotional state of the writer. Bickerstaff's story of
a man who accidentally shot his wife on their wedding day
involves two letters by the husband to the bride's father,
one, in joy, before the ceremony and a second, in misery,
after the fatal event (*T* 82). As he completes Caelia's
history, Bickerstaff includes her letter to the bigamist,
Palamede, which renders pathetically her inner condition:

> You, who this morning were the best, are now the
> worst of men who breathe vital air. I am at
> once overwhelmed with love, hatred, rage, and

disdain. Can infamy and innocence live
together? I feel the weight of the one too
strong for the comfort of the other. How
bitter, Heaven, how bitter is my portion!
How much have I to say; but the infant which
I bear about me stirs with my agitation. I
am, Palamede, to live in shame, and this
creature be heir to it. Farewell, for ever.
(*T* 198)

Mr. Spectator's account of Amanda, a precursor of *Pamela*,
employs three letters to substantiate his narration (*S*
375). Two are from the young lord to Amanda's parents,
the first proposing her as his mistress, the second re-
penting; in between is one from Amanda's mother to her
daughter, intercepted by the lover, which leads to his
change of heart. As in *Pamela*, the letter is a device of
plot as well as characterization. Other issues of the
Spectator using letters as plot devices include a story
about the addresses of the "old Beau" Escalus to Isabella,
which ends with their exchange of letters, and an anecdote
in which Ralph Trap sends himself a letter to snare his
spying rival, Jack Stint (*S* 318, 448). Bickerstaff contrasts letters of gallantry from John Careless and Colonel
Constant, written before their deaths in battle, to Romana,
who tells the Censor that she "ought to have taken Constant; but believed she should have chosen Careless" (*T*
30b). Style is also important in the nine brief letters
terminating the *amour* between Cynthio and Flavia, so-
called for "galantry Sake" (*S* 398). Like the "my story"
letters, these are also "miniature letter novels"[37] which
show how far Steele and Addison advanced beyond the letter
to the editor with which the *Tatler* begins in its eleventh
issue.

V.

The world of the *Tatler* and the *Spectator*, centered
on Bickerstaff and Mr. Spectator, and fleshed out by
clubs and correspondents, provides the context for varied
fictional forms, directly or silently approved by the

personae for the benefit and pleasure of their well-represented audience. The most frequently used form, the character, evidences the job of classification that Bickerstaff sees as part of his role (*T* 162) and the need for warning that Mr. Spectator cites: "When I meet with any vicious Character, that is not generally known, in order to prevent its doing Mischief, I draw it at length, and set it up as a Scarecrow" (*S* 205). Though most of the characters in these periodicals are not vicious, Mr. Spectator's hope to "make an Example of the Person" does suggest the utility of the form, for positive as well as negative sketches. The typing or classifying aspect of the character aids the personae's efforts to make their readers' society more comprehensible, despite Bickerstaff's whimsical claim that he has "not yet reduced . . . into any tolerable order" the members of the "soft sex" (*T* 162). He does list nineteen categories for males; however, in the same issue. Many terms in the characters suggest self-conscious, quasi-scientific inspection. For instance, Bickerstaff places the Political Upholsterer in "this species of men" (*T* 160), while Mr. Spectator introduces one type this way: "There is a Species of Women, whom I shall distinguish by the Name of Salamanders" (*S* 198). Correspondents label the jilt "a certain Species of Women" and the male jilt a "certain Species of Mankind" (*S* 187, 288). The Valetudinarian is "one of that sickly Tribe," but the freethinker belongs to "the Tribe of *Beaux Esprits*" (*S* 25, 234). Hotspur tells the Spectator of his new character: "You have in some of your Discourses described most sort of Women in their distinct and proper classes, as the *Ape*, the *Coquet*, and many others; but I think you have never yet said anything of a *Devotée*" (*S* 354). When Bickerstaff or Mr. Spectator classify readers, some accept their grouping voluntarily. After the Censor casts "the several conversable parts of mankind in this great city . . . into proper characters and divisions, as they resemble several instruments that are in use among the masters of harmony," he visits an "assembly of very fine women," who now look upon themselves in this way, providing a "female concert," gets letters from Nicholas Humdrum and Isabella Kit, and prints an advertisement for a Bass-viol (*T* 153, 154, 150, 160, 166a). The *Spectator's* antifeminist satire of "the Sex in their several Characters" of "Animals and Elements" evokes correspondence from Melissa, a bee, and the husbands of a filly and a cat (*S* 209, 211). But Addison and Steele do not subdivide the human species merely to help their readers understand it but also to aid them in judging it. After all, Bickerstaff hopes for the harmonious performance of his many instruments, and Mr. Spectator has an ecological balance in mind. Bickerstaff's suggestion that Will. Courtly serves as "a living instance of this truth" (*T* 30a) signals the primary evaluative function of the character--the example. The "living instance" proves an integral way for the *Tatler* and the *Spectator* to diversify their moral and social "truth."

Addison and Steele use this popular form more extensively and effectively than the editors of previous periodicals. Influenced by the example of La Bruyère more than by the seventeenth-century followers of Theophrastus, they situate most characters in the context of social or moral ideas, to serve as illustrations, and tend to individualize their types with names and other details or actions. Bickerstaff makes a suggestive remark about his method: "I would let [the country reader] know what I mean by a Gentleman, a Pretty Fellow, a Toast, a Coquette, a Critic, a Wit, and all other appelations in the gayer world, who are in present possession of these several characters; together with an account of those who unfortunately pretend to them" (*T* 21a). The remark implies that Bickerstaff will not depict, in Richmond P. Bond's words, "static subjects in a frozen scene" but

rather will present "persons in a convincing circumstance."[38] Bickerstaff's first characters are charming
social types, the rival toasts Clarissa and Chloe. He
begins to describe them as follows: "The beauty of Clarissa is soft, that of Chloe piercing. When you look at
Clarissa, you see the most exact harmony of feature, complexion, and shape; you find in Chloe nothing extraordinary in any of those particulars, but the whole woman ir-
resistible. Clarissa looks languishing; Chloe, killing;
Clarissa never fails at gaining admiration; Chloe, of
moving desire" (*T* 4b). Their names, their invented portraits by Charles Jervas, and their admirers in White's
Chocolate House give these illustrative characters a much
more intimate tone. In early issues Bickerstaff almost
always presents contrasting characters, either foiling
the exemplary with the ludicrous, as when the gentleman
Sophronius precedes the pretty fellow Jack Dimple, or by
pairing ridiculous types, as when Dactyle the wit accompanies Spondee the critic (*T* 21a, 29b). In these two
issues Bickerstaff first defines the type generally, then
introduces his representatives in action. For example,
we see Dimple admiring himself in a mirror at White's.
There are similar contrasts in the *Spectator*: Vocifer,
who "passes for a Fine Gentleman," and Ignotus, who is
one (*S* 75); Stephen Courier and Bridget Eitherdown, who
exemplify affected business and negligence (*S* 284). More
exuberant is Jenny Distaff's portrayal of the coxcomb,
beginning with a formal abstract character, quoted from
William Wycherley, which she demonstrates with her acquaintances, Lord Nowhere, Will Shoestring, Umbra, and
Flyblow, each fondly ridiculed in a slightly differing
way (*T* 38b). Mr. Spectator likewise describes four kinds
of female orators, and his correspondent, Charles Yellow
exemplifies the Jilt with Corinna, Kitty, Hyaena, Biblis,
and Chloe (*S* 247, 187). In later issues of the *Tatler*
and throughout the *Spectator* such contrasts of types or

53

varieties of a type are not so usual. With the memorable exceptions of the sketches of the club at the Trumpet and the Spectator Club, the most successful characters emerge from the authors' portrayal of illustrative individuals.

In his discussion of characters in the *Spectator* Donald Kay divides the form into two categories which he labels the "typical" and the "individual"; he also divides the former class between the formal Theophrastan kind and informal sketches in the manner of La Bruyère and argues that there is a general "loosening" in the direction of the short story.[39] If we accept Kay's divisions as a spectrum of possibilities, not as rigid distinctions, they are useful. For example, in the *Tatler* we find fewer of the more formal variety than in the *Spectator*. The sketches of Eugenius, "a Man of an Universal Good-nature" (*S* 177), and the Devotée (*S* 354) do not possess the kind of intimate detail they likely would in the *Tatler*; their rigid incremental structure, with clause after clause beginning with "he" or "she" makes them distant, though valuable examples. The "modest fellow" in the *Tatler* follows this pattern initially, but Bickerstaff typically introduces a relative to personalize the type in the next paragraph (*T* 52b). Amid Mr. Spectator's discussion of the pleasant fellow is a good instance of this formality:

> *Dacinthus* breaks his Word upon all Occasions both trivial and important; and when he is sufficiently railed at for that abominable Quality, they who talk of him end with, *After all he is a very pleasant Fellow*. *Dacinthus* is an ill-natured Husband, and yet the very Women end their Freedom of Discourse upon this Subject, *But after all he is very pleasant Company*. *Dacinthus* is neither in point of Honour, Civility, good Breeding, or good Nature unexceptionable, and yet all is answered, *For he is a very pleasant Fellow*. (*S* 462)

The name does little to particularize this sketch with its "pleasant" refrain. Only the epistolary presentation lessens our distance from the equally formal portrait of the "mercurial" friend (*S* 194).

Much more attuned to the sociability of the *Tatler*
and the *Spectator* are more informal characters like the
"Rural *Andromache*, who came up to Town last Winter," when
she was overheard by Mr. Spectator, or the "*Starer*" described by a correspondent, to whom the Spectator assigns
Will. Prosper (*S* 57, 20). We have already commented on
the success of letters in adding verisimilitude to the
character, especially when, like the Valetudinarian, the
typical figure describes himself. But Bickerstaff and Mr.
Spectator also know more about or interact with many such
characters in the middle range of this spectrum. Though
the sketches of the cunning Polypragmon (*T* 191a) or the
benevolent Manilius (*S* 467) move beyond stereotypes, still
more convincing are those like Eubulus, the monarch of Mr.
Spectator's coffee house at mid-day (*S* 49) or the dancing
virtuoso who disturbs Bickerstaff's repose (*T* 88b). In-
terestingly, Mr. Spectator uses Will Honeycomb to illustrate both the absent-minded and the pedant as a means to
particularize the reader's appreciation of the types (*S*
77, 105). The use of dialogue further individualizes
characters, like Mr. Spectator's passionate acquaintance
Syncropius: "If his Man enters the Room without what he
sent for, *That Blockhead*, begins he--*Gentlemen, I ask
your Pardon; but Servants now-a-days.*--The wrong Plates
are laid, they are thrown into the Middle of the Room;
his Wife stands by in Pain for him, which he sees in her
Face, and answers as if he had heard all she was thinking;
*Why, what the Devil! Why don't you take Care to give
Orders in these Things?*" (*S* 438). The ridiculous attitude
created by anger could not have been comparably explained
by precept.

Among the most thoroughly individual characters are
Bickerstaff's acquaintances, the Political Upholsterer and
Ned Softly; Sir Roger de Coverley's friend, Will Wimble;
and Mr. Spectator's correspondent, Nathaniel Henroost.
Each still clearly illustrates a type: the coffee-house

politician, the pretentious poet, the genteel younger son,
and the hen-pecked husband. The first three encounter
Bickerstaff or Mr. Spectator in a appropriate setting,
while the last sends his "Representation of an hen-peckt
Life," giving an "Account of my self and my own Spouse"
(*S* 176). The uxoriousness betrayed by this amiably self-
justifying letter suggests that the writer's role may be
partly voluntary. The use of circumstantial detail is
skillful. Henroost cannot express his religiosity because
his wife is a "violent Whig." So he soothes her with politics: "It is a common Practice with me to ask her some
Question concerning the Constitution, which she answers
me in general out of *Harrington's Oceana*: Then I commend
her strange Memory, and her Arm is immediately locked in
mine." The use of significant detail is also central to
Bickerstaff's meeting with Softly at Will's Coffee House,
where one of his foolish poems is the focus of the portrayal, along with his equally silly aesthetics. To
justify his line "*For ah! it wounds me like his dart*,"
Softly urges, "Pray, how do you like that 'Ah!' Does it
not make a pretty figure in that place? 'Ah!' It looks
as if I felt the dart, and cried out at being pricked
with it" (*T* 163). Bickerstaff never has to utter the
charge of false wit for the reader to think of it.

The Upholsterer and Wimble take us even further from
the typical character because each appears several times.
Bickerstaff first provides a brief introductory sketch of
his neighbor, telling us that he is "much more inquisitive
to know what passed in Poland than in his own family" as
prologue to their conversation in St. James Park (*T* 155).
This "extraordinary dialogue" about the King of Sweden
and the Upholsterer's "odd" friends on the bench particularize our belief in his shop's ruin. We later see the
Upholsterer in a coffee house reading aloud when Bickerstaff compares his obsession to Don Quixote's: "This
touch in the brain of the British subject is as certainly

owing to the reading newspapers, as that of the Spanish
worthy above mentioned to the reading works of chivalry"
(*T* 178). Bickerstaff receives two newsmongering letters
from the Upholsterer (*T* 160, 232a), which complete our
information about him. We also discover Will Wimble from
several perspectives. An "extraordinary Letter" and a
brief character given Mr. Spectator by Sir Roger precede
his appearance at the squire's estate. By the conclusion
of the issue Mr. Spectator has expressed pleasure at
Will's "Novelty" and "Compassion" for his situation, which
becomes the more generalized "Case of many a younger
Brother of a great Family, who had rather see their Children starve like Gentlemen, than thrive in a Trade or
Profession that is beneath their Quality" (*S* 108). The
charming particulars of Will's character arise from his
"Gentleman-like Manufactures and obliging little Humours,"
which are related in some detail. Mr. Spectator later
tells us of Will's presence at Sir Roger's dinner table,
where his rural manners cause difficulty for the town
guest and of his trip to the assizes with Sir Roger, when
Will's report of a fishing hole provokes Tom Touchy (*S*
119, 122). When Sir Roger tells the Spectator that "poor"
Will has been sued by Touchy, we also learn of his diversions at recent Christman festivities: "Our Friend *Will*
Wimble is as merry as any of them, and shews a thousand
Roguish Tricks upon these Occasions" (*S* 269). The Blooms
rightly judge Wimble's life to be "stifled by excessive
good breeding" which makes him "valueless" to himself and
his society;[40] but we need to keep in mind Sir Roger's
phrase "Our Friend," which suggests that his uselessness
does not deny his humanity. Characters such as Will
Wimble and the Upholsterer clearly move in the direction
of the story or the novel, where a writer like Smollett
could weave encounters with a functionless gentleman and
a coffee-house madman into a broader comic plot.

VI

Just as most of these characters in the *Tatler* and
the *Spectator* are recognizably English, many of the anecdotes and tales in the periodicals center on the English
family. Writing about one such early *Tatler* story Bonamy
Dobrée declares that "the lively realism, the sense of
middle-class actuality, are nearer to life than anything
that had so far been offered the public in the guise of
fiction."[41] This issue deals with a woman who is cured
by her second husband of the "fits" she used to manipulate
her first. Bickerstaff's circumstantial narration of her
wiser husband's reaction is vivid: "She immediately
fainted--he starts up as amazed, and calls for help--the
maids run to the closet--he chafes her face, bends her
forwards, and beats the palms of her hands; her convulsions
increase, and down she tumbles on the floor, where she
lies quite dead, in spite of what the whole family, from
the nursury to the kitchen, could do for her relief" (*T*
23a). Sin-e both reader and husband know she is feigning,
the situation is ludicrous. But the husband's generous yet
realistic words effect so thorough a cure that Bickerstaff
reports "she gave me this relation herself, to be communi-
cated for the benefit of all the voluntary invalids of
her sex." While this didactic remark concludes the story,
it remains, as T. O. Beachcroft suggests, a "compressed
version of a rather complex social comedy."[42] Bickerstaff
also tells a Lincolnshire version of *The Taming of the
Shrew* (*T* 231), which shows another husband more successful
in domesticating his wife than Nicholas Henroost, Antony
Freeman, and other hen-pecked husbands in the *Tatler* and
the *Spectator*. Also comic is "*The History of Tom Varnish*," which depicts a "man of wit and pleasure of the
town" who plans an intrigue with a merchant's wife (*T*
136a). The outcome reveals how thoroughly the *Tatler*
moralizes the novella form; instead of succumbing to the
clever gallant, Ballance and his wife foil his plot and
ship Varnish off in a chest.[43] These stories repeatedly

urge the integrity of the family against assaults from within or without.

Bickerstaff and Mr. Spectator present accounts of some good marriages, like that of Jenny Distaff and Tranquillus or that of Emilia and Bromius (*S* 302), but they and their correspondents more often relate the difficulties of matrimony, as we see in the anecdote of Harry Tersett and his wife, whose lives are "now at a Stand" (*S* 100), or in the longer story of Elmira and Osmyn, discussed earlier. Among the *Tatler*'s matrimonial tragedies is the account of the Irishman Eustace, who in murdering his wife after a brief quarrel, illustrates "how fatal surprises of passion are to the mind of man" (*T* 172). The attention given to Eustace's knife increases the horror of this bizarre event set in a commonplace life. Bickerstaff prefaces his story with suggestions that tragedy should not be limited to representatives of the upper class:

> I was thinking it would be of great use . . .
> to lay before the world such adventures as
> befall persons not exalted above the common
> level. This, methought, would better prevail
> upon the ordinary race of men, who are so
> prepossessed with outward appearances, that
> they mistake fortune for nature, and believe
> nothing can relate to them that does not hap-
> pen to such as live and look like themselves.

One practical reason for middle-class fiction is announced here. In the *Spectator* the correspondent who describes "a poor idle drunken Weaver" selling a winning lottery ticket purchased by his "faithful laborious Wife" expects Mr. Spectator to be expert in rendering such domestic difficulties: "This, Sir, is Matter of Fact, and would, if the Persons and Circumstances were greater, in a well wrought Play be call'd *Beautiful Distress*. I have only scetch'd it out with Chalk, and know a good Hand can make a Moving-Picture with worse Materials" (*S* 242). The oblique flattery shows how far the periodicals advanced

this kind of story. The problem of jealousy is handled
with some complexity in a letter from Philagnotes, relating the effects of his visit to a relative, now married
to a "wealthy Citizen," who believes that "he was made a
Member of too numerous a Society" (S 527). This portrayal
of jealousy's "Magnifying-Glasses" involves the kind of
realistic detail we expect: "I have writ to him to assure
him I was at his House all that Afternoon expecting to
see him: His answer is, 'tis only a Trick of hers, and
that he neither can nor will believe me. The parting
Kiss I find mightily nettles him, and confirms him in all
his Errors." This glimpse of unfounded jealousy shows
how effectively Addison and Steele use the letter form to
represent the "ordinary race of men."

Relations between parents and children also receive
the attention of Bickerstaff and Mr. Spectator in their
domestic fiction. The unnatural rivalry of mother and
daughter is the subject of an anecdote and a story (T 206;
S 91). In the first, "these jarring companions" Flavia
and Lucia vie for male attention, with the mother constantly reprimanding her daughter and the daughter frequently reminding suitors that Flavia is her mother.
Steele developed this sketch into a second version, setting the rivalry of Lady Honoria, a forty-year-old-widow,
with her daughter Flavia in a fuller social context. Tom
Wildair illustrates another kind of problem, the son
squandering his father's money. Here the father's patient
generosity leads to reformation: "Instead of that unthink-
ing creature he was before, he is now provident, generous,
and discreet" (T 60a). Mr. Spectator portrays "the amiable Fidelia" as one of the "small illustrious Number of
Heroines" who merit imitation and tells of her sacrifices
to care for her father (S 449); the story of two friends,
Eudoxus and Leontine, who exchange children after the
latter is widowed, concludes with the marriage of their
dutiful, loving children (S 123). Such exemplary conduct

contrasts with the parent-child conflicts that permeate the *Tatler* and the *Spectator*.

As evidence for the domestic lives of characters, in addition to letters, Bickerstaff and Mr. Spectator include a number of documents, and even a few journals. Bickerstaff uses his own will to satirize others; for example, he bestows his learning "upon the honorary members of the Royal Society" and his wit "among such as think they have enough already" (*T* 7a). But he lets the will of Nicholas Gimcrack ridicule its testator, a virtuoso, to "show this humour in its perfection" (*T* 216a). Bickerstaff prints other inventories for satiric reasons, such as the theatrical "movables" of *Ch--------r R-ch*, Esq. (*T* 42c). The bill of auction for a young man "carried off dead upon the taking away of his snuff-box" (*T* 113), itemizes the possessions of a fop, and a list of belongings stolen from Lady Farthingale by Bridget Howd'ee portrays its fashionable owner (*T* 245a). Mr. Spectator's survey of Leonora's library, while not a document, follows this listing method to satirize the frivolity and confusion of values it reveals (*S* 37). Although possessions effectively characterize their owners, more intimate portrayals arise from the week-long journals of a "sober Citizen" and of "a Maiden Lady of a good Fortune," Clarinda. The former shows that "our Hours may very often be more profitably laid out in such Transactions as make no Figure in the World, than in such as are apt to draw upon them the Attention of Mankind" (*S* 317), but the latter depicts "a modish State of Indifference between Vice and Vertue" (*S* 323). One other minor form related to letters and these other documents is the reader's mock petition, which both periodicals use occasionally. For instance, in the *Tatler*, William Jingle, Penelope Prim, and Deborah Hark petition about petticoats (*T* 113, 118b, 136c); in the *Spectator* Benjamin Easie petitions against a lady's fan (*S* 134), while Bartholomew Ladylove petitions for "Fawners"

(*S* 304). These documents, mostly used for ridicule, are another means of achieving an entertaining diversity.

VII.

Among other kinds of fiction in the *Tatler* and the *Spectator* are several in which neither English characters nor English settings are prominent. The dream, the allegory, the fable, and the oriental tale deal more indirectly with the world we have described as the basis of these periodicals by abstracting the subject matter from its English context. Bickerstaff and Mr. Spectator tell most of these narratives. The first allegory and the first dream in the *Tatler* suggest that Steele began using these forms as a polite way to discuss party politics. For instance, propaganda for the Whig Junto is transferred to Felicia, and the Duke of Marlborough is an unnamed warrior returning to a shadowy, unnamed isle (*T* 4e, 8c). The best political visions are not so specific. Bickerstaff dreams of "a happy region . . . inhabited by the Goddess of Liberty," who is seated between the "Genius of a Commonwealth" and the "Genius of Monarchy," surrounded by her train, but threatened by "two formidable enemies," led by Tyranny and Licentiousness (*T* 161). This fiction argues quietly for the reasonableness of the Whig position, as does the allegory of wax-work religions, in which a central matron symbolizing the Anglican Church is flanked by embodiments of Catholicism, Judaism, and Deism on her right and Presbyterianism, Anabaptism, Quakerism, and Atheism on her left (*T* 257). Moderation is the key to centrist policies in both these allegories. The only political vision in the *Spectator* comes in its third issue, where Public Credit is personified as "a beautiful Virgin, seated on a Throne of Gold" to validate Whig economic theories; again enemies appear to threaten the virgin until they are displaced by "Liberty, with Monarchy at her right Hand" and "Moderation leading in Religion" (*T* 3a). For an audience interested in entertainment as well as instruction,

Bickerstaff and Mr. Spectator found an appropriately good-natured method of political education.

But the dream is more likely to be the occasion for satire or philosophy. The vision of the Goddess of Justice uses the device of a mirror to ridicule the affectations of men and women. Bickerstaff describes its effect on documents: "The rays of this mirror had a particular quality of setting fire to all forgery and falsehood" (*T* 100). In the male world Justice restores property to true owners, children to actual parents, and positions to the meritorious; in the female world she ranks true rather than superficial beauty and punishes aptly "all females addicted to censoriousness" and "the loose part of the sex." Of this punishment Bickerstaff remarks: "It was a sensible affliction to me to see such a multitude of fair ones either dumb or big-bellied" (*T* 102). The extravagance of his satiric vision suggests ludicrously the moderation also needed in social life. One of Bickerstaff's dreams employs the analogous device of Ithuriel's spear, which has "a secret virtue in it, that whatever it was applied to, immediately flung off all disguise, and appeared in its natural figure" (*T* 237). The stripping away of affectation is rendered with mock-scientific plausibility in two of Mr. Spectator's dreams, which humorously recall a passage from Swift's *Tale of a Tub*: "Last Week I saw a Woman *flay'd*, and you will hardly believe, how much it altered her Person for the worse. Yesterday I ordered the Carcass of a *Beau* to be stript in my Presence; when we were all amazed to find so many unsuspected Faults under one Suit of Cloaths: Then I laid open his *Brain*, his *Heart*, and his *Spleen*; But, I plainly perceived at every Operation, that the farther we proceeded, we found the Defects encrease upon us in Number and Bulk."[44] The more genial dissections of a beau's head and a coquette's heart provide a satiric anatomy of the follies of these familiar types (*S* 275, 281). Will

Honeycomb submits two satiric dreams, his own ridiculing marriage and an allegorical one he has discovered warning women of beauty's decay (*s* 499, 301). The Scales and the exchange of griefs ordered by Jupiter, two more nonrealistic devices for moral instruction, involve Mr. Spectator himself (*s* 463, 558-59). In Bickerstaff's "unaccountable reverie," which "cannot be so properly called a dream as a delirium," a shilling narrates his "life and adventures," an amusing survey of human folly (*T* 249). There are other moral or philosophic visions and two literary ones, Mr. Spectator's dream about wit and a correspondent's journey to Parnassus (*s* 63, 514). The only attempt to relate these dreams directly to the ordinary world is the frequent suggestion that they arise from the reading or conversation of Bickerstaff and Mr. Spectator.

Both personae speak of allegories and fables together. After Menmius tells of Love's birth from Plenty and Poverty, Bickerstaff says: "I have been always wonderfully delighted with fables, allegories, and the like inventions, which the politest and the best instructors of mankind have always made use of: they take off from the severity of instruction, and enforce it at the same time that they conceal it" (*T* 90a). Before telling his "beautiful Allegory or Fable" of the marriage of Pleasure and Pain, Mr. Spectator distinguishes various kinds: "The Fables I have here mentioned are raised altogether upon Brutes and Vegetables, with some of our own Species mixt among them, when the Moral hath so required. But besides this kind of Fable there is another in which the Actors are Passions, Virtues, Vices, and other imaginary Persons of the like Nature" (*s* 183). Although he tells sixteen traditional, mostly animal fables,[45] Mr. Spectator's preference leads to his original relation of a "little kind of Allegory or Fable" depicting the conflict of Luxury and Avarice (*s* 55) and a "Heathen Fable relating to Prayers" (*s* 391). Bickerstaff tells a similar allegory of virtue and

64

pleasure (*T* 97), but he more often uses animal fables, even putting himself in the role of a "stout and honest mastiff" to fend off critics, depicted as nettlesome "curs" (*T* 115b). Following the example of AEsop "for figuring the manners, designs, passions, and interests of men, by fables of beasts and birds," Bickerstaff describes sharpers as a "pack of dogs" (*T* 59a); this fabulation continues for a few issues and evokes some correspondence. Mr. Spectator judges the fable the "Art of making Advice agreeable" because it "will appear to us, if we reflect, in the first place, that upon the reading of a Fable we are made to believe we advise our selves. We peruse the Author for the sake of the Story, and consider the Precepts rather as our own Conclusions, than his Instructions" (*S* 512). The intellectual activity required by fables and allegories proves yet another way to involve the reader in these periodicals.

Mr. Spectator gives some of his fables and allegories an oriental setting. Such an altered perspective, Arthur J. Weitzman contends, enables the editors to emphasize general truths, to discover "the constant and universal principles" of human life by holding an eastern mirror up to western society.[46] Of these oriental tales, some are borrowed, and a few are original. For example, Mr. Spectator tells "a very pretty Story in the *Turkish* Tales" to illustrate the Lockean concept of duration, an "Eastern Allegory" from the *Arabian Nights* to demonstrate the need for physical exercise, and "the Mistake of the *Dervise*" from *The Travels of Sir John Chardin* to depict man's transitory estate (*S* 94, 195, 289). He expresses his opinion about one such useful fiction, the story of Alnanschar, whose "chimerical Vision" of prosperity ruins his present condition: "The Fable has in it such a wild, but natural, Simplicity, that I question not but my Reader will be as much pleased with it as I have been, and that he will consider himself, if he reflects on the

several Amusements of Hope which have sometimes passed in
his Mind, as near Relation to the *Persian* Glass-Man" (*S*
535). These brief, borrowed fictions are clearly exemplary. The best known of the original oriental tales,
the "*Vision of* Mirzah," provides an allegorical glimpse
of the Christian's pilgrimage across the bridge of
"humane Life" to the "Mansions of good Men after Death,"
through Mirzah's meeting with a Genius (*S* 159). On the
other hand, the charming "Antediluvian" story of Shalum
and Hilpa lacks this ultimate concern and seems, unusually, to be told for its own sake (*S* 584-85). In the
mode of *The Turkish Spy*, using a foreign observer to comment on local morals and manners, are the "curious Observations" of King Sa Ga Yean Qua Rash Tow, one of four
Indian chiefs visiting London, and the letter to the King
of Bantam from his English ambassador (*S* 50, 557). While
the latter ridicules hypocritical forms of politeness,
the Indian's journal satirizes nominal Christianity,
political parties, and fashions. His description of a
sermon at St. Paul's Cathedral is characteristically
ironic: "There was indeed a Man in Black who was mounted
above the rest, and seemed to utter something with a great
deal of Vehemence; but as for those underneath him, instead of paying their Worship to the Deity of the Place,
they were most of them bowing and curtisying to one
another, and a considerable Number of them fast asleep."
We also find a more recognizable context in Will Honeycomb's importation of a Persian fair and a Chinese sack
sale to satirize the English marriage market (*S* 511).
Will tells, too, of Pugg the Monkey's letter, in which
the Indian belief in transmigration is used to dupe a
lady.

In addition to dreams, fables, and oriental fictions,
the *Tatler* and the *Spectator* employ other devices to distance the reader from the English milieu. Foreign settings, like the orient, are more frequent in the

Spectator, while non-realistic techniques, akin to the
dream, are prevalent in the *Tatler*. Both devices add
variety and stress the universality of the periodicals'
contents. Two of the most memorable stories in the *Spectator*, the history of Inkle and Yarico and the rivalry
between Brunetta and Phillis (*S* 11, 80), are set wholly
or partially in the Barbadoes. In each a native figure
is important--the betrayed Yarico and the "beautiful Negro
Girl" whose brocade matches that of the distressed Phillis.
The island of St. Christopher is the setting for a "wild
Tragedy" which involves the rivalry of two slaves for a
young woman. When they kill her and each other, Mr.
Spectator concludes: "We see, in this amazing Instance of
Barbarity, what strange Disorders are bred in the Minds
of those Men whose Passions are not regulated by Vertue,
and disciplined by Reason" (*S* 215). The exotic background
of the West Indies is an appropriate context for these
tales of passion. South America is the locale for Mr.
Spectator's histories of a "Male Commonwealth" and an
Amazonian "Female Republic," which allow him to emphasize
some elemental aspects of relations between the sexes (*S*
433-434). Of continental settings, France and Germany
are used most often. Mr. Spectator recalls his visit to
France (*S* 15), during which he also supposedly heard the
moving story of Constantia and Theodosius from a priest
in a stagecoach (*S* 163, 164). Their inability to win her
father's consent for marriage leads each to a monastic
life, in which they meet again, having learned the consolation of religion; separated in life, Constantia and
Theodosius are buried together. France is also the source
for the story of the male mummy, in which Monsieur Pontignan describes the "*Platonick* Hell" caused by two coquettes
(*S* 90), and for a letter in which the writer depicts the
death of Madame de Villacerfe, a "Heroine who is a Pattern
of Patience and Generosity" (*S* 368). Using the legendary
king of the Franks, Pharamond, and his invented friend

Eucrate, Steele created some "Pieces of secret History"
to illustrate current issues, such as dueling. Mr. Spectator comments aptly in one of these issues: "As humane
Life turns upon the same Principles and Passions in all
Ages, I thought it very proper to take Minutes of what
passed in that Age for the Instruction of this" (*S* 84).
Other essays in this series portray life in court and
country, including Pharamond's "Edict against Duels" (*S*
97, 76, 480). Germany is the setting for two domestic
conflicts: the intrigue of Eginhart and Imma (*S* 181) and
the saga of the Valentine family, where the "Want of
mutual Confidence and right Understanding between Father
and Son was fatal" (*S* 426). The remoteness of place and
time probably adds credence to Eginhart's walk in the
snow upon Imma's fair shoulders and to the Valentines'
skill in "the Hermetick Art." Algiers, with its pirates,
is an appropriately uncivilized context for the story of
a Castilian betrayed by his wife with the aid of a French
"Renegado" (*S* 198). The *Tatler* changes its scene much
less often. The tragic deaths of Philander and Chloe are
set in a Danish theater on an evening in 1679; Bickerstaff
suddenly breaks off his account, saying "I cannot go on"
and hoping that "so much virtue" could not "meet with so
great distress without a following reward" from Providence
(*T* 94a). Bickerstaff's most remote shift is to Nova
Zembla, Greenland, the setting for the episode of the
frozen words, supposedly taken from the travels of Sir
John Mandeville and translated for the reader's benefit.
With analogues in Rabelais and others, this incident more
likely conforms to Bickerstaff's comment: "One reads the
voyages . . . with as much astonishment as the travels of
Ulysses in Homer, or of the Red-Cross Knight in Spenser.
All is enchanted ground or fairy-land" (*T* 254). The tale
seems primarily designed for entertainment.

Several non-realistic devices in the *Tatler* are the
basis for satire. The first is Pacolet, Bickerstaff's

familiar, an appropriate companion for an astrologer. Since the familiar enables Bickerstaff to know little more than he later acquires on his own, Steele wisely abandoned this shadowy figure as a means of social intelligence. Similar, but limited to one issue, is Bickerstaff's magic ring, which transports him to various rooms (*T* 243). Boyce cites Pacolet's conversation with Socrates and a dead duelist (*T* 26b) and John Partridge's letter "*From the Banks of Styx*" (*T* 118a) as examples of "news from hell," a popular device in early eighteenth-century England.[47] In two series of papers Bickerstaff presides over courts designed to examine cases of human affectation. The first, the Court of Justice, begins in *T* 103, meets again in *T* 110, when the lover's phrase "I die for you" is ridiculed, and in *T* 116, which is the wonderfully exaggerated petticoat trial, and concludes with *T* 131, a vintner's case. Nearer the end of his Lucubrations Bickerstaff convenes the Court of Honor; he prints a description of its functions and selections from its "Journal" in six consecutive Tuesday issues (*T* 250, 253, 256, 259, 262, 265). A parade of familiar social types comes before this bench. For example, Charles Cambric, a linen merchant, is "indicted for speaking obscenely" to the prude, Lady Penelope Touchwood, in a coach (*T* 259). Though the jury finds the offending words, "linen" and "smock" apt to create images "not proper to be stirred up in the mind of a woman who was of the prosecutor's quality," Bickerstaff judges the prude's ears as guilty as the merchant's tongue and punishes both.

Besides printing oriental fables taken from the *Arabian Nights* or the *Persian Tales* Mr. Spectator and Bickerstaff retell many stories from other sources, classical, biblical, and modern. These twice-told tales include letters from Pliny and Cicero (*T* 149, 159; *S* 230), fables about noses and Pandora's box (*T* 260; *S* 471), and poetry paraphrased in prose from Homer, Ovid, Spenser, and Milton (*T* 6b, 117, 147a, 217a; *S* 391). The purpose of almost all is to illustrate some moral precept under consideration. The most coherent group of these narratives begins in *Tatler* 152 with Bickerstaff "meditating on the soul's immortality" and suggesting that it "may likewise be worth while to consider, what men of the most exalted genius, and elevated imagination, have thought of this matter." He completes this issue by retelling Ulysses's journey to the underworld from the *Odyssey,* later renders similar voyages from the *Aeneid* and Fénelon's *Télémaque* (*T* 154, 156), and concludes by saying:

> Prospects of this nature lighten the burden of
> any present evil, and refresh us under the worst
> and lowest circumstances of mortality. They
> extinguish in us both the fear and envy of
> human grandeur. . . . In short, the mind that
> is habituated to the lively sense of a here-
> after, can hope for what is the most terrify-
> ing to the generality of mankind, and rejoice
> in what is the most afflicting. (*T* 156)

Mr. Spectator retells two stories from Josephus's *Antiq-
uities of the Jews.* Introducing the first, Glaphyra's dream of her dead husband, he remarks that it is used "not so much for the Sake of the Story it self, as for the moral Reflections with which the Author concludes it" (*S* 110); the story of Herod and Mariamne "may serve almost as an Example to whatever can be said" about jealousy (*S* 171). While such twice-told tales vary the realism and setting of the *Tatler* and the *Spectator*, they also enhance the image of moral authority created for Bickerstaff and Mr. Spectator, who choose to include them.

VIII.

Now that we have described the general characteristics of fiction in the *Tatler* and the *Spectator*--the personae and their clubs, relatives, and correspondents, along with the varied forms and settings of their narratives--we can suggest how our *Guide* provides access to this fictional world. Each subsequent section contributes in a different way. Two chronological lists

depict briefly the contents of every issue of the
Tatler (subdivided by departments) and the *Spectator*, with
indications of narrators, subjects, and characters. We
include shorter descriptions of issues or departments containing no fiction (designated NF) to indicate the high
frequency of fiction. As implied in this introduction,
we define fiction broadly to include any sort of imagined
prose narrative, as well as the ongoing characterization
of the personae and their settings. Because we do not
try to classify every piece of fiction, we include much
that Kay could not fit into a specific genre in choosing
the one hundred examples of fiction discussed in his book.
In addition to anecdotes, characters, allegories, and
tales, we include almost all correspondence as fiction.
Though many letters are clearly fictional, few can be
accurately labeled non-fiction because of uncertain
attribution and likely editorial alteration. Our catalogues are inclusive rather than exclusive; they recognize
the shaping hand of Steele and Addison, which gives the
fiction such consistently high quality. Each catalogue
is accompanied by an index which arranges the pieces of
fiction among such categories as subjects frequently discussed, names of characters, narrative techniques and
forms, and authors. We have not tried to duplicate the
excellent index to Donald F. Bond's edition of the *Spectator* but have sought to complement it through our emphasis
on fictional strategies.

The final part of the *Guide* is a bibliography of secondary materials which contribute to our critical appreciation of the prose fiction in the *Tatler* and the *Spectator*. Although there are two earlier items, the bibliography essentially covers the two hundred years from essays
by James Beattie (1776) and Samuel Johnson (1781) until
1975. The numerous editions of and selections from these
periodicals are not listed, but published notes pertinent
to single issues are. The bibliography is annotated
descriptively.

One major purpose of this *Guide* is to make the *Tatler* and the *Spectator* more accessible to those interested in the development of prose fiction as well as to those interested in the periodicals themselves. That this body of fiction is not evaluated in a book like John J. Richetti's *Popular Fiction Before Richardson* (Oxford: Clarendon Press, 1969), typifies its neglect. While scholars with specialized interests--humor, the oriental tale, the character, epistolary fiction, magazine fiction --have added to our understanding of the fiction in the *Tatler* and the *Spectator*, few have assessed the relationship between this short fiction and longer fiction of the age. We hope that *A Guide to Prose Fiction in the* Tatler *and the* Spectator will facilitate such investigation through its documentation of the artful variety found in the periodicals' narratives. Because of its quality and influence, this fiction should be prominent in the study of eighteenth-century fiction. The *Guide* reflects our judgment that, in addition to containing the best short fiction of 1709-1714, the *Tatler* and the *Spectator*, taken as a whole, are the finest prose fictions of Stuart England's final years.

NOTES TO INTRODUCTION

[1] "English Short Fiction in the Eighteenth Century: A Preliminary View," *Studies in Short Fiction*, 5 (1968), 95.

[2] *The* Tatler: *The Making of a Literary Journal* (Cambridge, Mass.: Harvard Univ. Press, 1971), p. 156.

[3] *Short Fiction in* The Spectator (University, Ala.: Univ. of Alabama Press, 1975), p. 118.

[4] *The Short Story in English* (New York: Holt, 1909), p. 180.

[5] The editions used in preparing this study were *The Tatler*, ed. George Aitken, 4 vols. (New York: Hadley and Matthews, 1899) and *The Spectator*, ed. Donald F. Bond, 5 vols. (Oxford: Clarendon Press, 1965). Quotations from these texts are cited parenthetically, using the abbreviation *T* or *S* and the issue number.

[6] See C. N. Greenough, "The Development of the *Tatler*, particularly in Regard to News," *PMLA*, 31 (1916), 633-63; Robert W. Achurch, "Richard Steele, Gazetteer and Bickerstaff," *Studies in the Early English Periodical*, ed. Richmond P. Bond (Chapel Hill: Univ. of North Carolina Press, 1957), pp. 49-72; and Richmond P. Bond, *The Tatler*, Chapter III, "Current Affairs," pp. 44-70.

[7] *The English Novel in the Magazines 1740-1815* (Evanston, Ill.: Northwestern Univ. Press, 1962), p. 34.

[8] See Claude M. Newlin, "The English Periodicals and the Novel, 1709-40," *Papers of the Michigan Academy of Science Arts and Letters*, 16 (1931), 467-76.

[9] *Robinson Crusoe: An Authoritative Text, Background and Sources, Criticism*, ed. Michael Shinagel (New York: Norton, 1975), p. 3.

[10] *A Checklist of English Prose Fiction, 1700-1739* (Cambridge, Mass.: Harvard Univ. Press, 1960), p. viii.

[11] "Isaac Bickerstaff, Esq.," *Restoration and Eighteenth Century Literature: Essays in Honor of Alan Dugald McKillop*, ed. Carroll Camden (Chicago: Univ. of Chicago Press, 1963), p. 113.

[12] See Richmond P. Bond, "Isaac Bickerstaff, Esq." for an account of Swift's character and Steele's transformation of him.

[13] "The Ambivalent Spectator," *Papers on Language and Literature*, 9 (1973), 83-84.

[14] *Joseph Andrews*, ed. Martin C. Battestin (Middletown, Conn.: Wesleyan Univ. Press, 1967), p. 17.

[15] "Familiarity in the Addisonian Familiar Essay," *College Composition and Communication*, 16 (1965), 172.

[16] *Steele, Addison and Their Periodical Essays* (London: Longmans, 1959), p. 15.

[17] *The Rise of the Novel of Manners: A Study of English Prose Fiction between 1600 and 1740* (New York: Columbia Univ. Press, 1911), p. 95.

[18] *Satire and the Novel in Eighteenth-Century England* (New Haven: Yale Univ. Press, 1967), p. 59.

[19] Richmond P. Bond discusses the departments of the periodical in *The Tatler*, Chapter VII, "The Words and Ways of Bickerstaff," especially pp. 179-80.

[20] *The Clubs of Augustan London* (Cambridge, Mass.: Harvard Univ. Press, 1933), p. 203.

[21] Allen, p. 206.

[22] "The Periodical Essayists," *From Dryden to Johnson*, ed. Boris Ford (Hammondsworth: Penguin, 1957), p. 221.

[23] *Joseph Addison's Sociable Animal: In the Market Place; on the Hustings; in the Pulpit* (Providence, R. I.: Brown Univ. Press, 1971), p. 13.

[24] "Introduction," *The Spectator*, p. xxxiii.

[25] "The Augustan Author-Audience Relationship: Satiric vs. Comic Forms," *ELH*, 36 (1969), 656.

[26] *The Amiable Humorist: A Study in the Comic Theory and Criticism of the Eighteenth and Early Nineteenth Centuries* (Chicago: Univ. of Chicago Press, 1960), p. 102.

[27] Tave, pp. 102, 103.

[28] *Lives of the English Poets*, ed. George Birkbeck Hill (Oxford: Clarendon Press, 1905), II, 97.

[29] Donald F. Bond, "Introduction," *The Spectator*, p. xxxiv; Blooms, p. 16.

[30] Allen, pp. 176, 179.

[31] See Richmond P. Bond, *New Letters to the* Tatler *and* Spectator (Austin: Univ. of Texas Press, 1959), p. 6.

[32] "Meaning and Format: Mr. Spectator and His Folio Half-Sheets," *ELH*, 34 (1967), 483.

[33] *The Tatler*, p. 139.

[34] Donald F. Bond, "Introduction," *The Spectator*, p. xlii. Richmond P. Bond concurs:

> When we read the letters chosen for use we therefore cannot know how much the editor revised them and the compositor normalized their mechanics. We suspect, with some evidence from the letters in manuscript, that most of the correspondence required at least some editorial aid as well as the printer's usual help in capitalization, punctuation, and orthography.
>
> (*The Tatler*, p. 141)

[35] *Magazine Serials and the Essay Tradition 1746-1820* (Baton Rouge: Louisiana State Univ. Press, 1956), p. 9.

[36] *Told in Letters: Epistolary Fiction Before Richardson* (Ann Arbor: Univ. of Michigan Press, 1966), p. 150.

[37] Day, p. 267.

[38] Richmond P. Bond, *The Tatler*, p. 149.

[39] Kay, Chapter 2, "The Character," especially pp. 29-30.

[40] Blooms, p. 24.

[41] *English Literature in the Early Eighteenth Century 1700-1740* (Oxford: Clarendon Press, 1959), p. 80.

[42] *The English Short Story* (London: Longmans, 1967), I, 32.

[43] Newlin cites *Tatler* no. 198 and *Spectator* no. 198, in both of which sympathy is aroused for the rake's victim, as further examples of this process (p. 469).

[44] *A Tale of a Tub to Which Is Added the Battle of the Books and the Mechanical Operation of the Spirit*, ed. A. C. Guthkelch and D. Nichol Smith, 2nd ed. (Oxford: Clarendon Press, 1958), pp. 173-74.

[45] Kay, p. 55.

[46] "The Oriental Tale in the Eighteenth Century: A Reconsideration," *Studies on Voltaire and the Eighteenth Century*, 58 (1967), 1853.

[47] "News from Hell: Satiric Commuications with the Nether World in English Writing of the Seventeenth and Eighteenth Centuries," *PMLA*, 58 (1943), 434.

A CATALOGUE OF PROSE FICTION
IN THE *TATLER*

Tatler 1a. Tuesday, April 12, 1709. Steele. [Introduction].

In a brief introductory essay, Isaac Bickerstaff states the purpose and defines the format of his paper. Intended to instruct politic persons who neglect their own affairs for those of the State and who are known to be of strong zeal and weak intellect, it will, on Tuesdays, Thursdays, and Saturdays, report on gallantry, pleasure, and entertainment from White's Chocolate-house, on poetry from Will's Coffee-house, on learning from the Grecian Coffee-house, on foreign and domestic news from St. James's Coffee-house, and on all other subjects from Bickerstaff's apartment. The charge per issue will be one penny to pay reporters.

Tatler 1b. _____. *White's Chocolate-house, April 11.*

Bickerstaff tells the story of a young man, later named Cynthio, who has been undone by the glimpse he once had, while brushing his teeth at a tavern window in Pall Mall, of a young lady passing in a carriage. Unable to find her, he carries her picture in his bosom and pays attention to nothing else. As a result, he seems out of his senses when sober and most witty when he is drunk.

Tatler 1c. NF. _____. *Will's Coffee-house, April 8.*

A review of a performance of Congreve's *Love for Love*, given as a benefit for Thomas Betterton.

Tatler 1d. NF. _____. *St. James's Coffee-house, April 11.*

A brief account of political affairs in Europe.

Tatler 1e. _____. *From My own Apartment.*

Bickerstaff says, in a brief essay, that the almanac which came out in 1709 under the name of John Partridge is a fraud, since Partridge is dead, although his body may still perform its animal functions. Bickerstaff claims astrological powers and says he will use them in the future to point out the deaths of other men who appear to be alive. All men are thus given fair warning to mend their manners.

Tatler 2a. Thursday, April 14, 1709. Steele. *Will's Coffee-house, April 13.*

Bickerstaff tells of a young man who fell in love with a woman of great beauty but of equally great ill-nature. As a result, their marriage is very unhappy. Since there seems no way out of the situation, rather than tell the whole story Bickerstaff offers a poem on the match, entitled "The Medecine," by a friend, in which the two parties are named Miss Molly and Sir John.

Tatler 2b. NF. _____. *St. James's Coffee-house, April 13.*

Further reports on political events in Europe.

Tatler 2c. _____. *From my own Apartment, April 13.*

Bickerstaff boasts of his astrological powers; as proof of them he claims to know that no one has died in France who is younger than the French king since he reached his sixty-third birthday. The only exceptions to this are those who fell in battle against the British.

Tatler 3a. Saturday, April 16, 1709. Steele. *Will's Coffee-house, April 14.*

After giving a brief review of a performance of Wycherley's *The Country Wife,* a benefit for Mrs. Bicknell, Bickerstaff associates himself with the Society for Reformation of Manners and censures those who act badly in public, especially at the theater. He then moves on to Will's in search of wit and poetry. While there he attacks those who advise the writing of poetry by rules and those who presume to write poems on how to paint. He points to Mr. Dactile, who is writing a poem to a young virgin knitter telling her to knit major events of the Jacobite campaign into the pattern of a stocking.

Tatler 3b. NF. _____. *St. James's Coffee-house, April 15.*

A brief report on letters received concerning European political affairs.

Tatler 3c. _____. *From my own Apartment, April 15.*

Bickerstaff asks that all attend a benefit performance of Farquhar's *Beaux' Stratagem* being given for John Bickerstaff, his relative.

Tatler 4a. Tuesday, April 19, 1709. Steele. [Introduction].

In a brief introductory essay, Bickerstaff rejects the idea that he should do anything other than issue his opinions under the present arrangement. He will persist in his effort to inform his readers of the fashions and successes of the town, to entertain men of pleasure, but not to offend men of business.

Tatler 4b. _____. *White's Chocolate-house, April 18.*

Bickerstaff announces that all the town pants for Clarissa and Chloe. Each is charming, but in her own way, and Bickerstaff recounts the nature of their differences, both in terms of their appearance and manner and their effects on their admirers.

Tatler 4c. NF. _____. *Will's Coffee-house, April 18.*

A performance of the opera *Pyrrhus and Demetrius* provokes some negative comments on this type of dramatic entertainment.

Tatler 4d. NF. _____. *St. James's Coffee-house, April 18.*

A report on political affairs in Europe.

Tatler 4e. _____. *From my own Apartment, April 18.*

Bickerstaff reports on a letter from the island of Felicia, where conditions are said to be prosperous and well-run. Even though the king has recently died, political affairs are in the good hands of Camillo, Horatio, Martio, Philander, and Verono, each of whom is said to be a splendid person for his job.

Tatler 5a. Thursday, April 21, 1709. Steele. *White's Chocolate-house, April 20.*

Bickerstaff tells of Cynthio, who in his love of Clarissa provides an example of the old style of lover, a type not now much in evidence. Unfortunately, his beloved is in love with another, according to Mrs. Meddle. Wildair, who is the second gentleman involved, is not in love with Clarissa at all. Fortunately, Cynthio seems to be remembering things, so he may be coming back to his senses.

Tatler 5b. NF. _____. *Will's Coffee-house, April 20.*

A brief review of a book entitled *A Project for the Advancement of Religion*, by Jonathan Swift.

Tatler 5c. NF. _____. *St. James's Coffee-house, April 20.*

A report on European political affairs.

Tatler 5d. _____. *From my own Apartment, April 20.*

Bickerstaff tells the story of Unnion, a corporal, and Valentine, a private, who are engaged with the enemy at the siege of Namur. The two are in a dispute over a matter of love, but Valentine saves Unnion's life in spite of their rivalry. Bickerstaff sees in this story something of the greatness of the English, as especially exemplified in the person of the Duke of Marlborough.

Tatler 6a. Saturday, April 23, 1709. Steele. *Will's Coffee-house, April 22.*

Bickerstaff tells of a visit with a literary lady named Sappho, and a literary gentleman who remains nameless. Sappho tries to be a critic of modern authors; she has broken a pretty Italian fan over her discovery of the relationship between poetry and painting. Bickerstaff finds her comments good but so strangely mixed that he concludes they are the result of luck rather than reason or judgment. The gentleman tries to be a critic of classical authors; he claims that Virgil is more judicious in his epithets than Homer.

Tatler 6b. _____. *Grecian Coffee-house, April 22.*

Bickerstaff says that while the rest of the town is involved in being amused with the present, people here spend the evening inquiring into the past. He then gives the products of these labors, an attempt to put the events of the *Iliad*, Books I-X, in strict chronology.

Tatler 6c. NF. _____. *St. James's Coffee-house, April 22.*

A report on letters concerning European political affairs.

Tatler 6d. NF. _____. *From my own Apartment, April 22.*

A comparison of Caesar and Alexander.

Tatler 7a. Tuesday, April 26, 1709. Steele. [Introduction].

Bickerstaff apologizes for giving the account of the *Iliad* and blames it on the fact that he finds he is running out of wit. Without help, he says he will not last beyond another month; he encourages his readers to supply him with their comments on any subject. He also makes a long and detailed will disposing of his mental abilities and his body and making careful provisions for his funeral.

Tatler 7b. _____. *White's Chocolate-house, April 25.*

Bickerstaff and Colonel Ramble go for a walk in the fields, where they come upon a wedding party for Monsieur Guardeloop (Ramble's and Bickerstaff's French tailor) and Madame Depingle's maid. It is a wet morning, and the bedraggled party reminds Bickerstaff of the difficulties of marriage. As a result, he vows to stay away from all married people for at least 24 hours. He then goes to visit Florimel and her admirer, Colonel Picket, who are prime examples of the coquette and the coxcomb.

Tatler 7c. NF. _____. *Will's Coffee-house, April 25.*

A review of a performance of *Epsom Wells*, by Thomas Shadwell, given as a benefit for Mr. Bullock.

Tatler 7d. NF. _____. *St. James's Coffee-house, April 25.*

A report on letters concerning European politics.

Tatler 8a. Thursday, April 28, 1709. Steele. *Will's Coffee-house, April 26.*

Eugenio, whom Bickerstaff calls a "gentleman of just taste," complains to Bickerstaff about the false mannerisms displayed in English styles of acting, as exemplified in a production of the play, *The London Cuckolds*. Eugenio argues that proper use of the theater will encourage regular behavior among the people.

Tatler 8b. NF. _____. *St. James's Coffee-house, April 27.*

A report on letters concerning European political affairs.

Tatler 8c. _____. *From my own Apartment.*

Bickerstaff goes to bed with a volume of Virgil and dreams that he is on an island where the people are in great anguish over the death of a hero. Order is restored when a messenger comes with the news of peace in foreign wars.

Tatler 9a. Saturday, April 30, 1709. Steele. *Will's Coffee-house, April 28.*

Bickerstaff praises Congreve's *The Old Bachelor* and contrasts it to the work of most of the town's poets, which are rarely more than love sonnets to Phillis and Chloris. For contrast, Bickerstaff presents some lines of his relative, Mr. Humphrey Wagstaff, which describe morning in the city. He also tells of a meeting with Lord Timon, a character created by La Bruyère, and notes that he is being cheated by his servants, who ride in his coaches while he rides a horse.

Tatler 9b. _____. *White's Chocolate-house, April 29.*

Bickerstaff tells of Pastorella, who is converted from being a coquette because she overhears her aunt, one Parisatis, pray that she may behave in a more lady-like manner. The aunt is concerned that a Lord, struck by Pastorella's beauty, have honorable attentions, so Pastorella encourages this by forming herself "into the exact manner of Lindamira."

Tatler 9c. NF. _____. *St. James's Coffee-house,*
April 29.

A report on letters concerning political events abroad.

Tatler 10a. Tuesday, May 3, 1709. Steele. *From my own*
Apartment, May 1.

Jenny Distaff, Bickerstaff's half-sister, tells of her
relative and his amorous complexion. She then tells of
Colonel Ranter, who having seen Lady Betty Modish, now
acts in a more agreeable manner because he wishes to
please her. Jenny wishes a certain young man were
equally affected by her charms, but he has made laziness
a philosophy. Jenny discusses female writers, but is
interrupted by a packet of letters from Mr. Kidney at
St. James's Coffee-house.

Tatler 10b. NF. _____. *St. James's Coffee-house,*
May 2.

A report on letters concerning foreign political matters.

Tatler 11a. NF. Thursday, May 5, 1709. Steele. *Will's*
Coffee-house, May 3.

A brief discussion of the poetry of Jabez Hughes and of
the play *The Modern Prophets* by Thomas D'Urfey.

Tatler 11b. _____. *From my own Apartment, May 4.*

Bickerstaff, while protesting that pride in one's birth
is the greatest of vanities, reprints a letter from his
cousin, D. Distaff which traces the genealogy of the
"-staff" family, including Jacobstaff, the patriarch,
and his sons Bickerstaff, Longstaff, Wagstaff, Quarter-
staff, Whitestaff, Falstaff, and Tipstaff, his nephews
Distaff, Pikestaff, Mopstaff, Broomstaff, and Ragged-
staff, and his bastard grandchildren Pilgrimstaff and
Pipestaff. The Canes, the Clubs, the Cudgels, the
Wands, the Devil upon two Sticks, and Bread (the Staff
of Life) are not part of the family.

Tatler 11c. NF. _____. *St. James's Coffee-house,*
May 4.

Letters report affairs overseas.

Tatler 12a. Saturday, May 7, 1709. Steele. *White's Coffee-*
house, May 5.

Bickerstaff declares, in a preamble, that he will henceforth report what is sent him from those who have leisure and capacity for giving delight. The state of
public and private morality is at a low ebb, even
affecting the language. To illustrate this, he presents a scene observed in White's between Pip, a gentleman card-player; Trimmer, a gentleman becoming a cheat

at cards; Acorn, an honest, plain-speaking Englishman;
and Mr. Friendly, a reasonable man of the town. Pip
and Trimmer claim Acorn is an object of ridicule because he does not understand their "wit" and slang.
Friendly explains to Acorn that simplicity of behavior
is lost in the world.

Tatler 12b. NF. _____. *Will's Coffee-house, May 6.*

Bickerstaff reprints a poem by Ambrose Philips.

Tatler 12c. NF. _____. *From my own Apartment, May 6.*

Since the mail from Holland is not specific about events
abroad, Bickerstaff presents verses of Dryden from *The
Conquest of Granada*, Part II, i.

Tatler 13a. Tuesday, May 10, 1709. Steele. *From my own
Apartment, May 8.*

Bickerstaff describes a journey through Lincoln's Inn
Walks on which he meets a venerable gentleman who introduces himself as Bickerstaff's familiar, or guardian
angel. He reports on his last three assignments; the
first being Dictinna, who is seduced by Philander's
command of flattery and his comments on her friends,
Philander commends Flora and then deprecates Pastorella,
Mrs. Dimple, Mrs. Prim, Mrs. Dentifrice, and Mrs. Fidget;
the results of his skill in handling Dictinna will appear in nine months in the form of "a very remarkable
token." He also describes the brains and fates of his
other two recent assignments, a common swearer who is
cured by having to read his swearing and a compulsive
gambler who is still at the tables.

Tatler 13b. NF. _____. *St. James's Coffee-house,
May 9.*

Reports on more letters from abroad on foreign news.

Tatler 14a. Thursday, May 12, 1709. Steele. *From my own
Apartment, May 10.*

Bickerstaff says that his familiar has enabled him to
keep up his task of reporting on the moral state of the
town. Bickerstaff apologizes for his comments on Sir
Richard Blackmore's *Advice to the Poets* and hopes they
were made without ill-breeding. He then reports on
Verus, a magistrate of Felicia, who always gives a
scrupulously fair verdict, unlike two other judges,
Trick-Track and Tearshift.

Tatler 14b. NF. _____. *Will's Coffee-house, May 11.*

A brief report on John Bank's play *The Earl of Essex*
and Ben Jonson's *The Alchemist*.

Tatler 14c. _____. *White's Chocolate-house, May 11.*

Bickerstaff is told by a gentleman of a dumb fortune-teller who outdoes Partridge in his predictions. Many pay dearly for his hand- and head-gestures. One, a rich city widow, is told that she will have two more husbands. She has decided that they will be Frank Careless and Will Nice, both of whom give the appearance of being fine gentlemen, though one is a coxcomb and the other a fop. There is some suspicion that her maid will cause her to marry Tom Terrour, however.

Tatler 14d. NF. _____. *St. James's Coffee-house, May 11.*

More letters on foreign events.

Tatler 15a. Saturday, May 14, 1709. Steele. *From my own Apartment, May 12.*

Bickerstaff names his familiar, one Mr. Pacolet, and promises to take him into the city where he agrees to display his great knowledge of human nature. Mr. Pacolet accounts for this by telling of his birth and death by drowning at age 30 days, thus escaping the fate of becoming the heir to a great family, "lashed into a linguist till sixteen, running after wenches till twenty-five, and being married to an ill-natured wife till sixty."

Tatler 15b. _____. *White's Chocolate-house, May 13.*

Pacolet, Bickerstaff's familiar, makes him invisible so that they may prevent a nobleman-gambler from being cheated by his opponents in the game of life. The nobleman has pieces marked (only visible to Pacolet and Bickerstaff) with the inscriptions Good Fame, Glory, Riches, Honour, and Posterity. His opponents' pieces are marked Dishonour, Impudence, Poverty, Ignorance, and Want of Shame.

Tatler 15c. NF. _____. *Will's Coffe-house, May 13.*

A report on the performance of Susannah Centlivre's play *The Busy Body.*

Tatler 15d. NF. _____. *St. James's Coffee-house, May 13.*

News of a sea battle between French warships and English merchant ships.

Tatler 16a. Tuesday, May 17, 1709. Steele and Swift. *White's Chocolate-house, May 15.*

Bickerstaff is shown a letter from Bath which tells of the attempts of Florimel and Prudentia to hide the effects of age. They plot against each other and

84

compete for others' attentions. The high-point comes
when they stage rival plays for the entertainment of
the town; first Prudentia's play and then Florimel's
are in favor so that the ultimate outcome of the contest in doubt.

Tatler 16b. _____. *White's Chocolate-house, May 16.*

Bickerstaff writes a letter in defense of Castabella
and begs that he may ever live under her protection.

Tatler 16c. NF. _____. *St. James's Coffee-house,
May 16.*

More letters reporting on events abroad.

Tatler 17a. Thursday, May 19, 1709. Steele. *Will's Coffee-
house, May 18.*

A company, of which Bickerstaff is a member, discusses
the true nature of panegyric, with examples given from
Bacon's *Advancement of Learning* and from a pamphlet entitled *The Naked Truth.* Some of the conversants do not
like the latter work, but Bickerstaff praises it and
its author.

Tatler 17b. NF. _____. *St. James's Coffee-house,
May 18.*

More letters on foreign events.

Tatler 18a. Saturday, May 21, 1709. Steele and Addison.
From my own Apartment, May 20.

In a discussion of spelling, Bickerstaff tells of a cousin,
Humphrey Mopstaff, who wandered lost for a day because
his directions were spelled "beer" rather than "bear."
Bickerstaff also helps a man who cannot find his lodg-
ings because the statues in Stocks Market and Charing
Cross are so much alike.

Tatler 18b. NF. _____. *St. James's Coffee-house,
May 20.*

Extensive report on events overseas.

Tatler 19a. Tuesday, May 24, 1709. Steele. *From my own
Apartment, May 23.*

Bickerstaff laments the disrepute into which the title
Esquire has fallen. He traces the history of the term
and its honorable associations while lambasting those
who misuse it or betray its high calling. The true
squire, he says, is devoted to the service of ladies;
he will refuse to consider anyone a true squire who
cannot prove he has conquered a lady's obdurate heart,
led up a country dance, or carried a message between a
lady and her lover in secret.

Tatler 19b. NF. _____. *Will's Coffee-house, May 23*.

A brief report on performances of Susannah Centlivre's *The Busy Body* and Farquhar's *The Constant Couple*.

Tatler 19c. _____. *St. James's Coffee-house, May 23*.

In the midst of a discussion of events abroad Bicker-staff presents a letter from one Madame Maintenon to Monsieur Torcy, head of the French negotiating team with the victorious British armies. The letter shows Madame Maintenon urging Torcy to get as easy terms as possible from the British, especially since the French King, once so powerful, is now brought so low by the might of the British armies.

Tatler 20a. Thursday, May 26, 1709. Steele and Addison. *White's Chocolate-house, May 24*.

A young woman of thirty visits Bickerstaff with the complaint that her husband is impotent. She wishes a divorce, but Bickerstaff counsels the shame to come from public trial of the issue and urges on her the examples of nuns and older virgins. She says that her husband has been impotent only two weeks after a marriage of fifteen years and that the man is fifty years old. Bickerstaff can give no advice and so loses his client. He hopes, however, that the case will save Pastorella from a marriage to a man twenty years her senior.

Tatler 20b. _____. *Will's Coffee-house, May 25*.

Bickerstaff reports on a performance of *The Recruiting Officer* by Farquhar, discusses the breaking-up of May-fair, and reprints a letter on conditions in the theaters in Amsterdam.

Tatler 20c. NF. _____. *St. James's Coffee-house, May 25*.

A report on terms for the settlement of European wars.

Tatler 21a. Saturday, May 28, 1709. Steele and Swift. *White's Chocolate-house, May 26*.

Bickerstaff reports that a gentleman from the country has written asking for definitions of a Gentleman, a Wit, a Pretty Fellow, a Toast, a Coquette, and other characters of the "gayer world." He begins with characters of Sophronius, the agreeable Gentleman, and Jack Dimple, a Pretty Fellow, who tries to be a gentleman by imitating Sophronius, yet the former has good breeding by nature while the latter has it only through notice-able artifice.

Tatler 21b. NF. _____. *Will's Coffee-house, May 27.*

A report on a performance of Jonson's *Volpone*, with comments on the need for decorum in the theater.

Tatler 21c. _____. *From my own Apartment, May 27.*

Ephraim Bedstaff writes to tell of three women who are accused of witchcraft, but are proven to be only a keeper of a brandy and tobacco shop, the daughter of a butcher, and a baker of gingerbread men, by the testimony of the local priest. Ephraim also indicates that he has concluded that Bickerstaff is dying from the bottom up, since the amount of advertising in the *Tatler* is gradually increasing.

Tatler 21d. NF. _____. *St. James's Coffee-house, May 27.*

More reports on events in Europe.

Tatler 22a. Tuesday, May 31, 1709. Steele. *White's Chocolate-house, May 28.*

Bickerstaff finds Cynthio discussing love, as an authority, with his friends, the basis of his authority being his success with a certain young lady. The secret of his success, he believes, is his skill at ogling. Bickerstaff, through his familiar, learns that the lady in question is only flattered at her success. Pacolet steals a letter of the lady's to her friend Amanda in which she gives the relative merits of Cynthio, Beau Frisk, and Jack Freeland. She leans toward Frisk, because he loves her only because all the town does.

Tatler 22b. _____. *Will's Coffee-house, May 30.*

Bickerstaff says his chief business was to speak in favor of a benefit performance of *Hamlet* for the comic actor Cave Underhill. A gentleman says that comedy is to be encouraged in the town, but Bickerstaff hopes that tragedy will not be neglected, especially since he has the stuff of several tragedies in his commonplace book, including six lines of the farewell of a general, dying for love, and the declaration of the vanity of ambition by a politician, among other things.

Tatler 22c. _____. *From my own Apartment, May 30.*

Bickerstaff reports that Fidelia writes to tell of a woman of twenty-five who plans to marry a man of sixty, much against her relatives' wishes. Bickerstaff proposes one solution, which is to have the whole family go as a body to call the bride to the wedding tomorrow; he is sure that she will have second thoughts if no one opposes the match. Otherwise, we should applaud her choice, since clearly a fine young woman is what an aged rake deserves, since he has suffered so from the female sex in his former life.

Tatler 23a. Thursday, June 2, 1709. Steele. *White's Chocolate-house, May 31.*

Bickerstaff says that he finds he has a reputation for skill in medicine as well as in astrology. A gentleman writes for help with his wife, who is troubled with fits whenever her husband is upset with her. Bickerstaff says he knows the problem, and tells a tale to illustrate it and its cure. The tale concerns a woman whose husband gives her anything she wants because she has a fit when he denys her anything. He dies; his successor refuses to go along, so the woman, on threat of being abandoned by her new husband, stops having the fits.

Tatler 23b. _____. *From my own Apartment, May 31.*

Bickerstaff writes and dispatches by his familiar a letter to the King of France on the occasion of the King's refusal to sign the treaty with England. The letter asserts that Louis XIV has been misled in the conduct of his affairs and has misapplied his not-inconsiderable greatness. Louis should not prolong the suffering further for the sake of his ambition; instead he should recognize the needs of common humanity and end the war.

Tatler 23c. NF. _____. *St. James's Coffee-house, June 1.*

A report on further letters from abroad.

Tatler 24a. Saturday, June 4, 1709. Addison. *White's Chocolate-house, June 2.*

In a continuation of a former essay (see *Tatler* 21a) Bickerstaff gives the character of a Very Pretty Fellow --one who is a man of fashion, too careless to know when he offends and too sanguine to be upset if he knew it. Colonel Brunett is one example, as are three brothers recently landed from Holland. They are Hogshead, Culverin, and Musket, especially known for their skills in drinking. Others of this group are Joe Carry, Tom Drybones, and Cancrum. Bickerstaff goes on to describe a Toast, including Mrs. Gatty and Mrs. Frontlet, as one who is picked out by an admirer, yet her value is imaginary, her condition frail and dependent on the one who chooses her.

Tatler 24b. NF. _____. *St. James's Coffee-house, June 3.*

A report on more letters on events overseas.

Tatler 24c. _____. *From my own Apartment, June 3.*

Bickerstaff gives a letter from Bread, whom he welcomes
into the "-staff" family. The letter contains a poem
to Louis XIV which tells the King that all the world
despises him, urges him to surrender to the English,
and requests that he withdraw support from the pre-
tenders to the English crown.

Tatler 25a. Tuesday, June 7, 1709. Steele. *White's
Chocolate-house, June 6.*

Bickerstaff responds to a letter from a young lady
about her lover, lately wounded in a duel, by saying
that he finds dueling a barbarous custom. He tells a
brief story to indicate how duels come about, and gives
a letter which he says reflects the true nature of
challenges.

Tatler 25b. _____. *From my own Apartment, June 6.*

Bickerstaff relates the problems of giving advice, since
some of his friends have already made up their minds and
will get angry if his advice does not coincide with what
they already have decided to do. He has urged a friend
not to marry, only to learn they are already wed. He
has urged another friend not to pay his son's bills;
neither of them will speak to him now. Yesterday,
another friend asked him whether he should place his
son with Paulo or Avaro, two eminent men in the city.
Paulo is generous; Avaro, suspicious and stingy. From
Paulo the son will learn to gain and also to enjoy a
fortune, so the son is placed in his household.

Tatler 25c. NF. _____. *St. James's Coffee-house,
June 6.*

More reports on foreign events.

Tatler 26a.1. Thursday, June 9, 1709. Steele. *From my own
Apartment, June 8.*

Bickerstaff presents a letter, with instructions to Mr.
Kidney at St. James's and Sir Thomas at White's to take
notice, in which the correspondent wishes to be listed
among the ranks of Pretty Fellows (see *Tatler* 21a) because he is a seducer and rapist and leaver of plays
after the first act. He also draws swords at alehouses
and theatres and is a friend of Dr. Wall, the quack
doctor. He wishes, however, to have excluded from the
ranks of Pretty Fellows those who act in an effeminate
manner and those who have gone abroad to bully the
French now that a truce has been signed. Bickerstaff
agrees, but says that the correspondent is not a Pretty
Fellow either, but a Smart Fellow who hangs his cane on
his button and wears red-heeled shoes.

Tatler 26a.2. _____. *From my own Apartment, June 8.*

Bickerstaff gives Louis XIV's reply to his letter. The King agrees to take Bickerstaff's advice and sign the treaty. He invites Bickerstaff abroad, but Bickerstaff declines the invitation, because Louis' sense of justice is that of the gamester. Bickerstaff promises not to tell how Tom Cash came into his estate, if Bickerstaff receives from him payment of £200 in a week. He also expects £300 from Mr. Soilett for concealing double-dealings, and will return a fan to a certain lady if she will send word. He expects payment for every folly or vice committed in the town, on pain of having the truth told; everyone in town should pay up or mend his life.

Tatler 26b. _____. *White's Chocolate-house, June 8.*

Bickerstaff reports on his familiar's reaction to his campaign against dueling. Pacolet says that when he died, his soul went to judgement along with that of one killed in a duel. Pacolet's soul was welcomed with kindness and sent to heaven, while that of the man killed in a duel was received quite differently. He was called a fool of his own making. Socrates gets the man to admit that he read his will before signing it, but failed to learn the subject of the quarrel, in which he was only the second.

Tatler 27a. Saturday, June 11, 1709. Steele. *White's Chocolate-house, June 9.*

Pacolet having gone abroad for more information about dueling, Bickerstaff can continue to define the types of the town. He turns to the Rake, who acts constantly against his better judgement, yet has crowds of imitators. Noblis is such an imitator, but he is no rake though he drinks and uses bawdy language because he is not vicious against his will. A Coquette is a woman who lives in constant misapplication of her beauty. Chief among these is Mrs. Toss, who constantly practices those things which detract from her charms.

Tatler 27b. _____. *Will's Coffee-house, June 9.*

Bickerstaff reports on a poem from a gentleman to a lady in which the links between love and birds are explored. Bickerstaff finds this a just conception, but says the suitor must imitate the bird by talking constantly until she accepts his suit, then must remain silent ever after.

Tatler 27c. _____. *From my own Apartment, June 10.*

Bickerstaff reports that many young gentlemen write him for advice; one special plea is from Jeffrey Nicknack, in town from the university. Jeffrey reports that one

Charles Bubbleboy promised to sell him everything he
needed to become a gentleman, but when pressed for a
certificate of this fact said that he needed yet another sixty or eighty pounds. This is being obtained,
and Jeffrey wants to know what class of men Bickerstaff
will place him in when all is paid. Bickerstaff says
he will be able to help when he learns the shape of the
young man's snuff box.

Tatler 27d. NF. _____. *St. James's Coffee-house,*
June 10.

More reports from abroad.

Tatler 28a. Tuesday, June 14, 1709. Steele. *White's*
Chocolate-house, June 13.

Bickerstaff comments on a letter on the subject of
dueling. The correspondent says that he called a man
with his cane tied at his button and wearing red-
heeled shoes a Pretty Fellow; the man so-named took
offense and challenged the writer to a duel. Bickerstaff says the title "Pretty Fellow" is no cause for
offense, but laments the whole institution of dueling.
He points out that many nations do without it all together and that Englishmen who have mercenaries do ·
their fighting for them are despicable. He tells a
story of how Captain Crabtree and Major-General Maggot
had a misunderstanding, which came to involve Mr.
Jeffrey Stick and Tobias Armstrong, but all was settled
without fighting. Further comment on dueling awaits
Pacolet, who is attending a man wounded in a duel.

Tatler 28b. NF. _____. *St. James's Coffee-house,*
June 13.

More reports on events abroad.

Tatler 29a. Thursday, June 16, 1709. Steele. *White's*
Chocolate-house, June 14.

Bickerstaff reprints a letter from Tim Switch in response to his comments on dueling. Switch claims that
the popularity of dueling is from the same source as
the custom of wearing elaborate wigs--none other than
the desire not to seem peculiar. Dueling, he argues,
is a result of the dying-out of dragons; to impress the
ladies, young gentlemen must show their bravery in
single combat, to hold up the tradition of knight-
errantry. Bickerstaff agrees that Switch has hit upon
the cause of the problem, and gives a typical love-note
from a man who really says what he is supposed to feel.
In the note, the lover says that he will kill any man
who claims that he will die for his beloved.

Tatler 29b. _____. *From my own Apartment, June 14.*

Bickerstaff reports on a discussion between a critic
and a wit. Both are alike in their lack of judgement,
the former because he abuses his faculty; the latter,
because he neglects his. The critic spends too much
time on trifles while the wit depends too much on imagination without judgement. Jasper Dactyle is another
wit; he dominates the conversation because he has it
all rehearsed. Spondee is his companion critic; the
two stay together because they allow each other to
show off. They are compared to Novel and Oldfox in
Wycherley's *The Plain Dealer.*

Tatler 29c. NF. _____. *St. James's Coffee-house,
June 15.*

Bickerstaff reprints a letter from abroad which shows
that some of Louis XIV's subjects disagreed with his
decision not to ratify the preliminaries of the treaty
with England.

Tatler 30a. Saturday, June 18, 1709. Steele. *From my own
Apartment, June 16.*

Bickerstaff says that in time he hopes to be rewarded
for his efforts to raise the public morality; in the
meantime he must go on with his work, especially on the
subject of children. He reports on a ride about London
with three nephews who are constantly arguing among
themselves. The eldest, Mr. William, is arrogant,
while the youngest, Jack, has promise of being a fine
father, husband, and gentleman. Frequently men like
Sir William Scrip have a bad disposition but can make
money, while men like Sir Harry Wildfire have pleasant
dispositions but are always borrowing from the Scrips.
The third son is of the sort who will make a fine page
to a great lady; he is like Will Courtly who has the
disposition never to offend, for he personifies good
breeding.

Tatler 30b. _____. *Will's Coffee-house, June 17.*

Because the theaters are closed, the company discusses
the proper form of address to women in letters of gallantry. Bickerstaff's opinion is that letters should
be as close to actual speech as possible, since artificial speech tends to lose the lady. As an example,
Bickerstaff presents two letters to Romana. The first,
from John Careless, is highly artificial, but the second, from Colonel Constant, is grave and dignified.
Both died in battle, but Romana feels Careless is more
to be pitied than Constant.

Tatler 30c. NF. _____. *St. James's Coffee-house, June 17.*

Report on more letters from abroad.

Tatler 30d. _____. [Addendum.]

Bickerstaff gives notice to all persons who dress as they please, without regard for decorum, that they will be fined unless they change their behavior. There is no truth to the rumor that Bickerstaff has been bribed by the clothiers of the town to remain silent on this matter.

Tatler 31a. Tuesday, June 21, 1709. Steele. *Grecian Coffee-house, June 18.*

Bickerstaff replies to the charge that his dissertation against dueling lacks a display of learning, which is held to be the soul of all treatises. One of the gentlemen at the Grecian gives the results of his researches into the scope and history of dueling, giving examples from both the European and Oriental past. It also turns out that the antiquary, Humphrey Scarecrow, can demonstrate that many of the heroes of the past were really stage-fighters of the ancient Bear Garden, including Hercules, Typhonus, Theseus, Achilles, and others. The Bear Gardens of Greece and Rome formed models for the English version. Bickerstaff is called away in haste to measure the degree of affront between two gentleman.

Tatler 31b. Steele and Swift. *From my own Apartment, June 18.*

Bickerstaff hopes that his reputation is deserved, but finds in a letter from the country that he is not understood outside of London. The letter-writer says that a country gentleman, as learned as any man of the town except the barber, does not understand the meaning of the title "Toast." The correspondent also tells of a visit with Mistress Giddy, pretty but silly, and Mrs. Slim, a woman of understanding. The conversation is silly, but the three enjoy the exchange of witty repartee. Bickerstaff reprints the letter with the comment that pretty things said in company appear small when in print.

Tatler 31c. NF. _____. *St. James's Coffee-house, June 20.*

Report on more letters from abroad.

Tatler 31d. _____. Addendum.

A request for information about a surgeon's apprentice who attacked Bickerstaff's messenger while on the way

to the press and tore from his hand part of an essay on
dueling is given, along with the promise of satisfaction
from Mr. Morphew and a set of arguments to use on any
man in a passion to prevent quarreling. Bickerstaff
also says that he has taken the universities under his
charge to correct tutors and students alike.

Tatler 32a. Thursday, June 23, 1709. Swift and Steele.
White's Chocolate-house, June 22.

Charles Sturdy writes for help with his love for a professed Platonist, who discusses Platonism and rejects
all his advances. She uses formal language, calls her
footman Oberon, and refuses to admit to enjoying the
pleasures of the body. He wants to know if he could
put her on the rack to convince her that there is more
to life than the life of the mind. Bickerstaff says
that Platonic Ladies must be dealt with gently, through
flattery. He tells the story of a group of such ladies
who founded a nunnery; once, a Rake, came for a visit
and through flattery of Madonella, the projectrix of
the group, was able to gain admittance over and over
until the women yielded to the advances of the men.

Tatler 32b. NF. _____. *From my own Apartment, June 22.*

Bickerstaff claims that the evils of the town continue
to increase, especially the enormity of punning. Bickerstaff promises to prove that no man can be a man of
honor and a punster, and promises a collection of these
offenses.

Tatler 32c. NF. _____. *St. James's Coffee-house,
June 22.*

Further reports on events abroad.

Tatler 33a. Saturday, June 25, 1709. Steele. *From my own
Apartment, June 23.*

Mrs. Jenny Distaff, half-sister to Bickerstaff, reports
that Isaac is off in the country and has left things to
her. She will take the opportunity to discuss the
problem of keeping men in line with the rules of common
decency, and begins with a letter from Mr. Truman who
asks no more talk about the duel between Alexander and
Thalestris, since he buys the *Tatler* for his daughters
to read. Jenny objects to men who take liberties of
speech before women, and blames men for the folly and
coquetry of women. Men should learn the enjoyment of
a well-ordered and honorable life, rather than that of
a dissolute life. Women should not suffer the outrage
of society for their failings while men are permitted
theirs without censure. She tells how she was once
saved from the advances of a lord by the Lady Sempronia
and argues for the pleasures of conquering passion over
the pleasures of gratifying it.

Tatler 33b. NF. _____. *St. James's Coffee-house, June 24.*

More reports on foreign events.

Tatler 34a. Tuesday, June 28, 1709. Steele. *White's Chocolate-house, June 25.*

Bickerstaff reports on some of the cures for distemper which he has found effective, indicating that his cures have been conducted in private and not in public, as most mountebanks do. Mrs. Spy has been cured of her visual imperfection of rolling her eyes from one cox-comb to the next by an application of Bickerstaff's Circumspection Water, which has also cured Lady Petu-lant's husband of jealousy and Lady Gad's neighborhood of detraction. As a result, Bickerstaff is attractive to women, especially to Damia and Clidamira, who put on a charming dancing exhibit in the hope of earning the title of "very Pretty" among the female sex. Damia is found to be "very pretty," while Clidamira is only "pretty," since Damia's modesty reinforces the power of her charms.

Tatler 34b. _____. *From my own Apartment, June 27.*

Bickerstaff claims that because of a spare constitution he must walk frequently a mile or two to find fresh air; this convinces him of the value of travel for knowing the world. As Mr. Justice Overdo, a relative on his mother's side (and also from Jonson's *Bartholomew Fair*), found enormities by walking, so does Bickerstaff on a walk to a coffee-house in Chelsea. There, he meets a sage, a tooth-drawer named Mr. Salter, who is a member of the class of men Bickerstaff calls Odd Fellows. Mr. Salter is also of that group who dissipate their genius by being too attentive to too many things at once, in this case including music and the collection of odd objects.

Tatler 35a. Thursday, June 30, 1709. Steele. *Grecian Coffee-house, June 28.*

Bickerstaff attacks the habit of taking snuff; he cites by example a friend who could not go on with his tale because Bickerstaff hid his snuff box. Bickerstaff finds the taking of snuff a substitute for reflection and a cover for weakness of the brain. Worse than the man who uses snuff, however, are the borrower of snuff and the woman who uses snuff. Sagissa, one of the lat-ter, refused to quit after three years of Bickerstaff's arguments only to stop when a sneeze from snuff revealed a gallant hidden in her closet.

Tatler 35b. _____. *White's Chocolate-house, June 29.*

Bickerstaff reports that Cynthio, despairing of his love for Clarissa, has fallen in love with another woman with whom he is sure to succeed because he speaks to her with familiarity which does not overstep the bounds of proper deference. Bickerstaff gives a letter of Cynthio as an example; in it, Cynthio states that he will not use language of rapture, but will speak plainly and sincerely.

Tatler 35c. NF. _____. *Will's Coffee-house, June 29.*

Bickerstaff paraphrases *Hamlet*, III.ii. 1-49, as advice to actors which reflects the vices of the current stage as well as those of the Elizabethan.

Tatler 35d. _____. *From my own Apartment, June 29.*

Bickerstaff seeks advice, in preparation of his treatise on Punning, about a letter from one Elizabeth Potatrix, who claims that her family of trix is older and more honorable than the Staff family.

Tatler 35e. NF. _____. *St. James's Coffee-house, June 29.*

Report on events from abroad.

Tatler 36a. Saturday, July 2, 1709. Steele. *From my own Apartment, June 30.*

Jenny Distaff reports that she is now in charge, since Isaac has been called to the country, and will use the opportunity to deal with issues of interest to the fair sex. One, contained in a letter from Epsom written by Martha Tatler, reports on a scene involving Lady Autumn, a woman of good breeding, and Lady Springly, a "modern impertinence of the sex." Lady Autumn, angry with Lady Springly over her rival's preferment at a social gathering, initiates a name-calling and hair-pulling fight which soon involves their husbands and the neighbors.

Tatler 36b. _____. *White's Chocolate-house, June 30.*

Jenny reports on a man whose services to the fair sex have reduced him to such a state that he suffers the pains and torments of death, but seeks to remain in them by earning money from his diseases. This gentleman, one Africanus, is reported by Sir Thomas, a waiter of the establishment, to be a marvelous sight in his attempt to make a show of the end of his life. Africanus compares himself to Partridge, and refuses to admit his death. In response, Monoculus compares himself to Africanus, and says that they are opposites, since Monoculus is healthy yet fears death and Africanus is sick yet plans for the future.

Tatler 36c. NF. _____. *St. James's Coffee-house, July 1.*

More reports on foreign events.

Tatler 37a. Tuesday, July 5, 1709. Steele. *White's Chocolate-house, July 2.*

Jenny says that she does not visit White's, but receives guests who do and who testify that men talk as much as women. She gives her comments on Mrs. Alse Copswood, the Yorkshire huntress, and her brother-in-law, Tom Bellfrey, the most accomplished gentleman in the king-dom. Although he hates Italian music, he does frequent fox-hunts, with all their harmony between men and dogs. Robin Cartail and Jowler, Mr. Tinbreast and Sweetlips, Beau Slimber and Trips, Tom Bellfrey and Ringwood were among the male-dog combinations on one memorable hunt, the result being quite a show of music. Bellfrey showed his skills in dog-calling once at Lady Dainty's, which upset her dog Mr. Snippet. Jenny promises further tales of peculiar speakers, including the whisperer without business, the laugher without wit, and others.

Tatler 37b. _____. *Will's Coffee-house, July 3.*

Jenny reports on a speech of a gentleman on the subject of his play, which he says has been rejected by the players. He quotes from the play after stating a pre-face for the excerpt, which concerns Caesar speaking to his men at the Rubicon.

Tatler 37c. NF. _____. *St. James's Coffee-house, July 4.*

A brief report on foreign news.

Tatler 37d. _____. Addendum.

Jenny announces that she has written a treatise on the subject of life, as it affects women. One section con-cerns a reply of use to those married to persons of ill-breeding or ill-nature, while another deals with the words "I will," especially intended for virgins. Jenny also announces that a gentlewoman seeks a maid who can whisper, clear-starch, lisp, and tread softly.

Tatler 38a. Thursday, July 7, 1709. Steele. *From my own Apartment, July 6.*

Jenny gives a letter which she says illustrates the good effects of her brother's efforts in the *Tatler*. The letter, from A. B., praises Bickerstaff and tells of a pair of gentlemen who settle their differences through a fist-fight rather than dueling, as proof that it is possible to gain satisfaction without resorting to dueling. Jenny explains that one of the men in-volved sold the other a "bear," and explains this term. She then says she has called Isaac back to town, and prints a letter encouraging him to discuss whisperers without business and laughers without occasion.

Tatler 38b. _____. *White's Chocolate-house, July 6.*

Jenny gives the characters of a number of men whose fortunes or ambition in their follies have elevated them above the ordinary lot. The first is the man of business who keeps a customer waiting until he has drawn a crowd, then turns to whispering so that all may see how important he is and how inconsequential his customer is. Then there is Lord Nowhere, who pretends to know secrets when there are none; Will Shoestring, who works hard at showing off his teeth; Umbra, who displays his shallowness in his eagerness to become familiar; and finally, Flyblow, who is a notorious gossip. With the latter, Jenny is mad because he said she has wit and other virtues, but is not handsome.

Tatler 38c. NF. _____. *St. James's Coffee-house, July 6.*

More reports from abroad, plus the note that when any part of the paper is dull, there is a design in it.

Tatler 39a. Saturday, July 9, 1709. Steele. *Grecian Coffee-house, July 7.*

Bickerstaff tells of his visit to Oxford, made out of his love for his fellow man. Enraptured by his view of the life of man as a rational being, he turns only reluctantly to the town again. He finds that there is a difference in the way the Law term and the University term are determined, and discusses all the results, especially one man who has been sent to jail because he appeared in court on the wrong day. Even the dog that frequents the court at Westminster comes according to the Oxford calendar, so Bickerstaff is sure that the man will be vindicated.

Tatler 39b. _____. *From my own Apartment, July 7.*

Bickerstaff reports verbatim on a conversation on the subject of duels provoked by his comments on the subject. Mr. Sage argues that duels were unheard of among the Romans, Col. Plume claims that duels were out of favor among the officers of the Parliament army, and Sir Mark claims that duels were more in fashion among the Cavalier party, to promote the splendour of the Court. Col. Plume reports on the manner of Cavalier dueling, with a story of a dispute between Cornet Modish and Captain Smart, in which Major Adroit (Smart's second) is quickly defeated. Sir Mark concludes that he sees no reason not to leave the question of who is to die in a duel up to the toss of a coin.

Tatler 40a. Tuesday, July 12, 1709. Steele. *Will's Coffee-house, July 11.*

Bickerstaff says that the town is upset because of the fear that an inquiry into whether a wealthy man can keep his money if he is an idiot may set a precedent for other litigation. At Will's there is a gentleman who is sueing for his uncle's estate on precisely the grounds that the uncle has never exhibited any sign of reason. The case hinges on whether the abuse of reason is a sign of lack of it. The company at Will's hears the argument that lunatics are in the care of the Chancery, but fools are in the care of the Court. Renault objects, and another man argues that only a small valve makes the difference between a fool and a politician, as Pacolet the familiar would discover. He points out that fools and madmen may go to jail, but nothing happens to the many who are capable of reason but do not use it.

Tatler 40b. _____. *From my own Apartment, July 11.*

Bickerstaff reports on an evening visit of some ladies to sister Jenny, at which Sappho quotes Milton and Suckling in support of the idea that the best husband is a generous and protective lover. Jenny produces a letter from Mariana which argues to the contrary that there are two happy things allowed in marriage, a wife in her wedding sheets and in her shroud--or at least, so men believe. A lady present, playing with her dog, says that she is far more concerned for the dog Shock than for any man in England. Sappho leaves, upset at this display of levity which makes others think of women as inconsiderable things.

Tatler 40c. NF. _____. *St. James's Coffee-house, July 11.*

More reports on letters from abroad.

Tatler 41a. Thursday, July 14, 1709. Steele. *White's Chocolate-house, July 12.*

Bickerstaff laments the British love of the foreign. As an example he cites a detailed description of a mock battle to be held in the streets of London by the Artillery Company. Fortunately, a shower of rain prevented all the mock slaughter from taking place.

Tatler 41b. _____. *Will's Coffee-house, July 13.*

Bickerstaff describes the skill of a gentleman at Will's in managing with dexterity impertinent people, in this case Will Why-not, who asks questions not for information but to show how much he wants to know things. The friend also describes people who seek positions not because they are qualified but because it would be convenient for them to have such a job. An example is a man who has set up as a dancing teacher solely because he has broken his leg and cannot dance any more.

Tatler 41c. _____. *From my own Apartment, July 13*.

Bickerstaff quotes *As You Like It*, II.vii. 70-87 to indicate how he feels about those who write him claiming that Bickerstaff has referred to them in the *Tatler*.

Tatler 41d. NF. _____. *St. James's Coffee-house, July 13*.

More reports on foreign events.

Tatler 42a. Saturday, July 16, 1709. Steele and Addison. *From my own Apartment, July 15*.

Bickerstaff reports that his great-grandfather wrote a treatise on the subject of bribery which contains a digression arguing, in jingles and puns, that it is possible for a man to receive an injury and be aware that he deserves it. In support of this, Bickerstaff presents a poem from George Whetstone's *English Mirror* in which a poor man is less successful in bribing a judge than is a rich man.

Tatler 42b. _____. *Will's Coffee-house, July 15*.

A discourse on the subject of studying the taste of an age through examining characters in the comic dreams of the era is the setting for a character-sketch of the divine Aspasia, who is both learned and modest, noble and simple, with all other exemplary qualities of her age. She is contrasted with the restless Poluglossa, who is all appearance.

Tatler 42c. _____. *St. James's Coffee-house, July 15*.

Since by noon on this day no foreign mail has arrived, Bickerstaff takes the liberty of reporting on a sale of a magnificent palace and its contents taking place in Drury Lane (actually the props of Christopher Rich's theater), including Othello's handkerchief, a setting sun (a bargain), the imperial robes of Xerxes, only worn once, the complexion of a murderer, and so forth. Bickerstaff pleads for forgiveness on the part of his readers for this departure from routine.

Tatler 43a. Tuesday, July 19, 1709. Steele. *White's Chocolate-house, July 18*.

Bickerstaff writes that wit and merit are so little praised and encouraged by people of quality that authors are forced to turn to others for patronage. One example is Mr. d'Urfey, whose comedy, *The Modern Prophets*, was dedicated to a merchant-knight with a preface which is the model of dedicatory prose. Bickerstaff forbids all dedications to persons within the city of London, until the bankers Sir Francis, Sir Stephen, and the Bank will accept epigrams and epistles for

security on notes and the East India Company will accept heroic poems for sealed bonds. This would immeas-
urably improve the lot of writers and allow them to
take their proper place in society.

Tatler 43b. _____. *Grecian Coffee-house, July 18.*

Bickerstaff reports on a gentleman who plans to write a
system of philosophy which will be lively in both matter and language and thus will overcome the prejudice
that the learned are dry and dull. Bickerstaff provides
a sample, in which the creation of the universe is described in terms of a football game among the inferior
deities. The work will also contain a defense of the
first day of term according to the Oxford Almanac and
an argument against the wearing of buckles until 1714.

Tatler 43c. _____. *Will's Coffee-house, July 18.*

Bickerstaff reports on a discussion of the nature of
the True Sublime. After the discussion, one member of
the assembly says that the height of expressing greatness of soul is to be found in a modern poem--an honour
to the nation and to the language. The poem in question
is Addison's "The Campaign," from which Bickerstaff
quotes.

Tatler 43d. NF. _____. *St. James's Coffee-house,
July 18.*

Further reports based on letters from abroad.

Tatler 44a. Thursday, July 21, 1709. Steele. *White's
Chocolate-house, July 19.*

Bickerstaff reports on a conversation with Pacolet, his
familiar, who points out a walthy older Doctor who has
been disappointed in love and thus earns comparison
with AEsculapius in mourning over his unrequited love
of Hebe, the emblem of youth and beauty. The Doctor,
having treated his beloved in an illness, fell in love
with her and thus became her patient. All this provokes
Pacolet into a reflection on the impotence of wealth.

Tatler 44b. _____. *Will's Coffee-house, July 19.*

The company, gathered to purchase the remnants of the
playhouse mentioned in *Tatler* 42c, discovers that some
items had already been taken off by a gentleman of
Hampshire for a playhouse he is building near South-
hampton. Bickerstaff begs pardon of the town for misleading people in his account of the sale-to-be. He
also attacks a puppet-show man in Bath named Mr. Powell
for having a "profane lewd jester" named Punch speak
badly of Isaac Bickerstaff. Powell is but a tall puppet
himself, says Isaac, who would have all men automatons,
and therefore no more will be said of him.

Tatler 44c. _____. *From my own Apartment, July 14.*

Bickerstaff apologizes for haste in his discourse, but gives as excuse the fact that he was helping a friend, three years absent from the town, to decide that he cannot live in London since he cannot bear a jest. He has just been put on the northern coach.

Tatler 44d. NF. _____. *St. James's Coffee-house, July 20.*

Further reports on foreign events.

Tatler 45a. Saturday, July 23, 1709. Steele. *White's Chocolate-house, July 22.*

While on a walk, Bickerstaff is called to help the un-happy Teraminta, who once was simple in dress and pre-tension but who now is dressed only for revelling. She tells of her ruin at the hands of Decius, who has toyed with her virtue since her father's death and has im-prisoned her in his home. She asks Bickerstaff to pub-lish notice of her fate so that Decius will have to let her go.

Tatler 45b. _____. *Will's Coffee-house, July 21.*

Bickerstaff, to show that his attitude toward Mr. Powell, the puppeteer of Bath, is not totally fixed, announces that plays given by puppets are permitted in the univer-sities. Bickerstaff also asks Powell to help with a problem presented in a letter from Isaac's cousin Ben-jamin Beadlestaff, who says that Powell's Punch must be a "very pretty fellow" since he rarely leaves company without calling "Son of a whore" or the like, demanding satisfaction and dueling. He may also be another type who disturbs others with inappropriate ribaldry.

Tatler 45c. _____. *From my own Apartment, July 22.*

Bickerstaff reports on an evening spent with three Merry and two Honest Fellows. As a result of their merry-making and laughing, Bickerstaff is bruised and reflects on the animal-like qualities of men. He re-members fondly a conversation of a week ago with Florio, whose comments are always memorable. Also in the com-pany was Senecio, the best sort of good-natured old man, which leads Bickerstaff to conclude that the nat-ural man, rather than the artificial, is the best com-panion, and that a Merry Fellow is probably in fact the Saddest Fellow in the world.

Tatler 46a. Tuesday, July 26, 1709. Steele. *White's Chocolate-house, July 25.*

Bickerstaff reflects on the volumes written against Love the tyrant and is reminded of the Emperor Aurengezebe, a resident of London who has become wealthy through giving advice in political matters in a coffee-house. To escape the pressures of his life of wealth and power he comes to Will's to relax, where he has his attendants and his wenches for afterhours. He also frequently causes a stir in Drury Lane, where entertainments are prepared for him by Pandarus and Nuncio. These include the appearance of ravished ladies and wronged women. Pacolet says of this gentleman that he has fallen into an indecent old age and replays his earlier triumphs. Bickerstaff is instructed to put him and AEsculapius on the next bill of mortality of the metaphorically defunct.

Tatler 46b. _____. *Will's Coffee-house, July 24*.

Bickerstaff reports on a stir caused by a poem entitled "The Brussels Postscript" which is anonymous, but which turns out to be by Crowder, as a quote from Butler's *Hudibras* hints to the audience.

Tatler 46c. NF. _____. *St. James's Coffee-house, July 24*.

Instead of giving foreign news, Bickerstaff takes the opportunity to praise General Henry Withers for his service to his country.

Tatler 47a. Thursday, July 28, 1709. Steele. *White's Chocolate-house, July 27*.

Bickerstaff reports that Sir Thomas has given him details on events in Epsom, in which Sir Taffety Trippet, a fortune hunter of great and stupid vanity, is disturbing the tranquility of the town. Earlier, in Tunbridge, Sir Taffety courted the older of two sisters until the younger revealed to him that her sister had no fortune. He vanished, only to reappear now in Epsom where there is a young lady much sought after. Her friends fear that she will succumb to his advances.

Tatler 47b. _____. *Grecian Coffee-house, July 27*.

Bickerstaff describes how he cured Tom Spindle of low spirits, caused by the fact that he was almost finished with a great poem on the Treaty of Peace when news came that the French would not sign. Under the care of Dr. Drachm, he is helped by Bickerstaff's news that peace might yet be at hand again and by the reading of the "Brussels Postscript" and some heroic lines of Isaac himself. Bickerstaff says that one should go to a doctor with the same problem, and that he only treats those afflicted by the poetical vapors. For a friend in love, he sent for AEsculapius, who recognizes all the signs and recommends marriage.

Tatler 47c. _____. *From my own Apartment, July 27.*

Bickerstaff reports on a conversation on the subject of
tragical passion at which a gentleman recommends Shakespeare and draws on *Henry IV, Part I* for examples of
the true tragic style. Bickerstaff says that he will
put aside his own tragic efforts and turn to cares and
griefs beneath the level of tragic passion. For example,
he reports on the disconsolate Maria, who has lost her
lapdog, the beauteous Fidelia, and who mourns grievously.

Tatler 48. Saturday, July 30, 1709. Steele. *From my own
Apartment, July 29.*

Bickerstaff and Pacolet, his familiar, walk on Tower
Hill where they meet two men whom Pacolet says are
really superior beings who visit men for the purpose of
calling them from wrong pursuits or diverting them from
methods which will later lead them astray. These two
are Alethes and Verisimilis, guardians of Conscience
and Honour. Verisimilis wants to go it alone, for he
finds Alethes a limiting factor on his show in the
world. They have a third member of the group, Umbra,
who is the demon of credit. Alethes is the general
referee for mankind, while Verisimilis is the model for
soldiers and courtiers and Umbra is the model for merchants. Bickerstaff and Pacolet follow the three into
town and watch the stir they create. Men need, says
Pacolet, to keep all three in balance--and women too,
as the case of Lais is witness.

Tatler 49a. Tuesday, August 2, 1709. Steele. *White's
Chocolate-house, August 1.*

Bickerstaff comments that love is a much-misused term
because it can be a cover for lust. Philander upbraids
Bickerstaff for suggesting that the two could ever be
confused in reality, that one could think of Aspasia
and Sempronia at the same time. Philander describes
love in terms of the figure of Cupid and Lust in terms
of the figure of a Satyr; the first suggests that the
beloved does not want to give her lover anxiety, but is
looked on as a child insensible of her value, while the
second suggests that the lustful man prostitutes his
reason to follow his appetite. In these terms, Aspasia
is of the first Order of Love, since love is her effect
though never her design. Lucippe could learn from her
about the true nature of beauty and loveliness. Florio
and Amanda love each other and share their lives; as a
result they are happily married. Corinna, mistress of
Limberham, lives in constant apprehension because she
knows she is but a possession which can be disposed of
at any time. Worse is the fair Messalina, who is the
professed mistress of mankind, and her keeper Nocturnus,
who knows she is unfaithful to him with every available
man. The moral of all this is that life without

morality is wayward and only occasionally gives pleasure, but when lived under the rule of virtue gives enjoyment habitually.

Tatler 49b. NF. _____. *St. James's Coffee-house,
August 1.*

More reports on events abroad.

Tatler 50a. Thursday, August 4, 1709. Steele. *White's
Chocolate-house, August 2.*

Bickerstaff begins *The History of Orlando the Fair*, the
most renowned of heroes and lovers, who adds to his
natural charms by becoming a soldier and is still able
to suppress all rivals upon his return from foreign
duty. He falls in love with Villaria, the loveliest of
her sex, and addresses her as being the appropriate one
for his affections. Bickerstaff pictures Orlando stop-
ping his chariot to address a group of youths whom he
tells to go back to school and stop bothering him. He
gives money to one whom he believes to be his own son,
and rewards another who says he has never seen a man
such as Orlando. The eagle is Orlando's symbol.

Tatler 50b. _____. *From my own Apartment, August 2.*

Bickerstaff presents a letter from Powell, the puppeteer
of Bath, which responds to Bickerstaff's charges against
him. Powell writes to show how much he does not care
about Bickerstaff, but charges Isaac with spreading the
seeds of sedition among his puppets. Powell insists
that he has the right to do anything he wishes with his
puppets and warns Bickerstaff to be careful in any replies to this letter, or he may be in serious trouble.

Tatler 51a. Saturday, August 6, 1709. Steele. *White's
Chocolate-house, August 5.*

Bickerstaff continues with *The History of Orlando the
Fair*, who lives in glorious excess and complete tranquility until he is reminded that he cannot marry
Villaria because he is already married. This completely
deranges him so he turns to poetry for relief.

Tatler 51b. _____. *Will's Coffee-house, August 5.*

Bickerstaff reports that a man who attracts attention
for his ability to mimic bells and animal sounds is
quickly outdone by Tom Mirrour, a comic actor. Mirrour
then turns to Bickerstaff and imitates him so exactly
that all the company laugh except Bickerstaff. Pacolet
the familiar must explain to Isaac the significance of
the event, and say that Mirrour's fate as well as his
talent is in presenting others exactly as they are.
Sophronius is glad to see him because Sophronius has no

fear of being seen as he is, while Bathillus, who is all affectation, avoids meetings with Mirrour.

Tatler 51c. _____. *From my own Apartment, August 5.*

Bickerstaff reports that some writers have accused him of overstepping his proper bounds in his attacks on Powell of Bath, but protests that his function is to report all that is said which is unfit for the speaker to have said. This includes all flowers of rhetoric and refuges for malice, and Bickerstaff is preparing a mathematical sieve for the purpose of separating out this sort of material.

Tatler 51d. NF. _____. *St. James's Coffee-house, August 5.*

Further report on events from abroad.

Tatler 52a. Tuesday, August 9, 1709. Steele. *White's Chocolate-house, August 7.*

Bickerstaff relates the tale of how *Delamira resigns her Fan* to Virgulta. Delamira, much to the despair of milliners and other merchants, has decided to marry her Archibald. Virgulta, who has despaired of finding a man, asks Delamira to reveal her secrets. Delamira says she owes everything to her fan, a family heirloom with a picture of Cupid on it, and tells of the fan's success for Miss Gatty over Will Peregrine and for her over Will Sampler and Cymon the scholar. She gives the fan to Virgulta, and demands daily reports on its continued successes.

Tatler 52b. _____. *From my own Apartment, August 8.*

Bickerstaff and some ladies discuss the relative merits of men and women practicing the virtue of modesty. The women argue that it is becoming in all, but Bickerstaff and another man agree that while an ornament to women it is an impediment to men both in love and in business. As an example, the story of Nestor, the architect of Athens, is told. Nestor, because of his modesty, was never given his proper due and so Athenians were deprived of his skill in rebuilding their city. A bold discretion is required, exemplified in Varillus and in a grandson of Bickerstaff's who has risen quickly in the business world. A modest man is in doubt in all his actions, while a modest fellow is never in doubt; the latter is preferred.

Tatler 53a. Thursday, August 11, 1709. Steele. *White's Chocolate-house, August 10.*

Bickerstaff tells the story of *The Civil Husband*, which concerns the beautiful lady Elmira and her husband Osmyn. Although their love disappeared soon after their marriage, their nature was to hide the fact, and since love could not be revived, they remained civil to each other and retired to his estate in the North in the hope that one or the other would soon die and relieve them both of the problem. They there grew healthier, so they moved to Essex, where he died and she returned to town to begin a new life.

Tatler 53b. _____. *Will's Coffee-house, August 10.*

Mr. Truman criticizes Bickerstaff's second act of his tragedy, especially for depending on the retinue of his hero to make him magnificent. Mr. Truman says that Shakespeare is the model, especially his *Julius Caesar,* for making the hero magnificent through his passions, sentiments, and affections.

Tatler 53c. NF. _____. *St. James's Coffee-house, August 10.*

More news from abroad.

Tatler 54a. Saturday, August 13, 1709. Steele. *White's Chocolate-house, August 12.*

Bickerstaff discourses on the subject *Of the Government of Affection,* especially as it applies to Duumvir, who can govern his only to the extent of confining himself to a single mistress, with whom he divides his time with his wife. An example of passion uncontrolled by reason, Duumvir finds Laura, his wife to be insipid because she forgives him and takes him back, but he finds Phyllis, his mistress, full of spirit because she gets angry when he is away. Laura has no faults except that she is his wife; Phyllis, no virtues, except that she is his mistress. Bickerstaff laments Laura's treatment by Duumvir, and wonders if Chromius loved her in vain for only this. Laura now laments her choice; Duumvir has another wife in mind--Aglaura--in case he ever needs one.

Tatler 54b. _____. *From my own Apartment, August 11.*

Bickerstaff gives a letter from Jeoffry Chanticleer urging Bickerstaff to help reform the character and behavior of Stentor in St. Paul's Cathedral. Stentor's problem is that he is so loud in giving the congregational responses that he scares other people. Nor can he sing, yet he drowns out many other better singers. Chanticleer says that discord in a choir is like schism in the Church at large, and needs correcting. Bickerstaff gives yet another letter on the same subject, and says he has heard of dire problems such as frightened horses from Stentor's noises. He laments Lysander and Coriana, who swore to love till death, and now Lysander is seen all over town; thus, he is dead as a lover and Coriana is dead as his mistress.

Tatler 55a. NF. Tuesday, August 16, 1709. Steele. *White's Chocolate-house, August 15.*

Bickerstaff reports on the restoration to sight of a man born blind at Newington, by one Mr. Grant, oculist. Mr. Caswell, a minister, is present while the operation is performed. The man, upon seeing his mother for the first time, faints, and he must return to a state of darkness, only gradually getting used to seeing things in the light. He is especially concerned that his sight of Lydia, his beloved, will destroy their relationship, but decides that Lydia is the only woman in the world for him.

Tatler 55b. NF. _____. *St. James's Coffee-house, August 15.*

More reports on foreign events.

Tatler 56a. Thursday, August 18, 1709. Steele. *White's Chocolate-house, August 17.*

Bickerstaff reports that a young foreigner who is in his charge disturbs him with questions about the people of quality whom they meet. Many are rascals, but Bickerstaff wishes not to give the visitor such an impression of the country so he says they are tame hussars who are allowed in the city. Aletheus says that these people are the cause of the ruin of order, while Sophronius, with great energy, describes them as they really are, and outlines a company of pickpockets, called sharpers, including Monoculus, Will. Vafer, and Jack Heyday. Bickerstaff says that he finds all times and places have been inflicted by such people, and tells of Thersites and Pandarus, from Homer's *Iliad*. Their presence in England is due to the influence of the planet Mercury, as Partridge could testify, if he were alive.

Tatler 56b. _____. *St. James's Coffee-house, August 17.*

Bickerstaff presents a letter from Humphrey Kidney which tells the remarkable old ages of a number of people who recently have died in France.

Tatler 56c. _____. *From my own Apartment, August 17.*

Bickerstaff acknowledges the receipt of letters from Philanthropis and Emilia, and promises replies. He acknowledges that he would delight in reporting on the exploits of lower officers in the recent wars. He admonishes Stentor, saying that increased attendance on him is from his *Tatler* publicity, not from admiration of his voice.

Tatler 57a. Saturday, August 20, 1709. Steele. *Will's Coffee-house, August 19*.

Emilia complains to Bickerstaff that the people of the country do not recognize her as a wit, as did the people of London. Old Truepenny advises that the definition of wit is a local matter, and we should be aware of the company in which we make the best impression. Will. Ubi wants a companion so badly that he will welcome anyone, but wit can also be like Delia's beauty--no one values it because it is attainable by all. Emilia should be less humble; this would inspire her neighbors with a sense of her merit.

Tatler 57b. _____. *White's Chocolate-house, August 19*.

Tom Trump advises Bickerstaff that there are some notorious sharpers who are not properly of the fraternity of gamesters. One of these is Harry Coppersmith, who is a "creature who cheats with credit, and . . . a robber in the habit of a friend." Others are Sir Tristram and Giles Twoshoes, though the latter is bankrupt in his wit.

Tatler 57c. _____. *From my own Apartment, August 19*.

Bickerstaff translates from La Bruyère what he feels to be an elegant piece of raillery and satire; the piece describes the French from the perspective of a foreign traveler and finds them exceedingly curious. Bickerstaff also reports on a new sort of coxcomb in Hampstead, who spends his time fighting with the men and contradicting the women.

Tatler 58a. Tuesday, August 23, 1709. Steele. *White's Chocolate-house, August 22*.

Cynthio tells Bickerstaff that his passion for Clarissa has so come to dominate his life that he has energy for nothing else. Bickerstaff discusses precedents for this, especially the story of Scipio of Rome, who fell in love with a captive woman, but arranged to yield her up to her beloved Indibilis, who was told only to be a friend of Rome in thanksgiving for the return of his fiancé. Bickerstaff makes a claim for the enduring quality of solid virtue, after other fashions have passed.

Tatler 58b. _____. *Will's Coffee-house, August 22*.

Bickerstaff discusses the problem of London's changing language, as it came out in a conversation on the particle "for" between himself, Will. Dactyle the epigrammatist, Jack Comma the grammarian, and Nick Crossgrain the writer of anagrams. They are joined by the noble Martinus, who wishes to change the subject to "forasmuch." He is revealed in the course of the conversation to be a brisk entertaining fool with little learning.

Tatler 58c. NF. _____. *St. James's Coffee-house, August 22.*

Further reports on events abroad.

Tatler 59a. Thursday, August 25, 1709. Steele. *White's Chocolate-house, August 24.*

Bickerstaff, after AEsop, decides to call the sharpers of the town henceforth by the title of a pack of dogs. Actaeon, half man and half deer, is the natural prey of these dogs; the only way to save him is to break up the pack. Pacolet the familiar is sent out to find where they keep themselves. All are warned of a raffling-shop set up in Hampstead under the name of a maid Sisly by Signior Hawksly, the patron of the house-hold.

Tatler 59b. _____. *Will's Coffee-house, August 24.*

Obadiah Greenhat writes to Bickerstaff to praise his efforts, but protests that the Hampstead hero's character (*Tatler* 57c) cannot be new since Suckling knew of him sixty years ago. Bickerstaff agrees that he has been revealed to write nonsense here, but is not offended, because he has been put in company with Homer and Plato in the process. Bickerstaff discusses the Greenhat family, including Zedekiah, who told Beau Prim, who is impotent, that his mistress had rejected him because he had committed a rape. Prim, taking the bait, claims to have paid a hundred pounds to hush up the rape. Bickerstaff claims kinship with the Greenhat family; he will speak no ill of the dead, except of Partridge.

Tatler 59c. NF. _____. *St. James's Coffee-house, August 24.*

More reports on foreign affairs.

Tatler 60a. Saturday, August 27, 1709. Steele. *White's Chocolate-house, August 26.*

Bickerstaff reports on the adventures of Tom Wildair, a student of the Inner Temple, who lives such a dissolute life that he runs up great debts, to the dismay of his father Humphrey Wildair. The father sends the son a great deal of money--four thousand pounds--with the result that the son becomes a responsible young man.

Tatler 60b. _____. *Will's Coffee-house, August 26.*

Bickerstaff says that there is nothing so extravagant that someone will not practice it: for example, Harry Spondee, who carries on at great length about the

efficacy of well-applied nonsense, and Strephon, who
speaks nonsense to a great lady's woman, to the end
that she agrees to meet him at Rosamond's Pond. Only a
cold lover lets a lady know that he is in his right
mind.

Tatler 60c. _____. *From my own Apartment, August 26.*

Bickerstaff gives a letter addressed to smart fellows,
requesting them to meet Major Touchhole on the Artillery Ground for maneuvers. Bickerstaff now has in
press a pamphlet entitled "A Defense of awkward Fellows
against the Class of the Smarts."

Tatler 61a. Tuesday, August 30, 1709. Steele. *White's
Chocolate-house, August 29.*

Bickerstaff discusses the metaphor "fire" as applied to
humans, and finds it misleading. Last night he drank
with two such firemen, one a scholar and the other a
soldier. Both were quick to reach conclusions, but
both were superficial, since the former knew only books,
while the latter knew only men. Another of the sort is
Colonel Truncheon, who is always ready for a fight.
This sort of person is always impatient with slow service in drinking places. While the man of fire does
the wrong and persists in it, Marinus is the sort of
man who is vivacious in doing the right, in doing all
the offices of life eagerly and with pleasant moderation.

Tatler 61b. _____. *Will's Coffee-house, August 29.*

Bickerstaff responds to charges that his satire is too
harsh; he quotes a gentleman who says there is no other
defense against those who get by with doing wrong. He
explains the name *Coppersmith* and reports that Stentor
of St. Paul's has been rebuked for his voice by a noted
divine at St. Peter's.

Tatler 61c. _____. *From my own Apartment, August 29.*

Bickerstaff discusses the question of when women should
make beauty their chief concern. He urges women to be
natural in appearance, especially Cleomira, in the
expectation that every age has its own charms. He objects to the rudeness of Lady Wealthy's and Lady Plant-
well's children, and says that women today cannot compare with Sacharissa and Villaria of another day. Nor
does he like the manners of today's young women. Offspring Twig writes to report on the plans for a military maneuver in the city, run by Colonel Mortar and
Major Blunder.

Tatler 62a. Thursday, September 1, 1709. Steele. *White's Chocolate-house, August 31.*

Bickerstaff reports on a dog-kennel in Suffolk Street and gives a table of the occupants, including Jowler, Rockwood, Pompey, Ringwood, and an Italian greyhound, ten setting dogs, four mongrels, and twenty whelps. They are hungry, and have destroyed a wild boar of the north. Bickerstaff recommends deportation to America, for all these are great nuisances to everyone.

Tatler 62b. _____. *Will's Coffee-house, August 31.*

Bickerstaff reports on the propriety of words and thoughts. An odd gentleman argues that Harry Jacks deserved a statue for reporting on the French loss of Tournay because he was on the French side and it hurt him to admit its fall. Spondee finds this an odd conversation. Bickerstaff argues that no one is a better conversationalist than an accomplished woman, such as Lady Courtly.

Tatler 62c. _____. *From my own Apartment, August 31.*

Bickerstaff reports that he has lost esteem for Sallust because the writer did not give Cicero credit for his part in preserving the commonwealth and says that he prefers people to be honest about their self-interest. An example is a boatswain on Dampier's ship, who dissuades the crew from eating him by suggesting that Black Kate had made him unfit to eat and that he would be better drunk rather than eaten.

Tatler 62d. NF. _____. *St. James's Coffee-house, August 31.*

More reports on foreign events.

Tatler 62e. _____. Addendum.

Bickerstaff reports to booksellers that Mr. Omicron, the unborn poet, will write poems or prose and translate out of any language.

Tatler 63a. Saturday, September 3, 1709. Steele. *White's Chocolate-house, September 2.*

Bickerstaff discourses on the subject *Of the Enjoyment of Life with Regard to Others.* He argues that the Romans betrayed the glory of their ideals when they forced those people they conquered into humiliating positions rather than treating them with dignity. It is human nature, he concludes, for men to be more concerned about relative appearances than for a true sense of honor. Men would rather appear to be happy and actually be in pain than to be truly happy and be thought by the world to be miserable. Bromeo and Tabio are two examples of individuals who are locked in a

struggle to appear to the world to be better off than
they really are. The secret of success in this contest
is to obtain the high regard of one's opponent by pointing out to him places in which one is superior to him;
Gnatho is an expert in pursuing the skill of keeping
one's opponent off guard. Bromeo argues on the one
hand that men are purely concerned with pleasing themselves; on the other hand he also spends a great deal
of time trying to outdo Tabio in the eyes of the world.

Tatler 63b. _____. *Will's Coffee-house, September 2.*

Bickerstaff, Mr. Dactile, Will. Truby, and Humphrey Slyboots discuss some men's ability to make things seem
ridiculous. They agree that humor is important but only
in certain clearly defined situations. The Truby family
laugh on little provocation while the Slyboots family
smile only in occasions of great mirth; Bickerstaff says
that the differences between the two families are hereditary rather than psychological in nature; he realizes
however that these differences can result in disagree-
ments between members of the two families.

Tatler 63c. _____. *From my own Apartment, September 2.*

Bickerstaff presents a letter from Tobiah Greenhat, in
which Greenhat praises Bickerstaff for his ability to
admit his mistakes. Greenhat reports that his brother
Obadiah also sends his thanks; he also reports that
Madonella, who was thought to be dead, is in fact alive.
She and Epicene have decided to form a college for girls,
the purpose of which will be to instruct young ladies in
ancient languages rather than in the art of needlework.

Tatler 63d. NF. _____. *St. James's Coffee-house,
September 2.*

More reports on events abroad.

Tatler 64a. Tuesday, September 6, 1709. Steele. *From my
own Apartment, September 5.*

Bickerstaff gives an extensive report on the victory of
the Duke of Marlborough at Mons, a report brought to
him by Pacolet, his familiar.

Tatler 64b. _____. *Will's Coffee-house, September 5.*

Bickerstaff presents a letter from Josiah Couplet in
which Couplet applauds Bickerstaff's project of making
wit useful. Couplet says that this is the task which
should have been carried out by the best comedies, and
assures Bickerstaff that he will never run out of subject matter. Couplet then presents a character sketch
of Cleontes, who is a man of good family and good learning, a man who talks well and yet he appears to the
world only as one politely ridiculous. This is a result of his background and his training; he combines

some of the best qualities of the mind with some of the
worst of the heart; as a result, everybody is entertained by him but no one esteems him. Bickerstaff further reports that two Irish dogs, who belong to the pack
of London, are now missing. These, and other missing
dogs, may be kept by anyone who finds them.

Tatler 65a. Thursday, September 8, 1709. Steele. *Will's
Coffee-house, September 7.*

Bickerstaff reports on a conversation at Will's on the
subject of recent English victory. Instead of being
happy, many of the people involved in the conversation
are doubtful of the outcome and fearful that reports of
success were premature. Greenhat points out that one
of the men expressing dissatisfaction is a battle critic,
a person who is always suspicious and doubtful of the
way in which any report on military action is conveyed.
Sir George England reports that battle critics should
be silent because this victory is worthy of the sort of
praise given to victories in Roman times.

Tatler 65b. _____. *From my own Apartment, September 7.*

Bickerstaff prints two letters from his relatives on the
subject of the brotherhood of rascals. The writer of
the first letter says that Bickerstaff has been remiss
in his duty by not informing them of the dogs of London
coming to their part of the country. The dogs have
arrived, including among them Beau Bogg, Beau Pert,
Rake, and Tallboy. Beau Pert, a coxcomb, was able to
relieve Squire Humphry of four hundred guineas because
Pert is the perfect complement for Humphry, who is a raw
fool. Squire Humphry tried to recover his honor and
succeeded only in provoking a fight. Bickerstaff should
continue the struggle against these cut-purses. The
author of the second letter urges Bickerstaff to ac-
quaint Jack Haughty with the fact that the secret of
his meeting with the Swiss at the Thatched House is
known to all.

Tatler 66a. Saturday, September 10, 1709. Steele. *Will's
Coffee-house, September 9.*

Bickerstaff reports on a conversation about Eloquence
and Graceful Action. Lysander, who leads the discussion, argues that a man cannot be eloquent unless he is
also eloquent in action as well as in words. Lysander
cites classical examples to prove his theory, and among
contemporaries, points to the Dean, Daniel, and Parson
Dapper as examples of great oratory in the present day.

Tatler 66b. _____. *From my own Apartment, September 9.*

Bickerstaff reports on a letter from a young man who
wants to become a gentleman but who has trouble dealing

with women and wishes for Bickerstaff's advice. He has one thousand pounds per year, and is pursued by Mrs. Would-be. He lacks the education appropriate to his income and wishes to trade his income for establishment as a mercer. Bickerstaff consults Mr. Obadiah Greenhat on the subject; Greenhat is so pleased that he advises the young man be educated in a fashion appropriate to his income. This would mean turning into a sloven and drunkard, for this seems basic to the behavior of gentlemen of the town. Bickerstaff points out that many men with the title of gentleman act in a manner unbecoming to the title; Harry Lacker and Nokes Lightfoot are two examples. Bickerstaff forbids all persons who are not of the first quality or who do not have some important office from driving in Hyde Park with a team of six horses. Bickerstaff also presents a letter from Philanthropos in which the writer reports on the appearance of a new pack of dogs. This particular pack lives by taking advantage of young men who have just come into their fortunes.

Tatler 66c. NF. _____. *St. James's Coffee-house, September 9.*

Further reports on events abroad.

Tatler 67a. Tuesday, September 13, 1709. Steele. *From my own Apartment, September 12.*

Bickerstaff complains that his criticisms of people have had little success. Mr. Didapper still wears his red-heeled shoes, Stentor still roars, and Partridge still walks the streets at noonday. Bickerstaff says, however, that he will persist in his efforts; to help carry out his task of correcting mankind he will establish a Chamber of Fame, to which only 132 people will be admitted. All learned men are requested to submit their lists of the most justly famous men in the world to Mr. Bickerstaff. In the meantime, Bickerstaff will persist in trying to correct the ills of mankind. In pursuing this task Bickerstaff reprints three letters which he mailed recently to ladies in an attempt to correct certain aspects of their behavior. The first letter is to the current toast of the town, admonishing her to avoid looking so naturally beautiful because her beauty is costing Eleonora a great deal of money in her attempt to imitate this beauty artificially. The second letter is to a woman requesting her to take off the patches on the lower end of her left cheek on the condition that Bickerstaff will allow her two more patches under her left eye. The third letter is to two ladies of Essex Street admonishing them to spend less time gaping out their windows. Unfortunately, Bickerstaff finds that all the ladies involved refuse to change their behavior.

Tatler 67b. NF. _____. *St. James's Coffee-house, September 12.*

Further reports on events abroad.

Tatler 67c. NF. _____. *Will's Coffee-house, September 12.*

Bickerstaff argues that beginning writers should work hard on improving their skills in making a transition from one subject to the other. He gives an example of what he is talking about in a discussion of a wound received by the King of Sweden; his real purpose is to protest the lumping together of a wide range of subjects under a single heading.

Tatler 68a. Thursday, September 15, 1709. Steele. *From my own Apartment, September 14.*

Bickerstaff reports on the progress of the founding of his Chamber of Fame; he is amazed to see how many people nominate themselves. He also discovers that he has far more candidates for his dark room of men of evil fame than for his Chamber of Fame. Bickerstaff also reports that he knows there are many women who deserve to be locked with the pack of dogs but he is having difficulty coming up with appropriate names for them. If these women, however, do not stop their attacks on order, discipline, and virtue, Bickerstaff will be forced to proceed against them severely.

Tatler 68b. _____. *Will's Coffee-house, September 14.*

Bickerstaff reports that a letter asks him to discuss crying even as he has recently discussed laughing. Bickerstaff does so, suggesting that there is a close connection between laughing and crying. Bickerstaff finds, however, that many people use crying for their own ends, to gain our sympathy when it is not necessarily deserved. Bickerstaff finds examples of appropriate tears in Shakespeare's *Macbeth* and *Julius Caesar*; these examples suggest that the true art of expressing sorrow is found in bearing it with decency and patience. Tears are frequently the result of a mind too full to await words, which can be slow to express a person's feelings. Bickerstaff also reports that a tall, dangerous biter has broken loose from the London Pack and is now at Bath. This dog, named the Top, cheats at dice.

Tatler 69a. Saturday, September 17, 1709. Steele. *From my own Apartment, September 16.*

Bickerstaff discusses the nature and ends of education, which he sees as intending to raise people above the level of the vulgar; he believes, however, that the true nature of a gentleman is to be found in behavior

rather than in birth. The truly wise man thinks no man
is better than he unless he is more virtuous, and no
man worse than he who is not more full of vice. In
light of this discussion, Bickerstaff notes that he is
glad to receive a letter from Felicia, informing him
that Eboracensis has been appointed a governor of a
plantation. Bickerstaff believes that since Eboracensis
has read widely and also knows mankind, that he will be
a capable and able govenor.

Tatler 69b. _____. *White's Chocolate-house,
September 16.*

Bickerstaff presents a letter from Bridget Eitherside,
which describes the curious situation of two ladies who
are such close friends that they decide to marry the
same man rather than be separated from each other by
marrying different men. Bickerstaff comments that these
two constant friends, whose names are Piledea and
Orestea, are trying to deal with the very real problem
of preserving their friendship against the encroachments
of love. Unfortunately they will most assuredly run into the problem of jealousy. Bickerstaff cites as an
example an episode in Cervantes' *Don Quixote* in which
the Don delights in being praised by the Knight of the
Green Cassock; from this example, Bickerstaff draws the
conclusion that one of the two ladies will inevitably
be jealous of her former friend if their joint marriage
in fact comes about.

Tatler 69c. _____. *St. James's Coffee-house,
September 16.*

Bickerstaff reports that all the coffee houses are
filled with discussions of England's recent victory.
Mr. Kidney urges Bickerstaff to write a paper on the
subject of Valor; Bickerstaff agrees to do so in the
near future. Bickerstaff also reports on two gentlemen in a tavern who danced without clothes on; Bickerstaff claims that there is no wit in this practice.
Bickerstaff also reports on a chapel clerk who has been
found in bed with two women; he is urged to repent.
Bickerstaff also praises a clergyman for the brevity of
his sermon.

Tatler 70a. Tuesday, September 20, 1709. Steele. *From my
own Apartment, September 19.*

Bickerstaff presents a letter from a correspondent who
agrees with Bickerstaff that there are few men capable
of oratory in the best sense of the word. The correspondent argues that eloquence accompanied with the
appropriate voice and gesture will prevail over passion,
and that eloquence without voice and gesture is incapable of carrying out its purpose. To prove this point
the case of Cicero's Defense of Ligarius and his defense

117

of Milo are cited. Demosthenes, Hippocrates, and Horace are also discussed to provide classical precedents for proper oratory. While too little action in speaking makes the speech cold, too much action is also distracting, as the case of Stentor has already demonstrated. Bickerstaff also presents a letter from Jonathan Rosehat on the subject of oratory; Rosehat argues that the orator should appear to be as he would persuade others to be, so that his life is a part of his persuasive technique. Rosehat also claims to recommend to all orators the famous speaking doctor at Kensington, who claims to be able to make a good orator of a pair of bellows. Bickerstaff also presents a third letter from a correspondent who wishes that all young clergymen could read Bickerstaff's discussion on the subject of oratory.

Tatler 70b. _____. *White's Chocolate-house, September 19.*

Bickerstaff presents a letter from a correspondent on the subject of the inhabitants of the dog kennel in Suffolk Street in which the correspondent suggests that Pacolet, Bickerstaff's familiar, would find among the inhabitants the following: Towzer, a large French mongrel, Spring, a little French greyhoud, Sly, an old battered fox hound, and Lightfoot, a fine-skinned Flanders dog. The correspondent also informs Bickerstaff that Ringwood bites at Hampstead with false teeth.

Tatler 71a. Thursday, September 22, 1709. Steele. *From my own Apartment, September 21.*

Bickerstaff announces that as a result of his satires he has been warned about possible threats to his life and limb. Bickerstaff, however, is concerned about a letter from one A. J., in which the writer accuses Bickerstaff of accusing a man wrongly. Bickerstaff responds that if the writer can show any instance where he has injured a good man, he will be more than happy to acknowledge the offense as openly as the press can do it and abandon the *Tatler* forever. Unfortunately, he is most generally the subject of misinterpretation by those at whom his attacks were not directed; this is the case of a recent paper on the subject of Omicron.

Tatler 71b. _____. *Will's Coffee-house, September 20.*

Bickerstaff prints a letter from a correspondent who urges him to admonish the correspondent's vicar, whose conduct in preaching, reading prayers, and spending more time away from church than in it upsets him. Worst of all, he is so proud that he will visit the sick only once, unless they return his visit. Bickerstaff also presents a report by Mr. Greenhat on a performance of *Hamlet* in which Mr. Betterton played the central character. Bickerstaff also presents a letter from his relative Benjamin Beadlestaff, who assures Bickerstaff that his attack on ill-manners has had more of an effect in Oxford than it has had in London. As a result of Bickerstaff's efforts, the language, manners, and habits of the youths of Oxford are much reformed.

Tatler 72a. Saturday, September 24, 1709. Steele. *White's Chocolate-house, September 23.*

Bickerstaff says that he will turn now from attack upon vices to praise of notable characters. A correspondent asks him to tell the story of Paetus and his wife Arria, who lived and died in the reign of Nero. Paetus, happily married to Arria, is ordered by Nero to kill himself either with dagger, sword or poison under the threat of death by torture if he does not carry out the order within an hour. Arria, unable to endure the thought of living without her husband, stabs herself first; Paetus immediately followed her example. The depth of their devotion to each other survived them and is eternally enshrined in an epigram by Martial.

Tatler 72b. _____. *From my own Apartment, September 23.*

Bickerstaff presents a letter from a Quaker, who objects to the dullness and the inattention to the needs of his hearers of an Anglican divine. Bickerstaff agrees that many clergy are not sufficiently industrious in their jobs; he presents the character of Favonius as an example of one capable of defending religious truth against all dissenters, protecting all those under his care with his personal example and learning, visiting the dying and giving them comfort, and exhibiting in voice and behavior what Bickerstaff calls "a composed and well-governed zeal." Bickerstaff also presents a letter from The Trencher-Caps, who wish to know whether a chapel-clerk is a clergyman or layman; a half dozen bottles of wine ride on Bickerstaff's response. Bickerstaff informs them that he meant by his reference to chapel-clerk a drunken clerk of the church.

Tatler 73a. Tuesday, September 27, 1709. Steele. *White's Chocolate-house, September 26.*

Bickerstaff describes his confusion at receiving a letter from Monoculus, in which the writer accuses Bickerstaff of being an impudent fellow for mentioning him in an earlier *Tatler* (*Tatler* 36b). Monoculus says, "Rot you sir"; he assures Bickerstaff of his bravery and urges Bickerstaff to be careful. Bickerstaff prints his answer, in which he urges that a third party decide which of the two men is the more impudent. Bickerstaff urges Monoculus to "keep your temper, wash your face, and go to bed." Bickerstaff also presents a letter from Will. Trusty, in which the writer describes the society of a public house in terms of fellows at a college. This is, however, a college devoted to thieving; the current object of their interest is one Sir Liberal Brisk, who has just inherited a substantial estate. Pacolet, Bickerstaff's familiar, urges the writer to be plain in his address, and so he tells the story of Sir Liberal Brisk's being fleeced of his estate by Ace and Cutter. Brisk wishes his story to be known so that other young gentlemen can avoid his fate.

Tatler 73b. _____. *From my own Apartment, September 26.*

Bickerstaff describes an attempt by Sir Arthur de Bradly to influence the vote for Alderman for the ward of Queenhithe. A paper published by Sir Arthur promises to reward all those voting for him with a supply of coal. Everyone who votes for both Sir Arthur and his opponent Sir Humphry Greenhat will also be rewarded with a supply of coal.

Tatler 74a. Thursday, September 29, 1709. Steele. *White's Chocolate-house, September 28.*

Bickerstaff presents a letter which he received from Alexander Landlord, in which the writer urges Bickerstaff to publish in the *Tatler* a letter to a young lady so that he may meet her. Bickerstaff presents the letter to the young lady upon being assured that she is extremely attractive and that Landlord is sincere. The lady in question is the younger of two sisters; Bickerstaff says that if the elder is unmarried, the proposal from Landlord has no future.

Tatler 74b. _____. *From my own Apartment, September 28.*

Bickerstaff presents a letter from a correspondent who urges Bickerstaff to change the method of his attempts at reforming society. He argues that Bickerstaff is going about things the wrong way when he points out the vices of the town. A better approach is to praise virtue rather than denounce vice.

Tatler 74c. _____. *Grecian Coffee-house, September 29.*

Bickerstaff announces that he will, within the month, publish his first list of famous men; he requests further submissions of candidates for this list. Those in the race are warned not to attempt bribery; newswriters are excluded from consideration because their sense of fame is based on a desire to fill up space in their newspapers rather than as an interest in the difference between good and bad.

Tatler 74d. NF. _____. *St. James's Coffee-house, September 28.*

More reports on events abroad.

Tatler 75. Saturday, October 1, 1709. Steele and Addison. *From my own Apartment, September 30.*

Bickerstaff sets out upon the task of finding a husband for his sister Jenny. He assures his readers that she is chaste and modest; he seeks a man of modesty, vigor, and industry, as well as good health. Bickerstaff then begins a brief history of the family, which he traces back to Sir Isaac Bickerstaff, a knight of King Arthur's Round Table. The descendants of Sir Isaac have sought by various appropriate matches to overcome or compensate for various deformities in the family; thus, Sir Isaac's eldest son Ralph, who was very short, was married to a woman who was very tall. In like manner attempts have been made throughout the ages to compensate for various and sundry physical difficulties. In this regard, Bickerstaff seeks a husband for Jenny who will complement her outstanding characteristic, which is her wit. Bickerstaff's desire is for Jenny and her husband-to-be to produce children fit for any situation in which they find themselves. Bickerstaff urges that all marriage matches be made with great care, or the consequences will be disasterous for any family.

Tatler 76a. Tuesday, October 4, 1709. Steele. *From my own Apartment, October 3.*

Bickerstaff discusses the fact that many men's problems arise from within themselves, so that they are no man's enemy but their own. One example is Euphusius, who is full of good will; as a result everyone takes advantage of him. Euphusius is especially prone to get into trouble at the hands of the packs of dogs which feed upon him. All men of Euphusius' temperament are warned to be careful.

Tatler 76b. _____. *White's Chocolate-house, October 3.*

Bickerstaff reports that A. Landlord of *Tatler* 74a has heard from his lady, who wants love but not marriage. Bickerstaff is dismayed, and turns to the problem of Lovewell Barebones, whose lady is always accompanied by a kinswoman whose presence prevents Barebones from engaging in amorous advances. Bickerstaff's advice is for Barebones to find a lover for the beloved's confidant. Bickerstaff also presents a letter from a correspondent who praises satire as good means to reformation and defends Bickerstaff against all charges brought against him for the pursuit of his satirical method.

Tatler 76c. NF. _____. *St. James's Coffee-house, October 3.*

More reports on events overseas.

Tatler 76d. _____. Addendum.

Bickerstaff says that he has learned that a young gentleman has taken his claims for the death of John Partridge
too seriously and is sueing an elder brother for his
estate.

Tatler 77a. Thursday, October 6, 1709. Steele. *From my
own Apartment, October 5.*

Bickerstaff says that his task in the world would be
made much simpler if people habitually appeared to be
worse than they really are; unfortunately the reverse
is much more often the case. Bickerstaff describes,
however, the current fashion among the well-to-do of
pretending to be worse off than they really are. One
example is the Valetudinarian, who complains of stomach
trouble until noon and then eats everything available
after noon. Lady Dainty has a similar problem; because
she protests that her stomach is out of order, she eats
alone at 12:00 so that she may refuse to eat in public
at 2:00. Five years ago the fashion was to be blind;
now the fashion is to be lame. Other affectations which
have been popular include the use of a cane, lisping,
or deafness. There are also mental affectations; some
of these include atheism, marriage hating, quarrelsome-
ness, and other sorts of extravagancies.

Tatler 77b. _____. *St. James's Coffee-house, October 5.*

Bickerstaff reports no news from abroad, except a letter
supposedly from the Mareschal Boufflers to the French
King, in which the writer assures the King that though
his troops lost the battle, they fought magnificently
and yielded no ground. Bickerstaff also recalls all
physicians to their former places of practice from the
town of Bath, because there are now an excess of two
doctors per patient in that town.

Tatler 78. Saturday, October 8, 1709. Steele. *From my own
Apartment, October 7.*

Bickerstaff describes his method of working; he claims
that he has a scrutoire in which he has a drawer for
each of the many subjects which his writings have dealt
with, including hypocrisy, dice, patches, politics, love,
duels, and so forth. He has a special box for Pacolet
and another for Monoculus. He finds that his duel-box
is filled with letters from men of honor which are so
poorly spelled that they are hard to read. His love-
box is filled with letters from the fairest hands in
Great Britain which are almost as unintelligible as
those in the duel-box. Bickerstaff also reports on
nominations for the Table of Fame and reproduces some
extraordinary letters of nomination. The first, from
Ezekiel Stiffrump, a Quaker, fears that the Table of
Fame will only contain heathens, and therefore nominates

James Mayler, a Quaker thought by some of his followers to be Christ. The second letter urges Bickerstaff not to elect to the Table of Fame men who are dead, since they cannot pay for the honor. He assures Bickerstaff that he knows a person of quality who will be happy to pay one hundred pounds for admission to the Table. Bickerstaff assures this correspondent that he will be happy to consider the name if the hundred pounds is left with Bickerstaff's publisher. Lemuel Ledger writes in nomination of Dick Whittington, who set out in the world with a cat and died worth 350,000 pounds. Bickerstaff then sets aside public concerns for private concerns with a letter from T. B., who wishes to thank publicly a doctor who took care of him without insisting on payment. Bickerstaff joins in the praise of this physician. Bickerstaff also announces that all gentlemen of London who wish instruction in music, sports, poetry, and politics equip themselves with three dishes of Bohea and two pinches of snuff and come to the seat of learning at Smyran Coffee-house. Bickerstaff objects to letters signed by their writers "Faithful" or "Your Most Obedient" when such sentiments are not intended. Bickerstaff urges all readers to ignore the writing of a lunatic who will soon publish a work claiming to identify Mr. Bickerstaff's true identity.

Tatler 79. Tuesday, October 11, 1709. Steele. *From my own Apartment, October 10.*

Bickerstaff describes a meeting between him and his sister Jenny on the night before her marriage to her lover, the honest Tranquillus. Bickerstaff urges Jenny to remember that most quarrels in marriage arise over small incidents of disagreement, and therefore he urges her to be above arguing about trifles. While people who plan to marry usually agree on major issues, they overlook the fact that they must also work at agreeing on small issues. Sir Harry Willit and his lady are irreconcilable because she interrupted him by chasing a squirrel into his study while he was reading a grave and serious author. Sir Harry flew into a rage, but quickly recovered his tranquility; his wife then got angry with him because he so quickly got over his anger. She proceeded to her bed chamber where she tore her hair and named twenty coxcombs whom she felt would have treated her more the way she wished to be treated. As a result they have separated; both wish to reunite, but neither wishes to make the first step. With this advice, the bride proceeded to her wedding day, prepared by Mrs. Toilet, at the age of 23. The wedding was followed by a dinner attended by various members of the family, including Lepidus Wagstaff, who gave an oration on the subject of marriage ending with a quotation from *Paradise Lost*. The party was almost disrupted by a wag who made bawdy puns on the bride's entertainment that evening, but decorum was preserved by a rought-and-ready member of the family, a lieutenant of marines, who silenced the wag.

Tatler 80a. Thursday, October 13, 1709. Steele. *Grecian Coffee-house, October 12.*

Bickerstaff notices the high price of books and concludes that literature should be priced according to its language. Since Greek is so little understood and English is so widely understood, books in these two languages should be very cheap, while books in Latin should be expensive. He promises that the price of the *Tatler* will not increase.

Tatler 80b. _____. *White's Chocolate-house, October 12.*

Bickerstaff receives a letter from J. R. who announces that he was humiliated yesterday on a visit to Lady Haughty, who forced him to sit on a round stool in the company of people in arm chairs. The gentleman in question visits Bickerstaff, who sits him in an arm chair while placing himself in a chair with no arms. Bickerstaff examines the gentleman and decides that he needs to be treated for distemper of the spleen and assures him that all the world is not totally ill-natured.

Tatler 80c. _____. *From my own Apartment, October 12.*

Bickerstaff presents a letter from a correspondent who says that he has recently been injured in his left foot and hopes that he will not be considered to be an affected gentleman as well as an afflicted gentleman, since Bickerstaff's essay on affectations (*Tatler* 78). Bickerstaff agrees not to consider this an affectation so long as the gentleman in question does not have his limp for longer than five months.

Tatler 80d. NF. _____. *St. James's Coffee-house, October 12.*

A brief report on events abroad.

Tatler 81. Saturday, October 15, 1709. Steele and Addison. *From my own Apartment, October 14.*

Bickerstaff says that there are two kinds of immortality: the first is that enjoyed by the soul after this life, and the second is that imaginary existence through which men live on in their reputations. It is to celebrate this latter form of immortality that Bickerstaff establishes the Table of Fame. Yesterday, Bickerstaff says, he worked so hard comparing the lists of candidates for the Table of Fame which had been submitted to him that, upon going to sleep, he had a very remarkable vision. The dream is of a mountain which is difficult to climb because the pathways upward are protected by Sloth,

Ignorance, and Pleasure, as well as Death and Envy.
Those who attempt to climb this mountain use different
kinds of equipment, including swords, telescopes, and
rolls of paper, and many are not successful in reaching
the top. Those who do reach the top, however, are invited to take their place of honor inside a glorious
palace. Those who succeed in making the climb include
Alexander the Great, Julius Caesar, Homer, Socrates,
Aristotle, Virgil, Cicero, Hannibal, Pompey, Cato,
Augustus Caesar, Plato, and Archimedes. Bickerstaff
himself is put forth as a candidate for a place at one
of the lesser tables, but he is passed over for Robin
Hood.

Tatler 82. Tuesday, October 18, 1709. Steele. *From my own
Apartment, October 17.*

Bickerstaff, in a serious mood because of his discussions
of great men, meditates on the tragedy of those people
who love each other and yet have their happiness interrupted by tragedy when they least expect it. Bickerstaff finds such contemplation to soften the mind and
improve the heart; this he says is the purpose and function of Greek tragedy. In this vein, he tells two
stories to illustrate his point. The first story concerns a young gentleman who must go abroad on a long
voyage shortly after his marriage; unfortunately he returns home in a coffin. The second story is told in
letters from a young man to the father of his bride.
The first letter describes their happiness at the wedding, while the second letter describes the tragedy
which befell the couple when the bridegroom shot his
wife with a pistol he thought to be unloaded. As a
result the bridegroom shot the servant who loaded the
pistol and promises the father of his dead bride that
he will also kill himself. He begs the father's forgiveness.

Tatler 83a. Thursday, October 20, 1709. Steele. *From my
own Apartment, October 19.*

Bickerstaff describes a chance encounter with two people
who are discussing his account of the Table of Fame
(*Tatler* 81); the two people discuss whom they consider
to be the contemporary public figures whom they believe
Bickerstaff has hidden behind the classical names. Their
conclusions are based on their belief that all the people at the Table of Fame have bought their way into this
list of honor. Bickerstaff promises to explain all in
his last paper. Bickerstaff also prints a letter from
an admirer named Maria, who proclaims her love of Bickerstaff, not because of his looks but because of his
understanding. She says she is a "good agreeable woman,"
and she hopes that something will come of their relationship. She insists that she knows more of love than

Bickerstaff does of astronomy. Bickerstaff is flattered
by this, claiming that he is delighted with her praise
of his sense. Bickerstaff claims that at 63 he is too
old for love and therefore thanks her for her letter
but regrets he can only respond with another letter,
which he gives us.

Tatler 83b. _____. *Will's Coffee-house, October 19.*

Bickerstaff receives a letter from Solomon Afterwit, in
which the writer points to the difficulty a young man
has of saying the word "No" to anything in the city of
London. Bickerstaff promises to respond with a treatise
containing rules for a young man to go by in saying "No"
and for a young virgin to go by in saying "Yes."

Tatler 83c. NF. _____. *St. James's Coffee-house,
October 19.*

A vert brief report on foreign events.

Tatler 84a. Saturday, October 22, 1709. Steele. *From my
own Apartment, October 21.*

Bickerstaff responds to a letter from A. B., who suggests that the very heavy attendance of women at the Old
Bailey when a rape case is to be tried is an enormity.
Bickerstaff disagrees, arguing that since women are
chiefly the victims of such activity it is appropriate
for them to be in attendance. In fact, he argues that
juries in rape cases should consist of half men and
half women. There are many women who by long attendance at such trials know a sufficient amount of law
and anatomy to be competent judges of such cases. One
of these women is the learned Androgyne. Bickerstaff
concludes that modesty is in woman the most graceful
and becoming of virtues. The subject of modesty brings
Bickerstaff to a letter from the virtuous Lady Whittlestick, who offers the name of Lucretia as a candidate
for the Table of Fame. Bickerstaff also has a letter
from Mrs. Biddy Twig on the same subject; he responds
to both that although he knows Lucretia would have
graced the table, he knows she would not want to be in
the company of so many men without her husband.

Tatler 84b. _____. *Grecian Coffee-house, October 21.*

Bickerstaff communicates to the learned his interest in
bringing obscure merit into the public view; at the
same time, he promises to examine the merits of those
already known to the public for their virtues. The
first group to be examined will be those Frenchmen who
have written highly complimentary and also highly fictitious accounts of their own lives.

Tatler 84c. _____. *Will's Coffee-house, October 21.*

A friend expresses his sorrow for the enemies Bickerstaff has made, and says that for some, enmity is the greatest compliment they can give a man. Bickerstaff interrupts him to tell a fable of a man, awakened by a lizard, who starts to kill the lizard until he discovers that the lizard has awakened him to warn him of a poisonous snake nearby.

Tatler 85a. Tuesday, October 25, 1709. Steele. *From my own Apartment, October 24.*

Bickerstaff reports on a conversation with his sister Jenny provoked by the fact that Tranquillus requests that he and Jenny move from Bickerstaff's house to their own house sooner than expected. Bickerstaff realizes that Tranquillus and Jenny have argued and counsels Jenny to avoid argument for the sake of argument and to avoid taking pleasure in her power to give her husband pain. She and Tranquillus decide to remain with Bickerstaff a while longer. Tim Dapper, a dandy of the country and a relation of Tranquillus, stops by and makes everyone feel at ease by the delight he takes in himself.

Tatler 85b. _____. *White's Chocolate-house, October 24.*

Bickerstaff visits a lady who tells him the sad news of the death of Cynthio. After Clarissa married, Cynthio fell into despondency and went to the country to leave his thoughts of Clarissa behind him; unfortunately he found in the country only the opportunity to think about her all the time. As a result, he died. The lady who communicates this sad news to Bickerstaff asks for an epitaph for Cynthio's tomb; Bickerstaff promises to comply.

Tatler 86a. Thursday, October 27, 1709. Addison and Steele. *From my own Apartment, October 26.*

Bickerstaff presents a letter from John Thrifty, informing that Sir Harry Quickset, Sir Giles Wheelbarrow, Sir Thomas Rentfree, Andrew Windmill, and Mr. Nicholas Doubt plan to visit him. When these gentlemen come for a visit, they all show such courtesy to Sir Harry that the whole group can hardly do anything except wait on Sir Harry to act first. They retire to a public house, which had never seen such a display of men of high rank and country manners. Sir Harry concludes that the public house is too public for private business, and promises to return to see Bickerstaff again tomorrow.

Tatler 86b. _____. *Will's Coffee-house, October 26.*

Bickerstaff overhears a gentleman lecture a group of ten or twelve libertines on the subject of modesty, which he describes as a sure sign of a great and noble spirit. To prove his point, he tells the story of Ciscereius and Scipio in their competition for the office of praetor. Ciscereius obtains the office for Scipio but because of his modesty receives the honor though not the office. Similarly he tells the story of Pompey, who refused to accept the honors he felt were due to someone else. Finally he cites the example of Caesar, who upon his murder, tried to fall to his death so that he would appear to be in a decent posture.

Tatler 87a. Saturday, October 29, 1709. Steele. *Will's Coffee-house, October 28.*

Bickerstaff wazes rhapsodic to a cluster of critics on the subject of the dignity of human nature, and argues that it is exhibited at every level of human society. As an example he quotes a letter written by one John Hall, written from the battlefront, in which the correspondent, an ordinary soldier, shows a cheery attitude toward the rigors of battle, including the loss of friend. Bickerstaff argues that the gallantry of private soldiers arises from the same, if not from a nobler, impulse than that of soldiers from a higher order of society.

Tatler 87b. _____. *From my own Apartment, October 28.*

Bickerstaff announces that he is so moved by his reflections on the heroism of the common soldier that he proposes a way to divide the glory of a battle among the whole army by dividing it into shares. Of a total number of shares of ten hundred thousand, half go to the general, and the rest go to the officers and men, so that the Sergeant Hall of *Tatler* 87a. receives one share and a fraction of two-fifths. Bickerstaff concludes that even this amount of the glory would be sufficient to motivate a man to die for his country if the people of Britain express their appreciation of military heroism satisfactorily.

Tatler 88a. Tuesday, November 1, 1709. Steele. *White's Chocolate-house, October 31.*

Bickerstaff receives a letter from the country requesting that he explain the terms "gunner" and "gunster"; Bickerstaff informs his correspondent that gunners are people who tell lies with mischievous intent, while gunsters are those who tell lies only for entertainment. Bickerstaff divides the company of gunners into four types: the Bombadier, the Miner, the Squib, and the Serpent. The Bombadier is one who tells great lies which can panic a nation; the Miner tells lies which harm individuals; the Squib writes pamphlets; and the Serpent tells quiet lies which do great harms. There are many women adept at the role of Miner; a notable

female miner is Cleomilla. The gunster is harmless;
his lies are full of wind and harm no one.

Tatler 88b. _____. Addison. *From my own Apartment,*
   October 31.

   Bickerstaff is asked to come next door because a young
   man lodging there is making an enormous amount of noise
   and disturbing the whole house. Upon investigation,
   Bickerstaff discovers the young man to be a dancing
   instructor who is making the noise by leaping around
   the room practicing his technique.

Tatler 89a. Thursday, November 3, 1709. Steele. *Grecian*
   Coffee-house, November 2.

   Bickerstaff reports on a letter he has received from
   the country which praises Bickerstaff for the fine job
   he is doing correcting the morals of the country and
   for giving residents of the country something to talk
   about. Bickerstaff delights in this praise and compliments the author of the letter as clearly a man of good
   taste who is delightful company wherever he goes.
   Bickerstaff tells something of his past life, including
   his taking up the occult sciences.

Tatler 89b. _____. *From my own Apartment, November 2.*

   Bickerstaff and a correspondent both complain bitterly
   of those who visit when they are not welcome. Especially unfortunate are those who visit a man recovering
   from an illness; their visits may be so taxing that he
   may be visited into a relapse.

Tatler 89c. _____. *Will's Coffee-house, November 2.*

   Bickerstaff expresses his approval of a gentleman's
   objections to actors inserting their own words into the
   speeches they have been given to perform. It is as bad,
   he says, as those who have classical statues restored
   by contemporary stone-masons; the resulting work looks
   more disfigured than the original.

Tatler 90a. Saturday, November 5, 1709. Steele and Addison. *Will's Coffee-house, November 4.*

   Bickerstaff reports on a conversation on the subject of
   love. Menmius notices the remarkable similiarity in
   many artistic treatments of love; all these have in
   common their presentation of love as a soft torment, a
   bitter-sweet, a pleasing pain, or an agreeable distress.
   To illustrate his point, Menmius tells a story, from
   Plato, which recounts events at the birth of Beauty in
   which Poverty sleeps with Plenty and, as a result, gives
   birth to Love. Love is thus a joining of pleasure and
   pain.

Tatler 90b. _____. *From my own Apartment, November 4.*

Bickerstaff, in a pensive mood, recounts his reading of
a scene from Shakespeare's *Richard III*, in which Richard
reflects upon the inevitability of his fall. Bickerstaff then meditates on the different ends of good and
bad kings, and speculates on the death of the good king
William III.

Tatler 91. Tuesday, November 8, 1709. Steele. *From my own
Apartment, November 7.*

Bickerstaff recounts a visit from the woman who has professed her love to him under the name of Maria; she
turns out to be one of the top toasts of the town. Despairing of Bickerstaff's ever growing young again, she
has decided to marry someone else. She has two lovers,
Crassus and Lorio, and wishes Bickerstaff's advice on
choosing between them. Crassus is rich, but has no
other outstanding qualities; Lorio has a more limited
fortune, but is very agreeable in all other respects.
When she thinks of Lorio, she thinks of good companion-
ships; when she thinks of Crassus, she thinks of what
his wealth would buy. Bickerstaff insists that she is
leaving something out of her description, because he
cannot imagine why a woman of her good sense would wish
to marry Crassus. She admits that the problem is Clotilda, who is sure to marry Crassus if she does not,
and she cannot bear to think of Clotilda outshining her
in public. Bickerstaff says that the problem she has
is that she cannot be happy if she is afraid another
woman will be happier; he tells her of his courtship by
Miss Molly, a younger woman, who only sought his fortune. He concludes that no marriage can be a happy one
in which the object is only the satisfaction of vanity.
Bickerstaff then receives a letter from Nick Doubt, who
wonders if Bickerstaff did not write the letter of
praise in *Tatler* 89a himself. Bickerstaff protests that
he did not, but tells two stories to demonstrate that
sometimes authors do find ways of praising themselves.
The first concerns a poem to Maevius, which Maevius
finally admits that he wrote to himself. The second
story concerns Bavius, who, having his plays rejected by
the players, had a friend present a play to the players.
Roscius, the player, makes objections which the mock-
author is willing to accept, but Bavius is so upset by
them that he reveals his true identity as the playwright.

Tatler 92a. Thursday, November 10, 1709. Steele. *White's
Chocolate-house, November 9.*

Bickerstaff objects to the practice of praising someone,
and then ending the statement of praise with a qualifi-
cation. Bickerstaff argues that no men are perfect,
but that one man's failings are made up for by another's
perfections. Simplicius is not better than Latius

because he has certain qualities which Latius lacks. Unfortunately, Bickerstaff points out, the worst of mankind, libellers, receive much encouragement because some people enjoy having the faults of eminent men and women pointed out. The only one harmed by a libellous statement is the one who makes it, for he carries off the dirt and is therefore the filthiest creature in the street. Men should be equally prepared to ignore false detraction as false applause.

Tatler 92b. _____. *From my own Apartment, November 9.*

Bickerstaff reports on a letter from Charles Lillie, a seller of tobacco, who repeats his request to Bickerstaff that he be commented upon in the paper. Bickerstaff says that he is opposed to the taking of snuff but he admires Lillie's audacity, and therefore recommends him to all those who must indulge.

Tatler 93a. Saturday, November 12, 1709. Steele and Addison. *Will's Coffee-house, November 11.*

Bickerstaff asserts that the proper kind of letter to write a friend is a letter which says something to make the reader of the letter wish he were with the writer of it. Bickerstaff gives as a proper example a letter written from the top of the highest mountain in Switzerland; the writer describes the cold weather and the snow, but spends most of his time describing the inhabitants' practice of hiring themselves out as mercenaries early in life. If these soldiers-for-hire survive to age 50, they return home to much praise. One citizen boasts seven wooden legs in his family. Bickerstaff also describes what he considers the true purpose of travel and the best sort of traveller. Only those gentlemen should travel who would benefit from the experience. An acquaintance of Bickerstaff's says that he cleverly prevented his cousin Harry, a dull boy, from travelling abroad, and therefore prevented a member of his family from being laughed at all over Europe. Harry's older brother could only talk of his digestion and his escape from dangerous situations upon his return from abroad; for such people travel is a waste of time.

Tatler 93b. _____. *From my own Apartment, November 11.*

Bickerstaff reports that in response to rumors of threats on his life from those he has attacked in his papers, he is teaching himself the art of dueling with a sword. He has drawn on the walls of his chamber the figures of different sizes of men from eight feet in height to three feet two inches in height, within which he expects to find encompassed all the fighting men of Great Britain. He is learning about dueling from books; he feels that he is getting expert in the art. Although he has written against dueling, he sees no way to avoid it in some circumstances. He warns all who might threaten him that he will no longer put up with any affronts.

Tatler 94a. Tuesday, November 15, 1709. Steele. *Will's Coffee-house, November 14.*

Bickerstaff, claiming that gallantry to women is the heroic virtue of private persons, tells the story of Clarinda and Chloe, who grow up in the family of Romeo, the father of Chloe and the guardian of Clarinda. Philander, a fine young gentleman and friend of Romeo, visits the two ladies and falls in love with Chloe, though he does not reveal his choice. One night when they are all at the theater, the playhouse is set on fire. Philander rushes to the box, snatches up the lady and carries her to safety. He declares his love only to discover that the lady he has rescued is Clarinda and not Chloe. He rushes back into the theatre, reaches Chloe, proclaims his love of her, and the two perish together in the flames. Bickerstaff claims that the only way to accept such tragedies is to believe that those who are caught in them are immediately rewarded by Providence.

Tatler 94b. _____. *From my own Apartment, November 14.*

Bickerstaff reports that Mr. Charles Lillie, the perfumer of *Tatler* 92b, has written a letter of thanks for his mention in that essay. Bickerstaff reports that he has visited Lillie's shop and has discovered besides snuff an orange-flower water, which is good for use in the handkerchiefs of those who plead cases and as a gargle, to give "volubility to the tongue." It never fails to make a man pleased with himself, the first step in pleasing others. Mr. Lillie promises not to raise prices, in spite of his new notoriety. Bickerstaff also promises to publish his almanac on the 22nd of the month, and says that the appearance of the comparison of a woman's eyes to stars in its dedication will be the last time that this simile's use will be permitted. He says that on last Saturday night a gentleman strayed from the playhouse in the Haymarket. The lady who took him up is encouraged to restore him, for he is of no use to anyone but his wife.

Tatler 95. Thursday, November 17, 1709. Unknown. *From my own Apartment, November 16.*

Bickerstaff says that many people do not know the happiness they have and need to be reminded of it; this is especially true in the case of people who are married. Bickerstaff illustrates the joys of the married life by describing a dinner and evening he recently spent with an old friend, his wife, and their family. The old friend reminds Bickerstaff of his younger days, when he loved Teraminta. Most of the evening, however, is filled with the joy of getting to know the happy, vigorous, and growing children, and in hearing the father of the house praise his wife. He reminds Bickerstaff of his role in their courtship, and talks of his anxieties about her recent illness. Most of all, however, he praises her looks, her concern for him, and her excellence as a mother. The evening is in every way a delight, and Bickerstaff returns to his own family--which consists of his maid, his dog, and his cat--with sorrowful thoughts about his own bachelorhood.

Tatler 96a. Saturday, November 19, 1709. Addison. *From my own Apartment, November 17.*

Bickerstaff reports that his effort at correcting the morals and manners of his fellow Englishmen has met with some success and some failure; that is, he has many readers but few converts. This provokes him to report on the notion of Pythagoras, that all men who are no longer useful in the world are already among the dead, even if they still reside in the world. The living are only those who are in some way or other engaged in improving their own minds or in helping others. Bickerstaff promises to classify his countrymen in these terms, and he invites the dead to become alive by becoming good for something. Bickerstaff also notes that John Partridge, long dead, still claims to be alive, and calls Bickerstaff a knave for reporting otherwise. Bickerstaff considers this behavior unbecoming to a dead person.

Tatler 96b. _____. *From my own Apartment, November 18.*

Bickerstaff claims that his efforts have not had their desired effect; therefore he is refining his definition of coxcombs. A man with a cane upon his fifth button is now to be called Dapper. If he wears red-heeled shoes and a hat on the side of his head, he shall be known as a Smart. A man with his periwig in a twist is a Mettled Fellow, while a man with his upper lip covered with snuff is a Coffee-House statesman. Coxcombs will display themselves in this fashion; men of real merit will, however, avoid any peculiarities in their dress, gait, or behavior. Bickerstaff also says that country gentlemen, although they are well-behaved, frighten the town when they appear wearing red coats, an attire which makes some people think they are soldiers. Bickerstaff remembers one country gentleman, who, in his red coat, periwig, and cane, made it difficult for anyone to walk within several yards of him. About him, Bickerstaff quotes Terence: "Wherever thou art, thou canst not be long concealed."

Tatler 96c. NF. _____. *St. James's Coffee-house, November 18.*

A brief report on foreign affairs.

Tatler 96d. _____. Addendum.

Bickerstaff rejects the notion that he is in partnership with Charles Lillie (see *Tatlers* 92b and 94b); any man who says so is a knave.

Tatler 97. Tuesday, November 22, 1709. Addison. *From my own Apartment, November 21.*

Having in *Tatler* 96a declared most of the population to be dead, Bickerstaff says that he must now raise fresh recruits. Bickerstaff says he, with Xerxes, weeps when he surveys the populous city and sees how few of its inhabitants are, as a result of idleness, now living. In an attempt to bring to life some of those who are young, he retells a story of Prodicus, recommended by Socrates, of Virtue and Pleasure paying court to Hercules under the appearances of two beautiful women. Virtue appears as a noblewoman, modest, and unadorned, while Pleasure appears in makeup, with affectation mixed into her gestures. Pleasure promises Hercules all manner of delight, while Virtue promises him her attentions only if he goes through great pain and labor. Bickerstaff assures us that Hercules chose the life of Virtue over the life of Pleasure, and he recommends this life to all the youth of Great Britain.

Tatler 98a. Thursday, November 24, 1709. Steele. *From my own Apartment, November 23.*

Bickerstaff praises the frankness of Diana Doubtful in her letter to him, which he reprints. She describes herself as a woman in love, the object of whose affection is one Fabio. They are close acquaintances, and so he has told her of his love of Cleora, also a friend of hers. She is miserable because she cannot gain him by betraying Cleora, or being so immodest as to tell Fabio of her love for him. Bickerstaff says that a woman in love is like a ghost, because she may wander around her beloved, but lacks the power to tell him of her love. Bickerstaff encourages Diana to continue in her love for Fabio; he has already dispatched two gentlemen to woo Cleora, both of whom have a greater estate than Fabio. Bickerstaff's goal is to supply with the art of love all those who are sincere in their passions. The two gentlemen sent to pay court to Cleora are Orson Thicket and Walter Wisdom. The first is a man of the country who has been softened in his country manners by his love of Cleora, while the second is a young man who has just come into a great estate. The chase will begin at the next opera.

Tatler 98b. _____. *Will's Coffe-house, November 23.*

Bickerstaff reports on a conversation with an ancient friend who believes very strongly in the reforming power of poetry. He believes that licentious poems corrupt, while grave and serious poems elevate by delighting the passions to do the good and moving reason to accept it. When the fancy is bribed with the beautiful, moral improvement follows. The spokesman for didactic poetry quotes Virgil's *Aeneid* and Milton's *Comus* as examples.

Tatler 99a. Saturday, November 26, 1709. Steele. *Will's Coffee-house, November 25.*

Bickerstaff argues for the power of the theater to make a strong impression on the mind. He reports that the actors Hart and Mohun are especially good at making strong impressions on the audience through their acting. Bickerstaff laments the current state of the London stage, in which the plays presented only entertain the people and do not instruct them. Bickerstaff especially laments the attack upon his friend Divito by a mob incited by an attorney. This war on the peaceful empire of wit and the Muses Bickerstaff compares with the sack of Rome by the Goths and Vandals.

Tatler 99b. _____. *From my own Apartment, November 25.*

Bickerstaff gives to his good friends the Company of Upholders full power to bury all the dead who qualify under his recent definition (see *Tatler* 96a). Bickerstaff prints a letter from the Master of the Company of the Upholders, which complains that the walking dead of whom Bickerstaff has spoken are not, as they should, coming to him for proper burial. The Master feels that this is a great disgrace, for it means that coffin makers, embalmers, epitaph-mongers, and chief mourners will not get the kind of employment they should be getting. The Master urges Bickerstaff to instruct the walking dead to report to them for proper burial. He asks that the Company be empowered to take forcefully those who refuse to come on their own initiative. The Master also gives an advertisement to be printed in the *Tatler*, which announces that John Partridge will be forcefully buried on Tuesday, the 29th of November; any six of his friends are invited to be pall bearers.

Tatler 100. Tuesday, November 29, 1709. Addison. *Sheer Lane, November 28.*

Bickerstaff describes a vision which came to him after he walked alone in the garden of Lincoln's Inn, a dream of the Goddess of Justice coming down from the heavens to visit the male population of the country. A voice from the clouds proclaims that the purpose of this visit is to restore to every living person what is his due. First to be restored are all riches and estates or parts of estates to their rightful owners. The second is for all children to return to their true fathers. Thirdly the race of man is divided into men of virtue, men of

135

knowledge, and men of business. As a result of all this
setting of things aright, there are many dramatic changes.
Many who are rich become poor, while many who are poor
become rich. Many who have professed celibacy have to
acknowledge their children, while those the world has exalted have to acknowledge their subservience to others
whom the world has not recognized. Bickerstaff is delighted that all of his friends either keep their present posts or are advanced to higher ones. Bickerstaff
promises a later paper to deal with inequities among
women.

Tatler 101a. Thursday, December 1, 1709. *From my own
Apartment, November 30.*

Bickerstaff complains bitterly about those who print
pirated editions of books and sell them at a cheaper
price because they do not have to pay the authors anything for their work. This enrages Bickerstaff, not
only for his own work, but also for those who make a
modest sum by writing and who are dependent for their
health and well-being, and that of their families, on
what they can make through their publications. Notable
among these is Tom, who is fortunately dead, because if
he were still alive, he would be starved by the pirates
who would steal his work. Bickerstaff says that if the
pirating continues, it will be impossible to publish
fine editions of any book. Bickerstaff also reports
that Mr. Charles Lillie continues to have his blessing
as a seller of snuff and other potions. In fact, Bickerstaff has added magical powers to some of Lillie's
items. Lillie's wash-bowl will now restore a complexion within a week, while his orange-flower water will
give sincerity to a lover's advances.

Tatler 101b. _____. *Sheer Lane, November 30.*

Bickerstaff reports that while a number of walking-dead
persons have fled the city for the country, many others
still remain in the town and may be found at most of
the coffee-houses in and about Westminster. Bickerstaff
also asks his readers to help him in the corrections of
his publications, since he is so busy observing the
spots on the moon that he does not have time to search
out errors in his lucubrations.

Tatler 102. Saturday, December 3, 1709. Addison. *From my
own Apartment, December 3.*

Bickerstaff continues his report on his vision (see
Tatler 100) of the Goddess of Justice's visit to earth
to right wrongs and make sure that all get their just
desserts. In this part of the vision the Goddess of
Justice visits the world of women, all of whom endeavor
to put themselves forward to get their reward. Justice
declares that the ranking will be in terms of beauty,

and lets down the mirror of truth so that each woman
may judge herself according to her own image in the
glass. Many are upset by their image, as those who are
thought to be beautiful appear to be ugly; many who
have not thought themselves to be beautiful appear to
be so in the glass. Those who are found to be beautiful
are divided into three groups consisting of maids, wives,
and widows. The groups still being very large, the Goddess of Justice then delivers a number of edicts, one of
which is that all women who are hard on the conduct of
others will lose their power of speech, while the second
is that all women who have ever run the risk of being
pregnant will immediately become pregnant. An accom-
modation is made for this last group, whereby it will be
permissible for a woman's first child to be born within
six months of her marriage and for her last child to be
retained from birth for up to fourteen months after the
death of her husband. Bickerstaff concludes with a quotation from Milton's *Paradise Lost* Book VIII, 11. 546
and following in which is argued that virtue is venerable
in men but more lovely in women.

Tatler 103. Tuesday, December 6, 1709. Addison and Steele.
From my own Apartment, December 5.

Bickerstaff reports on the events of last Saturday, in
which he examined the pretensions of a number of people
who had applied to him for permission to carry canes,
use orange-flower waters, and other affectations. Bickerstaff describes the license he has prepared for the
use of the cane, which permits the bearer to carry it
anywhere within ten miles of London, so long as he does
not carry it under his arm, wave it in the air, or hang
it from a button. A similar form is prepared for the
use of snuff boxes and other affectations. Bickerstaff
first examines the petition of Simon Trippit to carry a
cane; Bickerstaff finds the cane to be ornate and its
carrier a prig. Bickerstaff only permits him to carry
it three days a week. Numerous others present their
petitions; most are rejected because their cases reveal
them to be pretentious or in need of medical attention.
A young lawyer who argues his case effectively is permitted to keep his cane so long as he wears it hanging
around his neck instead of from a button. Bickerstaff
permits a young dandy to wear spectacles so that he may
observe beautiful young ladies. He grants licenses for
men to carry orange-flower scented handkerchiefs on the
grounds that they, by doing so, are embalming themselves
and will make life easier for the company of Upholders.
Bickerstaff feels pleased that he has done some good for
the manners and morals of the town. He believes that
such follies lead to greater evil; at least, they reveal
a lack of that humble deference which is due to mankind
and also indicate some hidden flaw in the mind of the
person who commits them. He relates the story of a man

who stood out because he wore an unfashionable sword, although he was otherwise properly dressed. Bickerstaff says he had to wait 36 years for the man's folly to make itself known, but it finally did in the man's marriage to his own cook-maid.

Tatler 104. Thursday, December 8, 1709. Steele and Addison. *From my own Apartment, December 7.*

Bickerstaff reports on a visit from his sister Jenny upon the occasion of her husband Tranquillus' being out of town for a few days. Bickerstaff is delighted to see that Jenny has become decently matronlike in her appearance, and Jenny is delighted to report her love for and satisfaction in her husband. Jenny reports that her only anxiety is that she will not always appear beautiful to her husband and asks Bickerstaff to use his magical arts to make her appear always beautiful. Bickerstaff promises her, however, that she will always be able to please her husband if she herself always tries to please; he argues that fidelity, good humor, and complacency of temper will always outlive the charms of a pretty face and make its aging invisible to the beholder. Bickerstaff is delighted with Jenny's attitude and tries to reinforce it by telling a story about the opening of a coffin belonging to the body of a woman who, while living, was happily married. In the coffin are buried with her all the letters her husband wrote her both before and after their marriage. Bickerstaff compares, among the letters, one letter written before their marriage and one letter after; he is delighted to discover that the letter written after marriage states the writer's love for his wife even more strongly than he did to her in letters written when he was courting her. The daughter of the buried lovers happens by while the letters are being read, and bursts into tears upon being reminded of her dead parents. Bickerstaff assures her that her parents' constancy in their love has been rewarded by their continued union in a state in which there is no separation.

Tatler 105. Saturday, December 10, 1709. Steele. *Sheer Lane, December 9.*

Bickerstaff reports that he practices his fencing late into the night to defend himself against any potential attack. He sees this as an example of the fact that concern about reputation is the peculiar anxiety of the cultured class. To illustrate this point Bickerstaff tells the story of Will Rosin, the fiddler of Wapping, a man entitled to a quiet and happy life, who is the Corelli of Wapping as Tom Scrape is the Bononcini of Redriffe. Will's contentment in life has been disturbed by the fact that his wife, a widow much younger than he, has committed adultery with Boniface. Angered

because Boniface is about to be married to Mrs. Winifred
Dimple, she forces Will to swear upon the Bible that he
will not be angry with her and will reveal the name of
the one who has wronged her to the world. Will, discovering that he is a cockold, makes the whole thing
public; Boniface's father, angered at the breaking off
of the match, has Will arrested and recovers damages.
Bickerstaff attends the party designed to relieve Will's
misery; as a result, Will laughs the whole thing off.
Bickerstaff notes that in a noble family the issue would
have resulted in a long-drawn out feud rather than this
quick resolving of the matter. All this puts Bickerstaff
to mind of a poem entitled the "Dispensary," by Sir
Samuel Garth, which praises the nature of true honor.
Bickerstaff also reports that an old fellow has demonstrated to him a newly-invented door knocker; he also
demonstrates the different kinds of knocks appropriate
for different sorts and types of people.

Tatler 106a. Tuesday, December 13, 1709. Steele. *Will's*
Coffee-house, December 12.

While reading with pleasure one of his own papers, Bickerstaff is approached by an author who tells Bickerstaff
of a sonnet cycle he has composed to an imaginary mistress whose name is Flavia. He also has available a
collection of lampoons, a sketch for a heroic poem,
fifty heretofore unused similes, 23 descriptions of the
rising sun, and a number of observations upon life reduced to rhymed couplets. They are joined by two or
three critics who compare the letters found in the coffin (see *Tatler* 104) with Hamlet's speech (Act I, sc. ii)
in which he laments the all-too-recent marriage of his
mother to his uncle.

Tatler 106b. _____. Addendum.

Bickerstaff reports that Mr. Jeffery Groggram has sur-
rendered himself, admitted himself to be dead, and asks
for an internment by the Company of Upholders at a reasonable rate which will not impoverish his heirs. Because of his modesty, Bickerstaff pronounces Groggram
to be a live man and requires him to remain alive as an
example to obstinate dead men who will neither labor
for life nor go to their graves. Florinda requests that
she be designated a living woman because she has danced
the Derbyshire hornpipe in the presence of several
friends. Bickerstaff grants her request providing that
she can make a pudding by the 24th of the month.

Tatler 107. Thursday, December 15, 1709. Steele. *Sheer*
Lane, December 14.

Bickerstaff reports on a visit from a young man who is
deeply in love with Cynthia; unfortunately Cynthia is
in love with Quicksett. He wishes Bickerstaff to help

him cure his love for Cynthia. Bickerstaff first recommends travel abroad or joining the military; unfortunately, both these avenues of escape are closed to the
young man. Bickerstaff then suggests that the young
man retire to his country estate and forget about Cynthia by immersing himself in activities there; most of
all, he must avoid all sight of her. Bickerstaff says
that he conquered an unfortunate love for a lady at the
age of 30 by concentrating his mind on her ill treatment
of him, considering all her imperfections, and delighting in her ill treatment by her eventual husband. Bickerstaff also recommends that the young man avoid the
company of other men who have been disappointed in love;
he might also consider falling in love with another
woman. Finally, he recommends that the young man think
about the young lady in the company of her new lover
until he can do so with laughter instead of with tears.

Tatler 108. Saturday, December 17, 1709. Addison. *Sheer
Lane, December 16.*

Bickerstaff claims that he frequently attends the
theater to enlarge his thoughts and to find new ideas
which will appear in his lucubrations. In a recent
trip to the theater, however, he is thoroughly dismayed
to discover the audience delighting in an actor who per-
forms by twisting his body in strange and deformed
shapes. Bickerstaff is concerned that men can enjoy
seeing the human form so turned into ridicule. Nothing
pleases Bickerstaff more than seeing human nature presented in all its proper dignity; such writing encourages its audience to act virtuously and avoid the vicious. While classical literature does this, modern
French literature and its British imitators debase man
by refusing to distinguish him from animals. Bickerstaff says that a young man who took this attitude was
treated properly by his father who beat his son with
his stock and turned him out of the house, arguing that
if his son wished to consider himself no better than a
dog, then he could live like one. Bickerstaff then
quotes one of Sir Francis Bacon's passages in the *Advancement of Learning* to prove his point that poetry
which presents man in his best nature helps to improve
the moral state of mankind.

Tatler 109a. Tuesday, December 20, 1709. Steele. *Sheer
Lane, December 19.*

Bickerstaff reports on a tumult in his neighborhood,
caused a noblewoman and her entourage, who are in the
process of returning visits from other people who have
stopped by to see her. The people doing this visiting
never see each other because their mutual visitations
are made not from good will but out of fear of ill will.
Bickerstaff recommends that she set up an accounting

system to keep track of her visits. Bickerstaff says that nothing detracts from the esteem in which men of sense hold members of the fair sex more than the business of mutual visits. There are many impertinent people in the town who persist in visiting people of quality after their weddings and after funerals, not out of feeling but out of curiosity. As a result the true pleasures of life are lost in show, imposture, and impertinence. Bickerstaff regrets that so many women spend their time gratifying their eyes and ears instead of their reason and understanding; such attitudes give young women a false idea of life which results in their marriage to coxcombs and the abandonment of any chance for happy marriage.

Tatler 109b. _____. Addendum.

Bickerstaff reports that the Company of Upholders has complained to him of the obstinate behavior of dead persons who refuse to report for burial. Bickerstaff sets aside the following Wednesday as a day to hear both sides and to make decisions as to whether certain parties in fact deserve to be buried or not.

Tatler 110. Thursday, December 22, 1709. Addison and Steele. *Sheer Lane, December 21.*

Bickerstaff reports on his day of Judgement. Mr. Lillie acts as clerk and opens the session by reading a statement of its purpose, which is to pass judgement on those who are dead in reason. The first defendant is Mrs. Rebecca Pindust, who is accused of using the arts of the coquette to put to death several of her suitors. She defends herself by saying she practiced these purely to find herself a proper husband; Bickerstaff acquits her, but makes it a standing rule for the future that all those who write letters and promises to die for his beloved must either live for her or immediately be interred. The second defendant is one of Pindust's suitors who calls Bickerstaff Old Stiffrump and gestures constantly with his snuff box. Bickerstaff orders his snuff box taken from him; when this is done, he is struck speechless and carried off stone dead. The next defendants are an old man who talks constantly of his former mistress, one Madame Frances, and a young man who spends his time toasting women with whom he has never conversed. Bickerstaff orders both of them interred together. The next class of criminals are authors in prose and verse, who were judged to be living or dead depending on the quality of their work. The next group are old benchers of the Inns of Court, Senior Fellows of colleges, and defunct statesmen. All are ordered to be buried immediately. After adjourning the court, Bickerstaff is told of a new fashion in town in which women arrange their clothes so as to appear pregnant.

Bickerstaff says that he will investigate the matter; women are warned to avoid purchasing such a garment until Bickerstaff has had a chance to rule upon it.

Tatler 111. Saturday, December 24, 1709. Addison and Steele. *Sheer Lane, December 23.*

Bickerstaff is awakened in the night by the watchman; the lateness of the hour and the darkness of the night moves him to think about Shakespeare's *Hamlet*, Act I, sc. i, ll. 157-164, in which Marcellus discusses the time of night just before dawn. Bickerstaff laments this tendency of some Englishmen to abandon those manners of thinking which contribute to the happiness and well-being of mankind. Especially significant among these are atheists, who must consider man an insignificant creature incapable of rising above the animal level. To illustrate his point he describes a man who becomes a believer when he is in danger, such as in a storm aboard ship or when threatened by sickness or injury, but who is otherwise an unbeliever. Bickerstaff then states his own creed, which is never to pursue his own beliefs so far as to ridicule those of another.

Tatler 112. Tuesday, December 27, 1709. Steele. *Sheer Lane, December 26.*

Bickerstaff presents a letter, written by the author of the letter in *Tatler* 89, in which the writer laments the cruelty of his eldest son, Dicky, toward birds and other animals, but rejoices in the benevolence of his younger son toward the same creatures. Bickerstaff argues, and presents classical examples to prove, the point that spending an idle hour in contemplation of the variety of nature is an action of a noble and wise mind. Bickerstaff recommends such behavior to young gentlemen of the town who seem unable to do anything constructive in their idle moments. Bickerstaff prints his letter of reply to his country friend in which he urges him to put a stop to the actions of Dick the Tyrant and to praise the mercy of his younger brother. Bickerstaff also describes his delight in spending time watching his dog and cat before the fire.

Tatler 113. Thursday, December 29, 1709. Hughes. *Haymarket, December 23.*

Bickerstaff reports that the young man who died when his snuff box was taken away in *Tatler* 110 remains unburied; the Company of Upholders is to sell at auction his possessions to defray the cost of his funeral. These items include four pounds of scented snuff with three gilt snuff boxes, a very rich tweezer-case, six packs of cards, all the clothing of the dandy, and other various and sundry items of equipment for the coxcomb. Bickerstaff reports that while he has been correcting certain follies of the town others have broken out; these enormities include the petticoat referred to in *Tatler* 110. Bickerstaff presents a petition from William Jingle in which he describes an invention of a special chair to enable women wearing this petticoat to sit down. Bickerstaff promises to set aside next Tuesday for passing judgement on this article of clothing. Bickerstaff defines certain limited times and places at which the dead men who remain unburied may appear without molestation by the Company of Upholders. If at any time, however, they are found finding fault with any of the living, they are to be taken to the undertakers immediately.

Tatler 114. Saturday, December 31, 1709. Addison and Steele. *Sheer Lane, December 30.*

Bickerstaff describes a visit from the eldest son of the family described in *Tatler* 95, who reports to Bickerstaff that his mother is dying. They journey quickly to the house where they find Favonius, the clergyman, in attendance. Bickerstaff finds all the members of the family grieving intensely for their dying mother, except the woman herself, who is resigned to her fate. The woman dies, leaving her family in deep grief. Bickerstaff joins in the sorrow, considering the sad state of her husband, who is like a man who has lately lost his right arm. Bickerstaff quotes Milton's *Paradise Lost*, Book IV, 11. 639 ff. and Book II, 11. 557 ff. as poetic presentations of the love a man feels for a woman and the intense grief he feels at her death.

Tatler 115a. Tuesday, January 3, 1709-10. Steele. *Sheer Lane, January 2.*

Bickerstaff reports on a visit to the opera where the attendance is down because the contortionist mentioned in *Tatler* 108 was not in appearance. Bickerstaff is pleased by the performance of Nicolini but learns that Punchinello is more admired by female members of the audience. Bickerstaff notices that he had some difficulty keeping the female sex under control; while he is concerned about their petticoats, they go off to watch a puppet show run by Mr. Powell. Bickerstaff promises that if Powell does not cease his attacks, Bickerstaff will reveal all he knows about the man and his puppets. For example, Bickerstaff knows that Punch's head almost became a nutcracker. Bickerstaff promises to examine Powell's performances according to the critical categories of the French, who insist upon the unities of time, place, and action.

Tatler 115b. _____. *White's Chocolate-house, January 2.*

Bickerstaff gives the character of Sir Hannibal, a gentleman buried by the Company of Upholders because he,

a dead man, was found in public at an unlicensed hour.
The gentleman in question was often quick to speak when
he should have been silent; one of his hasty speeches
was a promise to kill Bickerstaff. Bickerstaff says
that he will henceforth bury all those whom he hears
intend to kill him. Bickerstaff prints a letter from
a disciple who wonders why Bickerstaff does not crush
immediately all those who threaten him. In response,
Bickerstaff presents a fable of a mastiff who is asked
by one of his puppies why he does not tear to pieces the
little dogs who bark at him. The larger dog responds,
"If there were no curs, I should be no mastiff."

Tatler 116. Thursday, January 5, 1709-10. Addison. *Sheer
Lane, January 4*.

Bickerstaff reports on the hearing into the matter of
the petticoat. The criminal, who was caught wearing
the petticoat, discovers that it is so large that she
cannot enter Bickerstaff's hall; when it is removed
from the lady it is too large to be unfolded completely
on the floor of the hall. In fact, when it is suspended
from the ceiling, it covers the entire assembly like a
gigantic canopy. The defense of the petticoat is that
it will be a great encouragement to the woolen and rope
industry, as well as an incentive to the preservation
of honor. Bickerstaff finds these arguments interesting but is persuaded to reject the garment because of
the great expense it would mean to husbands and fathers,
and because of the false security it would give young
virgins. The petticoat in question is sent to a gentlewoman who will make from it five normal petticoats for
her daughters. Bickerstaff says that he approves of
female adornments which compliment nature, but rejects
those, such as the petticoat in question, which distort
it.

Tatler 117. Saturday, January 7, 1709-10. Addison. *Sheer
Lane, January 6*.

Bickerstaff says that he likes best about himself his
concern for the well-being of mankind. He delights
especially in the rescues of good men and women from
danger or distress. Because history does not provide
sufficient numbers of such rescues to satisfy his interests, he delights in fictions which present the victory
of virtue over vice and the rescue of the hero or heroine from desperate circumstances. To illustrate his
point, Bickerstaff summarizes three such stories. The
first concerns a knight who happens to see his beloved
in the arms of another man. Instead of killing any of
them, he sets out on knightly adventures, eventually
discovering the man his beloved was embracing was in
fact her brother. The second story is that of Lucretia,
as told by Ovid. This royal virgin, raped by Neptune,

and offered anything she wants in return, requests that
she be changed into a shape which will prevent her from
every having to experience such an event again, and
therefore is turned into a man. The third story, Bickerstaff says, is from his own life. He tells of a dream
in which he saw his beloved fall into the sea from a
cliff. As a result of this dream, Bickerstaff always
reacts strongly to reading the description of Dover
Cliffs in Shakespeare's *King Lear*, Act IV, sc. vi, ll.
12-23.

Tatler 118a. Tuesday, January 10, 1709-10. Steele. *From
my own Apartment, January 8.*

Bickerstaff finds that he must kill some of the dead
again, because they refuse to stay dead. In this he
says that he imitates Evander, of Virgil's *Aeneid* (Book
VIII, l. 566). Bickerstaff presents a letter he has
received from John Partridge from his abode in hell.
Partridge says that he at first was very angry with
Bickerstaff for sending him there, but now he is delighted with all the people whom Bickerstaff has sent
after him to keep him company. Bickerstaff also presents a letter in which the author thanks him for the
tender portrait of the family in grief (*Tatler* 114),
and also for his descriptions of the dead. The author
says that these descriptions helped reform a country
squire of his acquaintance, who, having cared for nothing but his dogs, now has sold his dogs and intends to
become church warden next year.

Tatler 118b. _____. *From my own Apartment, January 9.*

Bickerstaff receives a petition from Penelope Prim
requesting that those who wear old-fashioned
petticoats which are too big for them should also be
forced to wear ruffs, bought from her. Bickerstaff
examines the case and notices that Dame Deborah Bickerstaff, his great-grandmother, and Mrs. Pyramid Bickerstaff, her sister, wore such garments; therefore, Bickerstaff agrees to Penelope's petition.

Tatler 119. Thursday, January 12, 1709-10. Addison. *Sheer
Lane, January 11.*

Bickerstaff, having recently been interested in the dis-
coveries made by use of the microscope, relates a discourse made to him by his genius while he was sleeping.
The content of his dream is the argument that the world
he knows contains many worlds in miniature, and is part
of the larger world of the universe.

Tatler 120a. Saturday, January 14, 1709-10. Addison. *Sheer
Lane, January 13.*

After thinking over the state of mankind in general,
Bickerstaff dreams that he is in a forest so large that

all mankind wanders lost within it. At the center of
the wood is an open plain, in which all of mankind has
divided itself into three groups, according to age, and
set off marching down three separate roads. Bickerstaff
joins the young group, The Band of Lovers. The road
soon grows narrow and hazardous, as each of the men in
this group chooses a woman who becomes his lover. The
women lead the men on chases through the forest; some
are quickly caught, while others lead their men on
chases through The Labyrinth of Coquettes. Along the
way many allegorical figures are encountered including
Hymen, Discretion, Complacency, Levity, Contention,
Cupid, and Jealousy. Many marry; others retire to The
Temple of Lust. The path of marriage in this allegorical forest appears to be hard at first but then becomes
easy, while the path of lust appears easy at first but
soon becomes more and more difficult.

Tatler 120b. _____. Advertisement.

Bickerstaff presents a letter advertising a benefit performance of Congreve's *Love for Love* for Thomas Doggett;
Bickerstaff is especially invited to attend. Bickerstaff replies that he will be happy to do so and will
make his entrance between the first and second acts,
provided that everything is ready for his reception.

Tatler 121. Tuesday, January 17, 1709-10. Addison. *From
my own Apartment, January 16*.

Bickerstaff reports a visit from a woman, in deep grief,
not for any human being, but for her lap-dog Cupid, who
is grievously ill. This provokes a discussion of mankind's affection toward animals on the one hand and his
disregard for the well-being and health of his fellow
human beings on the other. Bickerstaff gives two examples; the first of a Roman emperor, who thought of
making his horse a counsul, and the second English
country squires, who would rather kiss their hounds than
their wives. Bickerstaff does note one example in which
the affection for the animal is justified; this is the
case of a Turk, whose horse saved him in battle. Bickerstaff also notes that he has been prevailed upon to
permit free use of the farthingale until next February
20th.

Tatler 122. Thursday, January 19, 1709-10. Addison. *From
my own Apartment, January 18*.

Bickerstaff reports on his visit to the theatre to be
eyed by a Mr. Thomas Doggett and to be escourted home
by the Company of Upholders. He reports his delight at
the play, and especially at the warm reception given
his appearance by the audience at the play. Bickerstaff
says that this reception reminds him of Cicero's report
in his *De Amicitia* of the Roman audiences' response to

the story of Plyades and Orestes. Bickerstaff also remembers the response of the Athenian audience to a
speech of a covetous person, as reported by Seneca.
Bickerstaff also remembers Socrates' walking out of a
tragedy of Euripides in response to the equivocation of
Hippolitus on an issue of oath taking.

Tatler 123. Saturday, January 21, 1709-10. Addison. *From*
my own Apartment, January 20.

Bickerstaff continues his report on the dream he first
discussed in *Tatler* 120a. Having followed youth along
the pathway of love in the first part of his dream
vision, he now follows the middle aged group along the
Road of Ambition. At the end of this road are the
Temples of Virtue, Honor, Vanity, and Avarice. Each of
these temples contains an allegorical central figure;
other figures met along the way include Competency,
Corruption, Bribery, Extortion, and Fraud. The appearance of the allegorical figure of Poverty causes great
anxiety to those who are pursuing Ambition wrongfully.
Bickerstaff ends with a prayer to Poverty that if
Wealth is to visit him with her attendents Vanity and
Avarice, then he wishes Poverty to rescue him, accompanied by her companions Liberty and Innocence.

Tatler 124. Tuesday, January 24, 1709-10. Steele. *From my*
own Apartment, January 23.

Bickerstaff describes the excitement of those who have
bought lottery tickets as they await the announcement
of the winners. He has sold a couple of globes and a
telescope so that he might buy a ticket, but upon com-
puting the odds of winning, he has few expectations of
any success. He is concerned about the many who will
be disappointed when the winners are announced. Bickerstaff prints a letter from a correspondent who, finding Mr. Partridge to be dead, wishes Bickerstaff to use
his astrological skills in insuring his victory in the
lottery. Bickerstaff can offer little hope. Bickerstaff also presents a letter of thanks from John Ham-
mond, who appreciates the return of his watch.

Tatler 125. Thursday, January 26, 1709-10. Steele. *From*
my own Apartment, January 25.

Bickerstaff says that he agrees with Cicero that all
those who follow the principles of reason and virtue
are wise and all those who do not are madmen. According to this test, Bickerstaff believes that many of his
fellow citizens should properly be designated insane
and should be provided for. To this end, he proposes
that Bedlam be expanded to accommodate politicians
caught raving in a coffee-house, free-thinkers caught
publishing their ideas, moping lovers, and others who
persist in their frantic behavior for more than a month.

Tatler 126. Saturday, January 28, 1709-10. Steele. *From my own Apartment, January 27.*

Bickerstaff reports on a visit to Belvidera, who is the best sort of company because she is a woman of great good sense. While he is there, Lydia, a coquette, and Castabella, a prude, come in; Bickerstaff and Belvidera observe the pair and discuss the fact that they are really very much alike although they appear to be opposites. Bickerstaff proposes a test for the prude; drawn from the work of Madame de Bourignon, which argues that a woman is no prude unless she wishes to convey her virtue to her male beholders. Bickerstaff tells a story of a young coquette widow of France, who was revenged upon a Gascon, who claimed to others that he had bedded the widow, when in fact he had not. With the promise of a night in bed with her as his reward, she gets the man to spend the night disguised as a woman in the bed of the husband of a friend of hers; he is, all the while, really spending the night with her.

Tatler 127. Tuesday, January 31, 1709-10. Steele. *From my own Apartment, January 30.*

Bickerstaff argues that there is no more common human failing than pride; he plans to devote one entire section of his expanded Bedlam to its cure. As an example of a prideful man, Bickerstaff describes a cobbler upon Ludgate Hill, who has made himself a statue of a beau kneeling to him. Bickerstaff notes that many of the inmates of Bedlam believe they are people much superior to their real stations in life. Bickerstaff describes four people who are candidates for admission to the expanded Bedlam because of their pride. The first is a man who is poor but who acts as though he were rich. The second is a man who does everything he can to show the rest of mankind that he condemns them, but he is, personally, so inconsequential that no one pays any attention to him. The third is a man who boasts of his crimes, while the fourth is an old woman, useless to all, who brags about her blood, as though it were as valuable as that which glows in the cheeks of Belinda and sets half the town on fire.

Tatler 128. Thursday, February 2, 1709-10. Steele. *From my own Apartment, February 1.*

Bickerstaff prints a letter to Mopsa (the country maid in *Tatler* 124); the writer promises Bickerstaff a new pair of globes and a telescope if he will print the letter. The letter itself pledges the writer's love of Mopsa; it declares its writer a fool, but one who wishes to become wiser through marriage. Bickerstaff declares that the world is unkind to the ill-treated woman; he prints a letter from Statira, which tells of such a woman's distress. In her letter, Statira relates the story of her being woed two years by a man whom she thought loved her. She discovered to her sorrow that he quickly began to court a woman of a greater fortune than hers as soon as he himself came into an inheritance. Bickerstaff pledges to help avenge the lady.

Tatler 129. Saturday, February 4, 1709-10. Addison. *From my own Apartment, February 3.*

Bickerstaff reports that he has received a number of interesting letters from abroad. The first is from a correspondent in Amsterdam, describing satirical cartoons upon affairs prepared by Dutch draftsmen. One depicts European politics in terms of British and Dutch ships attacking a French man-of-war to take from her a long-boat with Spanish colors. Bickerstaff also receives a letter from Pasquin of Rome, in which the correspondent promises news of events in Rome if Bickerstaff will send him news of Great Britain. One thing he wants to know is a description of all the religions in England summarized in terms of hats. Pasquin reports on intrigues among the potential successors to the Papacy and on arguments over the relics of martyrs. Pasquin ends with a note: "P. S. Morforio is very much yours."

Tatler 130a. NF. Tuesday, February 7, 1709-10. *Sheer Lane, February 6.*

Bickerstaff remembers that the most polite Latin authors praised the glories of Rome. Bickerstaff therefore praises the glory of his own day, which he believes will shine as bright as any in the history of mankind. He also praises the Queen on her birthday and especially delights in the "glorious humility" with which she receives the splendid leaders, politicians, and soldiers who support her and serve her.

Tatler 130b. _____. Advertisement.

Bickerstaff explains that the name Pasquin of *Tatler* 129 derives from a statue in that city on which the private scandal of the city is generally posted. Morforio is the same sort of person. The mention of this person, a great wit as well as a great cripple, reminds Bickerstaff of Mr. Estcourt, for whom a performance of Ben Jonson's *The Silent Woman* will be presented next Thursday. Mr. Estcourt is a former apothecary of Bickerstaff's; therefore Bickerstaff's servant and maid will be allowed to attend this play on their one day off each year.

Tatler 131. Thursday, February 9, 1709-10. Addison. *Sheer Lane, February 8.*

Bickerstaff reports on a trial held before him of Tom Tintoret, Harry Sippet, and other chemical operators of

London who are engaged in the process of counterfeiting
wine by coloring water. The accused are charged with
causing all sorts of ill effects upon the English health
and reason; a drop of one of their potions causes Bickerstaff's cat great distress. Bickerstaff requests that
they poison none of his friends and find an honest livelihood; he then lets them go.

Tatler 132. Saturday, February 11, 1709-10. Steele. *Sheer
Lane, February 10*.

Bickerstaff proclaims the value of good conversation as
a way of relaxing before bedtime. He describes a club
of conversationalists who meet at the Trumpet; originally 15, it is now reduced to five, Bickerstaff the
best wit among them. The other members of the club are
Sir Jeoffrey Notch, a country gentleman who squandered
his estate early in life, Major Matchlock, who talks
only of his adventures in war, Dick Reptile, who laughs
at the company's jokes and brings his young nephew to
give him a taste of the world, and a fourth nameless
person, who always entertains the group with stories of
Jack Ogle. The conversation always follows the same
pattern; last night Bickerstaff did not arrive until
7:30, therefore missing the Major's account of the battle of Naseby and one story of Jack Ogle. Upon his
arrival Bickerstaff encourages Sir Jeoffrey to tell the
story of old Gantlett, which naturally leads to the
Major's account of Edge Hill fight, and another story
of Jack Ogle. Bickerstaff concludes that there is nothing worse than an old man whose stories grow longer and
longer and less and less interesting as he grows older,
and nothing better than an old man whose stories en-
lighten mankind. Bickerstaff is reminded of Homer's
comment about Nestor (*Iliad*, Book I, l. 249) and Milton's comment about Belial (*Paradise Lost*, Book II, l.
112 ff.) in which the two poets compare good conversation to the flowing of honey and the dropping of manna.

Tatler 133a. NF. Tuesday, February 14, 1709-10. Addison.
Sheer Lane, February 13.

Bickerstaff discourses on the value of silence, especially its eloquence and its indication of the presence
of a great mind. Along the way he notes examples from
Homer's *Odyssey*, Book XI, in which Ulysses responds to
the appearance of the ghost of Ajax with humble silence;
to Virgil's *Aeneid*, Book VI, in which the ghost of Dido
responds to Aeneas with silence; to Otway's *Venice Preserved*, Act V, in which Pierre bursts into tears instead
of requesting a friend to prevent his execution by stab-
bing him; and finally, to a comment of Lord Bacon, in
which he says that he will leave his memory to the regard of foreign nations and his countrymen, expecting
that after a time they will silently pass over it.

Tatler 133b. _____. Advertisement.

To oblige the Pretty Fellows, Bickerstaff reprints, from Dryden's translation, the passage from Virgil's *Aeneid*, Book V, in which Dido greets Aeneas with silence (mentioned in *Tatler* 133a).

Tatler 134. Thursday, February 16, 1709-10. Steele. *Sheer Lane, February 15*.

Upon being awakened by the crowing of a cock, Bicker-staff wonders if the bird in question is in fact a sleepy bellman forced to wake early and awaken others as penance for his laziness. He is then brought a peti-tion by a tall black gentleman who frequents the coffee-houses in the vicinity in which the petitioner, Job Chanticleer, wishes Bickerstaff to help obtain his re-lease from the hands of a "higgler," who plans to sac-rifice him in a cock fight. The gentleman who brought the petition and Bickerstaff discuss the kindness to animals exhibited by many people in the eastern nations. This moves Bickerstaff to consider the barbarity with which the English treat their animals in bull-baiting, bear-baiting, cock-fighting, and other kinds of inhuman-ity to animals. Bickerstaff wonders if this trait in the English character is also reflected in the English tendency to present violence upon the stage. Bicker-staff hopes that the English will give up the practice of attending cruel animal fights.

Tatler 135. Saturday, February 18, 1709-10. Steele. *Sheer Lane, February 17*.

Having been asked to discuss his meaning of the word "free thinker," Bickerstaff says that while he praises the great free thinkers of the past, he condemns the free thinkers of the present because their arguments are based on a Sophistry which tends to weaken and des-troy the very principles on which human freedom and dignity are based. The test of the value of a free thinker is whether his thought elevates the dignity of mankind or contributes to human happiness; modern free thinkers fail this test. Bickerstaff recounts the tale of a gentleman in France who spent a lifetime as a free thinker, gathering around him a group of disciples, only to request at his death that he be buried in the garb of a Christian monk. Bickerstaff also describes an event he observed in his youth, in which an old officer frightened a young free-thinking officer in-to submission by equating his own sword with that of the Lord, and of Gideon.

Tatler 136a. Tuesday, February 21, 1709-10. Steele. *White's Chocolate-house, February 18*.

Bickerstaff recounts the story of Mr. and Mrs. Ballance, a merchant and his wife happily married, who take a lodger, Tom Varnish. Varnish, immediately upon moving into the house, sends Mrs. Ballance a note proclaiming his love of her. Mrs. Ballance shares the note with her husband, and they plan Varnish's downfall. The result of the couple's playing games with Varnish is that he is put aboard ship locked in a chest with orders that the chest be thrown overboard. Bickerstaff says that he will not go on with the tale because Varnish has just returned from his travels and is eager to conceal the reason for his going abroad.

Tatler 136b. NF. _____. *St. James's Coffee-house, February 20*.

More reports on diplomatic events abroad.

Tatler 136c. _____. *Sheer Lane, February 20*.

Bickerstaff receives a petition from Deborah Hark, Sarah Threadpaper, and Rachael Thimble in which they request the exclusive right to wear and to sell big petticoats with ruffs. Bickerstaff responds by forbidding all persons but the petitioners and those who buy from them to wear the garments.

Tatler 137a. Thursday, February 23, 1709-10. Steele. *Sheer Lane, February 22*.

Bickerstaff describes a meeting with Dick Reptile, and their discussion of English abuses of languages, especially swearers and those who interject superfluous references to authorities in their conversations. Bickerstaff describes a meeting with an old army friend in Fleet Street; he discovers that his friend's speech is filled with swearing and references to hell and the devil. Bickerstaff concludes that such abuse of the language reflects a lack of good sense.

Tatler 137b. NF. _____. *St. James's Coffee-house, February 22*.

Bickerstaff is reminded, upon hearing of the departure of the Duke of Marlborough, of literary accounts of the significance of such a powerful figure's going forth. The first reference is to Shakespeare's *Henry the Fifth*, the Prologue; the second is to Shakespeare's *Julius Caesar*, Act III, sc. i, ll. 270-73; and the third is to Virgil's *Aeneid*, Book I, ll. 294 ff., quoted in Dryden's translation.

Tatler 137c. _____. Advertisement.

Bickerstaff makes brief reference to a number of items. First of all he announces that the benefit for Grimaldi will be held on the second of March. Second, he recommends procedures for making lightning in operas. Third, he announces that the true perfumed lightning is only sold by Mr. Charles Lillie. Finally, he requests a warm night cap from the lady who has chosen Bickerstaff as her Valentine.

Tatler 138a. Saturday, February 25, 1709-10. Steele. *Sheer Lane, February 24.*

Bickerstaff argues that a noble quality in a man is his ability to disregard the opinions of others. Bickerstaff's friend Mr. Hart, argues that actors only act well when they disregard the presence of an audience. Unfortunately, most actors, such as Will Glare, are so concerned about the applause of their audiences that they will struggle to evoke such applause; this bespeaks to Bickerstaff a superficial mind. Many men, if their actions could be invisible, would do ill rather than good. To illustrate this, Bickerstaff tells a fable from Plato's *Republic* of Gyges, who had a ring which made him invisible. Gyges used the ring to violate a queen and murder a king. But if secret injuries are detestable, secret kindnesses are even more beautiful because they are secret. In this regard, Bickerstaff announces that a citizen of London has made it possible for ten boys to attend St. Paul's School, the boys to be nominated by Bickerstaff. He requests that nominations be made to Mr. Morphew or Mr. Lillie.

Tatler 138b. _____. Advertisement.

Bickerstaff notes that a number of men called "whetters," have been drinking too much and then buying and selling stocks on the Royal Exchange. He forbids such people from engaging in commerce after the third half pint before the hour of one'o'clock. He also forbids any tavern near the Exchange to sell wine to such men unless it contains at least three parts cider; the master of these taverns must also have a certificate from Mr. Tintoret (*Tatler* 131). Bickerstaff also announces that the model of the intended expansion of Bedlam (*Tatler* 125) is now finished; all those wishing friends or relatives to be admitted to this house of madness are asked to come forward.

Tatler 139. Tuesday, February 28, 1709-10. Steele. *Sheer Lane, February 27.*

Bickerstaff says that he has found that women are more easily reformed than men. Many of the problems which women face, he has discovered, derive from the terms in which men flatter them. Mrs. Alice is praised not for her good qualities of devotion to her parents, her gentleness in behavior, and her modest behavior, but is instead praised as though she were a perfect creature, a resident of Arcadia, and a creature capable of causing the death of her suitors. Bickerstaff describes the effects of this kind of flattery by telling us of a

visit he made to the bedchamber of Flavia. Having given
his ring the magical power of invisibility (like that
of Gyges, *Tatler* 138), Bickerstaff visits Flavia's bedchamber where he finds her asleep with the poems of
Waller and a love note in which the lover says that
Flavia has caused him to suffer the pangs of hell.
Bickerstaff sees Flavia arise, read the letter, and
devote herself to makeup instead of to more useful
activities. Bickerstaff laments the effects of such
unrealistic flattery on women; he knows, he says, of
three goddesses in the New Exchange and two shepherdesses
in Westminster Hall.

Tatler 140. Thursday, March 2, 1709-10. Steele. *Sheer
Lane, March 1.*

Bickerstaff says that since the rest of the country is
concerned with other matters at the moment, he will deal
with letters written in response to issues raised in
recent issues of the *Tatler*. One letter wonders if the
call for nominations for free admission to St. Paul's
School is a joke. Bickerstaff responds that it is not,
and that two boys have been chosen. Strephon writes to
argue, supported by a quotation from Cicero, that most
vices and follies of the age arise because of man's inability to entertain himself. Dorothy Drumstick writes
that it is impolite to refer to women as "Madam": she
says that she writes wearing a thin under-petticoat,
and never did wear a farthingale (see *Tatler* 136).
Bickerstaff also receives a letter from Lydia, asking
that Bickerstaff not tell Mr. Pasquin (*Tatler* 129) of
the nature of the English church until manners in
church have been corrected. She refers to Lady Autumn,
who, along with her niece, curtsied during church service. She also objects to the taking of snuff in church.
Chloe writes to ask Bickerstaff if he is as good as he
seems to be. He responds with a letter in which he asks
Chloe if she is as ignorant as she seems to be.

Tatler 141. Saturday, March 4, 1709-10. Steele. *Sheer
Lane, March 3.*

While the attention of the town is drawn to other matters, Bickerstaff will again respond to letters concerning items in recent *Tatlers*. T. P. writes to ask Bickerstaff if his daughter should be put in a boarding
school. Bickerstaff promises a reply within a week.
L. T., N. F., and T. W. write that not only are there
"whetters" in the Royal Exchange, but there are also
men in the Chancellory office who are not only "whetters"
in the morning but also great singers of songs at midnight in the same taverns. Bickerstaff says that a
"whetter" is similar to a "snuff-taker," the only difference being in their choice of poisons for their
brains. Bickerstaff says that those who sing at night

may do so if they sing in places where they will not
disturb anyone. Those who do disturb others with their
song are similar to eavesdroppers who also push themselves into unwanted company. Bickerstaff also reports
that his Valentine has sent him a nightcap, which was
made by a relative in the reign of Queen Elizabeth. The
unfortunate lady pricked her finger while making the
nightcap and bled to death because of it. Bickerstaff
also presents a petition sent to him by those who live
near the site of his proposed mental hospital, claiming
that the preacher to the inmates of the hospital is himself mad, because lately he has only preached about
religious controversies. They are sure that he will
soon fall into ravings and foamings.

Tatler 142. Tuesday, March 7, 1709-10. Steele. *Sheer Lane,
March 6.*

Bickerstaff says that people are still concerned about
public affairs; from this concern there have been many
good results, including the fact that a toast of his
acquaintance has discovered that it is day before nine
in the morning. Bickerstaff says that he has been using the occasion to deal with the demands of his correspondents. One letter which concerns Bickerstaff
greatly is from a correspondent who claims that while
Bickerstaff has been favoring Charles Lillie he has
been ignoring his namesake Charles Mather, a toy man.
The correspondent describes the toy man's excellencies,
both as a toy maker and as a man who can use words so
well that he can convince people of the value of his
toys even when they at first do not believe him. His
pocket-books are especially good for holding addresses
of beautiful women; his seals are such that they improve the handwriting of young gentlemen, including Ned
Puzzlepost. His canes are excellent, and he will price
them according to the ability of the purchaser to pay.
Sir Timothy Shallow and Tom Empty, of radically different incomes, each bought the same cane and paid different prices. The correspondent also announces that
Mather will have for sale a new edition of snuff boxes
next Saturday, which will be in fashion until after
Easter. A gentleman who bought a diamond studded snuff
box may show it until Sunday night, if he will go to
church.

Tatler 143a. Thursday, March 9, 1709-10. Steele. *Sheer
Lane, March 8.*

Bickerstaff is surprised by a visit from his sister
Jenny, who urges Bickerstaff to move so that she may
visit him without spoiling her horses. Bickerstaff immediately writes her husband to tell him of her vanity
and to encourage him to be modest in enjoying his
moderate wealth.

Tatler 143b. _____. Advertisements.

Bickerstaff announces a stage coach soon to be leaving which will travel through all the rustic parts of England; this is for all Londoners who wish to write pastorals. Bickerstaff also notes that Mr. Powell refuses to take responsibility for those who woke up doctors and midwives in the middle of the night and sent them to people who did not need them. Bickerstaff also asks a shoemaker to take out of the window of his shop certain ladies' shoes which stir up irregular thoughts and desires in the youth of the nation. He is especially required to answer for slippers with green lace and blue heels. Bickerstaff also recommends the edition of Homer prepared by Joshua Baines, and says that he has worked a charm on the edition to prevent criticism of it.

Tatler 144a. Saturday, March 11, 1709-10. Steele. *Sheer Lane, March 10.*

Bickerstaff says that in a nation of free people there is no office more necessary than that of the Censor, which office he has chosen for himself. Bickerstaff says he especially objects to the rich who buy horses to pull their coaches and chairs and make it difficult for men of less wealth to walk the streets. He wishes to tax coaches and chairs and impound the horses; to this end he recruits the help of his friend Sylvius. Bickerstaff objects to those who do not deserve the honor of having themselves carried around in such a fashion and forcing ordinary mortals to ask, "Who is that?" Every carriage should, according to Bickerstaff, indicate in some way the name of its occupant.

Tatler 144b. _____. Advertisement.

Bickerstaff requests the names of all those who have become Beaus, Fops, and Coxcombs in the good town of Edinburgh, therefore corrupting the ancient simplicity in the dress and manners of Scotland. All offenders will be proceeded against in an appropriate way.

Tatler 145a. Tuesday, March 14, 1709-10. Steele. *White's Chocolate-house, March 13.*

Bickerstaff says he wishes to take up the question, posed in *Tatler* 141, of whether a young girl should be sent away to boarding school, but he is prevented from doing so because he has been requested to deal with the subject of Oglers. These creatures, gentlemen who spend their time in play houses and churches looking around them, are felt to be enemies by the females whom they usually spend their time looking at. Bickerstaff reports that in a recent visit to the theater, he saw Mirtillo, an Ogler, and Flavia, a Coquette, engage in an exchange of glances which reminded Bickerstaff of

nothing more than an interchange between a rattlesnake
and a squirrel. The two carry on an elaborate conversation with glances, each trying to gain control of the
other, throughout the entire play.

Tatler 145b. _____. Advertisement.

Bickerstaff receives a letter from one A. B. which says
that Bickerstaff in *Tatler* 139 forgot to mention the
angel in the Royal Exchange. He requests Bickerstaff
mention her in the hope that she will therefore become
his good angel.

Tatler 146. Thursday, March 16, 1709-10. Addison. *From my*
own Apartment, March 15.

Bickerstaff marvels at the fact that mankind can find
afflictions in everything. He presents a catalogue of
miserable people; the only thing that they all have in
common is that each has found a way to be miserable with
something another would find enjoyable. One complainer
longs for the divine Clarissa, while another, poor
Lavinia, is upset about the inconstancy of her lover,
Philander. One complains of a greyhound gone mad,
another complains of losing his wife, and another complains of the loss of money. Flavia mourns her parrot,
Mopsa mourns her neglect at a masquerade, while Clarinda
mourns the bad cold she caught at the same party. Some
are upset because they do not have the reputations they
wish, while others put all their hope in something which
does not deserve it. For example, Theron puts all his
hope in a running horse, Suffenus in a gilded chariot,
Fulvius in a blue string, and Florio in a tulip root.
In response to these reflections and upon reading some
of Homer's *Iliad*, Bickerstaff has a dream which to him
explains these events. In the dream, Jupiter having
distributed all the blessings of mankind and all the
calamities of human life, wishes to have them restored.
Messengers report that they have difficulty bringing
everything back because, all too frequently, the blessings have become calamities and the calamities have become blessings.

Tatler 147a. Saturday, March 18, 1709-10. Addison and
Steele. *From my own Apartment, March 17.*

Bickerstaff, proclaiming that reading is to the mind
what exercise is to the body, retells from Homer (*Iliad*,
Book XIV, l. 157 ff.) an allegorical fable addressed
especially to those of his correspondents who have complained that they have lost the favors of their husbands.
The fable has to do with Juno's attempts to recover the
affections of Jupiter by very carefully preparing herself for a deliberately accidental appearance before her
husband. She bathes herself in ambrosia, prepares her
hair, and appeals to Venus for a love charm, which the

love-goddess provides. Juno's preparations are effective; Bickerstaff suggests that care of the person and
her dress are extremely important for preserving a husband's affections.

Tatler 147b. _____. *Sheer Lane, March 17*.

Bickerstaff reports on receiving a present of a sample
of some wine to be sold at auction. He tries it, sleeps
on it, and confirms that it is "extra-ordinary French
claret." Bickerstaff says further that if others would
like him to evaluate their beverages, that he cannot
judge a liquor without examining at least three dozen
bottles. He says that others have tried to bribe him
with food but without success; in the future he will
evaluate and report on the best food available in the
city.

Tatler 148. Tuesday, March 21, 1709-10. Addison. *From my
own Apartment, March 20*.

Having promised in *Tatler* 147b to report on the food
available in the city, Bickerstaff urges all Englishmen
to eat beef and mutton. He recounts historical precedents for the English love of beef including the Earl
of Warwick, King Arthur, the Black Prince, and the Order
of Beefeaters. Bickerstaff attributes the success of
the English in battle to their diet; he finds French
cooking to be insubstantial. Bickerstaff recalls a meal
during the preceding summer in which a great deal of
French food was served; he found the food highly artificial and hard to digest. Bickerstaff says he prefers
all things simple and natural, including friends and
food.

Tatler 149. Thursday, March 23, 1709-10. Steele. *From my
own Apartment, March 22*.

Bickerstaff laments the large number of tyrannical, ill-
natured husbands who exist in England. He relates the
story of a visit to the family of a friend in which the
eldest daughter tells him a tale of a friend of hers
whose husband has tried to become her master rather than
her partner after their marriage. Bickerstaff has little
comfort for her except to say that it is a common occur-
rence. Although Sir Francis Bacon, in his *Essays*, asserts
that women should respect the wisdom of their husbands,
Bickerstaff says that marriage should be characterized
by mutual respect. As an example of what he means, he
quotes three letters of Pliny to his wife Calphurnia in
which Pliny expresses his respect for his wife. Bickerstaff ends the essay with a quotation from Milton, *Paradise Lost*, Book VIII, ll. 39. ff.

Tatler 150. Saturday, March 25, 1710. Steele. *From my own
Apartment, March 24*.

Bickerstaff presents a letter from a correspondent who
says that since Bickerstaff is a bachelor, he cannot
know from experience the true nature of marriage. The
author of the letter, an old married man, says that
couples, when they are married, know little of each
other and therefore shortly after the marriage find
much to disagree about. Having discovered this, they
begin to act like disappointed people; Philander finds
his Delia to be ill-natured and impertinent, while
Delia finds Philander to be surly and inconstant. The
solution is for each member of a couple to give the
other partner the benefit of the doubt in every situation. Unfortunately, some couples store up things to
feel resentful toward the other about. The author reports on a dinner he attended with a couple who spent
the whole evening expressing anger with each other indirectly. Many, however, succeed in their marriage;
Lovemore and his wife live in constant satisfaction with
each other so that their ordinary life is preferable to
the happiest moments of other lovers.

Tatler 151. Tuesday, March 28, 1710. Addison. *From my own
Apartment, March 27.*

Bickerstaff urges that women dress and adorn themselves
so that they display their natural beauty rather than
distort it artificially. Cleoria and Thalestris may
adorn themselves with jewels, but the jewels cannot
please so much as their natural charms. Unfortunately,
many women delight in extreme forms of dress which
Bickerstaff says reveal them to be trifling and superficial people. By the same token, many women are drawn
to artificialities in the dress of men, to their great
misfortune. Bickerstaff describes how his family prevented Marjorie Bickerstaff, his great aunt, from marrying throughout her life by insisting that she follow
each fashion as it came along, thus making her unattractive to each of her suitors in turn. Her chief protec-
tors are Sir Jacob, Bickerstaff's grandfather, and
Simon, Bickerstaff's great uncle. This discussion reminds Bickerstaff of a humorist mentioned by Horace,
named Eutrapelus, who did men mischief by presenting
them with gay suits.

Tatler 152. Thursday, March 30, 1710. Addison. *From my
own Apartment, March 29.*

Bickerstaff declares that he enjoys exploring the eternity to come, as well as the past and the present. He
especially enjoys, and here retells, Homer's account in
the *Iliad* of Ulysses' voyage to see Tiresis in Hades.

Tatler 153. Saturday, April 1, 1710. Addison. *From my own
Apartment, March 31.*

Bickerstaff tells of his delight in a picture which
shows all the great painters of an age playing musical
instruments which are appropriate to their styles of
painting. He uses his analogy to describe the different
talents in conversation in terms of musical instruments.
Drums are blusterers in conversation, lutes are sweet
and affable, trumpets are refined and fashionably educated, violins are lively, forward wits, hunting-horns
are rural wits, bass-viols are rough, and unpolished
speakers, bagpipes are dull, heavy, tedious story tellers, while those who are masters of all forms of conversations are harpsichords. Bickerstaff suggests
where each of these types of instrument-conversational-
ists might be found. Bickerstaff says he was for a
long time a drum, has since tried to become a lute, but
is degenerating into a bagpipe. Nicholas Humdrum writes
to say that he is having a concert at his house that
evening; in attendance will be a harpsichord, two lutes,
and a trumpet. He invites Bickerstaff to tune himself
and attend.

Tatler 154. Tuesday, April 4, 1710. Addison. *From my own
Apartment, April 3.*

Having told of Homer's description of the underworld in
Tatler 152, Bickerstaff now retells Virgil's account of
Aeneas' trip to the underworld.

Tatler 155. Thursday, April 6, 1710. Addison. *From my own
Apartment, April 5.*

Bickerstaff tells the story of the Political Upholsterer,
a man who becomes so involved in political affairs that
he begins to disregard all of his other appropriate concerns. While his wife and children starve, he is concerned about the King of Sweden. With the upholsterer,
Bickerstaff visits three or four politicians sitting
together in the upper end of the Mall. One of these is
an Asserter of Paradoxes; the conversation among the
group ranges over all the political intrigues and possibilities for conflict and its resolution throughout
Europe. At the end of the conversation, the Upholsterer
requests that Bickerstaff lend him half a crown; Bickerstaff lends him five shillings, with the promise of five
pounds when the Turk is driven out of Constantinople.

Tatler 156. Saturday, April 8, 1710. Addison. *From my own
Apartment, April 7.*

Bickerstaff here retells the story of Telemachus' journey to Hades, from Fénelon's *Télémaque*.

Tatler 157. Tuesday, April 11, 1710. Addison. *From my own
Apartment, April 10.*

While in the company of fine women, Bickerstaff describes
the musical instruments appropriate for the voices and

styles of speech of women. The most pleasing is a flute,
which is gentle and soothing to the ear because it keeps
the mind awake without startling it. The best of the
flutes is the hautboy because it has a sweet sound but
also a great strength and variety in its notes; the hautboy is as rare among women as the harpsichord is among
men. Another is the flageolet, which is shrill and sharp.
A prude is a virginal, a coquette is a kit, a country
woman is a Lancashire hornpipe, a Welch harp is a woman
concerned with her ancestry, a kettle drum is a loud,
bold, and masculine woman, and a dulcimer is a sweet and
melancholy woman who talks only of the countryside. A
friend, upon hearing this set of analogies, suggests that
he has been in love with every one. Bickerstaff concludes by proposing appropriately harmonious combinations
of instruments for marriage. Bickerstaff also announces
a benefit performance of a play for Mr. Betterton, to
which all of his disciples dead or living, mad or tame,
are invited to appear.

Tatler 158. Thursday, April 13, 1710. Addison. *From my own
Apartment, April 12.*

Bickerstaff tells the story of Tom Folio, a student of
printing, who is more concerned with the books' paper
and binding than he is with its contents. Bickerstaff
tries to discuss Virgil with Folio, but Folio can only
discuss the printing errors in the various editions. A
similar kind of pedant, according to Bickerstaff, is the
man who set a greater value on finding out the meaning
of a passage in Greek than on the author for having
written it. Bickerstaff concludes with some lines from
Boileau, *Satire IV*, which summarizes the character of
this sort of pedant.

Tatler 159. NF. Saturday, April 15, 1710. Steele. *From my
own Apartment, April 14.*

Bickerstaff laments the fact that the wits of England
have for fifty years inflamed the vices of the age
rather than tried to correct them. Marriage has been a
common topic of ridicule, with the result that many
marriages have been ruined which might have been saved.
Having presented an image of a good relationship between
a husband and wife in his quotation from Pliny's letters
in *Tatler* 149, Bickerstaff now presents translations of
four letters of Cicero to his wife Terertia to provide
more images of a good relationship between husband and
wife. Bickerstaff says he enjoys the image of this
great man of letters as a devoted husband.

Tatler 160. Tuesday, April 18, 1710. Addison and Steele.
From my own Apartment, April 17.

Bickerstaff reports that the Political Upholsterer disturbed him twice before he got up in the morning with

news of events abroad, which Bickerstaff would willingly
have learned later in the day. The Upholsterer also
left a letter full of political news, with the request
that all the gentlemen Bickerstaff met in the Mall earlier (see *Tatler* 155) would be delighted to receive five
shillings from Bickerstaff on the promise of the return
of a hundred pounds when the Turk is driven out of
Europe. Bickerstaff also presents a letter from Isabella Kit protesting Bickerstaff's selection of a base-
viol as an appropriate husband for her. He also has
received a letter from Tom Folio (see *Tatler* 158) suggesting that the bad state of the printing of Bickerstaff's papers reflects on Isaac's character.

Tatler 161. Thursday, April 20, 1710. Addison. *From my
own Apartment, April 19.*

Bickerstaff reports on a dream, inspired by his reading
"The Table of Cebes," in which he visits a pleasant
land hidden in the midst of the Alps, which is ruled
over by the Goddess of Liberty. On the Goddess' left
hand is the Genius of a Commonwealth, while on the
Goddess' right hand is the Genius of Monarchy. In the
Goddess' train are the several arts and sciences, including Eloquence, Plenty, and Commerce. Bickerstaff
finds that the landscape, though pleasant, is under
attack by two armies. Tyranny is the head of the first
army; behind her in her army are Barbarity, Ignorance,
Persecution, Oppression, Poverty, Famine, and Torture.
The other army is headed by Licentiousness, accompanied
by Clamor, Confusion, Impudence, and Rapine.

Tatler 162. Saturday, April 22, 1710. Addison. *From my
own Apartment, April 21.*

On the occasion of his first anniversary as Censor of
Great Britain, Bickerstaff reviews the achievements of
the past year. He says that he has modeled himself on
the office of the Roman Censor, whose job was to sort
the people into categories, look into the manners of
the people and check any growing luxuries, and punish
any offences according to the quality of the offenders.
In pursuing this, Bickerstaff says that he has divided
the residents of the city into the Dappers and the
Smarts, the Natural and Affected Rakes, the Pretty
Fellows and the Very Pretty Fellows, Pedants and Men of
Fire, Gangsters and Politicians, Cits and Citizens,
Free-thinkers and Philosophers, Wits and Snuff-takers,
and Duelists and Men of Honor. He has also reported
on excesses in dress and has begun to draw up lists of
the dead as punishment for various offences. Bickerstaff reports that Cato the Elder, his great predeces-
sor, was selected as Roman Censor on a platform of
strictness rather than that of leniency; Bickerstaff
promises to continue in this mold.

Tatler 163. Tuesday, April 25, 1710. Addison. *Will's Coffee-house, April 24.*

Bickerstaff reports on a conversation with Ned Softly, a man who fancies himself a poet. Ned insists that Bickerstaff go over with him, line by line, a poem entitled "To Mira on Her Incomparable Poems." He and Bickerstaff discuss Softly's friend Dick Easy's criticism of certain lines. The whole situation is an occasion on which Softly displays his supposed wit and learning to Bickerstaff.

Tatler 164. Thursday, April 27, 1710. Steele. *From my own Apartment, April 26.*

Bickerstaff surveys the vast number of letters he has received since becoming Censor of Great Britain, and hopes he has thus raised the revenues of the Post Office. Bickerstaff notices, as a result of a survey of these letters, that his popularity rises and falls in different parts of the city at different times. Bickerstaff delights in the praises some of the letters contain, and he says that the criticism keeps him from becoming too prideful. Many people comment upon his ancestry, criticising the behavior of his Aunt Marjorie or suggesting that Maud the Milkmaid is also one of·his relatives. He is most concerned, however, by the large number of letters which contain threats; as a result he has become an expert fencer and carries pistols with him at all times. Bickerstaff says that he is prepared for his death by writing a long letter describing the cause of his death. He models this behavior after that of a soldier, who, knowing he was to be executed, wrote a letter to his wife as though his death had already happened. As the events turned out, however, he was saved from dying; his wife, unfortunately, believing him to be dead, married another man. The soldier, not wishing to cause a stir, did not challenge the marriage since he knew that his wife had heard of his death by his own hand.

Tatler 165. Saturday, April 29, 1710. Addison. *From my own Apartment, April 28.*

Bickerstaff describes a particular kind of pedant, namely, the critic. The specific critic in question is Sir Timothy Tittle, who, like most critics, has a set of rules which he applies to all literature, judging it good or bad according to how closely it accords to these precepts. Bickerstaff reports on a scene in which Tittle visits his beloved, the eldest daughter of a friend of Bickerstaff's. After sitting for a while, acting exhausted and muttering phrases which no one understood, Tittle finally explains that he is exhausted because he has been at a play. His exhaustion derives from the fact that the playwright shifted the scene of the play's action a great deal, therefore violating Tittle's critical concept of unity of place. The young lady argues forcefully that the test of a play is whether it pleases or not rather than whether it accords to the rules. As a result of this argument, Tittle leaves; the lady is delighted that she is rid of such a foppish lover.

Tatler 166a. Tuesday, May 2, 1710. Steele. *White's Chocolate-house, May 1.*

Bickerstaff says that the world is overgrown with peculiar people; a good example is one Tom Modely, who believes that the only thing worth knowing is the fashion of the day. He stops Bickerstaff one day, corrects his behavior, and tells him of the fashion set by Lady Dimple and Mrs. Comma. Bickerstaff says that Tom is a member of the Order of the Insipids, whose business in the world is to be well dressed and whose greatest claim to fame is that he wears twenty shirts a week.

Tatler 166b. _____. *From my own Apartment, May 1.*

While Bickerstaff is observing the dancing of his milk-maid, Marjorie, Mr. Clayton appears to announce a performance of the masque *Arsinoe.* Bickerstaff requests that the performers tune the instruments before the audience comes in.

Tatler 166c. _____. Advertisements.

Bickerstaff announces that a bass-viol proposes to sell himself to a wife by running a lottery, at three pence a ticket, to raise ten thousand pounds. The fortunate woman who wins the lottery will be married to the gentleman. Bickerstaff also announces that he has been notified by several church wardens that ladies and gentlemen of too high a social state to be corrected have been misbehaving in church. Bickerstaff promises that those who have behaved in this manner must sell all their canes, cravats, bosom-laces, muffs, fans, snuff-boxes, and all other instruments of affectation; the money arising from this sale will be distributed to the poor and to the parishes in question.

Tatler 167a. NF. Thursday, May 4, 1710. Steele. *From my own Apartment, May 2.*

Bickerstaff presents a eulogy on the occasion of the death of the actor Mr. Betterton, and his burial in Westminster Abbey. Bickerstaff praises Betterton's acting and compares him with the great Roman Roscius, a performer praised by Cicero. The death of Betterton puts Bickerstaff to mind of Macbeth's speech (Act V, sc. v, ll. 19-26) in which the king compares life to an actor playing a role.

Tatler 167b. _____. Advertisement.

Bickerstaff says that it has been reported to him that
some have believed he encourages the Moving Picture and
Walking Statue and therefore are selling Walking Pictures; Bickerstaff says that he has ordered Pacolet to
take notice and to hang all such people in effigy.

Tatler 168. Saturday, May 6, 1710. Steele. *From my own
Apartment, May 5.*

Bickerstaff encounters an impudent young man who ridicules his role as Censor. Bickerstaff believes that
impudence is a vice, which proceeds from a basic inse-
curity about one's abilities. Bickerstaff encourages
all those who would have some impact on the world to
acquire self-assurance so that they may carry out their
goals with proper decorum. Bickerstaff recounts the
story of a visit to a Jesuit school, in which a gentleman who speaks well on the subject of the love of glory
is rewarded with the best shoulder of mutton. Bickerstaff receives a petition from Sarah Lately, who, having reached the age of sixty, requests four tickets in
the lottery for the Bass-viol because she has lived the
lifetime of four virginities. Isabella Kit writes Bickerstaff requesting that he establish a lottery for her
as well; she promises him a ticket and hopes that he
will be the winner of the lottery for her.

Tatler 169. Tuesday, May 9, 1710. Steele. *From my own
Apartment, May 8.*

Bickerstaff announces that, with summer approaching, he
has been invited by his relatives to spend a month or
two in the country. He would be glad to do so except
that he cannot drink enough to keep up with his country
relatives. He is dismayed by the fact that drinking is
a country vice; he believes that country-dwellers who
drink too much are incapable of appreciating what they
have by living in the country. No man, argues Bickerstaff, should be considered a true landlord of an estate
unless he can appreciate what he has. The true country
gentleman is one who truly understands his station and
delights in it. Bickerstaff presents a letter from his
cousin Frank Bickerstaff to illustrate the point; this
member of the Bickerstaff family is poor and lives ad-
jacent to a royal estate. He accepts his position and
delights in the little things of life, while his neighbor delights in the great things; each is happy, in his
own way.

Tatler 170a. Thursday, May 11, 1710. Steele. *From my own
Apartment, May 10.*

Bickerstaff says that he agrees with Seneca that nothing
that Fortune can give us is really our own; only our
intellectual possessions are our own because Fortune

cannot take those away, as it can wealth, glory and
power. With these thoughts in mind, Bickerstaff jour-
neys to the poor end of town, where he finds many people
blessed by Fortune who unfortunately deny her existence.
He meets a young woman who is organizing the government's
lottery. He addresses her as Dame Fortune, and requests
of her that she repulse the aggressive and the bold and
favor the modest and the humble.

Tatler 170b. _____. Advertisement.

Bickerstaff addresses Philander, who has written Clarinda
that he had lost his heart by a shot from her eyes and
requests that she see him and give him three sighs;
otherwise he will commit suicide in the Rosaman's Pond.
Bickerstaff requests that Philander present himself to
the coroner of Westminster or Clarinda, an old offender,
will be found guilty of willful murder.

Tatler 171a. Saturday, May 13, 1710. Steele. *Grecian
Coffee-house, May 12.*

Bickerstaff reports on a discussion of the origins of
titleos and honors. Timoleon argues that the practice
arose when men fell away from the standards of the
Golden Age, to set apart those who continued to act
virtuously. Urbanus reports on the honor given by the
Emperor of the Mohocks to their landlord on a recent
visit to England; they called him Cadaroque, after the
strongest fort in their part of the world. Minucio
argues that the business of the Indians was arranged
beforehand. Minucio, concerned more with incidentals
than with major issues, then gets involved in a discussion of the distances from parts of London to another.
Bickerstaff ponders the poverty of imagination which
causes men to contradict each other on no grounds.

Tatler 171b. _____. Advertisement.

Bickerstaff reports that his aerial messenger reports
that an auction of pictures held recently was conducted
honestly with no "screens" present; all false buyers at
auctions will henceforth be known as "screens."

Tatler 172. Tuesday, May 16, 1710. Steele. *From my own
Apartment, May 15.*

Bickerstaff says that mankind has always to be on guard
that he not injure others because of his ungoverned
passions. This is especially true, he says, among close
friends and acquaintances, because those whom we only
know casually can only injure us slightly, while those
whom we know well can injure us severely. Nowhere is
this more true than in the marriage relationship, where
the possibility for injury is great indeed. To illustrate his point, Bickerstaff tells the story of Mr.

Eustace, who became so angry with his wife that he stabbed her repeatedly with his dagger. The unfortunate woman soon died, as did her husband, after being shot by a policeman.

Tatler 173. Thursday, May 18, 1710. Steele. *Sheer Lane, May 17.*

Bickerstaff says that he has had great difficulty in learning to fence because he had to unlearn bodily movements learned as a youth while practicing the use of the back sword. This leads him to comment upon the state of education for the young in England which he finds to be abysmally bad, because young men are all taught the same subjects whether they have any need for them or not. The son of a woman in Bickerstaff's neighborhood tells Bickerstaff what he knows of Horace. His translation is ludicrous. Bickerstaff says that the young man should be spending his time in more practical pursuits because he will never be able to understand Horace and does not need to anyway. The study of Horace, and of classical literature in general, should be reserved for those who are capable of a life in the Court; those not so suited should be taught a trade.

Tatler 174a. Saturday, May 20, 1710. Steele. *From my own Apartment, May 19.*

Having dealt with the lazy by declaring them dead, Bickerstaff now proposes to deal with their opposite number, those who are impertinently active and enterprising. He first comments unfavorably upon Dr. Trotter and Dr. Langham, astrologers who are earning a great deal by attempting to predict the outcome of the national lottery. Two others whose energies are put to useless ends are the Lady Fidget and Will Voluble, the former because she visits too much and the latter because he talks too much. Lady Fidget visits because she is envious of all those who have good fortune; she visited Flavia after her bout with the smallpox and has never been back because Flavia was not altered by the disease. Bickerstaff promises to comment on Will Voluble at a later time. He proposes that all those whose activities do not contribute to the well being of mankind be forced into inactivity by sending them to his expanded Bedlam.

Tatler 174b. NF. _____. *St. James's Coffee-house, May 19.*

Further reports on events abroad.

Tatler 175a. Tuesday, May 23, 1710. Steele. *From my own Apartment, May 22.*

Bickerstaff says that he hopes to further our understanding of the proper function of men and women by

describing the nature of the male and the female life
at different stages in its growth. His examples are of
Mrs. Elizabeth and her brother William. In early adult-
hood, Mrs. Elizabeth is her father's delight, her
mother's companion, and the object of great admiration
by young men; at the same time, her brother William is
only beginning to acquire the skills and talents he will
need in adult life. Later, after she marries, she has
little to do but be a good wife and mother; her brother,
however, is entering into the years in which he will
fulfill his early promise. The goal of a woman's life
should be to be pleasing, while the goal of a man's life
should be to become wise; those who give up these goals
forfeit their claims to life, while those who seek to
achieve these goals by erroneous means should be taken
into custody for their false industry. Bickerstaff
breaks off abruptly because he is afflicted by a toothache.

Tatler 175b. NF. _____. *St. James's Coffee-house,
May 22.*

More reports on events abroad.

Tatler 176a. Thursday, May 25, 1710. Steele. *From my own
Apartment, May 23.*

Bickerstaff, having broken two pipes and his spectacles
while suffering the pain of a toothache, is moved to
reflect upon those heroic spirits who seem to rise
above the pains of living. Bickerstaff feels that this
ability is the highest achievement of human life. Men
are to be judged not by what they are like, but by what
they do; for example, Eucrates, Martius, and Aristaeus
are examples of men who have brought their will into
accord with their reason and therefore have become perfect masters of themselves in all circumstances.

Tatler 176b. _____. *Sheer Lane, May 24.*

Bickerstaff presents a letter from J. B. in which the
author says that he has so many diversions open to him
that he does not know where to begin; he requests Bickerstaff's help to find a way of doing nothing. This letter is accompanied by a letter from J. B.'s daughter
S. B. who requests that Bickerstaff instruct her father
to marry off his daughter before he begins to do nothing.

Tatler 177. Saturday, May 27, 1710. Steele. *Sheer Lane,
May 26.*

Bickerstaff announces that Mr. Penkethman, the comedian,
has dedicated his theatrical efforts to Bickerstaff and
wishes Bickerstaff to recommend them to the world. This
provokes Bickerstaff to think about the matter of dedications in general. Bickerstaff applauds the Roman

practice, as exemplified by Pliny in tribute to Martial,
of speaking the truth simply and directly, so that all
the world knows the dedication is deserved. He objects
to flowery dedications, full of untruths, which he feels
are an insult to the person who would otherwise be
honored. To illustrate his point, Bickerstaff prints
his response to the dedication by a female author of
her poems to him, with a adaptation of Virgil's *Aeneid*,
Book II, ll. 583-84, which roughly translated runs,
"There is no glory in a woman's punishment."

Tatler 178. Tuesday, May 30, 1710. Steele. *Sheer Lane,
May 29.*

Bickerstaff delights in the portrait of Don Quixote,
presented by Cervantes; he especially delights in the
way in which Cervantes presents the Man of LaMancha's
growing madness. Bickerstaff remarks that many of his
contemporary Englishmen are also far gone in as visible
a madness as the Don's. An example of the sort is Bickerstaff's friend the Upholsterer, who uses many words
but makes no sense, a malady which Bickerstaff attributes to reading too much political news in the newspapers. The papers in question include the *Postman*, the
Letter, and the *Courant*; Bickerstaff feels that reading
these papers is affecting the British mind much as reading too many books about chivalry is affecting the Spanish. By telling the Upholsterer that he is being taken
to the Bastille, Bickerstaff is able to convey him to
his lunatic asylum.

Tatler 179. Thursday, June 1, 1710. Steele. *From my own
Apartment, May 31.*

Bickerstaff delights in reprinting a letter from T. S.,
describing the joys of country life. The correspondent
goes into great detail describing his greenhouse, which
contains marble walks, statues of Venus, Adonis, Diana,
and Apollo, all manner of fruit trees, as well as two
grottoes from which his wife sings and his daughter
plays the lute.

Tatler 180a. Saturday, June 3, 1710. Steele. *From my own
Apartment, June 2.*

Bickerstaff responds to a letter in which the correspondent accuses him of criticizing the lower classes of
mankind severely while treating with more gentleness
persons of quality. Bickerstaff agrees that there is
some truth in the charge, and says that it is a great
injustice that so many people of quality and power permit their affairs to be conducted by hirelings rather
than by themselves. In the olden days, the distinctions
among British classes were in terms of wealth, generosity, and hospitality; now, however, they are usually
described in terms of debtor and creditor. Bickerstaff

promises to begin publishing lists of those people of quality who do not know the nature of the affairs of their own families. Bickerstaff quotes the philosophers Epicetus, Sallust, and Cicero to support his notion that those who are rich should be responsible in their wealth and in their treatment of those who lack wealth.

Tatler 180b. _____. Advertisement.

Bickerstaff announces a stage-coach to leave at 6 from Nando's Coffee-house to Mr. Tiptoe's dancing school.

Tatler 181. Tuesday, June 6, 1710. Steele. *From my own Apartment, June 5.*

Bickerstaff says that since life is too short for a sufficiency of true friendship or goodwill, some wise men have adopted the practice of taking some time to mourn lost friends. In following this procedure, Bickerstaff remembers all the melancholy and sorrowful circumstances of his life. He especially remembers the death of his father, and his mother's grief. After some time spent thinking of his sorrows, Bickerstaff is interrupted by a servant who brings him some samples of wine to be put on sale next week. As a result, Bickerstaff sends for three friends with whom he spends a delightful evening, until 2:00 a.m., enjoying the consuming of two bottles per man.

Tatler 182. Thursday, June 8, 1710. Steele. *Sheer Lane, June 7.*

Bickerstaff says that all of his beaux have become shepherds and his belles wood-nymphs; even the theaters are closed for a vacation. One of the great things about the theater, Bickerstaff says, is that in the theater all sorts and conditions of men are gathered to enjoy themselves in each other's presence, a sight which should be pleasing to the wise man. Although some say Bickerstaff praises the theater too much, he wonders if any man can praise too highly something he extremely likes. Eugenio delights in showing off his art; Crassus, his countryside; and Bickerstaff, the theater. Bickerstaff praises two actors, Wilks and Cibber, each a perfect actor in his own way. Bickerstaff announces that he has a young poet under his tutelage; he has arranged for a performance of Cibber's *The Careless Husband* to show this young author a well-written play, well-acted.

Tatler 183. NF. Saturday, June 10, 1710. Steele. *From my own Apartment, June 9.*

Bickerstaff laments the fact that more men are not public spirited. He praises the civic-mindedness of the Greeks and Romans and says that the English would be more public-spirited if they only put to use the many good qualities in their possession. An example of the public-spirited man is Regulus, who having been taken prisoner by the Carthagenians, was sent to Rome by them in an attempt to exchange for him some of their own countrymen. Regulus took an oath to return to Carthage if he was unsuccessful; he pleaded with his Roman countrymen to force him to return by not giving up the prisoners, since the prisoners were young and vigorous and he was old and of little use to anyone. This example of self-sacrifice Bickerstaff finds to be the highest expression of true partriotism.

Tatler 184. Tuesday, June 13, 1710. Steele. *From my own Apartment, June 12.*

Bickerstaff says that people's behavior at weddings indicates how the rest of their lives will go, while their behavior at funerals tells a great deal about their inward state. It is appropriate to mourn the dead, but it is also appropriate to delight in the happiness of those who marry. Since a successful marriage is the goal of both sexes, Bickerstaff believes it appropriate for unmarried women to dress in such a way that unmarried men are aware of their physical charms. He applauds an ancient custom of allowing men and women who intend to be married to live together as lover and mistress for a brief time before the actual wedding. He says that the delight in the nuptial bed can be treated with decency as well as gaiety, but this is rendered difficult in contemporary England by the "insipid mirth of certain animals" called "wags." Such "wags" delight in making bawdy suggestions about everyone. Bickerstaff hopes that these people will not bother his brother Tranquillus, and Tranquillus' wife Jenny, Bickerstaff's sister, who will attend the play with Bickerstaff tomorrow evening in the clothes they wore on their wedding day.

Tatler 185. Thursday, June 15, 1710. Steele. *From my own Apartment, June 14.*

Bickerstaff receives a letter from Sylvia telling of her father's objections to her love affair with Philander, a man of considerably less fortune than she. Bickerstaff urges Sylvia's father to consider the calamity of unhappiness in love, and to consider whether true happiness in marriage can be bought at any price. To illustrate his point he tells a story, in which Antiochus, a young prince, fell in love with the young Queen Stratonice, who was his mother-in-law and wife to his father the old King Seleucus. Erasistratus, a physician, called to attend the young man in his lovesickness discovered the source of his problem and informed the King; upon being informed that his son's illness was due to his love for his mother-in-law, the

King immediately gave orders and the young Queen, to show her obedience, generously exchanged the father for the son.

Tatler 186a. Saturday, June 17, 1710. Steele. *Sheer Lane, June 16.*

Bickerstaff says that while all men want honor, respect, and glory, most men instead exhibit vanity, pride, and ambition. The problem, he says, is one of appearances; if men were in fact honorable, they would receive honor, but instead they try to appear honorable and therefore prevent themselves from achieving it in reality. Damasippus is an example of this situation; he is good-natured, well-bred, and well-fashioned, but he throws away all his good attributes because his single goal in life is to gain the good opinion of everyone he talks to. Bickerstaff tells of walking in an Inn of Court, and seeing a young man practice pleading a case before a jury by delivering his plea in a nightgown standing before a mirror; to Bickerstaff this young man will surely achieve honor because he is concerned about doing his job well rather than appearing to be successful in the eyes of others. Bickerstaff accuses Machiavelli of being the first one to teach that the pursuit of ambition is worthy any cost.

Tatler 186b. _____. Advertisement.

Bickerstaff announces that he has received two letters postage-due, one of them, from Ireland, declaring that he has grown dull. Bickerstaff requests that all correspondents please pay the postage on their letters.

Tatler 187a. Tuesday, June 20, 1710. Steele. *From my own Apartment, June 19.*

Pasquin writes to Bickerstaff more gossip of Rome and the Pope; he declares that the church of Rome is especially upset that a work of Henry Dodwell which attempts to demonstrate the mortality of the soul, has not been burned in England. He declares that Bickerstaff's Roman readers wish a list of all the mortal and immortal men within the dominions of Great Britain. A young Englishman in France awaits a decision of British grammarians about the English use of the word "revolution" before he goes to Rome to become a Cardinal. An Englishman of Pasquin's acquaintance says that Bickerstaff will never find a place large enough to hold all the lunatics he has found in the country. The same Englishman also says that Bickerstaff is at the height of his reputation, yet he may fall, as Hannibal did, not by force of Roman arms but by the envy and detraction of his countrymen.

Tatler 187b. _____. *Will's Coffee-house, June 19*.

Bickerstaff reports on the indifferent reaction of a number of people to an account of the British victory at Douay. Harry English, observing the lack of enthusiasm, concludes with Bickerstaff that the English are very unlike the old Romans.

Tatler 188. Thursday, June 22, 1710. Steele. *From my own Apartment, June 21*.

Bickerstaff receives a letter from an unknown correspondent who wonders how the greenhouse of *Tatler* 179 can grow grass inside it, since grass needs rain as well as sun and fresh air. This oversight reminds Bickerstaff of the Biblical account of Moses' striking a rock. Another letter to Bickerstaff objects to his approval of the love of Sylvia and Philander (*Tatler* 185). This correspondent says that marriage is far too serious a matter to be left to children, and that marriage should come first with love following afterwards. The correspondent is very upset that his eldest daughter Winifred is causing a commotion in the house because she has fallen in love and is using Bickerstaff as proof that she should be allowed to do so. Bickerstaff says that few men are so indifferent about marriage as this correspondent; more are like the characters in Shakespeare's *Othello*, in which love-relationships are the most important things in their lives. Having praised Wilks and Cibber in *Tatler* 182, Bickerstaff is asked by William Bullock and William Penkethman to give his assessment of them. Bickerstaff agrees, and discovers that Penkethman eats cold chicken, is dexterous at getting under a table, and has a great deal of money, while Bullock is more talented at eating asparagus, is active in jumping over a stick, and is the taller man.

Tatler 189. Saturday, June 24, 1710. Steele. *From my own Apartment, June 23*.

Bickerstaff describes two different families for the purpose of showing the success the first family has had in the rearing of children and the failure of the second family in the same undertaking. The account of the first family is contained in a series of letters which have been given to Bickerstaff; the letters show the early propensity toward literature of the eldest son, now a scholar, and the early tendency toward generosity of the younger son, now a war hero. The parents of these sons delight in them and live their lives over again through them. The second family is a branch of the Bickerstaff family, headed by Samuel Bickerstaff, one of Isaac's cousins. In this family there are also two children—Tom, 19, and his sister, Mary, 15. The father is so worried that his children will be taken advantage of by the rest of the world that he puts constraints on their

every move and constantly keeps them where he can watch
them. The family is now in town, and Bickerstaff finds
that the two children constantly fight with each other
and have no idea about proper conduct of themselves in
the world. The son is to be sent to the Inn of Court,
but his father insists that he tell him everything that
happens; he is more concerned that his son not have some
of his linen stolen by a laundress than he is that his
son become a successful lawyer.

Tatler 190. Tuesday, June 27, 1710. Steele. *Sheer Lane,
June 26.*

Bickerstaff says that he has received a number of letters objecting to his introduction of politics into the
pages of the *Tatler;* he has especially received an in-
comprehensible letter from one Aminadab, a Quaker, who
reminds Bickerstaff of those who have fallen because of
their own words. He urges Bickerstaff to think of this
and take tobacco. Another correspondent writes for advice on the management of his estate, and Bickerstaff
assures him that he is in the right (with reference to
the succession to the English throne). Bickerstaff
also addresses a letter to Louis XIV of France suggesting that some of his advisers are working against his
best interests in their advice about which party of
Englishmen he should favor.

Tatler 191a. Thursday, June 29, 1710. Steele. *From my own
Apartment, June 28.*

Bickerstaff gives a character-sketch of Polypragmon,
who makes it his business to appear more cunning, clever,
and ambitious than he really is. This gentleman does
all the ill that he can, but he pretends to do much
more than that. He rarely ever appears in public, seeking to appear mysterious to increase his power. All
this Bickerstaff finds a true contradiction of the only
means to a just reputation, which is simplicity of manners.

Tatler 191b. _____. *Will's Coffee-house, June 28.*

Although Bickerstaff says that wit and pleasure are at the
lowest ebb in the town, a gentleman informs him that
Cibber's burlesque, *The Rival Queens; or Humours of
Alexander the Great* is to be performed. This provokes
Bickerstaff to say that Bluster is inconsistent with
the character of a hero, for to be plain is not to be
rude but to be civil. In the play Lee's *Rival Queens;
or the Death of Alexander the Great*, burlesqued by Cibber, Alexander is presented as a monster of lust and
cruelty, as if the way to make him a hero were to make
his character as little like that of a worthy man as
possible. Cibber objects to this concept of the hero,
and Bickerstaff agrees with him.

Tatler 192. Saturday, July 1, 1710. Addison. *From my own Apartment, June 30.*

Bickerstaff retells an account of a journey taken by a coach full of his friends as far as Land's End. The conversation on the journey began in good humor but quickly various members of the party began to fall out with each other for one reason or another, until Mr. Sprightly fell asleep, and no one was left to keep everyone in good humor. Similar events happened on another coach on the same journey, so Bickerstaff sees the experience of these two coaches as a picture of human life, because in the relationships between men and women, few make it in good-humor all the way to the end. The best attributes for a successful journey are cheerfulness and constancy. Bickerstaff concludes this paper by telling a story about a shipwreck during which one couple chose to die together while the husband of the other couple chose to try to swim for safety. The whole shipload was rescued, but the couple who decided to die together separated shortly thereafter while the other couple remained happily married until the end of their lives.

Tatler 193. Tuesday, July 4, 1710. Steele. *Will's Coffee-house, July 3.*

Bickerstaff says that he has received a number of letters from people objecting to his recent stand on political issues; nevertheless he feels that he has done the right thing. Upon coming to Will's to escape the controversies he is asked by Mr. Thomas Doggett to attend a benefit performance of *The Old Bachelor* to be given for him on Thursday. Bickerstaff promises to recommend attendance to all his friends, and is given a letter from J. Downes the prompter. Downes is concerned that a gentleman of the Inns of Court--a deep intriguer--has become sole manager of the theatre. He has, unfortunately, thrown out the British actors and brought in foreign ones instead. The letter, really an attack on the ministry of Harley, describes the theatre-director in Machiavellian terms.

Tatler 194. Thursday, July 6, 1710. Steele. *From my own Apartment, July 5.*

To provide rules for the conduct of virtuous amours, Mr. Bickerstaff "transproses" the tenth canto of the fourth book of Spenser's *Faerie Queen*, in which Sir Scudamore describes the progress of his courtship to Amoret.

Tatler 195. Saturday, July 8, 1710. Steele. *Grecian Coffee-house, July 7.*

Bickerstaff says that a number of the learned world are unhappy with his comments on political affairs. One,

Cato Junior, writes to suggest that Bickerstaff would be better off if he turned his attention to the large number of abuses in the country which he has as of yet not treated. Bickerstaff says that he plans to take up the broader concern of the state of Love in the island of Great Britain; at the same time, he has instructed Don Saltero (see *Tatler* 34 and *Tatler* 221) and Dr. Thomas Smith (*Tatler* 103) to bring him lists of those who are no better trained than they, yet who practice medicine beyond their training. Bickerstaff says he is also working on a plan to achieve the marriage of every unmarried woman over the age of 25 in the country. He presents a letter to Amanda in which he encourages her to come to town to participate in his marriage program, the goal of which is to relieve all British females who are at present "devoted to involuntary virginity."

Tatler 196. Tuesday, July 11, 1710. Steele. *From my own Apartment, July 10.*

Bickerstaff is asked by an old acquaintance to prepare a paper on the subject of the behavior of great men to those who seek to do them service in return for financial reward. He is especially concerned about those great men who lead those who would do them service to expect appropriate return for their service, and then never provide it. Bickerstaff believes that such a patron is more unjust than those who took the Upholders' goods without paying for them. Unfortunately, Bickerstaff says, many persist in expecting reward when none is forthcoming; two of these are Will Afterday and Harry Linger. Bickerstaff has discussed the matter with Dick Reptile and Dick Estcourt at his club; they agree that nothing is worse than a patron who gathers a group around him for companionship by promising them future reward. On the other hand, nothing is more beautiful than the life of a patron who does reward his dependents in an appropriate fashion.

Tatler 197. Thursday, July 13, 1710. Steele. *Grecian Coffee-house, July 12.*

Bickerstaff delights in the dedication to him of a work entitled *Epistolarum Obscurorum Vivorum*, which he finds to be a collection of letters from some profound blockheads, written in honor of each other; he considers the great amount of useless work done by scholars in reprinting in the present day the follies of the past. Ralph Shallow is one of this sort, a man of barren genius but fertile imagination. The true use of learning is to enoble and improve man's natural faculties, not to disguise his imperfections. Bickerstaff also thanks Dorenda and promises to answer her letter and take her advice.

Tatler 198. Saturday, July 15, 1710. Steele. *From my own Apartment, July 14.*

Bickerstaff recounts the history of Caelia. The lady, of great humility and constant cheerfulness but of little fortune, was met in St. Paul's Cathedral and wooed by Palamede, a learned, genteel, and wealthy young man; the two fell in love and prevailed on his father to permit their marriage. She accidentally discovers that he is already married secretly to a woman in the country. She rejects any and all attempts at reconciliation, and says that she and her soon-to-be-born child will and must live in shame.

Tatler 199. Tuesday, July 18, 1710. Steele. *From my own Apartment, July 16.*

Bickerstaff laments that there is no appropriate way to protect a young woman from being ruined by her choice of husband. Nor is there any way to punish sufficiently the young man who has deprived Caelia (*Tatler* 198) of any chance of happiness. Bickerstaff describes some of the ways in which parents try to protect their children by arranging the marriage themselves, with the help of Coupler the Conveniencer, who helps set up marriage settlements. Bickerstaff objects that such externally-arranged marriages ignore the pleasures and graces of life. He is diverted from thinking about the subject by the need to prepare a marriage settlement between John and Mary, who wish to be married and seek his advice.

Tatler 200. Thursday, July 20, 1710. Steele. *From my own Apartment, July 19.*

Bickerstaff presents a letter from Caelia, in which she writes to ask his advice about whether she should marry Philander or Silvius. Philander is young, well-educated, and wealthy; Silvius is also young and rich, but not so well educated. Bickerstaff urges that she marry the man with an education. He also receives a letter from Diana Forecast, who urges that he publish his plan for getting all the unmarried virgins of 25 years and more to the altar. Bickerstaff offers one proposal for solving this problem, which is to establish a lottery, the purpose of which will be to advance each of ten young ladies, 2,500 pounds to enable them to marry a man appropriate to their stations in life. Bickerstaff urges comment on his proposal.

Tatler 201a. Saturday, July 22, 1710. Steele. *White's Chocolate-house, July 21.*

Bickerstaff expands upon his claim that a great source of all the ills of the country is the impertinent way in which English men treat English women. Bickerstaff believes that the way to increase the number of amiable women and to lessen the number of unhappy women is to promote the success of well-grounded passions. To promote this, he presents a letter from a man urging his suit upon the woman he loves. He also presents a letter which Bickerstaff hopes is from the beloved, in which she says that she wishes the man who loves her would talk of love with her in spite of the fact that she urges him not to.

Tatler 201b. _____. *From my own Apartment, July 21.*

Bickerstaff receives a Mr. Mills, the player, who urges Bickerstaff to attend a benefit performance of *Hamlet* to be given for him on Wednesday. Bickerstaff laments that many spectators prefer parts to be overacted and therefore prefer Sir Harry Wildair to actors who act naturally. He is also visited by Mr. Elliot, who wishes to know who will win the lottery. Bickerstaff tells him because he is impressed by Mr. Elliot's bookkeeping methods.

Tatler 201c. _____. Advertisement. *From the Trumpet in Sheer Lane, July 20.*

Bickerstaff announces that the story tellers who frequent this place are permitted to tell stories, so long as they do not repeat the same story in a given night. He also asks his love correspondents to vary the names they choose, because he is overstocked with Philanders.

Tatler 202. Tuesday, July 25, 1710. Steele. *From my own Apartment, July 24.*

While wandering in Stepney Churchyard, Bickerstaff discovers a gravestone with the inscription "Here lies the body of T. B." The notion of a man who wishes to be remembered by only the first letters of his name provokes Bickerstaff to reflect on human vanity and the imperfect attainment of ambition. Bickerstaff is reminded of a story from Plutarch of the philosopher Cineas, who asked Pyrrhus what he truly wished to do. He was told by the king that he wished to make merry; the philosopher responded with a question as to what prevented the king from doing that now. An old friend of Bickerstaff's lost a major's post 40 years ago, and has ever since spent his time criticizing the achievements of others. Since, however, ambition is part of human nature, it is necessary for men to form goals which they can really attain. A fellow conversationalist at the Trumpet argues that life should be measured in quality rather than quantity, and that every man can aspire to be generous. Bickerstaff is interrupted in his reflections by a crowd of people who wish to know if they have won the lottery; Bickerstaff informs them that the winners will be the wisest and the fairest. Mr. Elliot reports that he has prepared all the bookkeeping for the lottery.

Tatler 203a. Thursday, July 27, 1710. Steele. *From my own Apartment, July 26.*

On the occasion of the first drawing for the lottery, Bickerstaff reflects on the nature of fortune. He notices the reactions of those in the crowd, especially one man, holding seven tickets, whose hopes and fears rise and fall as each ticket is drawn. Bickerstaff argues that wealth is valuable to a man's character only in the way it is applied, not in the mere having of it. He argues that "The true greatness of mind consists in valuing men apart from their circumstances, or according to their behavior in them." Bickerstaff quotes Dick Reptile to support his argument. He also prints a letter he has written to Chloe on the occasion of her winning the lottery; he hopes that wealth will not take away her other virtues.

Tatler 203b. _____. *Grecian Coffee-house, July 26.*

Bickerstaff receives a letter from his country gardner (see *Tatler* 179) who responds to the argument made in *Tatler* 188 that it is impossible to grow grass under glass. The correspondent says that with proper watering, mowing, and rolling, it is possible to achieve a beautiful grass-plot under a glass roof.

Tatler 204. Saturday, July 29, 1710. Steele. *From my own Apartment, July 28.*

Bickerstaff objects to the common errors in manners of address between persons of the same or of different quality; he especially objects to the impertinent use of title, when combined with a paraphrastical way of saying "you." He gives two examples of this error: the first involves a fish monger who, while apologizing to a magistrate, refers to him as "his worship" and "his honor"; the second, a shoemaker who, while fitting a nobleman's shoes, refers to him as "his lordship" over and over again. What all this artificial regard for quality can lead to is seen in Tom Courtly, of whom Bickerstaff gives a character-sketch. Tom is very strict in performing what he calls his "respects"; however, title is all Tom knows of honor, and civility all he knows of friendship.

Tatler 205. Tuesday, August 1, 1710. Fuller. *From my own Apartment, July 31.*

Bickerstaff proclaims that every man has two basic desires in life, to keep himself alive and to have children. He promises to discuss the latter subject in more detail as time goes by; he will now address himself to the former subject. He is especially concerned with an excess of activity in self-preservation--gluttony. He proposes a new sort of man, the Dozer, who is in subjection to his appetite. There are two ways of erring in this situation: the first is to be an eater, or one who eats too much and too long; the other, to be a swallower, who eats what he eats too rapidly. He ends by quoting a sermon of the learned Dr. South upon the Ways of Pleasantness. The jist of Dr. South's remarks is that men who eat too much sacrifice time, their most precious commodity.

Tatler 206. Thursday, August 3, 1710. Steele. *From my own Apartment, August 2.*

Bickerstaff says that the general purpose of men in conducting their lives is to gain either the affection or the esteem of those with whom they converse. The man who is always trying to please is easy to control because those who know him can deal with him by giving him as much of what he wants as they chose to. There is another type of man, however, who pleases simply because that is his natural inclination. Jack Gainly and his sister Gatty are examples of those who brighten up the company they keep. The opposite kind of people are Flavia, and her daughter Lucia; the mother looks young for her age, the daughter older, so they are rivals instead of companions, especially for the attention of Colonel Lofty. Bickerstaff says that he will pass most of his time with the facetious Harry Bickerstaff, but the prudent William Bickerstaff will be the executor of his will.

Tatler 207. Saturday, August 5, 1710. Steele. *From my own Apartment, August 4.*

Bickerstaff, having received some Latin verses in praise of him from a young admirer, comments upon the relationship between youth and age. He describes a dinner at which his three nephews and a beautiful lady of the city are invited to dine with Bickerstaff. In the reactions of the woman to the three nephews, Bickerstaff soon perceives the differences among the three which their different educations are producing. The lady at first is delighted with the young courtier of the group because he can tell her about Lady Lovely and all the fashions of the day. When the Oxford student quotes his translation of Theocritus, she quickly turns her attention to him. Only the nephew studying to be a merchant seems unconcerned with impressing the lady. Bickerstaff describes the difficulties of communication which arise among people of different educational backgrounds. He also presents a letter from Chloe (see *Tatler* 203) in which the young lady says that her modesty in receiving a benefit of 400 pounds a year is not from humility but from disappointment in not having received 1,000 pounds a year; she hopes that her behavior will become humble rather than disappointed with time.

Tatler 208. Tuesday, August 8, 1710. Steele. *From my own Apartment, August 7.*

Bickerstaff meets an old acquaintance who delights him by telling him that he looks well, but disappoints him because he reminds Sir Isaac of their days at Lady Brightly's, an era which Bickerstaff would like to forget. This provokes Bickerstaff to reflections on the subject of flattery. Because all wish to be flattered, Bickerstaff says that the flatterer is a powerful creature; he gives an example from Terrence of a flatterer who cheated a coxcomb out of his livelihood. Appropriate flattery is exhibited by a young man who wakens Sir Jeffrey at the club by snoring so loud; Sir Jeffry is delighted to find a younger man more lethargic than he. The best flatterer Bickerstaff knows of is one who conceals his flattery under a spirit of contradiction; when Lady Autumn disputed him about something that happened at the revolution he replied angrily, "Pray, Madam, give me leave to know more of a thing in which I was actually concerned, than you, who were then in your nurse's arms."

Tatler 209. Thursday, August 10, 1710. Seeele. *From my own Apartment, August 9.*

Upon being asked by a friend for an appropriate subject for a painting, Bickerstaff tells the story of Alexander the Great and Philippus, his physician. Having been told that Darius, Alexander's enemy, had bribed Philippus to poison the general, Bickerstaff trusted in his physician and was delighted with his loyalty. Bickerstaff says that the appropriate purpose of art is either to cause us to think agreeable thoughts of absent friends or elevating ideas about eminent people.

Tatler 210a. Saturday, August 12, 1710. Steele. *Sheer Lane, August 10.*

Bickerstaff finds himself in conversation with a lady of quality who spends her time condemning the faults of another woman of the city. Bickerstaff describes to the woman's face her own failings, and urges her to reform her servants before she tries to reform those people of her own station in society. Bickerstaff also receives a letter from a woman who says that she has been a virgin for 27 years and asks for help in avoiding becoming an old maid. Bickerstaff says that he needs more information; that a woman is not a maid until she is 15 and therefore the woman in question may either be 28 or 43, and he needs to know which.

Tatler 210b. NF. _____. *St. James's Coffee-house, August 11.*

Further reports on events abroad.

Tatler 211. Tuesday, August 15, 1710. Steele. *Sunday, August 13.*

Bickerstaff says that if men and women simply got together on Sunday in church with their minds at leisure from the cares of this life and their bodies dressed in their best attire then that would be sufficient justification for the Sunday observance, but it is made an especially good occasion by the added mention of devotion and contemplation of the next life, which helps a person avoid corrupting his present life in the other six days of the week. Although it is possible to pretend to devotion, it is harder to pretend to this particular quality than to other human qualities. Although Lotius tries not to appear pious, his efforts in behalf of others suggests that there is some piety in him. Caelicola is a man of great wisdom, yet he delivers his decisions not as a wise man but as a humble man. Bickerstaff concludes with a quotation from Dr. South, to the effect that the pleasure of the religious man is the greatest pleasure of all.

Tatler 212. Thursday, August 17, 1710. Steele. *From my own Apartment, August 16.*

Bickerstaff prints a letter from Plain English in which the correspondent asks him to explain the nature of a truly well-dressed woman (see *Tatler* 151). Bickerstaff answers that a simplicity of manners is the highest achievement of a woman; appropriate dress reflects this quality, so that her distinction is due to her manner rather than to her dress. Unfortunately, some women such as Araminta, always try for an effect, and therefore never appear before their husbands without a hood on. The lean Miss Gruel makes herself less attractive than she might be because she deliberately wears her hair in the modern fashion. Flavia, on the other hand, exemplifies the proper relationship between composure of looks, dignity of thought, and naturalness of dress. Bickerstaff also receives a letter from J. L., in which the writer says that he was surprised by a man wearing a mask; he thought the man a thief, but he made no such attempt. Bickerstaff responds that the man had just recovered from smallpox. The correspondent of *Tatler* 210 who was asked for the exact length of her maidenhood responds that she is 28 years old and in the twelfth year of her virginity. The correspondent also wants to know if a woman may live as a maid any more years than she is courted. Another correspondent writes to ask Bickerstaff to explain the phrase, "He expressed as much bravery as conduct."

Tatler 213a. Saturday, August 19, 1710. Steele. *Sheer Lane, August 16.*

Bickerstaff says that he finds he must explain the distinction between simulation, a pretense of what is not, and disimulation, a concealment of what is. Bickerstaff is particularly concerned that some Englishmen are trying to appear to have evil habits which they really do not. Tom Springly recently pretended to have a romantic meeting with a married woman; he was seen shortly thereafter reading the responses at Evening Prayer.

Tatler 213b. _____. *Sheer Lane, August 17.*

Bickerstaff receives a letter from Richard Traffic, who says he is offended by the portrait Bickerstaff drew of his young merchant in *Tatler* 207. He says that merchants can make heroic lovers and tells a story of Tom Trueman to illustrate his point. The young gentleman, having fallen in love with the beautiful Almeira, his master's daughter, discovered that the merchant who was employing him was about to go bankrupt. Trueman went abroad and was able to save the merchant 10,000 pounds. Shortly thereafter Trueman's uncle left the young man a considerable estate, so that he could ask Almeira's father to let her marry him. Trueman was granted the wish; the father also offered to turn over the business and the 10,000 pounds to the young man. Trueman refused both, and retired to the country with his bride. Because he had refused a woman who would bring with her 20,000 pounds, Trueman's love of Almeira cost him 30,000 pounds. Charles Lillie notes that Mr. Thomas Trueman is henceforth entered among the heroes of domestic life.

Tatler 214. Tuesday, August 22, 1710. Steele. *From my own Apartment, August 21.*

Bickerstaff says that in every party there are two sorts of men: the rigid, who act upon principle and will not change under any circumstances; and the supple, who change their opinions according to the needs of the day. Because sometimes things can change very quickly, Bickerstaff has devised a Political Barometer, a State Weather-Glass, which anticipates all changes and revolutions in government through the rising and falling of a magical liquid. After many changes, Bickerstaff is delighted that his glass has lately returned to Settled Fair. He quotes Virgil's Aeneas (*Aeneid*, Book VI, ll. 103 ff.) to the effect that as a result of his glass he anticipates changes in fortune. Some friends of Bickerstaff's have used his knowledge of political changes to increase their wealth; Bickerstaff says that he uses it to know when to retire from public life.

Tatler 215a. Thursday, August 24, 1710. Steele. *From my own Apartment, August 23.*

Lysander reports to Bickerstaff from the country that his life of retirement and quiet has been interrupted

by a flatterer while he was reading Virgil's *Georgics*.
Bickerstaff sees this as an example of superficial human
behavior, which results from acting all the time in a
way that is occasionally pleasing. A lady from Bath
reports on her journey where she was bothered by a common flatterer and a common jester. Both these two, who
have annoyed Corinna, are the results of a barrenness
of imagination. Bickerstaff prints a letter from Rebecca
Midriffe, who relates the sad case of her elder sister,
a widow for six months, who has remarried. She is now
about to give birth to a child and wonders which husband
is the legal father. Bickerstaff says it is a difficult
case but that although there is no remedy for the mother,
the law gives the child the right to chose the father.

Tatler 215b. _____. Addendum.

Bickerstaff prints a petition from the Company of Linen
Drapers protesting the new-fashioned women going essentially naked above the waist. The greatest offender is
Mrs. Arabella Overdo; as a result of this the petitioners
are in the danger of losing the advantage of covering a
ninth part of every woman of quality in Great Britain.
Bickerstaff says that before he answers this petition
he wishes to examine the offenders himself.

Tatler 216a. Saturday, August 26, 1710. Addison. *From my
own Apartment, August 25.*

Bickerstaff says that nature is full of wonders; therefore, he would not discourage the exploration of any of
its aspects. The study of small things, however, should
be a diversion and not the central activity of one's
life. Bickerstaff calls those who devote themselves
entirely to the study of trivial and insignificant things
by the title of Virtuoso. He presents the will of
Nicholas Gimcrack, a Virtuoso, who leaves his wife a
box of butterflies, his daughter Elizabeth a recipe for
preserving dead caterpillars, his daughter Fanny three
crocodile eggs. To his friends and other relations he
leaves equally insignificant items.

Tatler 216b. _____. Advertisement.

Bickerstaff says that in spite of the presence of im-
posters, John Partridge continues to be dead.

Tatler 217a. Tuesday, August 29, 1710. Steele. *From my
own Apartment, August 28.*

Bickerstaff says that overhearing a conversation while
passing a neighbor's house reminds him that he needs to
comment upon a particularly outrageous group of women
who are known as Scolds. Such women always insist that
their modesty has been insulted, while they violate a
basic cannon of modesty by their outrageous vocal

behavior. The Bully and the Scold are male and female versions of the same basic attitude of mind. To illustrate the nature of this situation, Bickerstaff retells in contemporary language a conversation between Adam and Eve from Milton's *Paradise Lost*, Book IX. One cure for this behavior would be for the woman in question to see herself raging in a mirror; Lady Firebrand was so upset by her appearance that she broke the mirror.

Tatler 217b. _____. Advertisement.

Bickerstaff promises to be wittier than he has been of late, such improvement to begin as of October 1.

Tatler 218. Thursday, August 31, 1710. Addison. *From my own Apartment, August 30.*

Bickerstaff describes an early morning walk in the country; he is reminded of a passage in Milton's *Paradise Lost*, Book IX, 11. 445 ff. Driven to take shelter by a sudden rain storm, Bickerstaff overhears two or three men discussing ancient and modern heroes. The conversation turns out not to be about men but about tulips, which the gardeners have named after great men. Bickerstaff finds that the flowers he likes are not the ones valued by the gardeners; Bickerstaff finds one of the gardeners to be afflicted with Tulippomania, signifying that he is rational on every subject except tulips. Bickerstaff returns home feeling great pleasure in the bounty of Providence in giving man such beautiful things to look at.

Tatler 219a. Saturday, September 2, 1710. Steele. *From my own Apartment, September 1.*

While Bickerstaff praises an easy manner of conversation, he objects strenuously to something he saw this evening when two wits imposed themselves upon a gentleman whom they did not know, yet treated him as if they knew him well. Tom Mercett is such a wit; he thinks it pleasant to say to a man's face what his enemies say about him behind his back, so long as he says it in a witty and pleasant manner. Bickerstaff believes conversation one of the great delights of life; unfortunately, Mercett disrupts conversation because his sole ambition is to be witty rather than to be pleasing. Bickerstaff's reflections on conversation are interrupted by the delivery of a letter from a lady who objects to Bickerstaff's translation of the speech between Adam and Eve (*Tatler* 217). She scolds Bickerstaff, but promises to forgive him if he will describe Mrs. Sissy Trippit according to the description which she provides.

Tatler 219b. _____. Addendum.

Joshua, because he is a general lover who has put a great deal of money into clean gloves for offering his hand to ladies, wishes to be known as an esquire; Bickerstaff agrees.

Tatler 220. Tuesday, September 5, 1710. Addison. *From my own Apartment, September 4.*

Having been praised for his Political Barometer, Bickerstaff now describes his Ecclesiastical Thermometer, the purpose of which is to predict changes and revolutions in the church. The Thermometer, having been invented at the time of the English Reformation, is now used to distinguish between the High and Low Parties in the church. The scale on the thermometer runs from Ignorance to Ignorance through Persecution, Wrath, Zeal, Church, Moderation, Lukewarmness, and Infidelity. Bickerstaff records fluctuations in the thermometer around London and throughout England.

Tatler 221. Thursday, September 7, 1710. Addison. *From my own Apartment, September 6.*

Bickerstaff receives a letter from Lady Gimcrack, telling of the life and death of her eccentric husband (*Tatler* 216a). He also receives a letter from a lady who agrees with Bickerstaff that the Scold is a lamentable creature, but says she has found it extremely hard to break this habit. Bickerstaff says that he has recently made the acquaintance of a doctor who proposes to cure all vices and defects of the mind by inward medicines or outward applications. To cure the Scold, he has instructed a cold bath, arranged with a long pole so that a Scold may be totally immersed in the cold water a number of times until she has lost completely the power of speech. A woman who enters the bath with a passionate tongue emerges from it "as silent and gentle as a lamb."

Tatler 222. NF. Saturday, September 9, 1710. Addison. *From my own Apartment, September 8.*

Bickerstaff reports that letters from Nottingham have informed him that young ladies of that city have been kept up late at night by riotous lovers who perform with violins and bass-viols in the streets between the hours of 12:00 and 4:00 in the morning. Bickerstaff finds that young Britons have a natural tendency to break windows; when they grow older, they fall in love and tend to enjoy languishing under them. Considering the climate of England, this habit of singing late at night under one's lady's window is an unnatural way of acting in England. Bickerstaff believes that the custom originated in Italy, where eunuchs started it as a way of expressing their love for their mistresses, while men of hoarser voices were expressing their passions in other ways. Italy is an appropriate place for such activities to originate because of the soft climate and because of the innate musical genius of the Italians. Unfortunately, if the British lover practices this kind of courtship for very long, he will die of some disease contracted in the early morning air. Bickerstaff finds a Miltonic allusion to such practice (*Paradise Lost*, Book IV, 11. 760 ff.). Englishmen, however, have such a lack of musical talent that they only find themselves wishing to sing when they are drunk.

Tatler 223. Tuesday, September 12, 1710. Steele. *From my own Apartment, September 11.*

Bickerstaff is urged by Clarinda, Flavia, and Lysetta to present his proposal for marrying off all the unmarried women of England. Bickerstaff feels that the legal and financial complications of marriage are the source of much of its unhappiness. He proposes that the Legislature fix a set value on every woman, with different rates for the maid and the widow, so that if we are in fact to buy and sell women, it will be done justly. Bickerstaff proposes some rules for the settlement of financial affairs in marriage, and says that all men who break them shall become Pretty Fellows, Smarts, Squibs, H-Horns, Drums, and Bagpipes, while all women who break the laws shall become Kits, Hornpipes, Dulcimers, and Kettle-drums. Bickerstaff believes that making marriage cheap and easy will go a long way toward discouraging the vices which now surround it.

Tatler 224. NF. Thursday, September 14, 1710. Addison. *From my own Apartment, September 13.*

Bickerstaff says that when news is otherwise in short supply, he delights in the advertisements in the newspapers which he sees as conveying the news about the mercantile world in much the way that the regular part of the newspaper conveys news of the political and social world. Advertising is one way in which small men have of getting on the same pages with great men who make political and social news. Advertisements also are places in which controversies among merchants can be carried out. Advertisements are also a place in which the world can be told where it may get anything it needs for all the ills and necessities of life. The art of writing advertisements involves catching the eyes of the reader and in using a style which will make its claims convincing. Bickerstaff presents an advertisement for lavender as an example of skill in this form. Bickerstaff objects to some advertisements including one for Carminative, Wind-expelling pills.

Tatler 225a. Saturday, September 16, 1710. Steele. *From my own Apartment, September 15.*

Bickerstaff praises conversation as one of the most pleasant activities of life, but he objects to those

who use the familiarity of conversation to say unpleasant things about the person one is conversing with.
Such indiscreet familiarity is practiced by Eusebius,
who has wit, humor, and spirit, but who puts all these
to the end of making himself and those he converses with
feel contemptible. The goal of good conversation is to
hide rather than to uncover the infirmities of oneself
and one's friends. Bickerstaff also receives a letter
from Plain English who says that he has already started
being more witty, not putting off this until the first
of October. Bickerstaff says that he has changed his
plan and intends to be witty until the first day of
October.

Tatler 225b. NF. _____. *St. James's Coffee-house,
September 15.*

Another report on foreign events.

Tatler 226. Tuesday, September 19, 1710. Addison. *From my
own Apartment, September 18.*

Following his plan to transmit to posterity accounts of
everything monstrous in his own time, Bickerstaff presents a letter from a correspondent who tells the story
of Margery, who practiced medicine in men's clothing
under the name of Dr. John Young. The correspondent
compares her with Kirleus (see *Tatler* 14), but says that
a she-quack is a strange creature indeed. She is described as an Aesculapius without a beard and is said
to have resembled certain statues of Apollo. Having had
an illegitimate child early in life, Margery went to
London to recover her reputation, but instead became a
man and then a doctor. Because of her attempts to disguise her voice, she became known as the Squeaking Doctor; she married twice, both of the wives having children. Saltero, who has a museum in Chelsea, has on display a curiosity which enabled the doctor to carry on
his/her imposture.

Tatler 227. Thursday, September 21, 1710. Addison. *From
my own Apartment, September 20.*

Bickerstaff reports on a visit from a young man who is
jealous of his cousin, since both of them hope to in-
herit the estate of an uncle. Bickerstaff praises the
young man for admitting his jealousy and hopes that
through conversation the young man's envy can be changed
into emulation. Bickerstaff notes that only noble minds
can appreciate the good qualities in others; shallow
minds can only see their faults. Bickerstaff says that
Milton's devil (*Paradise Lost*, Book IV, 11. 358 ff.) is
similarly incapable of being pleased by the paradise of
God's creation.

Tatler 228. Saturday, September 23, 1710. Steele. *From my own Apartment, September 22.*

Apologizing for not having anything of his own to contribute, Bickerstaff turns this paper over to his correspondents. The first letter is from High Church, who wishes for advice because he has been offered a well-paying position if he will also marry Mrs. Abagail. He wonders how the body of Mrs. Abagail can be annexed to the cure of souls. Bickerstaff sees no problem with this, since many noblemen have married the daughters of wealthy merchants with the same goals in mind. T. Philomath writes that he is about to issue his almanac for the next year and wishes Bickerstaff to lend him the state weather-glass so that he may forecast political weather instead of regular weather. Bickerstaff refuses this request. A third correspondent says that he is planning to set himself up as a writer of advertisements and offers Bickerstaff some samples of his work, which Bickerstaff presents without comment.

Tatler 229. Tuesday, September 26, 1710. Addison. *From my own Apartment, September 25.*

Bickerstaff notices that all of creation preys upon itself; every creature has creatures who live upon him. This comforts Bickerstaff because of all the small wits and scribblers who have found employment by commenting upon Bickerstaff's work. Bickerstaff says that many people would be out of work if he quit writing his paper; he, however, threatens to deal harshly with those who do not appreciate what he has done for them. He tells the story of a fox, who when troubled with fleas, goes into a pool of water with a piece of wool in his mouth, stays under water until all the fleas have moved to the piece of wool, and then casts off the wool. He quotes Spenser's *Faerie Queene*, Book I, canto I, vs. 22 & 23 to illustrate his point. He also tells a fable of owls, bats, and other birds of the night who get together and abuse their neighbors, including the sun. The sun retorts that he could burn all of them up, but will have his revenge by simply shining on.

Tatler 230. Thursday, September 28, 1710. Steele and Swift. *From my own Apartment, September 27.*

Bickerstaff receives a letter from a man, learned in languages, who expertly lays open many of the faults in everyday speech and grammar. The correspondent objects to authors of works in history, politics, and the *belles lettres*, they exhibit ignorance and want of taste as well as corruption of the English tongue. The correspondent presents a letter written in the style he objects to; the letter refers to Tom, the French King, the Jacks, and Will Hazzard and is filled with misspellings, slang expressions, and outrageous grammatical constructions. He urges Bickerstaff to publish an annual *Index*

Expurgatorius, which would list all corruptions of the language.

Tatler 231. Saturday, September 30, 1710. Steele. *From my own Apartment, September 29.*

Bickerstaff tells the story of a gentleman in Lincoln-shire whose ill-tempered daughter is tamed by her husband. He comes to fetch the ill-tempered daughter while riding on a skeleton of a horse, tended only by a favored hound. When the dog does not do what he is ordered to do, the master shoots him dead. Soon after the horse stumbles and is run through by the gentleman with his sword. The wife is forced to drag the saddle home. Shortly thereafter, at an assembly, the lady displays her new-found devotion to the wishes of her husband. Bickerstaff also receives a letter, with a dozen bottles of wine, saying that more of this vintage will be sold on Thursday following. The correspondent claims that Will Hazzard was cured of his hypochondria by three glasses of the wine; it has proven to have other medicinal purposes. Bickerstaff tries it with some friends and approves it in every way.

Tatler 232a. Tuesday, October 3, 1710. Steele. *From my own Apartment, October 2.*

Bickerstaff receives a letter from his friend the Political Upholsterer, who is more deeply involved in foreign affairs than ever. He gives Bickerstaff a brief summary of current events, and evaluates for him the current newspapers. Bickerstaff comments that the Upholsterer's devotion to the King of Sweden has reduced him to a low condition of both reason and fortune. Bickerstaff is concerned that political arguments have been taken up by the silliest of women and that they are having a negative effect on relationships between women and their lovers.

Tatler 232b. _____. Advertisement.

Bickerstaff announces that he has received Silvia's letter from Bath and promises that Tom Frontley will bring her into the company of the city.

Tatler 233. NF. Thursday, October 5, 1710. Steele. *From my own Apartment, October 4.*

Bickerstaff says that a good way to calm anxiety is to think about the adversities and misfortunes of people higher on the social scale than oneself; by this means the problems of the lives of people in lower stations will appear more insignificant. As an example, Bicker-staff retells the story of Joseph (Genesis, Chap. 37 ff.). Bickerstaff especially elaborates on the emotional reunion of Joseph and Benjamin in Egypt.

Tatler 234. Saturday, October 7, 1710. Steele. *From my own Apartment, October 6.*

Bickerstaff receives a letter from a man who finds the cause of the English failings in language and speech to lie in the faulty school system; he especially objects to too-early training in Latin and Greek, and proposes instead an early and thorough grounding in the native tongue. The correspondent recounts a story in which a certain author brought a poem to Mr. Cowley, who instructed the author to attend to the poem's grammar. The author protested that he did not wish to go back to school, whereupon Cowley told him that it would not do him any harm. Bickerstaff also receives a letter from W. E. who urges that those who stay away from church in the winter should pay the doctors' bills of those who come to the cold, empty churches and catch cold.

Tatler 235. Tuesday, October 10, 1710. Steele. *From my own Apartment, October 9.*

Bickerstaff is concerned about families in which parents distinguish their children from each other by loving them unequally. Bickerstaff gives as an example a household of his acquaintance, in which the father adores the eldest daughter, Mrs. Mary, for her wit and beauty, and the mother loves the youngest daughter, Mrs. Biddy, for her coquettish manner. Therefore they ignore Mrs. Betty, the middle daughter, who has therefore become a woman of a great deal of merit and is the favorite of everyone who knows the family. Another unfortunate situation arises when a parent praises his own children at the expense of all others. Lady Goodly loves all her children the same, but she constantly finds fault with the children of others. Her daughter Betty cannot dance as well as Mrs. Frontinett, but she is much more the gentlewoman; by the same token Mrs. Rebecca is not as witty as Mrs. Clapper, yet she is the better person because she is more discreet. Bickerstaff says he only knows of one family of his acquaintance in which the father lives gracefully with his children; his method is to urge kindness among the children and promise that he would consider the best child the one that was the best brother or sister.

Tatler 236. Thursday, October 12, 1710. Steele. *From my own Apartment, October 11.*

T. B., an Irish relative of Bickerstaff's, writes Isaac from Dublin to tell him the history of the migration of frogs into Ireland. All the Irish frogs having been expelled by St. Patrick, a number of virtuosos during the reign of King Charles II attempted to return them to that country. Unfortunately, the first frog brought back got seasick off the Irish coast, while the second died on a Rings End car on the way to Dublin. All other

191

attempts failed, until an ingenious physician and a good protestant, to show his zeal against popery, brought several barrels of frogs to Ireland where they have since overrun the country. Bickerstaff concludes that much mischief in England has been done by the fellows of the Royal Society, who consist of men opposed to nobility and breadth of learning, instead favoring narrowness and dullness.

Tatler 237. Saturday, October 14, 1710. Steele. *From my own Apartment, October 13.*

Bickerstaff reports that he returned home early and spent the time before bedtime reading Milton's *Paradise Lost*, Book IV. He is especially struck by the description of Ithuriel's spear (ll. 797-819) which he thinks would be a great advantage for any Minister of State. Having read this passage, he falls asleep and dreams that he has the spear and that he uses it to test the truthfulness or falsity of people he meets. One lady who seems to be modest and demure turns out to be a mere prostitute, while another turns out not to be the virgin she claims to be. He tests with the spear a number of people; only one turns out to be what he claims to be. Unfortunately that person is a man who boasts of his debauches and his affronts to religion. In general those who appear good disappoint him when tested by the wand of truthfulness, while those who appear bad anyway turn out to be worse. He is delighted that two people of great reputation turn out to be worthy of it. Upon waking from the dream he is delighted to remember that when he took the spear in hand he who was an old, decrepit man turned out to be a very handsome, jolly, well-dressed man.

Tatler 238. Tuesday, October 17, 1710. Steele and Swift. *From my own Apartment, October 16.*

Bickerstaff says that storms at sea are so frequently described by ancient poets and copied by modern poets that descriptions of storms in modern poetry are well worth skipping over. While Bickerstaff says that Virgil has achieved the best sea-storm with his Tempest and the best Land-Shower poem as well, he will devote the rest of this paper to presenting the description of a City Shower, done by his kinsman Mr. Humphrey Wagstaff. The poem describes the coming of the shower and the consequences of its washing the garbage out of the city.

Tatler 239. Thursday, October 19, 1710. Addison. *From my own Apartment, October 18.*

Bickerstaff says that no man should criticize the work of another if he has not distinguished himself by his own performances. He is especially concerned by a modern who has criticized him by trying to show that Horace

and Virgil were more modest than Isaac, and that Isaac
is a very conceited old fellow, as vain as Cicero or Sir
Francis Bacon. Bickerstaff says he does not mind the
attacks on him, but is particularly concerned about the
attacks on Cicero. He presents the criticism directed
against him by this writer. Bickerstaff finds the criticism ridiculous, and says it is analogous to the performance of a wag whom he met in a coffee-house; the
wag criticized a poem of Atterbury by finding in it a
ridiculous description of Flavia, where in fact the
poem is gentle, delicate, and beautiful. After responding vigorously to the criticism, Bickerstaff promises
his reader to ignore such in the future and spend all of
his time in caring for the public morality.

Tatler 240. Saturday, October 21, 1710. Addison. *From my
own Apartment, October 20.*

Bickerstaff praises medicine, and says that he himself
has joined the study of astrology to that of medical
science. Bickerstaff also claims that poetry and medicine have the same foundation--that is, good sense.
Bickerstaff argues that it adds to a man's credibility
if he is a master of two different sciences; quacks and
charlatans know this and always lay claim to a wide range
of accomplishments. Bickerstaff describes one doctor
whose advertising argued that he knew of the green and
red dragon, and had discovered the female fern seed; the
connection between this and the practice of medicine was
unclear, but it helped the man to a successful practice.
Another succeeded by posting the word Tetrachymagogon,
which also attracted curiosity and business. Some benefit from oddities of birth such as being the seventh son
of the seventh son or not having been born at all such
as the Unborn Doctor. Others succeed in combining medicine and poetry, such as Dr. Case, who advertised as
follows:
> *Within this place*
> Lives Dr. Case.

Bickerstaff points out that if doctors tend to deal in
poetry, then apothecaries tend to deal in oratory. Bickerstaff says that his cure for most things is abstinence.
While a colleague has proposed a pill against the earth-
quake, Bickerstaff says that many would be helped by a
fortnight of water-gruel.

Tatler 241a. Tuesday, October 24, 1710. Steele. *From my
own Apartment, October 23.*

Bickerstaff regrets that the art of spending one's time
agreeably is so little thought about that what most people do is drink. A drunkard is a vicious person; therefore, Bickerstaff proclaims all drunkards suicides.
Drunkards never know the satisfaction of youth, but skip
directly from childhood to manhood and are as decrepit

as soon as they are of age. Bickerstaff says that he
is one of these gentleman's godfather; the man in question, now thirty-three, is already an old man. The
worst situation is when the drunkard is married; the
wretched Astrea, the perfection of beauty, is condemned
to a life-sentence of being married to a drunkard.
B. B. writes Bickerstaff to urge his attention to a matter at St. Paul's; many of the congregation have lapsed
into an unconcerned silence and motionless posture.
Scoto-Britannus writes to object to a man who uses ex-
cessively the phrase, "The best of any man in England."

Tatler 241b. _____. Advertisement.

Bickerstaff says that Humphrey Trelooby has protested
that he was defrauded of half-a-crown which he was
charged for a tour of the Cathedral of St. Paul while
wearing his own hair, a pair of buck-skin breeches, and
a hunting-whip. Bickerstaff says that no one can charge
a country gentleman under the age of 25 more than six
pence for a tour of the cathedral.

Tatler 242. Thursday, October 26, 1710. Steele. *From my
own Apartment, October 25.*

Bickerstaff is upset to hear a companion praise Tom
for his spiteful wit and satire. Bickerstaff argues
that good-nature is necessary for the best satirist.
The proper objects of satire are those which incite
the best minds to the greatest indignation. Bickerstaff
believes the best satirists to have been Horace and
Juvenal; he gives a brief summary of each man's career.
Unfortunately, Bickerstaff finds that many people who
try to be satirists in the present day are not qualified for this role. The nature of true satire is its
impersonality; when the subject of satire arises from
a personal issue, then it is merely a misunderstanding.
Bickerstaff quotes with pleasure a friend at Oxford who
said that he could not take revenge on a person who had
done him wrong until he had forgiven the person.

Tatler 243. Saturday, October 28, 1710. Addison. *From my
own Apartment, October 27.*

Bickerstaff tells the story of Gyges and his ring (see
Tatler 138). He claims that he now has the ring in his
possession, and makes use of the fact that it makes him
invisible to visit the bedchambers of rakes, coquettes,
and covetous people whom he finds to be very restless
and light sleepers. Bickerstaff finds the covetous man
on his death bed; he is dismayed to discover that the
man's dying words were to ask how bank stock traded on
the Royal Exchange that day. He also visits the bedchamber of a poet whom he thought to be a lunatic because the poet is trying a variety of rhymes. He takes
off the ring and appears in his true person just in time
to frighten a man breaking into a neighbor's house.

Tatler 244. Tuesday, October 31, 1710. Steele. *Will's Coffee-house, October 30.*

Bickerstaff says that he is concerned because many people, while trying to get an education, become eloquent before they have anything to say. Tom Varnish is all rhetoric and no substance; people flock to him because they like to hear his manner of speaking, rather than the content of his speech. Bickerstaff finds other problems with the way men address the world; Urbanus offers his opinions hesitantly, while Umbratilis steals Urbanus' opinions and expresses them with confidence. Bickerstaff finds the enemies to good company are the clown, the wit, and the pedant. The clown tries to be rough and manly, while the wit tries to be sharp and clever and the pedant has read much and understands little.

Tatler 245a. Thursday, November 2, 1710. Steele. *From my own Apartment, November 1.*

Bickerstaff presents a list of stolen goods given him by the Lady Farthingale, stolen from her by her servant Bridget Howd'ee. The list of stolen goods includes all the equipment--clothing, pictures, makeup, needlework, jewelry, and letters--of a coquette. The letters are from Philander, Strephon, Amyntas, Corydon, and Adonis; the lady promises fifty guineas' reward for the return of the whole and ten pounds for the packet of letters alone, with five going to the recoverer of the letters from Philander.

Tatler 245b. _____. Postscript.

Bickerstaff receives a letter from Pompey, a young Turk, now christened, who wishes to know if he should still dress as a Turk.

Tatler 246. Saturday, November 4, 1710. Steele. *From my own Apartment, November 3.*

Bickerstaff says that in spite of all he and others can do, the topic of conversations inevitably seems to turn to the faults of people known to the conversationalist. The problem with this type of conversation, Bickerstaff says, is that all mankind is imperfect; therefore, to say that man is imperfect is to say no more than that he is human. Nevertheless, there are many who need correction; one is a man whom Bickerstaff writes and urges to button his waistcoat from his collar to his waistband in the wintertime. Another Bickerstaff writes urging him to wear his jeweled cross with a black ribbon if it is a token of an absent lover, but if it is a reward for heroism in battle, he may continue to wear it with a red ribbon. Plumbeus and Levis are two people who practice the bad habit of criticizing each other for things they cannot help and overlooking those things

which can be easily changed. In addition, each is trying to become something that he cannot be and refusing
to become that which he can. Another problem is the
old, who instead of thinking of how well they spent
their lives, spend their time being concerned about the
ridicule of those younger than they. Dick Reptile urges
old men to say to their younger critics, "Prithee don't
mind him; tell him thou art mortal."

Tatler 247. Tuesday, November 7, 1710. Steele. *From my
own Apartment, November 6.*

Jenny Distaff, Bickerstaff's half-sister, answers a letter from Disconsolate Almeira, who says that a young
gentleman has for some time courted her, but refuses to
take the step of asking her to marry him. She wishes
to tell him good-by, but would like Bickerstaff's advice.
Jenny says that the woman is afflicted by the most common of any evil that attends womankind; Almeira is subject to the common failing of women, which is to value
the merit of their lovers based on the grace of their
address rather than the sincerity of their hearts.
Women should judge men according to their reputation
among other men; in this way they will avoid finding
themselves married to the outcast of the male sex. Jenny
says some of the fault for men behaving this way is due
to the taste of the wits in the previous generation,
since a libertine on the throne helped to make the language and the fashion turn in emulation of his behavior.
Unfortunately, she says that some of the fault must lie
with women, who all too frequently are drawn to the one
who is most lovely rather than the man who acts the best.
Jenny concludes with a story of Clarinda, who, being
wooed by a Strephon, a man of sense and knowledge of the
world, and Cassio, who is rich and wise, fell in love
with Damon, who was neither, at a ball; from that point
on, the most reasonable of women became the most unrea-
sonable.

Tatler 248. Thursday, November 9, 1710. Steele. *From my
own Apartment, November 8.*

Bickerstaff describes a lady he met while riding in En-
field Chase, who ability, beauty, and grace he finds
unforgettable. He says that outdoor activities enrich
the beauty of women, as Virgil describes in the *Aeneid*,
Book I, ll. 315 ff. He remembers that Cibber's comedy
The Ladies' Cure describes a woman who tries to appear
unhealthy, but whose natural robustness shines through
her attempts to appear otherwise. Dyctinna, a woman
recently come to town, illustrates the fact that a
healthful body and a cheerful mind make a woman as ir-
resistably charming as she is inimitable. Unfortunately
many women such as Palestris are too lazy or like Lady
Goodday are too busy at trivial things. Bickerstaff
proposes to help the fair sex by establishing a female

library which will divert but also improve women in
their femininity.

Tatler 249. Saturday, November 11, 1710. Addison. *From my
own Apartment, November 10.*

Bickerstaff is visited by a friend who would attack
those men who in trying to be busy all the time engage
in a series of trifling and insignificant actions. He
says that none have been as active as a shilling which
he sees lying on Bickerstaff's table. This incident
provokes a dream which Bickerstaff has upon going to
bed in which the shilling tells its tale. He describes
his adventures from his birth as an ingot in a little
village of Peru, his travel to England in a convoy of
Sir Francis Drake, his being made into a coin with the
face of Queen Elizabeth on it, and his travels from hand
to hand throughout the world. His adventures include
being locked up in a chest by a miser, being held by a
superstitious old woman, being used to raise soldiers
against the King during the Civil Wars, and finally serving as the inspiration for a poem by John Phillips,
entitled "The Splendid Shilling."

Tatler 250. Tuesday, November 14, 1710. Addison. *From my
own Apartment, November 13.*

Bickerstaff recalls his establishing a Court of Justice
last winter, and reviews some of its more celebrated
cases. This year he proposes a Court of Honor, which
he again will preside over. To Bickerstaff's right will
sit several men of honor, while women of virtue will sit
to his left as his assistants. All are invited to appeal for redress to this court who have received short
bows, cold salutations, supercilious looks, unreturned
smiles, distant behavior, or forced familiarity. Other
issues to be decided by the court are how much a man
may wave his cane while telling a story without insult-
ing his hearer, what amount of contradiction does it
take to make a lie, whether a man of honor may take a
blow from his wife, and whether asking pardon is appropriate atonement for treading upon another's toes. For
the purpose of deciding cases in this court, Bickerstaff
has acquired a pair of scales, together with appropriate
weights, which he will use to help him reach decisions.

Tatler 251. NF. Thursday, November 16, 1710. Steele. *From
my own Apartment, November 15.*

In a lengthy essay, in which he quotes Jeremy Collier,
Shakespeare's *Macbeth* (Act II, sc. 2, l. 40), and Abraham Cowley, Bickerstaff argues that the satisfaction
with one's own thoughts is necessary to an easy and
happy life. The way to this state, he argues, is to
judge ourselves by our own standards and not by those
of the rest of the world.

Tatler 252. Saturday, November 18, 1710. Steele. *From my own Apartment, November 17.*

Bickerstaff presents a letter from a man who criticizes him for being too harsh on those who drink wine (*Tatler* 241a). The writer argues that wine frequently is necessary for releasing man's wit, when used in moderation, as it does with an acquaintance of the writer. Bickerstaff agrees that wine may frequently elevate a conversation to the level of wit and good humor, but he argues that Caska goes too far when he adds the effects of drinking to his natural impudence. Sir Geoffrey Wildacre also goes too far when he takes his son drinking with him. Bickerstaff says that the key is moderation, in drinking as in all things. He also presents a letter from Ralph and Bridgett Yokefellow, in which the writers ask why certain things are required in education, even when the student is not gifted in that direction. Their son and their daughter are being asked to learn to play the spinet and to make verses, while the girl has no ear and the boy is a blockhead.

Tatler 253. Tuesday, November 21, 1710. Addison and Steele. *From my own Apartment, November 20.*

Bickerstaff presents an extract of the *Journal of the Court of Honor*, prepared by Charles Lillie. Lillie describes the assembly of the Court of Honor; twelve men of the Horse Guards are impanelled as the jury, with Mr. Alexander Truncheon, as the foreman. After a moment of silence, Mr. Bickerstaff addresses the jury, and argues that while the streets are filled with crimes of all sorts, the most serious are those for which there is no legal remedy. This court, he says, will address itself to the points of honor; those arguing before the court are urged to speak simply and directly, avoiding excessive verbiage and the words *also* and *likewise.*

Tatler 254. Thursday, November 23, 1710. Addison and Steele. *From my own Apartment, November 22.*

Bickerstaff declares his delight in travel-books, especially those of Sir John Mandeville and Ferdinand Mendez Pinto. Bickerstaff retells an adventure from Mandeville's work in which the traveler and the crew of the ship he is sailing on land in a place where it is so cold that their words freeze in the air before they reach the ears of the one to whom they are spoken. Eventually, when the weather warms enough for the frozen words to melt, all the things that had been spoken are finally heard, although at inappropriate times. Some of the things which are now heard were originally said in private, so that a number of romances, heretofore concealed, are now revealed. The melting words of the English language hiss with the *s*'s of the English language, the Dutch

unfrozen words sound harsh, and the French words dis-
solve so quickly upon melting that no one ever hears
them.

Tatler 255. Saturday, November 25, 1710. Addison. *From my
own Apartment, November 24.*

Bickerstaff receives a letter from a clergyman asking
his advice on the place of sweetmeats in his diet; Bickerstaff responds by saying there is no reason why clergy
should not eat dessert as readily as any man. Bickerstaff says that the custom of the clergy retiring before
dessert began by accident and should be dropped. Bickerstaff says that special treatment of the clergy deters
many able men from entering that profession; he quotes a
poem by Oldham, which addresses itself to this point.

Tatler 256. Tuesday, November 28, 1710. Addison and Steele.

Bickerstaff presents a copy, done by Charles Lillie, of
the *Journal of the Court of Honor.* The first case is
that of Thomas Gules, who indicts Peter Plumb, for putting on his hat while Gules is left bare-headed for two
seconds. Plumb is punished by forfeiting his hat to the
Court and by being forbidden the use of the streets of
London by him or any of his family, who must all remain
in their coaches. Dathan, a peddling Jew, and T. R., a
Welshman, are indicted by the keeper of an alehouse in
Westminster for breaking the peace and two earthen mugs
in a dispute about the antiquities of their families.
They are punished by being tossed in the same blanket.
Richard Newman is indicted by Major Punto for using the
words, "Perhaps it may be so," during a dispute with the
Major. Bickerstaff proclaims the great harm which has
come to England by the use of the word *lie* and bans it
from use in the language.

Tatler 257. Thursday, November 30, 1710. Addison and Steele.
From my own Apartment, November 29.

Bickerstaff says that while every nation is distinguished
by its peculiar productions, Great Britain is especially
noted for its varieties of religions, which are currently
on display in a wax works now touring Germany. Bickerstaff receives description of this exhibit from a friend,
who does so in elaborate detail. The curtain before the
exhibition contains a tapestry showing a many-headed
hydra; the music is produced by a discordant collection
of an organ, a bag-pipe, a groaning-board, a stentorophonic
trumpet, and several other disagreeably-sounding wind
instruments. The show consists of seven figures, the
central one of which is a woman, cheerful and dignified,
dressed in the garments of Queen Elizabeth's time. This
figure represents the Church of England, while a woman
next to her covered with ornaments and with a painted
face represents Popery. On the other side of the woman

representing the Church of England is another woman,
sickly and splenetic, who represents Presbyterianism.
A man counting money among the ruins of the temple represents Judaism, while a half-naked, awkward country
wench represents Deism. A man looking with horror at
a silver basin of water represents Anabaptism, while a
man in very plain garb represents Quakerism. Another
group represents the Family of Love, while yet another
group represents the Sweet Singers of Israel. Across
from these figures, and many other figures representing
other varieties of English religion, is a statue dressed
in a fool's coat pointing at the group, laughing and
shaking his bells.

Tatler 258. Saturday, December 2, 1710. Steele. *From my
own Apartment, December 1.*

Bickerstaff presents a number of letters, including one
from J. S., M. P. and N. R., in which the correspondents
ask if Bickerstaff really intends for them to use the
word British instead of English and Scot. The letter
uses this distinction over and over in an attempt to
make it ridiculous. Another letter objects to a
neighbor's use of the phrase, "A person of my quality."
Another letter, from a young lady, asks the use of
Ithuriel's spear to determine which of her lovers loves
her best. Bickerstaff wonders if a touch of her fan
would have the same effect as a touch of the spear.
T. W. writes that he has been treated better since Bickerstaff wrote in favor of treating clergymen with honor
and allowing them to eat sweetmeats. Q. Z. writes to
praise Bickerstaff's account of Nova Zembla (*Tatler* 254)
and the story of Talicotius (*Tatler* 260) in which is
more of the same. Th. Cl. writes to propose a plan for
dealing with the large number of single people in the
country.

Tatler 259. Tuesday, December 5, 1710. Addison and Steele.

Charles Lillie continues his *Journal of the Court of
Honor.* Elizabeth Makebate is indicted for stealing the
hassock from under Lady Grave-Airs; she is also accused
of stealing the petticoat of Mrs. Mary Doelittle. The
lady is convicted and forced to plead for mercy before
the court. The first lady of the women's jury begs
permission, since women cannot get dressed before church
is half over, to send in a footman to keep their places
until they arrive. Charles Cambric is indicted for
speaking obscenely to Lady Penelope Touchwood. The
accused is a linen-draper, who is charged with discussing women's underwear in the presence of the lady; he
is forced to stand in the court gagged, while the lady
stands opposite him with her hands to her ears. Edward
Callicot is indicted as an accomplice of Cambric, but
is acquitted. Josias Shallow is indicted by Dame Winifred Dainty, for ruining her reputation by paying court

to her. The jury judges him Ignoramus. Ursula Good-
enough is accused by the Lady Betty Wouldbe, for saying
that she is painted. Upon discovering that the lady
brought the charge only to have her complexion compli-
mented, the woman is ordered to wear her mask for five
months. Benjamin Buzzard is indicted for telling Lady
Everbloom that she looked well for a woman of her years.

Tatler 260. Thursday, December 7, 1710. Addison and Steele.
From my own Apartment, December 6.

Bickerstaff says that Montaigne has discussed thumbs in
his *Essays* and Swift has discussed ears in his *Tale of
A Tub*; he will present an essay on the subject of noses,
taking a text from Butler's *Hudibras*. To do so, Bickerstaff tells a fable about a liaison between Mars and
Venus, the result of which was a little Cupid who shot
men's noses instead of their hearts. To repair diseased
noses, Bickerstaff relates, Talicotius began the practice of repairing them by grafting skin. To avoid the
problem which he encountered early on of creating a mismatch in the color of skin between the new nose and the
old face, he gathered a group of skin-donors of all
complexions. The skin for the noses always came from
servants, creating a situation in which for the first
time servants led their betters by the nose. One unfortunate Englishman of Bickerstaff's acquaintance lived
such a prodigal life that he used up five noses. Bickerstaff urges the young men of the town to remember that
nose-replacements are no longer available; they therefore should not act like the ordinary town rakes, who live
as though there were a Talicotius at the corner of every
street.

Tatler 261a. Saturday, December 9, 1710. Steele. *From my
own Apartment, December 8.*

Bickerstaff says that the philosopher must be concerned
with only the most practical proposals for bettering
society and not spend much time with the impractical,
such as that of the renowned Talicotius; those who
spend time on impractical proposals are fit only for
the attentions of the Society of Upholders. A practical proposal, however, is that of Thomas Clement, for
raising 250 pounds to pay every child baptized who is
born in wedlock. Bickerstaff applauds this proposal,
and feels that it will increase the number of legitimate
births in the country. Another practical proposal is
that of a correspondent who proposes to use some of his
lottery winnings to place half-a-dozen youths with Mr.
Moore, a riding master. Bickerstaff also praises one
Celamico, who left his entire estate to a man to whom
he owed no debt.

Tatler 261b. _____. Advertisement.

Bickerstaff gives notice of a coming meeting of the Court of Honor.

Tatler 262. Tuesday, December 12, 1710. Addison and Steele.

This issue continues the *Journal of the Court of Honor.* Timothy Tretall is indicted by several women, friends of his sister, who accuse him of a rude affront by forcing them to sit at the table in order according to their ages. The women, Mrs. Frontly, Widow Partlett, Mrs. Fidget, Mrs. Fescue, and Mrs. Mary Pippe, are successful in their suit because Bickerstaff concludes he has treated a serious matter too lightly, and orders him to treat them to dinner again with all due respect to decorum. Rebecca Shapely is indicted by Mrs. Sarah Smack for saying that she was dressed in an objectionable manner, i.e. that the heels of her silk slippers were two inches high, that she wore a steel bodice, and a false rump. The lady is cleared of wearing the heels and the bodice, but found guilty of the rump; therefore she is punished appropriately. The Lady Elizabeth Prudely is accused by William Trippett of refusing him her hand, as he offered to lead her from her coach. The woman involved is ordered to marry the gentleman or to pay him half-a-crown for gloves and coach-hire. Mrs. Flambeau is accused by a Lady Townly of not visiting her since her marriage to Sir Ralph; because of intricacies of the rules involving visits, Bickerstaff puts the case under advisement. Richard Sly is accused by Winifred Lear of breaking a marriage contract; she alleges that he ogled her twice in opera, three times in St. James' Church and once at Powell's Puppet-Show. Bickerstaff orders the man to be exposed in public as a false ogler. Another false ogler, caught ogling a lady of the grand jury, is seized and prosecuted upon the statute of ogling.

Tatler 263. Thursday, December 14, 1710. Steele. *From my own Apartment, December 13.*

Bickerstaff discovers that an old friend from the country is in town, and he goes to visit at 8:00 in the evening, only to discover that his friend has gone to bed. This provokes Bickerstaff to a discussion of the hours of rising and sleeping in England; he finds that the old hours of going to sleep at 8:00 and rising at 6:00 are still observed by animals and in the universities, but nowhere else in the country. The fashion now is to sleep away the morning and stay awake late into the night. Bickerstaff believes that if man were true to his nature he would be awake while the sun shines and sleep while the sun is set. He is also concerned that the dinner hour has moved back from 12:00 noon until 3:00 in the afternoon, therefore forcing supper to be postponed as well. He believes that the person who does not rise early in the morning misses much of the beauty of nature; to demonstrate this he quotes Milton's passage in *Paradise Lost*, Book V, 11. 1 ff. in which Milton describes the coming of dawn in Paradise.

Tatler 264. Saturday, December 16, 1710. Steele. *From my own Apartment, December 15.*

Bickerstaff quotes Boccalini and John Donne to support his contention that those who are too long-winded in their story-telling do injury to mankind. While an author may be put down when he becomes tedious, a man may be challenged to a duel for walking out on the telling of a story. Bickerstaff says that his kinsman, Mr. Humphrey Wagstaff, argues that the life of man is too short for a story-teller, but he says story-telling is permissible if the teller pleases his audience rather than himself. Bickerstaff declares that he has invented a watch which records minutes instead of hours; each story-teller is allowed three minutes for his story henceforth. The watches are sold by Charles Lillie, with instructions as to their use.

Tatler 265. Tuesday, December 19, 1710. Addison and Steele.

Bickerstaff continues the *Journal of the Court of Honor*, as compiled by Charles Lillie. At this proceeding of the Court, Henry Heedless is indicted by Colonel Touchy because Heedless removed a feather from the shoulder of the Colonel by knocking it off gently with the end of his walking stick. The charge is brought because it is claimed that the shoulder is the tenderest part of a man of honor; Bickerstaff orders the coat of the prisoner to be cleaned of dust by beating it with a stick, and the case is dismissed. Benjamin Busy is indicted by Jasper Tattle for looking at his wife three times while Tattle was giving an account of the funeral of his first wife. Tattle is discovered to be a notorious story-teller, who detained a gentleman this morning to hear several witty things of his five-year-old son. Bickerstaff dismisses the charges and forces the prosecutor to pay damages to the prisoner for the prisoner's losses while listening to this tale. Sir Paul Swash is indicted by Peter Double for not returning a bow given him by Double at the playhouse. Bickerstaff orders the prisoner not to bow to anyone without speaking his name, so that there will be no confusion in public places. Oliver Bluff and Benjamin Browbeat are indicted for fighting a duel. Each is found to be wearing protective armor; when this armor is removed, neither is interested in proceeding with the duel. The court is adjourned until after the holidays.

Tatler 266. Thursday, December 21, 1710. Steele. *From my own Apartment, December 20.*

Claiming that there needs to be a study of the art of growing old, Bickerstaff says that too many aging men, instead of studying to become wiser, persist in being the same sort of fools they were when younger. Bickerstaff finds more foolish old men than old women, because women's goals in life are more easily attainable than men's. A contrary case is presented by Bickerstaff's old friend Sam Trusty, who reports on a visit to the homes of two elderly ladies. The first, Lady Camomile, has taken up the practice of writing to her elderly friends in the neighborhood as though they were young ladies who lived far away; Mrs. Furbish is addressed as Divine Cosmelia, who writes to Lady Camomile as the Charming Lucinda. His second visit is to the home of Mrs. Feeble, the former Betty Frisk, who lives with a shock dog, a monkey, a great grey squirrel, and a parrot. During his visit, the old lady coughs, causing all the animals to break out in loud barking, chirping, and chattering, creating a general uproar. After being bitten by the monkey, Trusty leaves, and promises Bickerstaff that the next woman to make him ridiculous will be a young one.

Tatler 267. NF. Saturday, December 23, 1710. Addison. *From my own Apartment, December 22.*

Remembering that the Roman Catholic Church, as well as the Anglican Church, set aside times of special devotion, Bickerstaff remembers that great Englishmen have always been devout churchmen as well as imminently learned and knowledgable men. His example is Sir Francis Bacon; Bickerstaff presents a prayer written by Bacon, which he feels is appropriate to the Christmas season.

Tatler 268. Tuesday, December 26, 1710. Steele. *From my own Apartment.*

Bickerstaff announces that he has been given a gift of port wine and a petition from Lloyd's Coffee-house, in which the customers propose that a pulpit be installed at every coffee-house in town for the use of coffee-house orators. All announcements of public events, all explanations of political activities, and all discussions of politics, plays, sermons, business, or poetry, take place from this pulpit. Bickerstaff agrees with this proposal, and proposes an additional item for every coffee-house, namely an elbow-chair, into which anyone who tells a story longer than one minute in length be placed. Only two sorts of men would be exempt from being placed in the elbow-chair; the first those who have the skill of parodying and ridiculing the speech of others, and the second those who treat the company and thus pay for their audience. Bickerstaff quotes with pleasure a comment of Epictetus, to the effect that no man should tell his dreams in public. Bickerstaff also quotes Horace and a translation of Horace by Oldham, in which the poet satirizes those who speak so much that they run the risk of being the death of their listeners.

Tatler 269a. Thursday, December 28, 1710. Steele. *From my own Apartment, December 27.*

Bickerstaff promises to be more faithful in responding to his correspondents and gives two letters which demand immediate answers. The first is from Ebenezer, who writes to complain that his beloved is rude and ill-mannered in her treatment of him. Bickerstaff counsels that such behavior is always cured by neglect. Patient Friendly writes to complain of those who make jests of disagreeable subjects and persist in their jests the more the subject is found disagreeable to the listener. Bickerstaff says that such behavior either proceeds from pride or from a barrenness of invention; only those with a poverty of imagination speak obscenely or in such a way that they irritate their listeners.

Tatler 269b. _____. Advertisement.

Bickerstaff reminds Plagius that while he is an excellent preacher, he does not need to be so eloquent with his customary congregation. Mr. Dogood is asked to consider that his story attacks a weakness, and not a folly, of mankind.

Tatler 270a. Saturday, December 30, 1710. Steele. *From my own Apartment, December 29.*

Even though there are many who persist in offending by their manner of dress, Bickerstaff says that he is pleased that others are offended by this as well as he. He presents a letter from his cousin, Felix Tranquillus, in which the writer praises Bickerstaff for his objections to extremes in dress and adds his support to objections to men wearing laced hats, wigs tied up with ribbons, or embroidered coats. Bickerstaff also presents a petition from Ralph Nab, a seller of hats, who writes to object to the use of gold and silver lace on hats, because this custom induces men to wear their hats, thus making them last longer, and because the application of such adornment means that a hat can be worn longer than it should be. Nab proposes that Bickerstaff consider this practice one day in his Court of Honor. Bickerstaff also presents a petition of Elizabeth Slender, in which the writer objects to clergymen who wear long powdered wigs. Bickerstaff says that those who dress in such a way that they appear to be of a higher class of society than they really are betray a

secret vanity. Bickerstaff announces his plans to deal
with Pretty Fellows in Holy Orders. Bickerstaff also
presents a letter, which he obtained from Tom Trot, in
which Penitence Gentle tells Mr. Ralph Incense that she
did not understand half of his sermon but that she found
his manner in the pulpit very fine. She wonders if he
is trying to win her to heaven, or to himself.

Tatler 270b. _____. Advertisements.

Bickerstaff announces that Mr. Proctorstaff is received
as a kinsman, and the distressed son of Aesculapius is
urged to be more particular.

Tatler 271. NF. Tuesday, January 2, 1710-11. Steele.

Richard Steele, being informed by his printer that there
are enough of these papers to make four volumes, declares
that he has come to the end of his desire to address the
world in the character of Isaac Bickerstaff. He says
that his purpose in creating the character of Bickerstaff was to delight his reader and add the weight of
reason to the agreeableness of wit. The general purpose
of this exercise, he says, has been to recommend truth,
innocence, honor, and virtue as the chief ornaments of
life. He appreciates the acceptance which has greeted
the paper, and says that the best parts of it have been
written by others than himself. To his farewell, he
recommends himself to the mercy of his readers.

INDEX TO *TATLER* CATALOGUE

Steele: T2a, T3a, T6a, T8a, T9a,
T17a, T22b, T27b, T30b, T37b, T17a,
T22b, T27b, T30b, T37b, T40a, T41b,
T43c, T44b, T45b, T46b, T51b, T53b,
T57a, T58b, T59b, T60b, T61b, T62b,
T63b, T64b, T65a, T66a, T68b, T71b,
T83b, T84c, T87a, T89c, T94a, T98b,
T99a, T106a, T187b, T191b, T193,
T244

Characters

A--Abigail T228
   Ace T73a
   Acorn T12a
   Actaeon T59a, T76a
   Adonis T245a
   Aescupalius T44a, T47b, T270b
   Africanus T36b
   Afterday, Will T196
   Afterwit, Solomon T83b
   Aglaura T54a
   Aletheus T48, T56a
   Alice T139
   Allegorical Personifications
T44e, T100, T102, T120a, T123,
T131, T157, T161, T170a
   Almeira T213b
   Amanda T22a, T49a, T195
   Amelia T56b
   Aminadab T190
   Amoret T194
   Amyntas T245a
   Androgyne T84a
   Antiochus T185
   Aramenta T212
   Aristaeus T126a
   Armstrong, Tobias T28a
   Arria T70a
   Aspasia T42b, T49a
   Astrea T241a
   Aurengezebe T46a
   Lady Autumn T36a, T140, T208
   Avaro T25b
B--Ballance, Mr. and Mrs. T136a
   Barebones, Lovewell T76b
   Bathillus T51b
   Bavius T91
   Beadlestaff, Benjamin T45b,
T71b.
   Bedstaff, Ephraim T21c
   Bellfrey, Tom T37a
   Belinda T127
   Belvedira T126
   Biddy, Mrs. T235

Bickerstaff, Deborah T118b
   Frank T169
   Harry T206
   Jacob T151
   John T3c
   Pyramid T118b
   Ralph T75
   Samuel T189
   Simon T151
   William T206
   Black Kate T62c
   Bluff, Oliver T265
   Blunder, Major T61c
   Bogg, Beau T65b
   Boniface T105
   Bradley, Sir Arthur de T73b
   Brightly, Lady T208
   Brisk, Sir Liberal T73a
   Bromeo T63a
   Browbeat, Benjamin T265
   Brunett, Colonel T24a
   Bubbleboy, Charles T27c
   Busy, Benjamin T265
   Buzzard, Benjamin T259
C--Caelicola T211
   Caelia T198, T199, T200
   Callicot, Edward T259
   Calpurnia T149
   Cambric, Charles T259
   Camillo T4e
   Cancrum T24a
   Careless, Frank T14c
      Jack T30b
   Carry, Joe T24a
   Cartail, Robin T37a
   Cash, Tom T26a.2
   Caska T252
   Cassio T247
   Castabella T16b, T126
   Celamico T261a
   Chanticleer, Jeffrey T54b,
      Job T134
   Chloe T4b, T94a, T140, T203a,
T207
   Chloris T9a
   Cinder, Elizabeth T270a
   Cineas T202
   Clapper, Mrs. T235
   Clarinda T94a, T146, T170b,
T223, T247
   Clarissa T4b, T5a, T35b, T58a,
T85b, T146
   Clement, Thomas T261a
   Cleomilla T88a

208

Whittlestick, Lady T84a
Why-not, Will T41b
Wildacre, Geoffrey T252
Wildair, Humphrey T60a
    Sir Harry T5a, T201b
    Tom T60a
Wildfire, Harry T30a
William, Mr. T30a, T175a
Willit, Sir Harry T79
Windmill, Andrew T86a
Wisdom, Walter T98a
Would-be, Lady Betty T66b, T259
Y--Yokefellow, Bridget T252
    Ralph T252

Narrative Forms

Allegories (other than dreams):
T4e, T44b, T50b, T63c, T69a, T97,
T147a, T193, T214, T220, T257
    Character: T4b, T9a, T12a, T14a,
T21a, T24a, T25b, T26a, T27a, T29b,
T30a, T34b, T36a, T37a, T38b, T41b,
T42b, T45c, T47a, T48, T49a, T52b,
T54b, T57b, T61a, T64b, T66a, T72b,
T76a, T77a, T85a, T88a, T106a, T111,
T115b, T126, T127, T132, T135, T145,
T146, T155, T158, T160, T163, T165,
T166a, T174a, T176a, T178, T186a,
T191a, T197, T204, T206, T208, T211,
T212, T216a, T217a, T219, T221,
T225a, T232a, T244, T248, T266
    Contrasted examples of one
type: T4b, T24a, T25b, T38b, T57b,
T61a, T66c, T77a, T88a, T135, T146,
T174a, T176a, T208, T217a
    Contrasted types: T14a, T21a,
T27a, T29b, T30a, T36a, T42b, T45c,
T48, T49a, T61a, T126, T132, T186a,
T206, T212, T244, T248, T266
    Presented by narrators other
than Bickerstaff: T26a, T36a, T38b,
T42b, T48, T49a, T54b, T64b, T66a,
T160, T216a, T221, T232a, T266
    Dream Visions: T8c, T81, T100,
T102, T117, T119, T120a, T123, T146,
T161, T237, T249
    Fables: T43b, T84c, T90a, T115b,
T138a, T147a, T229, T260
    The Dogs of London (sharpers):
T59a, T62a, T64b, T65b, T66b, T68a,
T70b
    The Instruments of London:
T153, T157, T160, T166c, T168

Narratives paraphrased or
Translated: T6b, T56a, T58a, T69b,
T72a, T86b, T117, T122, T133,
T147a, T149, T152, T154, T156,
T194, T202, T209, T217a, T233,
T260
Narrative series: The Story of
Cynthio: T1b, T5a, T22a, T35b,
T58a, T85b
    Orlando the Fair: T50a, T51a.
    Vision of the Goddess of
Justice: T100, T102
    the Upholders and the "living
dead": T62, T76d, T96b, T97, T99b,
T101b, T103, T106b, T109b, T110,
T113, T115b, T118c, T122, T162,
T261
    the Court of Justice: T103,
T110, T116, T131
    the Court of Honour: T250,
T253, T256, T259, T262, T265
    Visits to the Shades: T152,
T154, T156
    Visits to the beloved family:
T95, T114
    the Chamber of Fame: T67a,
T68b, T74c, T78, T81, T83c, T84a
    the Political Upholsterer:
T155, T160, T178, T232a
    Tales: of domestic life: T2a,
T9b, T23a, T53a, T60a, T79, T85a,
T95, T104, T143a, T150?, T172,
T189, T231
    Of intrigue and gallantry:
T1b, T5a, T16a, T22a, T33c, T35b,
T44a, T46a, T50a, T51a, T54a, T58a,
T69b, T85b, T98a, T105, T128, T136a,
T213b, T247
    Of pathos: T5d, T45a, T82,
T94a, T114, T198
    Of satirical adventure: T13a,
T15b, T26b, T32a, T52a, T80b, T126,
T192, T243, T254
    Issues or departments with no
fiction: T1c, T1d, T2b, T3b, T4c,
T4d, T5b, T5c, T6c, T6d, T7c, T7d,
T8b, T9c, T10b, T11a, T11c, T12b,
T12c, T13b, T14c, T14d, T15c, T15d,
T16c, T17b, T18b, T19b, T20c, T21b,
T21d, T23c, T24b, T25c, T27d, T28b,
T29c, T30c, T31c, T32b, T32c, T33b,
T35c, T35e, T36c, T37c, T38c, T40c,
T41d, T43a, T43d, T44d, T46c, T49b,
T51d, T53c, T55a, T55b, T58c, T59c,

T62d, T63d, T66c, T67b, T67c, T74d,
T76c, T80d, T83c, T96c, T130a,
T136b, T137b, T159, T174b, T175b,
T183, T205, T210b, T222, T224,
T225b, T233, T251, T267, T271

Narrative Techniques

Isaac Bickerstaff

As narrator only: T1a, T1b,
T1e, T2a, T3c, T4e, T5d, T7a, T9b,
T14a, T21a, T22c, T23a, T23b, T24a,
T25a, T27a, T27b, T28a, T29a, T29b,
T32a, T39a, T40b, T41a, T41c, T42a,
T42c, T43a, T44b, T44c, T46a, T50a,
T51a, T51c, T52a, T53a, T54a, T56c,
T57a, T57c, T59a, T59b, T60a, T60b,
T61b, T62a, T62c, T63a, T67a, T68a,
T68b, T69a, T69b, T69d, T71a, T72a,
T73b, T74a, T74c, T75, T76a, T76b,
T78, T82, T84a, T87b, T88a, T89a,
T94b, T96a, T96b, T97, T98a, T99a,
T101a, T105, T106b, T113, T118a,
T118b, T125, T128, T129, T130b,
T136a, T138a, T183b, T140, T143b,
T144a, T144b, T145a, T146, T147a,
T152, T153, T154, T156, T159, T162,
T164, T166c, T167b, T169, T170b,
T175a, T176a, T177, T180a, T182,
T185, T186b, T188, T190, T191a,
T194, T195, T198, T200, T201a,
T205, T209, T211, T212, T213a,
T214, T216a, T216b, T218, T220,
T223, T228, T229, T231, T232a,
T232b, T233, T236, T239, T240,
T241b, T242, T246, T252, T254,
T255, T260, T261a, T268, T269a,
T269b, T270a, T270b

As transmitter or eyewitness:
T4b, T5a, T6b, T8a, T8c, T11b,
T12a, T12b, T14c, T16a, T17a, T18a,
T22a, T24c, T26a, T26b, T27c, T31a,
T31b, T35a, T40a, T42b, T43b, T43c,
T45b, T46b, T47a, T47c, T49a, T53b,
T54b, T55a, T56a, T58b, T62b, T63b,
T64a, T66a, T71b, T72b, T73a, T77a,
T80a, T84b, T86b, T89c, T90a, T90b,
T92b, T93a, T94a, T98b, T99b, T108,
T111, T112, T115a, T134, T135,
T141, T142, T151, T168, T171a,
T172, T174a, T176b, T184, T186a,
T187b, T189, T191b, T197, T199,
T204, T215, T217a, T219a, T221,
T225a, T235, T238, T241a, T244,
T257, T264

As actor: T3a, T4a, T6a, T7b,
T9a, T13a, T15a, T15b, T19a, T20a,
T20b, T22b, T25b, T30a, T30b,
T34a, T34b, T41b, T44a, T45a,
T45c, T47b, T48, T51b, T52b, T57b,
T58a, T61a, T61c, T65a, T66b, T79,
T80b, T81, T83a, T84c, T85a, T85b,
T86a, T88b, T91, T93b, T95, T100,
T102, T103, T104, T106a, T107,
T109a, T110, T114, T116, T117,
T119, T120a, T121, T122, T123,
T124, T126, T127, T131, T132,
T137a, T139, T143a, T147b, T148,
T149, T155, T157, T158, T160,
T161, T163, T165, T166a, T166b,
T167a, T170a, T173, T178, T181,
T192, T193, T196, T201b, T202,
T203a, T206, T207, T208, T210a,
T227, T237, T243, T248, T249,
T250, T253, T256, T259, T262,
T263, T265, T266

Bickerstaff's associates

Jenny Distaff as narrator:
T10a, T33a, T36a, T36b, T37a,
T37b, T37d, T38a, T38b, T247

Pacolet: T13a, T14a, T15a,
T15b, T22a, T23b, T26b, T27a,
T28a, T40a, T44a, T46a, T48,
T51b, T59a, T64a, T70b, T73a,
T78, T81, T119, T167b, (narrator
in T13a, T15a, T26b, T44a, T48,
T119)

Charles Lillie: T92b, T94b,
T96d, T101a, T103, T110, T129,
T137c, T138a, T140, T142, T166,
T200a, T213b, T250, T253, T256,
T259, T264, T265

Kidney of St. James Coffee-
House: T1d, T10a, T26a.1, T56b,
T69c, T174a, T268

Sir Thomas of White's Chocolate House: T16a, T26a.1, T36b,
T47a, T73a

Other non-epistolary narra-
tive associates: T14c, T42b,
T45a, T49a, T60b, T66a, T90a,
T93a, T257

Letters

To Bickerstaff: T11b, T20b,
T21c, T24c, T26a, T27c, T28a,
T29a, T31b, T32a, T33a, T35d,
T38a, T45b, T50b, T54b, T59b,
T61c, T63c, T64b, T65b, T66b,
T68b, T69b, T70a, T70b, T71a,
T71b, T72a, T72b, T73a, T74a,

T74b, T76b, T78, T80b, T80c, T83a, T83b, T84a, T86a, T89a, T89b, T91, T92b, T93a, T98a, T99b, T112, T115b, T118a, T120b, T124, T128, T129, T140, T141, T142, T145b, T150, T153, T160, T168, T169, T176b, T179, T185, T187a, T188, T190, T193, T195, T200, T201a, T203b, T207, T210a, T212, T213b, T215a, T219a, T221, T225a, T226, T228, T230, T231, T232a, T234, T236, T241a, T245b, T247, T252, T255, T258, T261, T269a, T270a

Issues containing two letters: T26c, T38a, T54b, T65b, T71b, T72b, T73a, T89a, T118a, T124, T141, T176b, T195, T200, T201a, T221, T228, T234, T241a, T247, T252, T269a

Issues containing three or more letters: T70a, T78, T128, T140, T160, T188, T190, T212, T258

To Jenny Distaff: T36a, T40b.

Of praise or blame: T21c, T31b, T33a, T38c, T59b, T63c, T64b, T65b, T71a, T73a, T76b, T84a, T89a, T115b, T118a, T140, T160, T188, T190, T195, T213b, T219a, T225a, T252, T258

Seeking advice or assistance: T27c, T28a, T32a, T54b, T65b, T66b, T68b, T69b, T71b, T72a, T72b, T74a, T78, T80c, T83a, T83b, T92b, T98a, T99b, T120b, T124, T128, T140, T141, T145b, T153, T160, T176, T185, T188, T190, T200, T201a, T210a, T212, T215, T228, T241a, T245b, T247, T252, T255, T258, T269a, T270a

Narration or description: T11b, T21c, T29a, T31b, T36a, T38a, T40b, T45b, T54b, T61c, T63c, T64b, T65b, T66b, T69b, T70a, T70b, T71b, T73a, T80b, T84a, T93a, T98a, T112, T128, T129, T142, T150, T169, T179, T185, T187a, T193, T207, T213b, T215a, T221, T226, T230, T232a, T234, T236, T241a

From Bickerstaff to characters: T16b, T23b, T67a, T73a, T83a, T103, T112, T120b, T140, T143a, T190, T T195, T203a, T246

Between characters: T16a, T19c, T22a, T30b, T35b, T60a, T72a, T74a, T82, T87, T104, T128, T140, T164, T198, T201a, T230, T270a

As alleged source: T2c, **T4e**, T11c, T16a, T21a, T22c, T23a, T25a, T47a, T56c, T57a, T57b, T57c, T66b, T69a, T76b, T84a, T88a, T94b, T129, T133b, T135, T146, T164, T170, T180a, T186b, T189, T215a, T222, T232b, T246

Exemplary letters: T25a, T149, T159

Mock Petitions: T103, T113, T118b, T134, T136c, T141, T168, T215b, T219b, T268, T270a

Subjects frequently discussed

Bickerstaff and his paper: T1a, T1e, T2c, T4a, T7a, T26a.2, T30a, T31b, T34b, T38a, T38c, T56c, T61b, T67a, T71a, T71b, T73a, T74b, T78, T84c, T91a, T101a, T160, T164, T175a, T176a, T217b, T225a

Church, Clergy, conduct in: T54b, T70a, T71b, T72b, T166c, T239, T255, T269b

Conduct of men, young and old: T1b, T2a, T5a, T7b, T14c, T21a, T22a, T22c, T24a, T25b, T26a.1, T26b, T27a, T28a, T30a, T32a, T34a, T41b, T44a, T45a, T45c, T46a, T56a, T60a, T60c, T73a, T78, T80b, T80c, T86a, T86b, T92a, T100, T102, T109, T110, T113, T125, T127, T144b, T146, T149, T162, T165, T168, T173, T174a, T191a, T196, T200, T203, T204, T205, T206, T207, T211, T213a, T213b, T214, T215a, T216a, T217a, T219a, T219b, T244, T247, T252, T256, T260, T266, T268, T270a

Conduct of women, young and old: T2a, T4b, T5a, T7b, T9b, T16a, T21a, T24a, T27a, T31b, T33a, T34a, T36a, T37d, T40b, T42b, T44a, T45a, T47c, T56a, T57a, T61c, T62, T63c, T67a, T68a, T80b, T84a, T98a, T100, T102, T109, T110, T113, T11y, T121, T126, T140, T142, T145a, T146, T166c, T175, T178, T184, T200, T202, T210a, T211, T212, T215b, T221, T224a, T248, T250, T252, T266

215

Country life and standards of conduct: T19a, T31b, T44c, T53a, T57a, T85a, T98a, T118a, T121, T169, T179, T188, T189, T215a, T241b, T263

Courtship: T1b, T2a, T4b, T7b, T9b, T10a, T13a, T14c, T15a, T19a, T22a, T24a, T25a, T27b, T29a, T30b, T32a, T33a, T34a, T35a, T36b, T37d, T44a, T45a, T47a, T49a, T51a, T52b, T58a, T60b, T69b, T74a, T75, T76b, T83a, T90a, T91a, T94a, T98a, T120a, T126, T128, T145a, T168, T170d, T176, T185, T188, T198, T201a, T201c, T206, T207, T213a, T213b, T258

Dress, especially fashionable, of men and women: T6a, T21a, T30d, T32a, T43b, T52a, T77a, T100, T102, T103, T113, T115, T116, T118b, T136, T140, T142, T143b, T147a, T151, T166a, T166c, T212, T215b, T245b, T248, T270a

Language, uses and abuses: T2a, T3a, T6a, T6b, T9a, T12a, T13a, T14a, T18a, T24c, T27b, T29b, T31b, T32a, T32b, T35b, T35d, T38a, T38b, T38c, T42a, T43c, T44c, T46b, T47b, T51a, T57a, T58b, T62e, T66a, T70a, T76b, T78, T80a, T90a, T91a, T98b, T106a, T137a, T143b, T158, T163, T165, T197, T201c, T204, T209, T219a, T230, T234, T238, T241a, T242, T244, T245a, T253, T254, T256, T258, T268, T269a

Marriage and the family: T7b, T15a, T20a, T22c, T23a, T25b, T37d, T40b, T47b, T49a, T51a, T52a, T53a, T54a, T72a, T76b, T79, T82, T85a, T85b, T91a, T94b, T95, T102, T104, T105, T114, T118a, T120a, T126, T136a, T149, T150, T155, T164, T172, T185, T192, T195, T198, T199, T200, T210a, T215a, T227, T228, T235, T241a, T260

Peace and war: T2c, T5d, T8c, T19c, T23b, T24c, T26a.2, T26b, T29c, T41a, T47b, T48, T50a, T56c, T y1c, T65a, T69c, T77b, T87a, T87b, T129, T164, T187b, T209

Politics: T4e, T14a, T42a, T46a, T73b, T84b, T96b, T160, T161, T162, T190, T193, T195, T214, T220, T237

Theater: T8a, T9a, T16a, T30b, T37b, T41c, T42c, T43a, T44b, T47c, T51b, T53b, T64b, T82, T89c, T90b, T94a, T94b, T98a, T99a, T108, T115a, T120b, T130b, T134, T137c, T138a, T145a, T165, T166b, T182, T184, T188, T191b, T201b, T248

A CATALOGUE OF PROSE FICTION
IN THE *SPECTATOR*

Spectator 1. Thursday, March 1, 1711. Addison.

Mr. Spectator gives a brief account of his life, including his mother's dream that he would be a judge, his education at the University, his travels in Europe, and his present circumstance as a spectator, in the city's public houses, of the species of mankind. Urged by his friends to make public his observations, he proposes, aided by a group of gentlemen who meet as a club on Tuesdays and Thursdays, to present a daily "Sheet-full of Thoughts . . . for the benefit of my Contemporaries."

Spectator 2. Friday, March 2, 1711. Steele.

Mr. Spectator introduces, with brief character sketches, the members of his club. They are Sir Roger de Coverley, a middle-aged country gentleman and a bachelor; the gentleman of the Inner Temple, Sir Andrew Freeport, a London merchant; Captain Sentry, a retired military officer; Will Honeycomb, a man of fashion; and the Clergyman, a man of able mind, high moral character, but weak health.

Spectator 3. Saturday, March 3, 1711. Addison.

Mr. Spectator reports on a dream in which he visits the Great Hall of the Bank of England where the Virgin of Publick Credit sits enthroned, surrounded by bags of gold. A woman of delicate condition, the Virgin thinks debt away when a group of six Phantoms enter. The Phantoms are Tyranny and Anarchy, Bigotry and Atheism, and Genius of a Common-Wealth and the pretender to the throne. The lady revives when a second group of Phantoms enters, including Liberty and Monarchy, Moderation and Religion, and Genius of Great Britain and Prince George.

Spectator 4. Monday, March 5, 1711. Steele.

Mr. Spectator describes the satisfactions of his life of solitude and silence. To prove how much silence communicates, he recounts how much Will Honeycomb learned from his silent attention to a young lady at the opera. Mr. Spectator praises women and urges them to contribute their observations to his paper.

Spectator 5. Tuesday, March 6, 1711. Addison.

Mr. Spectator describes the extravagances of some opera
producers in creating their scenic effects, including
the release of large numbers of sparrows during performances. This discussion is prompted by comments he
heard while on a walk made by a man carrying a cage
filled with the small birds. So many sparrows have been
released that there is some anxiety over whether the
birds will enter other operas at inopportune moments.
Mr. Spectator recalls that some discussion was given to
producing as an opera the story of Dick Whittington and
his cat; this was given up when the threat of an invasion of mice was realized.

Spectator 6. Wednesday, March 7, 1711. Steele.

Mr. Spectator laments the Abuse of Understanding. He
regrets the unhappy affectation of being wise and witty
rather than honest and good-natured. To illustrate his
point, he recalls Sir Roger de Coverley's telling him
that he believes only "Men of fine Parts deserve to be
hanged." Mr. Spectator takes him to mean that reason
should govern passion and those with greater powers of
reason should be punished more severely for lapses of
it. In Mr. Spectator's view, only what is natural
should be held laudable; as a result Mr. Spectator
laments the tendency to make fun of old age rather than
to respect it. To illustrate his point he tells a story
from Plutarch of an elderly Greek who had trouble getting a seat at the theatre in Athens. The Athenians
promised him a seat, but then denied it to him; the
Lacedemonians respected his age and gave him a seat, to
the spontaneous applause of all.

Spectator 7. Thursday, March 8, 1711. Addison.

Mr. Spectator visits the family of a friend and finds
the entire family upset because the wife has had a bad
dream. This leads to a discussion of human fancy to
which the narrative of various old women's superstitions
contributes. He remembers being in the company in which
several people left the room when the number of the company was discovered to be thirteen. Other women of his
acquaintance spend their time frightening people by
claiming to be able to make prophecies of evil to come.
Mr. Spectator urges trust in God as a remedy for such
fears.

Spectator 8. Friday, March 9, 1711. Addison.

Mr. Spectator presents a letter from a Director of the
Society for the Reformation of Manners, who objects to
the immorality he sees in "midnight masks." Another
letter protests the ladies of low quality who masquerade
at these affairs as ladies of quality. Mr. Spectator

refuses comment until he has had the chance to investigate the charges personally.

Spectator 9. Saturday, March 10, 1711. Addison.

To illustrate his point that man is a Sociable Animal, Mr. Spectator describes the nature of men's clubs in England. He describes the meeting place of the Club of Fat-Men, their opposite number the Society of Scare-Crows' Skeletons, the Club of the Kings, and others. He especially describes the Hum-Drum Club, the Mum Club, the Club of Duelists, the K-Cat Club, the B-State Club and the October Club. He ends his paper by presenting the Rules of the Two-Penny Club.

Spectator 10. Monday, March 12, 1711. Addison.

Mr. Spectator delights in the success his paper has achieved in so short a time. He singles out a number of groups of people whom he feels would especially benefit by regular reading of his paper. These include well-regulated Families, who set apart an hour every morning for tea and reading his paper; the Fraternity of Spectators who are either so lazy or so rich that they may consider the world their theatre; the Blanks of Society, who having nothing in their minds need something to 'talk of; and all members of the female world, who need more serious matter with which to occupy their time than the world usually provides. Mr. Spectator knows that some well wishers wonder if he can maintain the quality of the paper over a long period of time; he promises to stop doing the paper as soon as his wits grow dull.

Spectator 11. Tuesday, March 13, 1711. Steele.

Mr. Spectator, previously introduced by Will Honeycomb, visits Arietta and describes her as a woman visited with profit by everyone who has pretence to wit or gallantry; her conversation is such a mixture of "Gaiety and Prudence that she is agreeable both to the young and the old." To a man who would belittle women, she tells a fable of a lion and a man, from Aesop, which reveals that mankind's claims to superiority over animals is presumptuous. She also tells the story, from Ligon, of Thomas Inkle, an Englishman, who is aided and protected in America by Yarico, an Indian girl whom he finally sells into slavery. Mr. Spectator is so moved by this story that he leaves the room in tears.

Spectator 12. Wednesday, March 14, 1711. Addison.

Mr. Spectator describes his difficulty, upon arriving in London, of finding suitable lodging. He had to leave his first two lodging places because those who rented him his rooms would not give him the solitude he needed. His current lodgings are much more agreeable

because his landlady and her daughters leave him completely alone, which is much to his liking. This leads
him to remember an event last winter in which a number
of girls from the neighborhood sat around the fire telling ghost stories which frightened everyone in the room,
especially a little boy. Mr. Spectator says that he
disapproves of such stories because they may permanently
affect the imaginations of young people. Mr. Spectator
argues that whatever Spirits exist are creations of God
and therefore not threatening to humans. He concludes
with an image drawn from Milton's *Paradise Lost*, Book
IV, which pictures Celestial Spirits praising God.

Spectator 13. Thursday, March 15, 1711. Addison.

Mr. Spectator comments lightly upon the appearance of a
lion in a recent opera; he has discovered that three
different people have played the part of the lion. The
first was a Candle-snuffer, who was of too testy a temperament for the part and overdid it. The second was a
tailor, who was too mild-mannered for the part. The
third and present lion is a Country Gentleman who plays
the role for diversion. Mr. Spectator repeats the claim
that the lion and the actor who kills him in the opera
have been seen smoking a pipe together between acts;
the story is told to suggest that the combat on stage
is merely a sham, but Mr. Spectator assures us that such
familiarity occured only after the lion has been killed
on stage. This description is given to demonstrate poor
taste of London audiences.

Spectator 14. Friday, March 16, 1711. Steele.

Mr. Spectator suggests that the public entertainment of
the day is more childish than that of 25 years ago. He
receives a letter from the actor who portrays the lion
in a current opera; the actor insists that the battle
exhibits the valor of the warrior's character and the
fierceness of the lion. Mr. Spectator also presents
several letters which he feels have to do with "The
Elegance of our present Diversions." One correspondent,
a clergyman, regrets that his parishioners have deserted
his church to attend a puppet show run by Mr. Powell of
Tatler fame. Among this group is Mrs. Rachel Eye-bright.
He urges Mr. Spectator to get Powell to schedule his
performances for other than church time. Another correspondent, the Undertaker of the Masquerade, objects
to the outlandish costumes and behavior of his audiences.
Another correspondent presents a review of Powell's puppet show and the current opera; he finds both outlandish
in their use of animals on stage as well as for other
reasons, but he prefers the performance of Mr. Powell.

Spectator 15. Saturday, March 17, 1711. Addison.

Mr. Spectator tells of a trip to France on which he met
Cleanthe who gave up one lover for the pomp and riches

another could give her. He discusses "this unaccountable Humour in womankind, of being smitten with everything that is showy and superficial." He claims that true happiness is of a retiring nature, an enemy to pomp and noise. Aurelia exemplifies this because she finds happiness in a retired life away from pomp and noise; Fulvia is her opposite, because she lives a life of perpetual motion and restlessness. Virgil's Camilla, a character in his *Aeneid*, is a classical example of this problem in women.

Spectator 16. Monday, March 19, 1711. Addison.

Mr. Spectator reports that a number of correspondents have urged him to satirize extremes of fashion including the Muff now in fashion, fringed gloves, and other such foppish apparel. Mr. Spectator says that he will not devote time to specifics of fashion, but address himself to the causes of such excesses. Other correspondents have reported on private scandals; Mr. Spectator says that he will deal with groups of such criminals but not individual cases. Yet another group of correspondents urges him to take notice of the excesses of others; again, he will deal with human frailty wherever it occurs but not to the increase of controversy. He offers a letter from Charles Lillie, in which the perfumer offers to accept advertisements for the city of Westminister and the duchy of Lancaster. Mr. Spectator approves of this request.

Spectator 17. Tuesday, March 20, 1711. Steele.

Mr. Spectator praises those ugly people who accept their deformities with grace and humor. He offers as an example Shakespeare's Falstaff. In this regard he presents a letter from Alexander Carbuncle, a resident of Oxford, who tells him of the Ugly Club. This correspondent presents the rules of the club and reports on verses of praise sent to Mrs. Touchwood, Mrs. Andiron, Mrs. Vizard, and Nell Trot. Mr. Spectator finds this correspondent appropriately mirthful about human deformity; he comments upon his own short face and hopes he is sufficiently accepting of it to be made a member of the Merry Club.

Spectator 18. NF. Wednesday, March 21, 1711. Addison.

Mr. Spectator offers a history of the nonsense known as Italian opera, and its performance in England.

Spectator 19. Thursday, March 22, 1711. Steele.

Mr. Spectator presents an extended character of the Envious Man, with examples from Bacon's *Essays*. He describes Will Prosper, a man who makes it his business to torture envious men by telling them tales designed to aggravate their distress at the good fortune of others.

Spectator 20. Friday, March 23, 1711. Steele.

Mr. Spectator says that he is concerned with the Correction of Impudence; to this end he presents an extended character of the Impudent Man. His starting point is a letter from S. C. who describes the type man known as the "Starer." Will Prosper agrees to stare against this man in defense of the ladies whom he makes uncomfortable.

Spectator 21. Saturday, March 24, 1711. Addison.

Mr. Spectator regrets that the three great professions of Divinity, Law, and Physick all have too many practitioners who starve one another because there are too many men competing for too little work. He describes the conduct of these superfluous members of the great professions; Vagellius is an example of a man who has become a lawyer not because he is counted in this area but because his parents insisted he go into it. Many of these professionals bring dignity to their calling, but too many are superfluous practitioners who give their professions a bad name.

Spectator 22. Monday, March 26, 1711. Steele.

Mr. Spectator says that one of his major roles is to comment on the sad state of the theater in England. To illustrate this, he presents a group of letters from various actors who describe how well they have performed a series of bizarre and unusual roles. The first letter, from Thomas Prone, describes how effectively he played the role of Lyon; he must die at the hands of Camilla, and is so struck by her charm that he dies like a man. The second letter is from William Screne, who describes his performance in the role of a Chair and a Pump. Ralph Simple writes the third letter, in which he describes his performance as the Flower Pot. Another describes the actor's performance of the passion of Thirst. The final letter is from an actor who has performed the role of the King of Latium; he protests his demotion from the role of King to the role of common soldier. The paper concludes with an advertisement for a doctor who claims success in curing a variety of people, including four Scaramouches, three Nuns, and a Morris Dancer. He claims to be able to pull teeth from people of fashion without their having to remove their masks.

Spectator 23. Tuesday, March 27, 1711. Addison.

Mr. Spectator argues that nothing betrays a base, ungenerous spirit more than "the giving of secret Stabs to a Man's Reputation." He urges that great men should behave toward the wits of their age with generous civility. To demonstrate this he presents several narratives to illustrate possible responses of great men

to sharp criticism of them. The generous include Socrates, who acted generously in spite of Aristophanes'
satire of him as he approached his death. Julius Caesar
responded to Cotellus' satire of him by inviting the
poet to dinner; Cardinal Mazarine bestowed an Abbey on
Quillet, who had published derogatory verses on the
churchman. Sextus Quintus was not so generous to Pasquin; after the unfortunate wit had satirized the Pope's
rise from low estate, the churchman had his tongue cut
out and his hands chopped off. The possible effects of
satire Mr. Spectator describes by telling a fable of
Sir Roger L'Estrange in which a frog tells some boys
who are stoning him, what is play for them is death for
him.

Spectator 24. Wednesday, March 28, 1711. Steele.

Mr. Spectator attacks the impertinence of insignificant
people who plague men of significance simply to be seen
in their company. Thomas Kimbow, an old tavern humorist,
writes that although he wishes solitude, he is plagued
nightly by a group of people who seek him out because
he provides room and a good fire. Will Fashion writes
to urge Mr. Spectator no longer to take off his hat to
Fashion in the park because he is afraid that his mistress will believe he and Mr. Spectator are more intimate than they really are. Mr. Spectator says that
women are also plagued by this problem; he presents a
letter from Mary Tuesday who urges the woman to whom
she writes no longer to seek her company because the
two women have nothing to offer each other. The paper
concludes with an advertisement announcing that Kidney
is no longer at St. James' Coffee-house, his place having been taken by John Sowton.

Spectator 25. Thursday, March 29, 1711. Addison.

Mr. Spectator offers a letter from a Valetudinarian who
describes himself as the type of person who imagines
himself to have every disease he reads of. Although he
desperately tries to remain in good health balancing
all of his activities, he remains constantly in ill
health. Mr. Spectator discusses such Imaginary Sick
Persons; he claims that they in fact endanger their
health by the measures they take to try to preserve it.
As a remedy he quotes a fable in which a farmer is
given by Jupiter control over the weather of his own
estate. After a year of trying to regulate the weather,
with resulting poor crops, the man returns control of
the weather to Jupiter.

Spectator 26. Friday, March 30, 1711. Addison.

Mr. Spectator says that when he is in a serious Humour,
he walks by himself in Westminister Abbey and looks at

223

the tombstones. He finds the common destiny of all men a cure for envy, inordinate desires, and the pretensions of mankind.

Spectator 27. Saturday, March 31, 1711. Steele.

Mr. Spectator says that many men protest that the agony of their labors is greater than any reward they get from their work. He says that no man can live comfortably in retirement till he has learned to live amid the noise of the world. He presents three letters given him by his friend the Clergyman; R. O. thanks the Clergyman for urging him to be good to someone every day. T. D. asks why his dear Chloe is looked on so harshly by pious men. R. B. describes the contest he feels in his own mind between Reason and Fashion.

Spectator 28. Monday, April 2, 1711. Addison.

Mr. Spectator satirizes Projectors by offering a letter from one who wishes to get rid of the strangely faked signs in London and insists that the sign of every shop should reflect the wares that are sold within. A second correspondent plans to exhibit a pair of monkeys in London; he feels that his monkeys are better men than many of those who are men by birth.

Spectator 29. NF. Tuesday, April 3, 1711. Addison.

Mr. Spectator criticizes the excesses of the Italian opera, especially the use of Italian Recitativo with English words.

Spectator 30. Wednesday, April 4, 1711. Steele.

Mr. Spectator reports on the establishment of a Set of Sighers in Oxford University, who permit each other the privilege of describing the favors their beloveds have shown toward them. A similar group of Lovers in London was known as the Fringe-Club; these men, however, were incapable of expressing their love except in their dress. The patron of this club was Don Quixote. A correspondent writes to describe the Amorous Club, also of Oxford, whose members spend their time drinking to the health of their mistresses. They are opposed to excess and insisted recently that a young student who described his beloved, Elizabeth Dimple, as Elizabetha, refer to her as Betty. The writer says that Albina, who has six Voteries in the Amorous Club, is one of Mr. Spectator's readers.

Spectator 31. Thursday, April 5, 1711. Addison.

Mr. Spectator reports on a conversation he overheard in a coffee-house in which a Projector entertained his audience with a plan for an opera entitled *The Expedition of Alexander the Great*. The plot of the play enables the opera to include a wax works, a group of performing monkeys, violent murder, and a puppet show run by Mr. Powell. This Projector assures Mr. Spectator that for a mere ten thousand pounds he can procure a musician from Switzerland who can make an organ sound like a drum.

Spectator 32. Friday, April 6, 1711. Steele.

Mr. Spectator presents a letter from a correspondent from the Ugly-Club of Oxford, in which the writer tells Mr. Spectator that he has been accepted as a member. The letter describes the meeting of the Club at which Mr. Spectator's membership was accepted; it also discusses those who are overly concerned with the appearance of their shapes. This group includes Lady Ample, Miss Cross, Squire Lath, and Madame Van Brisket. Some of the members wonder if Mr. Spectator might not, in fact, be ugly only because he is wearing a mask; the president overcomes this objection by telling a story which claims that the wits of every age are entitled to wear whatever masks they please.

Spectator 33. Saturday, April 7, 1711. Steele.

Mr. Spectator tells of two daughters of a friend of his. The first, Latitia, is one of the "Greatest Beauties of the Age." Her sister, Daphne, is not "remarkable for any charms in her person," but, because she is good humored, is the first of the two sisters to get married. Mr. Spectator presents excerpts from an old letter to "Profess'd Beauties" in which the correspondent urges them to concern themselves with the pleasing of others rather than the preservation of their beauty; Sophronia is presented as a model of innocence, piety, good humor, and truth; Milton's description of Eve in *Paradise Lost*, which stresses her grace and dignity, is given as an example to young women.

Spectator 34. Monday, April 9, 1711. Addison.

Mr. Spectator describes a meeting of the Spectator Club during which the various members discuss the effects on the public of the *Spectator* papers. Will Honeycomb is worried about the effects on some ladies of Mr. Spectator's criticism of the opera. Sir Andrew Freeport is sure that the papers have done great good. The Templar praises the paper's wit, while Sir Roger de Coverley wonders at the attention given by serious men to the foolishness of the age. Captain Sentry urges discretion in dealing with the army, while the Clergyman urges the continuing harsh treatment of vice. Mr. Spectator resolves to continue his efforts in improving the virtue of the realm.

Spectator 35. Tuesday, April 10, 1711. Addison.

Mr. Spectator comments on the difficulty of writing successful humor; he agrees with Shadwell that much of what
passes for humor in the country is the Offspring of a
Distempered Brain. To illustrate his point he presents
an allegory, after the manner of Plato, in which Humor
is seen to be the Offspring of Wit and Mirth. Wit's
father was Good Sense, whose father was Truth. Unfortunately there is about in the realm an imposter named
False Humor, the son of Frenzy and Laughter and the
grandson of Nonsense and Falsehood. Mr. Spectator gives
a character of False Humor, saying that he differs from
True Humor as a monkey does from a man.

Spectator 36. Wednesday, April 11, 1711. Steele.

Mr. Spectator offers a letter from an actor in which
the performer says that he and other fellow actors are
in agreement with the effort to remove from the stage
everything other than the representation of human life.
All actors who make a living representing the inhuman
are being dispatched to the Projector of *Spectator* 31
for his monstrous opera. Salmoneus writes that his
position as Thunderer to the playhouse has been taken
from him; he wishes Mr. Spectator's help in getting a
place in the opera of the Projector. The paper concludes with an advertisement in which a widow, the
daughter of Thomas Prater and Latitia Tattle, announces
that she has established a school for the instruction
of talking birds. She promises, within a year, to be
able to teach birds all the languages and words they
need to become appropriate companions for young ladies
of fashion.

Spectator 37. Thursday, April 12, 1711. Addison.

Sir Roger de Coverley directs Mr. Spectator to take a
letter for him to the home of Leonora, where he examines
her library with great care. He finds that the books
are grouped by size; although all the books are richly
bound, quite a number are counterfeit. He offers a
catalogue of the lady's books, finding that many were
bought only because they were popular or because she
had met their authors. Those books she had bought for
her own use tended to be works which only divert the
imagination. A widow, Leonora has turned all her interests into a love of books and retirement. Since
most of her reading is in the area of Romance, she has
transformed her country home into an artificial wilderness designed to stir the emotions. Mr. Spectator regards her with a mixture of admiration and pity, for he
can only wonder at how she might have improved if her
reading had been more carefully selected.

Spectator 38. Friday, April 13, 1711. Steele.

Mr. Spectator reports on a conversation with a very handsome lady and gentleman and notes how much their beauty and wit have been turned into deformity and absurdity by affectation. This leads to a long meditation on the consequences of affectation and the desire for public applause. Mr. Spectator closes with a letter he has written to a witty man, telling him that he must learn to wait for the praise he so much desires.

Spectator 39. NF. Saturday, April 14, 1711. Addison.

Mr. Spectator presents a lengthy discourse on the subject of tragedy.

Spectator 40. NF. Monday, April 16, 1711. Addison.

Mr. Spectator continues his discussion of tragedy and its current state in England.

Spectator 41. Tuesday, April 17, 1711. Steele.

Mr. Spectator offers a letter from a man asking his advice on how to get rid of a wife because her beauty is entirely artificial and applied. Mr. Spectator allows that the man has justice on his side. Calling such women Picts, he presents a lengthy character which stresses the inherent falsehood of such overly painted women. Will Honeycomb relates to Mr. Spectator a strange adventure with a Pict, whose entire business in life is to gain the hearts of male admirers. The lady goes to great lengths to snare men and then treats them with great cruelty. Honeycomb's attachment to her is cured by seeing her without her makeup. Mr. Spectator says that only Lindamira, because of her delicate complexion, should be permitted the wearing of makeup. Statira as an example should be a model for her sex, since her features are enlivened by the cheerfulness of her mind. The paper concludes with an advertisement for a position by a young gentlewoman of the House of Grotesque, who paints the finest flesh color in town.

Spectator 42. NF. Wednesday, April 18, 1711. Addison.

Mr. Spectator continues his discussion of tragedy, here based on examination of Aristotle's *Poetics*.

Spectator 43. Thursday, April 19, 1711. Steele.

Mr. Spectator describes the Club of Dull Fellows, a group of men who from vacancy of thought, involve themselves in things for which they are unfit. He presents a letter from Abraham Froth of Oxford; Froth describes his club and its detailed discussions of political and economic matters. Mr. Spectator points out that such men only concern themselves with novelty and never reach

a conclusion about anything. Such men move Mr. Spectator to urge that everyone in the country be taught a
craft to fill the time of those whose minds are incapable of dealing appropriately with serious subjects.

Spectator 44. NF. Friday, April 20, 1711. Addison.

Mr. Spectator discusses various means of moving audiences to pity and fear in tragedy.

Spectator 45. Saturday, April 21, 1711. Addison.

Mr. Spectator says that he wishes peace with France, but
wonders if the influx of French fashion which would result from such a peace would not be detrimental to the
well being of the nation of England. Many women of the
realm are already overcome with French fashion; Will
Honeycomb takes Mr. Spectator to visit a woman who, in
the French fashion, has spent a great deal of time getting ready to greet guests in her nightgown. Sempronia
has adopted the French fashion of receiving guests and
talking politics while she is getting dressed. Mr.
Spectator says that such behavior opens women to great
danger; he urges discretion and modesty as an alterna-
tive. He tells how a woman, affected by French manners,
disrupted the performance of *Macbeth* by talking throughout the play. Mr. Spectator finds such behavior childish; he cites another example, from La Bruyère, of people who deliberately used difficult words in their conversations so they could murder the pronunciation of
them. He concludes by noting that the imitation of
French fashion is so widespread that English women can
learn such extremes of behavior without leaving the
country.

Spectator 46. Monday, April 23, 1711. Addison.

Mr. Spectator describes his method of working in preparing his papers. One of his working papers, a jotting-
down of ideas for papers, was lost; it fell into the
hands of a cluster of people in Lloyd's Coffee-house and
was finally read aloud by the boy of the House. The
reading of the paper produces great merriment in the
House and much speculation as to its source. One citizen proposes that the paper be carried to a Secretary
of State; a young Oxford Scholar, who happens to be present, ridicules this suggestion. Mr. Spectator resolves
this situation by obtaining the paper and using it to
light his pipe. He presents a letter from a correspondent who says that he is married to a Gospel-Gossip, a
Quaker woman, who spends all her time at lectures and
church meetings. She constantly invites the preacher
and his family for dinner, when she and her husband are
alone she becomes a Sermon Popgun; constantly discharg-
ing Texts, Proofs, and Applications at her unfortunate
husband. A second letter is from an Ogling-Master, who

proposes to teach his art. He will teach the Church
Ogle in the morning, and the Play-house Ogle by candle-
light. He is the author of a work entitled *The Compleat
Ogler*.

Spectator 47. Tuesday, April 24, 1711. Addison.

Mr. Spectator quotes Hobbes on the subject of laughter
and its value in human life. Because of the importance
of laughter, every country values its wits, those merry
wags known in England as Jack Puddings. Everyone becomes a wit on April Fool's Day, including Mr. Spectator's landlady who on that day sent all of her children
on foolish errands. Unfortunately, some men try to make
every day April Fool's Day; these men, known as Biters,
are really full of pride instead of merriment. Frequently this merriment comes at the expense of Butts,
men who constantly find themselves the object of wit
and raillery. Dull Butts never get the best of the
situation, but Witty Butts can frequently turn the situation into a joke on their ridiculers. Falstaff was a
hero of this species of Butt.

Spectator 48. Wednesday, April 25, 1711. Steele.

Mr. Spectator writes the Ugly Club accepting with pleasure his admission to that society. He says that he
will soon come for a meeting and bring along an old
Beau and a modern Pict as new candidates for membership.
Hecatissa writes Mr. Spectator to learn if women may be
admitted to this select company. Another correspondent
says that he is a man of such vanity that he wears
fashionable ill-fitting shoes even though he has the
gout. A correspondent from Epping writes that a Company
of Players in his neighborhood are so poor that their
ragged costumes make the noble characters they perform
in tragedies appear ridiculous. He hopes that Mr. Spectator will send to this Company some of the outlandish
equipment he has banned from the London stage. The only
part which they can perform with propriety is that of
Justice Clodpate.

Spectator 49. Thursday, April 26, 1711. Steele.

Mr. Spectator reports on the behavior of men in coffee-
houses, where the important thing is to know whether one
should be a speaker or a hearer. Beaver the Haberdasher
will let no one talk, from 6:00 until 7:45 a.m., on the
subject of political affairs in Europe other than himself. At a quarter to eight, center stage of the coffee-
house is taken over by students at the Inns of Court.
Eubulus dominates conversation around the middle of the
day. Mr. Spectator promises to describe those who reign
supreme in the coffee-house in the afternoon and evening and to conclude with the History of Tom the Tyrant,
who holds forth between the hours of 11:00 and 12:00 at
night.

Spectator 50. Friday, April 27, 1711. Addison.

Mr. Spectator reports on the reactions of four Indians who recently visited London. He describes their reactions to buildings, the people, and the customs in this country which is so strange to them. Their account, given to Mr. Spectator's friend by the Upholsterer, includes their description of St. Paul's Cathedral. Their understanding of the country is made more difficult because one of their guides is a Tory and the other is a Whig; each guide presents a very different picture of the things they see. The Indians find the actions and dress of many fashionable people to be particularly mysterious.

Spectator 51. Saturday, April 28, 1711. Steele.

Mr. Spectator presents a letter from a lady who complains of the immorality of the theater. This provokes Mr. Spectator to a discussion of bawdry in the theater, which he attributes to a dearth of invention. In doing this, the playwrights appeal to the appetites of their audience. Apicius, for example, delights in a description of a delicious meal, while Clodius, delights in a description of a wanton beauty. Mr. Spectator urges that men of wit who write for the stage turn their attention to elevating the morals of their audiences rather than playing to their appetites.

Spectator 52. Monday, April 30, 1711. Steele.

Mr. Spectator receives a letter from Hugh Goblin Praeces, welcoming him to membership in the Ugly Club and announcing that they have reserved a seat for the Pictish Damsel, Mr. Spectator's candidate for membership in the Club. Only those picts who have a face like Dr. Carbuncle's will be admitted. The letter also urges that Mr. Spectator marry Madame Hecatissa. Mr. Spectator agrees to the match, with the reservation that he wonders if she will choose him over other members of the Club. Another correspondent wonders if the laughter that resulted from Mr. Spectator's paper on April Fool's Day does not contradict his theory of laughter. Mr. Spectator replies that the laughter was directed at the characters described in the paper and at the Ideot, the German Courtier, the Gaper, the Merry-Andrew, the Haberdasher, the Biter, the Butt, and not at him.

Spectator 53. Tuesday, May 1, 1711. Steele.

Mr. Spectator presents a letter from a correspondent who praises his criticism of women who wear too much makeup, and urges that he educate men to respond to women's virtue and not to their appearance. Anna Bella writes that she hopes Mr. Spectator objects only to fivolous conversation between men and women and not that conversation governed by the Rules of Honour and Prudence. Mr. Spectator refuses to answer this letter until Anna Bella has provided a description of those she calls the Best Bred Men in the World. A splenetic gentleman, who has acquired this delicacy by reading the best authors, urges Mr. Spectator to inform men of fashion that they do not have the Spleen if they cannot talk without the help of a glass at their mouths or understand each other without smoking pipes. Another correspondent, a reformed Starer, urges that Mr. Spectator censor women who encourage Starers. These women, called Peepers, are not happy unless they are the object of the attention of a Starer. One such woman used an elaborately decorated fan and her eyes to call attention to her beautiful Bosom in church. Mr. Spectator says that this woman, because she used both Fan and Eyes, is to be considered a Pict. Latinus writes to announce a performance of music for his benefit and the benefit of others in his situation.

Spectator 54. Wednesday, May 2, 1711. Steele.

Mr. Spectator receives a letter from Cambridge, telling him of a sect of Philosophers which has been founded there, called the Loungers. Taking their cue from classical philosophers, such men spend their time in idle pursuits. Mr. Spectator elaborates the description of this Club by claiming that such men are content with being part of mankind without distinguishing themselves. They are constantly in motion and pay attention only to the present.

Spectator 55. Thursday, May 3, 1711. Addison.

Mr. Spectator says that the activities of most men arise either from the Love of Pleasure or the Fear of Want. The former can degenerate into Luxury; the latter into Avarice. To illustrate this, Mr. Spectator presents, from Dryden's translation of Persius, a conversation between Avarice and Luxury. To illustrate his point further, he presents a fable of a war between Avarice and Luxury. Luxury's generals are Pleasure, Mirth, Pomp, and Fashion, while Avarice's officers are Hunger, Industry, Care, and Watchfulness. Avarice's chief counsellor is Poverty. Their war is for Universal Monarchy of the Hearts of Mankind. Luxury's chief counsel is Plenty.

Spectator 56. Friday, May 4, 1711. Addison.

Mr. Spectator gives a friend's report on what the visiting American Indians think about religious matters. The account, provided by a Visionary named Marraton, describes his visit to the underworld, describes his meeting in the underworld with his former wife Yaratilda, who is in the process of preparing a beautiful place for him to live after his death.

Spectator 57. Saturday, May 5, 1711. Addison.

Mr. Spectator discusses the proposition that men and women should concern themselves only with those changes which are appropriate to their sex. He gives a list of those who violate this principle, including a young man who spends his time discussing fashion and a young woman who spends her time discussing fox hunting. Camilla and Penthelisea spend their time arguing political matters. He accompanies Will Honeycomb on a visit to a lady who has allowed a doctor to dominate her life instead of her husband Truelove.

Spectator 58. Monday, May 7, 1711. Addison.

Mr. Spectator sets out to describe the true nature of wit. One example of false wit is the use of acrostics or shaped verses. This false wit is in evidence in England; a writing master has written the entire Old Testament in a wig. A Poetical Lover known to Mr. Spectator intends to practice this false wit by presenting his mistress with verses made in the shape of her fan. He also hopes to write a poem shaped like a ring.

Spectator 59. NF. Tuesday, May 8, 1711. Addison.

Mr. Spectator continues his discussion of false wit, concluding with an illustrative quotation from Butler's *Hudibras*.

Spectator 60. Wednesday, May 9, 1711. Addison.

Mr. Spectator continues his discussion of false wit, by focusing on anagrams. One Lover of whom Mr. Spectator has heard spent half a year working on an elaborate anagram on his beloved's name, only to discover at the end that he had spelled it wrong. He expresses his surprise that so learned a man as Menage would indulge in the composition of anagrams. He quotes a description of Menage in which the man describes his composition of an anagram.

Spectator 61. NF. Thursday, May 10, 1711. Addison.

Mr. Spectator continues his discussion of false wit, this time focusing on the pun.

Spectator 62. NF. Friday, May 11, 1711. Addison.

Mr. Spectator continues his discussion of wit.

Spectator 63. Saturday, May 12, 1711. Addison.

Mr. Spectator concludes his discussion of wit by relating a dream-vision, in which he was transported into the country ruled by the Goddess of Falsehood, the Region of False Wit. Everything in the country is false

in appearance; the landscape is dominated by a temple
of the God of Dullness. The god's attendants include
Industry and Caprice. Offerings to the god include
shaped verses and anagrams as well as acrostics. He
discovers a battle in progress between the forces of
Truth and the forces of Falsehood. The frontiers of
the realm are inhabited by a species of Mixed Wit; some
of these ally themselves with Truth while others ally
themselves with Falsehood. At length, the Goddess of
Falsehood disappears when faced with the light of the
Goddess of Truth. When the reign of Truth is established in this realm, all changes as appearances fall
away to be replaced by realities. The figures of Wit
and Truth are accompanied by Heroic Poetry, Tragedy,
Satyr, Rhetoric, Comedy, and Epigram.

Spectator 64. Monday, May 14, 1711. Steele.

Mr. Spectator notes in the actions of a courtier and a
"dealer in Silks and Ribbands" the extent to which the
fashions of royalty affect people of much lower stations
of life.

Spectator 65. NF. Tuesday, May 15, 1711. Steele.

Mr. Spectator presents an extensive review of Etherege's
comedy *The Man of Mode, or Sir Fopling Flutter*. He discusses the character of each of the major roles in the
play and concludes that it is a "perfect Contradiction
to good Manners, good Sense, and Honesty; . . . there
is nothing in it but what is built upon the Ruin of
Virtue and Innocence."

Spectator 66. Wednesday, May 16, 1711. Steele.

Mr. Spectator presents a letter from Celimene, who
writes to inquire of him how best to educate a young
country woman recently come to town who knows nothing
of the way in which women of the city conduct themselves.
Celimene is concerned that this woman does not know the
"Language of Lurks and Glances," among other standard
equipment of the city coquette. Another correspondent,
having been involved in helping Celimene draft her letter to Mr. Spectator, also urges Mr. Spectator's comments on the subject of "Fine Breeding," because he is
afraid that this woman, having been brought up to exhibit "that plain thing called Good Breeding, may be
spoiled by learning the ways of the town." These letters provoke Mr. Spectator into a discussion of the education of children; his thesis is that people neglect
the education of the minds of their daughters and the
bodies of their sons. Parents try to make their daughters agreeable; as a result women in the prime of life
are out of fashion and neglected. One such woman is
Cleomira, who dances elegantly but whose simplicity of
thought raises admiration in her beholders and not loose
hope.

Spectator 67. Thursday, May 17, 1711. Budgell.

Mr. Spectator paraphrases at length a Dialogue of Lucian, in which the philosopher defends at length the practice of dancing. He presents a letter from a correspondent whose daughter has been under the instruction of a dancing master named Rigadoon. Upon going to an exhibition of the dances she has learned, he is at first delighted with her dancing, but he is soon so concerned with the familiarity with which some of the male dancers handle his daughter while dancing that he seizes the child and takes her home. Mr. Spectator says that his correspondent had reason to be concerned but that he would have had even more reason if he had seen the kissing dance which Will Honeycomb has described to Mr. Spectator. Mr. Spectator concludes that dancing is an extremely useful thing to know, but that it is indeed open to abuse. He says that he practices country dancing with his landlady's eldest daughter. This number ends with a Postscript containing a letter from J. Graham, advertising an exposition of Italian paintings forthcoming at Covent Garden.

Spectator 68. NF. Friday, May 18, 1711. Addison.

Mr. Spectator discusses at length the subject of friendship, with references to Cicero, Martial, and the Book of Ecclesiasticus.

Spectator 69. Saturday, May 19, 1711. Addison.

Mr. Spectator says that there is no place in London which he so enjoys visiting as the Royal Exchange, in which he has the opportunity to observe so many Englishmen and foreigners engaged in the private business of mankind. In his visits to the Exchange, he is known only to his friend Sir Andrew Freeport and an Egyptian merchant. Mr. Spectator observes that the Exchange makes London a kind of emporium for the whole world. Because in comparison to other countries, England is a bound island, the English merchants in their commerce with other parts of the world do their country a great service, while they are building their own private fortunes. Commerce unites mankind. Mr. Spectator weeps tears of joy at the sight of so many people happily engaged in pursuing their business.

Spectator 70. NF. Monday, May 21, 1711. Addison.

Mr. Spectator praises literature which appeals to people of every degree and station of life. Such works are those which describe nature in an appealing way and which are founded on an important "Precept of Morality"; such works as the "Old Song of Chevy Chase" and epics of Homer, Virgil, and Milton, have these qualities in common. Mr. Spectator compares favorably and at length the English ballad with these great epics.

Spectator 71. Tuesday, May 22, 1711. Steele.

Mr. Spectator insists that the conquest of human passion is difficult. He urges that all passion, including love, be refined to greater elegance than they come to us from nature. As an example of a refined example of love, he presents a lengthy quote from Dryden's "Cymon and Iphigenia." To compare with this elegance, he presents a letter from "an enamour'd Footman in the Country" to his beloved. The letter, from James the Country Bully to Betty the Country Coquette, uses the language of contemporary Romances. Mr. Spectator offers a revision of the letter in which the language of love is made more elegant.

Spectator 72. Wednesday, May 23, 1711. Addison.

Mr. Spectator presents a friend's account of the Everlasting Club, whose membership is so arranged that the Club sits day and night, so that no member ever lacks company. The Club, begun toward the end of the Civil Wars, sat without interruption until the Great Fire of London, at which time it was dispersed for several weeks. The steward at the time of the Great Fire refused to leave his chair until he had emptied all the bottles then upon the table; he is remembered with · great respect by present members of the Club. The Club keeps careful records of its history, including a tally of all tobacco smoked and all liquid refreshment consumed. The fire in the Club is always kept burning; a woman is retained for the sole purpose of keeping the fire going. This Club looks upon all others with contempt; the ordinary conversation of the Club concerns the adventures of its own members in perpetuating the Club's drinking and smoking activities.

Spectator 73. Thursday, May 24, 1711. Addison.

Mr. Spectator discusses at length man's perfectability and love of praise; he finds that the Wise Man seeks goodness, while the Fool tries to be better than others. The desire for admiration is especially ripe among women; Mr. Spectator therefore defines a category of women known as Idols. Everything that such women do is directed at the goal of gathering male worshippers. Mr. Spectator defines such women in detail, with allusions to Milton, Ovid, and Chaucer. The beautiful Clarinda, "one of the greatest *Idols* among the Moderns," is such a creature because she is constantly involved with adorning her person and attracting attention to herself. In many cases, the woman outlives the Idol, because marriage and old age undeify women.

Spectator 74. NF. Friday, May 25, 1711. Addison.

Mr. Spectator continues to praise the "old Song of Chevy-Chase," by comparing it favorably to Virgil's *Aeneid*.

Spectator 75. Saturday, May 26, 1711. Steele.

Mr. Spectator reports that a lady of his acquaintance has objected strenuously to his calling Dorimant, of the play *Sir Fopling Flutter*, a Clown. Mr. Spectator defends himself by saying that no man should be praised who violates the commonly accepted standards of behavior of his country; Dorimant clearly does so. Mr. Spectator then gives character sketches of Vocifer, who does not deserve to be called a fine gentleman, and Ignotus, who does because he acts on the basis of great and noble motives.

Spectator 76. Monday, May 28, 1711. Steele.

Mr. Spectator discusses the kind of person who makes the best friend; he finds that only those men who are well-ordered in their personal lives are constant in their friendships with others. As an example, he tells the story of Pharamond of France, a nobleman so humane that he was able to make everyone feel equal to him. With his close friend Eucrate, he made his court a place of wit and humor agreeable to all.

Spectator 77. Tuesday, May 29, 1711. Budgell.

Mr. Spectator describes Will Honeycomb as a man who is Absent, even though he is physically present, because he thinks of nothing at all, or because his mind is distracted by thoughts of something other than the immediate situation. On one occasion, he threw his watch into the river and put a pebble in his watch pocket because his mind was distracted. On one occasion, in a coffee-house, Will broke off a description of Moll Hinton which he was giving to a group of listeners when he saw his friend Mr. Spectator approach. Mr. Spectator points out that this malady of mind affects some men who are caught up in their studies and other men who are caught up in passions; he describes La Bruyère's "Absent Man," Menalcas, as an example. Menalcas frequently appears in public half dressed because he has forgotten to finish dressing; on one occasion, he swallowed dice and threw his glass of wine and water on the Backgammon board.

Spectator 78. Wednesday, May 30, 1711. Steele.

Mr. Spectator presents a letter from a man of Cambridge who offers for his consideration two other letters. The first claims that the Club of Ugly Faces was originally founded at Cambridge; accounts of the founding members are given in copious detail. One prospective member, insisting that he was not all that ugly, offered as proof his being kissed by a woman in the street in London; unfortunately for him the woman turned out to be a pickpocket. Another was proved to be so ugly that he caused a pregnant woman to miscarry and frightened two children into fits. Mr. Spectator is invited to join the Society of the Ugly Faces to go along with his membership in the Ugly Club of Oxford. A petition comes from Who and Which, who protest the encroachment of That into their proper usage in the English language.

Spectator 79. Thursday, May 31, 1711. Steele.

Mr. Spectator says that a number of his female correspondents have taken him to task for objecting to their behavior. One correspondent, protesting her youth, says that she will put off marriage in favor of the pleasures of the town which her innocence and virtue can get for her. She notes in a postscript that since her lover does not know she likes him, she is not engaged. Upon the theory of Will Honeycomb that "A Woman seldom writes her mind but in her Postscript," Mr. Spectator suspects that this woman will change the object of her affections ten times before she is married; he believes that men and women alike lack the love of laudable things. In contrast to this attitude, he describes Eudosia, who combines good breeding with all the arts of life. Her goodness is so much a habit that it would be as hard for her to think an erroneous thought as it would be for Flavia, a fine dancer, to enter a room ungracefully. He also offers a letter from Hecatissa, on the subject of how little people really understand their true minds. This correspondent says that many women spend too much time before the mirror because Mr. Spectator has not yet offered them the catalogue of a female library which he has promised. Philautia, an Idol, spends hours worshipping herself at her looking-glass. The religious books offered for women encourage a false sense of religious duty; one woman under the spell of these books plays cards for hours, leaves the game for an hour of prayer, and then returns to her cards. Dulcianara insists on speaking her mind to everyone about everything, and therefore is a nuisance both to her family and to her acquaintances. Thus, Mr. Spectator's catalogue of books for women is desperately needed.

Spectator 80. Friday, June 1, 1711. Steele.

Mr. Spectator recounts the history of Brunetta and Phillis, two beautiful women born on the same day in the same year who grew up as close friends. In spite of this, when they reached the age of 15, they became bitter rivals for the attentions of men. Phillis eventually married a man from Barbadoes and moved there to live as a queen surrounded by servants; Brunetta was not happy until she had married the man who owned the adjoining estate in Barbadoes. Not to be matched, Phillis acquired for herself an exquisite brocade dress. Brunetta had the final word, because she had a similar dress made for one of her black serving-women. Phillis has now returned to England in unconsolable despair. Mr. Spectator also presents a Postscript, a letter from That, who claims that Who and Which are inferior words.

Spectator 81. Saturday, June 2, 1711. Addison.

Mr. Spectator describes a visit to the opera in which he discovers two groups of women who seem to be at odds with each other. One group of women had patches on the right side of their foreheads, another group had patches on the left side of their foreheads, while a third group had patches arranged indifferently. He discovered, upon inquiry, that those with patches on the right sides of their faces were Whigs; those with patches on the left side were Tories; while those with patches arranged indifferently were politically neutral. In this context, he discovers that Rosalinda, a Whig, is very upset because she has a beautiful mole on the Tory side of her forehead; in a similar situation is Nigranilla who, because of a pimple, has to patch on the Whig side. Mr. Spectator discovers that more Tory-patchers attend the theatre, while more Whig-patchers attend the puppet show. Mr. Spectator urges that English women take the role of women in the battle between the Romans and the Sabines, in suing for peace rather than encouraging war. Mr. Spectator urges, with allusions to Greek precedent, that the proper place for women is in the home; therefore, women should stay out of politics.

Spectator 82. Monday, June 4, 1711. Steele.

Having encountered a former acquaintance of his who has been reduced from wealth to poverty, Mr. Spectator offers his reflections on the subject of debt and the sort of person who falls into it. He marvels that so many men can run the risk of financial ruin with so little forethought; Jack Truepenny, a friend of Sir Andrew, exemplifies the sort of man whose credulity destroys all of his other merits as well as his fortune.

Spectator 83. Tuesday, June 5, 1711. Addison.

Mr. Spectator says that when the weather is too bad for walking outdoors, he enjoys visiting art galleries with small groups of friends. After one such visit to a museum, he has a dream in which he finds himself in a large gallery in which the works of dead painters are arrayed on one side of the room while the works of living painters are displayed on the other. The artists at work on the living side of the gallery include Vanity, Stupidity, Fantasque, Avarice, and Industry. Another artist busily at work retouching his own work is Envy. Mr. Spectator is delighted with the realistic portraits of people he finds on the dead artists' side of the gallery.

Spectator 84. Wednesday, June 6, 1711. Steele.

Mr. Spectator continues the story of Pharamond by giving a character of Eucrate, Pharamond's close friend. Eucrate is described as being a compassionate man who is especially devoted to relieving the distress of those injured by unusual circumstances of nature or human nature. Once Eucrate brings before Pharamond the unfortunate Spinamont, who is deeply upset because he has killed his closest friend in a duel.

Spectator 85. Thursday, June 7, 1711. Addison.

Mr. Spectator declares that he reads every piece of printed paper that comes his way, regardless of its source. He claims that he has by humorous means run across a wide variety of fascinating items, including a ballad entitled the "Two Children in the Wood" which he discusses at length and compares favorably to Horace.

Spectator 86. Friday, June 8, 1711. Addison.

Mr. Spectator stresses the value for understanding human nature of reading the appearance of men's faces. To prove his point he tells a story of Socrates' visit to a Physiognomist, during which Socrates is described as a man having many serious faults. Socrates says that he might well have such faults if he had not conquered them through his philosophy.

Spectator 87. Saturday, June 9, 1711. Steele.

Mr. Spectator says that he has offered his papers in an attempt to enable people to become more aware of the significance of their behavior. To offer proof of some success in this, he prints a letter from Rosalinda, in which she, because of her oval face, wishes to participate in the Ugly Club along with Mr. Spectator and Hecatissa. She says that she has also begun to patch her face differently on both sides. Another correspondent complains that six or seven coffee-houses in the city are dominated by Idols, who sit all day to be adored by their worshippers. As a result, those who wish to use these coffee-houses for other purposes are prohibited from doing so.

Spectator 88. Monday, June 11, 1711. Steele.

Mr. Spectator receives a letter from Philo-Britannicus, who praises Mr. Spectator for his efforts at bettering the morals of the world. He hopes, however, that Mr. Spectator will turn some attention to the corruption of manners among the servants of the land, especially grooms. Mr. Spectator agrees, and says that he feels the misbehavior of servants is an evil which touches all of mankind. He attributes much of the corruptions of men-servants to the practice of giving them board-

wages; such practice enables them to frequent public
houses and imitate the behavior of their masters. Mr.
Spectator has overheard servants talking to each other
as though they were their masters. Along with public
houses, servants cause the most trouble at the entrance
of Hyde Park, while their masters are riding. Here,
servants have been known to carry on romances with
women of quality in the clothes and manners of their
masters. He recounts one meeting of a servant with
master while both were escourting ladies; the gentleman
behaved himself in an appropriate way and embarrassment
was prevented on all sides. Mr. Spectator promises more
discussion of this subject.

Spectator 89. Tuesday, June 12, 1711. Addison.

Mr. Spectator announces that the subject of this paper
is Love; he will take special notice of that category
of lovers known as Women of Dilatory Tempers, who have
the habit of lengthening the time of their courtship
greatly without either dismissing their lovers or agreeing to marry them. One letter on the subject, from a
lawyer, claims that he has been pursuing the same young
lady through a lengthy career at the law with no final
results. Such women are to be called Demurrers; a letter from Thirsis claims that his mistress has been de-
murring for seven years. Philander claims that his
Sylvia has demurred marriage with him until she is now
past the age of childbearing. Strephon writes that his
beloved has made an old man of him by her constant delays in their relationship. Finally, Mr. Spectator
prints a letter from Sam Hopewell, a pleasant man who
has at last married a Demurrer. Hopewell says that he
first began to love Martha at the age of twenty-two;
they were not married until 50 years later. She is
still, to Hopewell, a very charming old woman; he hopes
that Mr. Spectator will send a congratulatory letter or
perhaps an Epithalamium on the occasion of their long
delayed marriage. Mr. Spectator concludes with a list
of three points which he hopes will overcome the Folly
of Demurrage. The first is the shortness of life; the
timorous woman may die before she has made up her mind
about marriage. The second is the even shorter life of
beauty, while the third is the strange behavior shown
by some women of 60 years, who have not previously fallen
in love. He concludes his paper with a lengthy quotation from Milton's *Paradise Lost*, Book VIII, which is a
description of Eve as a modest and yet not unduly reti-
cent lover.

Spectator 90. Wednesday, June 13, 1711. Addison.

Mr. Spectator begins with an account of Plato's concept
of the permanent effects that passions of the body have
on the soul while it is in residence in the body. Such

impressions are permanent; the torture of a voluptuous man after death is in having desires that he cannot gratify. Mr. Spectator refers to the use of this notion by contemporary divines, by the ancients in the images of Tantalus, and by Virgil, in the sixth book of his *Aeneid*. To illustrate his concept of tantalism, or Platonic Hell, he tells a story from Monsieur Pontignan of a Love-Adventure of last summer. Having wooed energetically two beautiful women, M. Pontignan had every reason to expect the delights of a full-fledged affair with each of them. Unfortunately, the two women played a trick on him by getting him to let them bind him hand and foot so that he could not move. Having thus secured him, they proceeded to join him in bed, wearing only their nightgowns. The French gentleman assures us that spending the night close to so beautiful a pair of women without being able to move was far more than he would ever want to do again.

Spectator 91. Thursday, June 14, 1711. Steele.

Mr. Spectator tells the story of the Lady Honoria, a widow of forty years, and her daughter Flavia, a young woman of 15. The two women are companions more than they are mother and daughter; they are also, to some extent, rivals for the attention of gentlemen in the town. Even as the two women try to outdo each other, so do their principal lovers--Dick Crastin, the admirer of Honoria, and Tom Tulip the pretender to Flavia. Once, when Crastin recited part of a poem by Rochester to greater effect than Tulip had recited lines from Ovid's *Art of Love*, Tulip retaliated by casting aspersions on the virility of Crastin. In response, Crastin challenged Tulip to a duel, an appointment that Tulip never kept. Flavia, disappointed in her lover is now fallen in love with Crastin. Mr. Spectator promises more of this *History of the Rival Mother*.

Spectator 92. Friday, June 15, 1711. Addison.

Mr. Spectator receives a letter from Leonora, who tells him of the importance which the *Spectator* papers have for her. She strongly encourages Mr. Spectator to deliver on his promise of a list of books recommended for ladies. Mr. Spectator reports that since promising to deliver such a list he has gotten lots of assistance in preparing it. Booksellers have invariably recommended titles published by them. Husbands write recommending books that would severely regulate the lives of women. A number of women themselves have written urging the inclusion of books and plays about love rather than Manuals of Devotion or Books of Housewifery. Coquettilla is especially concerned that women not be forced upon their knees, while Florella desires a book against Prudes. Mr. Spectator also thanks Men

241

of Learning, who have also offered their suggestions. He has found the task of preparing this list to be extremely difficult, but he promises to get on with it. He is delighted that a number of ladies of the town seem to be improving themselves as a result of his Speculations. Mr. Spectator also informs us that Tom Tattle is an Impertinent Fellow, that Will Trippett has begun to act suspiciously, and that Frank Smoothly will soon become a Coxcomb.

Spectator 93. NF. Saturday, June 16, 1711. Addison.

Mr. Spectator notices that while all men complain of the shortness of life, few know how to spend their time with profit. He suggests a number of methods including the Exercise of Virtue, Prayer, Reading, Useful Diversions, Friendship, and the Arts.

Spectator 94. Monday, June 18, 1711. Addison.

Mr. Spectator continues his discussion of the best ways to spend one's time in an argument, based on Locke, that time spent in study, reading, and the pursuit of knowledge not only lengthens life but also turns all of it to the studious man's advantage. Mr. Spectator also notes Mallebranche's observations on this subject. He then retells two "Eastern Fables" to illustrate the importance of learning. The first, from the *Alcoran*, describes a visit with God, on which the Angel Gabriel took Mahomet, which took only the briefest amount of time. The second tale, also of Mahomet, tells how a Sultan of Egypt doubted the truth of the first story about Mahomet. As a result, Mahomet had the Sultan insert his head in a tub of water, whereupon he immediately found himself in a strange country where he lived long enough to marry and have seven sons and seven daughters. Reduced to a desperate state of poverty, he plunged himself into the sea to wash himself before prayer only to find that he was immediately returned to the tub where he began. Mr. Spectator goes on to claim that the hours of a wise man are lengthened by his Ideas, although the hours of a Fool are shortened by his passions.

Spectator 95. Tuesday, June 19, 1711. Steele.

Mr. Spectator receives a letter from a correspondent who urges Mr. Spectator to discuss General Mourning more deeply than he did in *Spectator* 64. The correspondent especially objects to those who establish elaborate rules and regulations for grief, and judge the depth of a mourner's feelings according to how much he lives up to their pre-ordained images. A second letter, from Annabella, declares her appreciation of Mr. Spectator's efforts on behalf of women. Annabella says, however, that Mr. Spectator should not praise women for being

more scholarly than men (see *Spectator* 92); real praise
of women would be of their improvement in the spheres
of being better daughters, wives, mothers, and friends.
She recommends for the education of women Fénelon's
treatise *The Education of a Daughter* as a work which
belongs on Mr. Spectator's list of books for women.

Spectator 96. Wednesday, June 20, 1711. Steele.

Thomas Trusty writes to complain that in *Spectator* 88
Mr. Spectator finds no place for the Good Servant, and
goes on to tell his story, presenting himself as an
example of such a man. He describes his birth to a
tenant of the family of Sir Stephen Rackrent, who hired
him to accompany his son Harry to school. When his
young master dies, Tom must find other means of employment. His first is as servant to a young man of the
Temple, who spends most of his time writing love letters
and frequenting Public Houses. Dismissed when his master marries, Tom then becomes a go-between for a young
woman, who also lets him go when she marries. He then
spends some time with a good family, until he finds his
master in an embrace with the chambermaid; he leaves
this position in haste. He uses his experiences to draw
the conclusion that in many cases servants are of higher
moral character than their masters.

Spectator 97. Thursday, June 21, 1711. Steele.

Mr. Spectator tells the story of a conversation between
Pharamond and Eucrate on the subject of duels; as a
result of this conversation, Pharamond subsequently
issues a "Edict against Duels."

Spectator 98. Friday, June 22, 1711. Addison.

Mr. Spectator discusses the variety of ways in which
women, in his memory, have worn their hair. To describe
the excesses of hair-shaping, he tells the story of a
woman who forced her hair into towering spires, until
she heard a Monk, Thomas Conecte, preach against this
subject. Mr. Spectator argues that women's natural
beauty is best; anything which alters nature is of
necessity less attractive.

Spectator 99. Saturday, June 23, 1711. Addison.

Mr. Spectator describes how at a meeting of his Club
the subject of conversation was the chief Point of
Honour among men and women; the conclusion is that among
men it is Courage and among women it is Chastity. Mr.
Spectator recounts the pattern of Courage from Books
of Chivalry, in which the knight, having fallen in love,
must demonstrate his courage by trying to defeat enemies
more powerful than himself for seven years before he can
expect his lady to take notice of him. In Spain, Mr.

Spectator reports that it is as wrong for a lady to
glance accidentally at her lover out a window as it is
right for him to show his passion for her by fighting
bulls. The great violation of honor among men is to
accuse another man of lying; this affront can only be
settled, at the moment, by fighting duels. Mr. Spectator finds dueling to be an unfortunate way of settling
a question of honor; he illustrates this by telling a
brief story of how a French gentleman and an English
gentleman almost came to blows because the French
gentleman was using dueling language to talk about
something else. Mr. Spectator concludes by urging that
when the dictates of honor go contrary to those of religion and equity, they are deprivations of human nature.

Spectator 100. Monday, June 25, 1711. Steele.

Mr. Spectator says that since so much of a man's life is
filled with sickness, ill-humor, and idleness, every man
should cultivate a predisposition to be pleased and satisfied with his lot in life. Men when they are ill
should keep to their chambers, instead of appearing in
public; Sir Roger de Coverley always orders some Posset-
drink for anyone he hears planning to be out of order;
as a result, those who are around him always have a
cheerful disposition. Mr. Spectator praises those who
have obtained the blessings of a reasonable mind; as an
example of the cost of not achieving such an acceptance
of advancing age, Mr. Spectator tells the story of Harry
Tersett and his lady, Rebecca Quickly. Having married
each other and satisfied their desires, they now find
that their lives have come to a standstill; the passage
of time makes both of them tedious. Varilas is given
as an example of a man who has good humor and therefore
is welcomed to every group.

Spectator 101. Tuesday, June 26, 1711. Addison.

Mr. Spectator agrees that censure is a risk that all
public men run; only the passage of time gives us a true
sense of great men and small in any age. He then tries
to imagine how a historian, three hundred years hence,
will describe the reign of Queen Anne and Mr. Spectator
himself. This future historian describes briefly Mr.
Spectator's external appearance, his friendship with
Sir Roger de Coverley, and his descriptions of life in
eighteenth-century London. The last part of this imaginary historical account is not given, because Mr.
Spectator says that it is far too laudatory.

Spectator 102. Wednesday, June 27, 1711. Addison.

Mr. Spectator presents a letter from a correspondent
who describes an Academy which the correspondent has
established for training young women in the Exercise
of the Fan. Women are instructed how to "Handle your

Fans, Unfurl your Fans, Discharge your Fans, Ground
your Fans, Recover your Fans and Flutter your Fans."
The letter then describes in detail the training program which women in the Academy are put through so that
each of these maneuvers can be properly learned. It
concludes by describing a work entitled *Passions of
the Fan*, which is a scholarly study of the use of fans
by women.

Spectator 103. Thursday, June 28, 1711. Steele.

Mr. Spectator's Club is reminded by the Clergyman-member
that excessive use of civilities in conversations with
each other really represents a debasement of language.
The Clergyman calls the Club's attention to a sermon of
Archbishop Tillotson on the subject of Sincerity. Mr.
Spectator quotes the sermon at length.

Spectator 104. Friday, June 29, 1711. Steele.

Mr. Spectator declares how nice it would be if no one
transgressed against "that Rule of Life called Decorum,
or a Regard to Decency." As an example of indecorous
behavior, Mr. Spectator discusses an Equestrian Order
of Ladies which is described to him at length by a correspondent. The correspondent, having seen a woman
dressed in men's attire riding with a group of horse-
men, traces the history of this practice and concludes
that it goes awkwardly with English modesty.

Spectator 105. Saturday, June 30, 1711. Addison.

Mr. Spectator gives a character of Will Honeycomb, who
feels that as a result of his wide experience in the
world he has the Knowledge of Mankind, which he feels
is the Learning of a Gentleman. He contrasts this kind
of learning favorably with the learning of those who
have acquired their knowledge from books. Mr. Spectator analyzes the strengths and weaknesses of the two
different kinds of learning and finds that both types
are, in the final analysis, two different kinds of
pedantry. He also describes the Military Pedant, the
State-Pedant, and the Book-Pedant. Learning of any
sort will not make a man wise, if he has a natural
tendency to be vain or arrogant.

Spectator 106. Monday, July 2, 1711. Addison.

Mr. Spectator goes to the country with Sir Roger de
Coverley. He notes the high regard all of Sir Roger's
servants have for the distinguished older gentleman.
Sir Roger plays a fatherly role to all those in his
household, including his servants. During this visit
he tells Mr. Spectator of how he found the man who
serves as the parson for his parish; he describes the
parson as a man who has always asked favors for others

but never asked for anything for himself. Mr. Spectator hears the Clergyman preach and wishes that more of the country clergy would follow his example.

Spectator 107. Tuesday, July 3, 1711. Steele.

Mr. Spectator describes with praise the even-handed and economical way in which Sir Roger conducts his household. Because he is respected for his benevolence, Sir Roger lives like a prince rather than a master in his household. Sir Roger is a model of the man of honor and generosity. Mr. Spectator concludes his paper with an elaborate description of a painting of Sir Roger which hangs in his portrait gallery. The picture depicts a servant saving Sir Roger from drowning.

Spectator 108. Wednesday, July 4, 1711. Addison.

While Mr. Spectator is staying with Sir Roger, a neighbor named Will Wimble sends Sir Roger a huge fish which he had caught that day. Sir Roger describes, in a lengthy character, Will Wimble as a country gentleman who is an expert in all the country arts of hunting and fishing. In the midst of the character sketch, Wimble arrives to have dinner and pleasant conversation with Sir Roger and his guest. Mr. Spectator says that Wimble is an example of the young man whose family would rather that he starve as a gentleman than prosper in a trade or profession.

Spectator 109. Thursday, July 5, 1711. Steele.

Sir Roger and Mr. Spectator walk in Sir Roger's portrait gallery; Sir Roger describes with delight these paintings of his ancestors. They first examine two portraits, one of a beautiful lady and the other of a knight of the Tudor era who won her affections in a tournament. They then examine a group of three portraits, of three sisters. Two of the sisters died, and the third was carried away by a gentleman of a neighboring estate. The next portrait is of a man who at one time owned the estate; having more wit and manners than judgement, he plunged the estate into debt. The debt was paid off by another man, whom Sir Andrew Freeport claims was one of the children of the woman carried away by a neighboring gentleman. The last portrait they examine is of Sir Humphrey de Coverley, a man of great integrity, honesty, and foresight. The discussion of paintings is ended by a call to dinner.

Spectator 110. Friday, July 6, 1711. Addison.

Mr. Spectator takes a walk in the ruins of an Abbey and speculates on the nature of ghosts. Sir Roger tells him that so much of his house was thought to be haunted that he had the entire place exorcised by his chaplain.

Mr. Spectator says that the enormous amount of evidence
for the existence of ghosts suggests that those who believe in them are more reasonable than those who do not.
He offers the theory of Lucretius as to the nature of
ghosts, and concludes with a story from Josephus concerning the dream of Glaphyra, daughter to King Arch-
ilaus. The lady, married to her third husband, dreamed
that she saw her first husband reproach her for her re-
marriage; she died soon thereafter.

Spectator 111. Saturday, July 7, 1711. Addison.

Mr. Spectator describes some reflections of his on the
subject of immortality of the soul, which he engaged in
while walking in Sir Roger's Woods. He offers several
arguments for the soul's immortality, and says he especially delights in the notion that the soul perpetually
progresses toward perfection.

Spectator 112. Monday, July 9, 1711. Addison.

Mr. Spectator describes a country Sunday at Sir Roger's;
Mr. Spectator finds that Sunday has a great civilizing
effect on mankind. The two go to church, where Sir
Roger has provided everyone with a cushion and a Book of
Common Prayer; he will allow no one to sleep in church
but himself. In the middle of this day's service, Sir
Roger calls out to John Matthews to stop disturbing
the congregation by clicking his heels together. Mr.
Spectator delights at the understanding that exists between Sir Roger and his chaplain, and their united effort
of doing good.

Spectator 113. Tuesday, July 10, 1711. Steele.

While on a walk, Sir Roger tells Mr. Spectator about his
disappointment in love with the Perverse Widow. This
leads Sir Roger to a lengthy discussion of his life,be-
ginning with his assumption of the estate at the age of
22. While serving as sheriff, he met the Widow, who
captivated the court in which she was to make an appearance. Sir Roger praises the Widow as a woman of dignity,
composure, and civility. After describing her at length,
Sir Roger is overcome, and Mr. Spectator must lead him
back to the house. The paper ends with an epigram of
Martial which describes how a woman can dominate a man's
thoughts.

Spectator 114. Wednesday, July 11, 1711. Steele.

Mr. Spectator describes a dinner at Sir Roger's attended
by a number of country gentlemen. This leads Mr. Spectator to a discussion of economy in men's affairs, which
he finds has the same affect upon a man's fortunes as
good breeding has upon his conversation. One of the men
at the dinner drinks too much; it, therefore, does not

surprise Mr. Spectator to learn that although he is a
wealthy man, he is greatly in debt. To illustrate his
point further, he tells the story of Laertes and Irus;
Laertes and Irus are neighbors, but Irus conducts his
affairs out of a fear of poverty and Laertes conducts
his by the shame of it. Irus only buys what he has to
have, while Laertes buys things he doesn't need. Mr.
Spectator quotes Cowley approvingly, and concludes by
saying that everyman should set himself a sum of money
which he will not exceed in his spending.

Spectator 115. Thursday, July 12, 1711. Addison.

Mr. Spectator praises the healthy body which results
from living in the country. Sir Roger's fine physical
condition is an example of the benefits of exercise
gained in the country, especially from hunting. Sir
Roger tells Mr. Spectator that when the Perverse Widow
is being especially cruel to him he would double his
efforts in fox hunting. Riding, to Mr. Spectator, is
the most effective form of exercise he knows. Mr. Spectator concludes this paper by saying that when he was
younger, he learned the art of shadow boxing to keep
his body in healthy condition.

Spectator 116. Friday, July 13, 1711. Budgell.

Mr. Spectator again praises Sir Roger for getting so
much exercise in the country; he describes a rabbit hunt
on which he recently accompanied Sir Roger. Mr. Spectator finds the barking of the dogs, the fresh air, the
sounding of the horn, the exercise on the ride, and the
echoes of all the sounds from the neighboring hills to
be an invigorating experience. The rabbit, having been
caught, is not killed, but is let go in Sir Roger's
orchard where other Prisoners of War are held. Mr.
Spectator quotes Pascal's objections to hunting; he rejects them because he is convinced of the good health
which results from hunting. He resolves to go hunting
with Sir Roger twice a week during his stay.

Spectator 117. Saturday, July 14, 1711. Addison.

Mr. Spectator says that on some subjects, such as witchcraft, a man should be neutral, refusing to take sides
so as to avoid making errors. There are sufficient reports of witches for Mr. Spectator to believe there must
be some substance to the belief, but so many of the people who are supposed to be witches are really mentally
diseased, that Mr. Spectator feels he cannot take a
stand on either side of the issue. Sir Roger and Mr.
Spectator, while walking in the woods, encounter Moll
White, who is claimed by many to be a witch. They visit
her home, finding it a wretched, disgraceful place for
a human being to live. Sir Roger's chaplain has kept
him from bringing charges of witchcraft against the poor

old woman. This leads Mr. Spectator to conclude that many witches are merely unfortunate old women whose old age has brought with it a deliriousness of mind and the fancies of the poor person's townspeople.

Spectator 118. Monday, July 16, 1711. Steele.

Mr. Spectator describes how delightful it is for a city man to walk in the woods. While on such a walk, Sir Roger tells Mr. Spectator how the Perverse Widow keeps him off balance. Sir Roger warns Mr. Spectator to avoid people who share confidences with each other. Orestilla has a great fortune and is therefore very suspicious of new acquaintances; Themista, her confidant, is just as careful of all whom she speaks to. In the midst of this discussion, they run across Mr. William, Sir Roger's Master of the Game, and Betty, with whom he is in love. Sir Roger and Mr. Spectator observe William say he will kill himself if he cannot have the love of Betty. Betty asks him about his feelings toward Susan Holliday; William tells her not to believe a word that Kate Willow has said. This is, for Sir Roger, evidence of the danger of trusting confidants; he decides to move the wedding date of the two forward before they run into other kinds of difficulties. Sir Roger goes on to tell Mr. Spectator he is not sorry he has had the unhappy love relationship with the Widow, because the thought of her makes him feel beautiful. He concludes by saying that he would give ten pounds to hear her argue with Sir Andrew Freeport about trade.

Spectator 119. Tuesday, July 17, 1711. Addison.

Mr. Spectator's adventures in the country lead him to compare the country with the city especially in terms of behavior and good breeding. Mr. Spectator points out that while manners in the town have taken on a certain casualness, manners in the country still preserve the formality of an earlier age. The excessive politeness of some country people is an annoyance to Mr. Spectator who objects to eating a cold dinner at Sir Roger's because carrying out ceremony prevented the meal from being eaten hot. Will Wimble is especially bothersome in his excessive pursuit of manners. Another point of difference is that gentlemen of the city have begun to use coarse language; such abandonment of modesty **has,** fortunately, not yet reached the country. A third point of difference is that people in the country still wear the clothes of an earlier era; they have not yet adopted the fashions of town.

Spectator 120. Wednesday, July 18, 1711. Addison.

Sir Roger delights in Mr. Spectator's curiosity about his chickens. This leads Mr. Spectator to a series of reflections on the instincts of animals in caring for

their young and pursuing their two main passions, lust
and hunger.

Spectator 121. Thursday, July 19, 1711. Addison.

Mr. Spectator observes a hen followed by a brood of
ducks on Sir Roger's estate and reflects at length on
the subject of instinct. Quoting Locke, Cicero, and
others, Mr. Spectator points out that animals, while
they lack reason, share with man all the lower parts of
human nature.

Spectator 122. Friday, July 20, 1711. Addison.

Mr. Spectator says that a man's first concern should be
to avoid the reproaches of his own heart, while his second should be to escape censure by the world. With this
in mind, he describes a trip with Sir Roger to the
Country-Assizes. They make the journey with Will Wimble;
he talks to a couple of men whom Sir Roger describes to
Mr. Spectator. The first is a man who kills animals to
give him more meat in his diet; the second, Tom Touchy,
a man who has at one time or another sued everyone in
town on little or no provocation. On this occasion, he
threatens to sue Will Wimble for fishing in the wrong
part of the river. Mr. Spectator is delighted with the
honor paid his friend Sir Roger by those around him.
On the way home, they find a former servant of Sir
Roger's has had a painting of the good gentleman hung
over his tavern, which he has named The Knight's Head.
Sir Roger says he is too much flattered by this, and
encourages the former servant to alter the painting and
rename the inn The Saracen's Head. The honor paid his
friend makes the travels very pleasant for Mr. Spectator.

Spectator 123. Saturday, July 21, 1711. Addison.

Sir Roger and Mr. Spectator meet a spoiled young man,
who like others of their type feels that he does not
have to work at anything to be successful in the world.
This leads Mr. Spectator to tell the story of Eudoxus
and Leontine, both of whom began life with small estates.
Eudoxus became a lawyer and gathered a small fortune.
Leontine sought knowledge and improvement of his mind.
At the age of forty, both men decided to retire to the
country; they both married and bought estates near each
other. Eudoxus' estate was much larger than Leontine's.
Eudoxus had a son named Florio, and Leontine had a daughter named Leonilla. To make sure that each child had
the proper upbringing, the two men swapped children.
Florio, seeing the poorness of his supposed father,
realized that he had to make his own way in the world,
and threw himself into his studies and became a successful lawyer. Florio and Leonilla fell in love with each
other but despaired of marrying because of the disparity
in their fortunes. Ultimately, however, the exchange

of children was revealed, and the two happy children
were united in marriage.

Spectator 124. Monday, July 23, 1711. Addison.

Mr. Spectator describes the difficulties as well as the
rewards of preparing his paper, and promises to continue
his rural speculations to the end of the month. He is
not at all concerned when men of no taste or learning
reject his papers; to illustrate why, he tells the Fable
of the Mole. The Mole, trying to improve his eyesight,
gets a pair of spectacles, but his mother reminds him
that while glasses might be good for men they are of no
use to a mole. Those who are not interested in his
paper are therefore considered to be moles.

Spectator 125. Tuesday, July 24, 1711. Addison.

Sir Roger tells Mr. Spectator a story of his youth in
which a group of people accused him of being a Papist
because he asked for St. Ann's Lane and also ridiculed
him when he asked for Ann's Lane. This is evidence to
Mr. Spectator of the ill effects of a spirit of division
in the country; division weakens morals and understand-
ings, destroys common sense, and wrecks the virtue of
the nation. Mr. Spectator quotes Plutarch to the effect
that one should not hate one's enemies because such
hatred leads to a general viciousness of mind. Mr.
Spectator also objects to the way in which party spirit
obscures the perception of truth on either side of an
issue. He also objects to the way in which party division promotes the spread of scandalous stories whether
true or false about men in public life. Mr. Spectator
encourages the establishment of an honest Body of
Neutral Forces, to promote the recognition of merit on
both sides and the common rejection of villany.

Spectator 126. Wednesday, July 25, 1711. Addison.

Mr. Spectator continues his plans for forming an Association for Honest Men of all Parties with a document
designed to bring this association into being. He describes the benefits of such an association and uses
as a fable lore from Siculus about an animal called the
Ichneumon, who spends his time breaking crocodile eggs,
therefore preventing crocodiles from overrunning Egypt.
Ordinary men spend their time trying to destroy men of
eminence; Mr. Spectator hopes that his Association will
limit this violent tendency among Englishmen. Mr. Spectator further describes Sir Roger de Coverley and Sir
Andrew Freeport as men of different principles and financial interests. The old knight is concerned with
land; his friend, with money. Sir Roger's support of
the Tory party and Sir Andrew's support of the Whig
party never go beyond good-humored banter between the
two of them; other people, however, take party division

more seriously. Evidence of the heat of party division
is the refusal of gamblers to admit a member of parliament who had taken an unpopular vote to their games.
Mr. Spectator stops Will Wimble from telling malicious
stories about a great man and is thus considered a
Fanatic.

Spectator 127. Thursday, July 26, 1711. Addison.

After having heard Sir Roger read Dyer's *Letter,* Mr.
Spectator reads him a letter in which the correspondent
laments the deplorable state to which women have sunk
since Sir Roger left London for the country. Having
abandoned tall wigs under Mr. Spectator's urging, they
now have adopted wide bottoms, created by using the
Hoop-Petticoat. Some men consider this fashion an omen
of political misfortune; others, a cover for pregnancy.
Even as Alexander the Great buried the armor of giants
to make people think he commanded an army of giants,
even so people in the future would think the women of
the day were of monstrous size if they could see only
these items of dress. One of the most disturbing things
about them is that they make the streets even more
crowded than they are.

Spectator 128. Friday, July 27, 1711. Addison.

Mr. Spectator discusses the differences in temperament
between men and women and describes several couples to
give examples. Unfortunately, light-headed women tend
to attract light-headed men. Faustina, married to Marcus Aurelius, preferred the more foolish sort of man.
She reared her son Commodus to be such a person; as a
result he became the most foolish and abandoned Tyrant
ever to head the Roman Empire. In a similar vein, Mr.
Spectator points out Sir Roger's neighbors, a country
couple consisting of a wife, an old coquette, who wishes
to be in the town, and an old Rustick, who refuses to
take her. In contrast, Mr. Spectator describes the marriage of Aristus and Aspatia, who are a perfect combi-
nation of vivacity and gravity. The children combine
the qualities of both parents and are models of benevolence and satisfaction.

Spectator 129. Saturday, July 28, 1711. Addison.

Mr. Spectator notes that great portrait-painters never
paint people in the fashions of the day because they
are always changing. He laments that people who live
in the country all too often follow the outlandish fashions of the city. He presents a letter from a lawyer
on the dress of women he noticed while riding the
Western Circuit. The further he moves from London, the
older the fashions are; nevertheless, whatever the age
of the fashion, those who pursue it, pursue it to extremes. A woman, who spent the winter in London, causes

a stir in Cornwall when she shows up in church wearing
one of the oversized Hoop-Petticoats then fashionable
in the city. The correspondent promises further reports
on outlandish fashions in the country at a later time.

Spectator 130. Monday, July 30, 1711. Addison.

While riding in the fields, Sir Roger and Mr. Spectator
encounter a band of gypsies. Sir Roger describes their
customs and habits, and the two stop to have their fortunes told. Sir Roger is pleased that his fortune contains the promise of marriage with his Widow. His pleasure lasts only so long as it takes to discover that his
pocket has been picked. To conclude his paper, Mr. Spectator tells the story of a man who is reunited with his
wealthy father after spending some years with gypsies.
He becomes a successful public figure, finally serving
as ambassador to some of the countries in which he wandered as a gypsy.

Spectator 131. Tuesday, July 31, 1711. Addison.

Even as Sir Roger hunts on the boundaries of his estate,
Mr. Spectator says that he has spent a month on the
boundaries of his middle estate. He discovers that Sir
Roger's neighbors are beginning to talk strangely about
him. Will Wimble fears that he is a murderer, while a
justice of the peace fears he is a Jesuit. Some people
fear he is a conjurer and point to his association with
Moll White. Other of Sir Roger's friends are afraid
that he is being imposed upon by a freeloader. Since
Will Honeycomb has written urging him to return to the
city and since some of his city friends believe he is
in love with one of Sir Roger's dairy maids, Mr. Spectator says that he sets out for London tomorrow.

Spectator 132. Wednesday, August 1, 1711. Steele.

Mr. Spectator describes his return journey from the
country to the city. His companions in the coach include Mrs. Betty Arable, a woman of wealth; her widowed
mother; young Squire Quickset, her cousin; Ephraim the
Quaker, Arable's guardian; Mr. Spectator; and a recruiting officer. Their conversation begins disagreeably,
with the soldier claiming he will be a suitor of either
the widow or her daughter and the Quaker telling him to
mind his own business. The soldier is good humored
about this retort to his advances, and the journey becomes increasingly pleasant with every passing mile.

Spectator 133. Thursday, August 2, 1711. Steele.

Mr. Spectator describes the mixture of terror with delight which comes from the contemplation of death. He
cites examples of Socrates, Phocion, Niocles, and
Epaminondas, as men who faced their deaths not only with

realistic apprehension but also with good humor. Mr. Spectator then tells of an incident in which he went to visit a friend with the intention of kidding him about his intended marriage, only to discover that he was dying. Mr. Spectator recounts for us the soliloquy he gave to the young man's mother in an attempt to make her grief more bearable.

Spectator 134. Friday, August 3, 1711. Steele.

Mr. Spectator catches up on his correspondence by presenting a series of letters which arrived during his stay in the country. The first, from George Trusty, praises Mr. Spectator's abilities in improving the moral character of his readers. He recommends that the *Spectator* be read for six successive mornings with half an ounce of Virginia tobacco. The person who follows this regimen is guaranteed to become open, obliging, officious, frank and hospitable. William Wiseacre writes that he wishes to enroll his daughter and his son in the Fan School so that they will learn the discipline of handling this object of fashion. The paper concludes with a petition of Benjamin Easie, who having observed a woman well-trained in the use of the fan, wishes that a school be established to teach gentlemen how to handle their snuff-boxes in an equally capable fashion.

Spectator 135. NF. Saturday, August 4, 1711. Addison.

Mr. Spectator says that he is delighted to have been born an Englishman, primarily because of the splendor of the English language.

Spectator 136. Monday, August 6, 1711. Steele.

Mr. Spectator offers a letter from a self-professed liar. The author of this letter suggests that there are sufficient numbers of his sort of person in London so that they should form a Club, called *The Historians*. As evidence of his skill in lying, he tells a story of his cousin, supposedly a volunteer in the Russian army. After giving other examples of his habit of lying, the correspondent makes clear that he is the sort of person who would rather tell a lie than appear ignorant.

Spectator 137. Tuesday, August 7, 1711. Steele.

Mr. Spectator expresses his concern over those servants whose masters do not allow them the happiness to which they are entitled. He presents a letter from Ralph Valet, in which the correspondent says that his master is the exact opposite of Sir Roger de Coverley. An unhappy person, Valet's master keeps him under constant surveillance and is constantly finding fault with his behavior. Another letter, from a Patience Giddy, describes her life as a servant to a Lady and her Woman.

The Lady is indecisive in her choice of garments and must dress and undress twenty times before deciding on what she will wear each day; this results in her two servants running into each other over and over as they rush around finding new choices of clothing. Mr. Spectator describes a servant in worse condition, a boy of 14 who must carry the garments of a very fat Master. In contrast to this mistreatment of servants, Mr. Spectator describes the household of Pamphilio, who treats his servants as human beings and thus has a happy household.

Spectator 138. Wednesday, August 8, 1711. Steele.

With examples from Cicero, Mr. Spectator describes the story-teller who spends most of his time describing circumstances, so that he never gets around to the point of his tale. A similar person is the preacher who tries to prove the obvious in his sermons. Another type is the kind of man who raises arguments over inconsequential subjects. Mr. Spectator ends this issue with an *Advertisement* for Exercises of the Snuff-Box, to be taught at Charles Lillie's; Mr. Spectator assumes that before long Snuff-Box users will be trained to take on the Regiment of Fans, which have been lately trained.

Spectator 139. NF. Thursday, August 9, 1711. Steele.

Mr. Spectator offers an essay on the subject of mankind's love of glory; he offers as examples the King of France and the Emperor of Russia.

Spectator 140. Friday, August 10, 1711. Steele.

Mr. Spectator offers a series of petitions from his readers. Lydia Novell writes to learn if her Suitor really loves her; his words to her are impassioned, but his actions are temperate. Another correspondent writes to ask Mr. Spectator's comment on the despicable state of letters; he finds that contemporary writers imitate only the superficial qualities of a Milton, a Cowley, or or an Ovid. Betty Saunter writes to know if Dimpple should be spelled with one or two "p's." Parthenope criticizes Mr. Spectator's information on petticoats. Another correspondent writes to urge care in the mixing of wine and conversation. Rachel Basto objects to Female Gamesters, who waste their time at the Ombre Table. Finally, Parthenia writes urging Mr. Spectator to help her, as he has helped Eleonora, to learn some useful books for her to read.

Spectator 141. Saturday, August 11, 1711. Steele.

Mr. Spectator says that he has received requests from actors who wish him to lower his standards for good acting. Some of their requests he will tolerate for a season, but hopes that such practices will not survive

the return of people of condition and taste to the
theaters. He presents a letter from a correspondent
who complains about over-tricky stage craft. Having
heard that Moll White was to play a role in Shadwell's
The Lancashire Witches, the correspondent went to see
the play, and sits next to a neighbor of Sir Roger de
Coverley. The correspondent finds the play a poor imitation of Shakespeare's *Macbeth*, and objects to the way
in which the witches' powers are presented. He believes
the moral of the play has little to do with its contents.

Spectator 142. Monday, August 13, 1711. Steele.

Mr. Spectator offers a series of letters as Images of
a Worthy Passion. The first letter is to Mr. Spectator
from Andromache; she offers a series of letters from
her deceased husband to illustrate love in its best
sense and to oppose the false notion of Gallantry in
Love. The first letter offers Andromache her suitor's
undivided attention and devotion. The second offers
his prayers that God reward her for her innocence and
protect her in all her doings. A third letter objects
to the way in which business distracts him from his
expression of his love, while a fourth looks forward to
conversation and companionship with her. The next letter asserts that all of his ambition and health is in
loving her,while the final letter protests that nothing
can take away from his esteem for her.

Spectator 143. Tuesday, August 14, 1711. Steele.

Mr. Spectator discusses what men expect of their acquaintances; companions should join in with the spirit
of the group rather than distract from its pleasures.
Cottilus is a good companion because, although he has
been beset by many misfortunes, he has made peace with
the world and is able to enjoy companionship and tranquillity. Uranius has overcome pain by concerning himself with hope for the world to come. Mr. Spectator
concludes this discussion with a long quotation from
Thomas Burnet, to the effect that consolation in this
world comes from aspirations to happiness in the world
to come.

Spectator 144. Wednesday, August 15, 1711. Steele.

Noting that "beauty has been the Delight and Torment
of the World ever since it began," Mr. Spectator describes those women of the town who are dangerous because of their looks. Amaryllis is naturally beautiful, while Dulcissa is beautiful because of her Art.
Merab possesses both Beauty and Wit, but each is at
war with the other. Albacinda is a destroyer who makes
her admirers more hopeful than they should be. Eudosia
combines beauty and Nobility of Spirit, while Eucratia
epitomizes the kind and submissive sort of beauty.

Omnamante is a model of deceit, for she combines an outward appearance as innocent as Lucrece with a mind as
wild as Cleopatra; she constantly changes roles to control her admirers. Mr. Spectator concludes with a warning against valuing beauty too highly.

Spectator 145. Thursday, August 16, 1711. Steele.

Mr. Spectator offers letters from a series of correspondents protesting various enormities. The first correspondent compliments Mr. Spectator on his description of
frivolous Disputants and adds to the list Wagerers who
constantly insist on making bets over frivolous questions.
A second correspondent objects to those who sing or
whistle in Public Rooms. The third letter is from a
female correspondent who insists that an old bachelor
who has been annoying her and her female companions
marry one of them soon or they will expose him as a
clown. The final correspondent is a woman who, while
pointing out that she has reduced the size of her petticoat, insists that men have imitated the same fashion
in the size of the skirt of fashionable men's coats.

Spectator 146. NF. Friday, August 17, 1711. Steele.

Mr. Spectator says that the highest pleasure our minds
are capable of enjoying with composure is the reading
of sublime thoughts expressed by men of genius and eloquence. As examples, Mr. Spectator offers a passage
from Cicero describing Socrates' speech upon hearing of
his impending execution and a passage from Thomas Burnet,
Theory of the Earth on the magnificence of the world.

Spectator 147. Saturday, August 18, 1711. Steele.

Mr. Spectator offers a letter from a correspondent who
comments at length upon the way in which services are
read in the Church of England.

Spectator 148. Monday, August 20, 1711. Steele.

Mr. Spectator's correspondents inform him of the new
evils which they have noticed in the town. His correspondent of *Spectator* 145 writes that the Voluntary-Singer
has now become a dancer as well. Mr. Spectator declares
him an Outlaw. He then gives the character of the Loud
Speaker, another kind of Impertinent which the sober
people of England may run into in mixed company. Another
Imperinent closely related to the Loud Speaker is the
Whisperer who disturbs the tranquillity of society
equally as much. In response to the complaint of some
ladies of the town that they have been visited by a man
wiser than they, Mr. Spectator writes letters to the
dancing Outlaw and the wise man arranging for them to
change places so that each will have an audience appropriate to his conduct. In his letter to the wise man,

257

he remarks that wisdom is unappreciated by many women, who find it impertinent.

Spectator 149. Tuesday, August 21, 1711. Steele.

Mr. Spectator receives a letter from Sylvia, a widow, who writes for advice on which of two men to marry. Mr. Spectator replies that if Strephon and Florio are equal in their characters, the richer is the man to choose, but if they are not equal, the better man is the proper choice, regardless of his wealth. Mr. Spectator goes on to describe the sorts of people who make up insipid marriages, vexatious marriages, or happy marriages.

Spectator 150. Wednesday, August 22, 1711. Budgell.

Upon hearing an advertisement for a pamphlet entitled *The 99 Plagues of an Empty Purse*, Mr. Spectator discusses at length the point "that few things make a Man appear more despicable, or more prejudice his Hearers against what he is going to offer, than an awkward or pitiful Dress." To demonstrate this, Mr. Spectator describes the conduct of Victor and Atticus. He concludes by telling a story of the different treatment accorded a man dressed poorly and a man dressed fashionably in a tavern. The man dressed poorly is in fact the father of the well-dressed man, who has chosen this costume to impress upon his son the need to be more cautious in his spending.

Spectator 151. Thursday, August 23, 1711. Steele.

Mr. Spectator presents a lengthy description of the Man of Wit and Pleasure of the Town. Much of Mr. Spectator's information about these Coxcombs comes from Will Honeycomb, who finds the Town dull without some of them around. Mr. Spectator finds that such creatures, because they pursue pleasure as their chief goal in life, distort the true image of man and miss out on most real human pleasures. Given to intemperance in all its forms, such men age themselves prematurely.

Spectator 152. Friday, August 24, 1711. Steele.

Mr. Spectator reports on the pleasure of conversation with military men whose courage and generosity come from thought and reflection. In an evening walk with Captain Sentry, Mr. Spectator marvels at the ability of soldiers to deal with their fear of death. Sentry describes the ease with which soldiers come to look upon the possibility of death, and tells a story of two friends in the army who seem to be very close, but one of them is able to take the death of the other very philosophically.

Spectator 153. Saturday, August 25, 1711. Steele.

Mr. Spectator discusses at length the impertinence of man's wish to be younger than he is. He give an anecdote of two older gentlemen, one of which wishes he were younger, while the other accepts the passing of the heat of youth with wisdom and gratitude. With quotations from Cicero, Mr. Spectator finds the life of the mature man to be preferable to the life of the young man.

Spectator 154. Monday, August 27, 1711. Steele.

Mr. Spectator presents a letter from a Simon Honeycomb, in which he explains why he found it necessary to become a Man of Wit and Pleasure so that he could please the ladies. Simon reports that while he was still a virgin, women of virtue treated him coldly and made jests about him. After a summer of sensuous delight, he finds himself much better received among the fashionable in town. Having now married a splendid woman, he regrets his earlier life of debauchery.

Spectator 155. Tuesday, August 28, 1711. Steele.

The Idol, referred to in *Spectators* 73 and 87, writes Mr. Spectator a letter to protest that it is difficult for a modest woman to keep a public house because men who frequent her establishment enjoy saying immodest things to see her reaction. Mr. Spectator says that this woman is not alone; a number of women in business have notified him that men enjoy taking advantage of the commercial relationship to say bawdy things in their presence. Mr. Spectator finds such behavior on the part of men to be unconscionable. He concludes with a letter from a milliner, who says that she is a Beauty, as described in *Spectator* 144, who is treated badly because she is not a noble woman. She says that Albacinda, Eudosia, and all the rest of the noble Beauties would be treated as she is if they were at her station in life.

Spectator 156. Wednesday, August 29, 1711. Steele.

In an essay on the subject of the reigning beauties in town, Mr. Spectator presents a character of the Woman's Man. The purpose of such a man is to entertain, and Bareface, an impudent Toad, is one who is successful in this enterprise. Will Honeycomb points out that one strategy for pleasing a woman is to be known as pleasing to her rival. Mr. Spectator laments the number of women who are pleased by affected men.

Spectator 157. Thursday, August 30, 1711. Steele.

Mr. Spectator discusses at length the Latin word *indoles*, which means a natural disposition to a particular art, science, profession, or trade. He feels that attention should be given to this quality in individual young people as plans are being made for their education. From classical literature, Mr. Spectator gives examples of Alexander, Cassius, Scipio, and Marius as men whose specific talents were visible from their youth. Mr. Spectator laments the current state of education in England and argues that no man who is not interested in the subject can be forced to enjoy it. He particularly objects to the practice of flogging as punishment in school. This issue of the *Spectator* concludes with an advertisement for a horse offered by Enos Thomas.

Spectator 158. Friday, August 31, 1711. Steele.

Mr. Spectator offers a series of letters from his correspondents. The first objects to Mr. Spectator's quoting from Cicero, and to his honoring virtue in women. To this correspondent, honor in a woman is only peevishness. He says that Mr. Spectator would be worthy of applause if he had described Corinna as charming though inconstant, and found something in human nature to explain Zoilus' fondness for her. A Gentle Reader writes to say that she and her companions will not give up the attentions of any Woman's Man until men of sense think fit to relieve them. Another correspondent asks Mr. Spectator to devote his attentions to the subject of Good Breeding, because the correspondent is distressed at the affected behavior of Gigglers and Oglers in church on Sunday last. A fourth correspondent proclaims himself a Woman's Man; he reports that a fine lady, upon hearing Mr. Spectator's paper on the Woman's Man dismissed it with a laugh, and said that men only want what the girdle surrounds.

Spectator 159. Saturday, September 1, 1711. Addison.

Mr. Spectator presents an Oriental tale from *The Visions of Mirzah*. The narrator of this tale describes a meditation on the subject of Man as Shadow and Life as Dream. While contemplating this subject, he hears music played by a Genius of the mountain who presents him with an allegorical vision of human life. Life appears to be filled with pitfalls, but it offers the opportunity of great reward for virtuous living.

Spectator 160. Monday, September 3, 1711. Addison.

Mr. Spectator provides an extensive discussion of the nature of a Genius, with many classical allusions. He concludes with a brief narrative illustrating the idea that all too frequently the abilities of geniuses are wasted on trivial subjects. In his narrative, a shepherd put as much effort in learning to juggle eggs without breaking them as he might have put into becoming a great mathematician.

Spectator 161. Tuesday, September 4, 1711. Budgell.

Mr. Spectator receives a letter from a correspondent in the country who claims that he saw Mr. Spectator at Sir Roger de Coverley's. He describes events at a festival held in a neighboring Parish, and especially notes the conduct of a ring of Cudgel-Players who were breaking each others' heads to make an impression on their mistresses' hearts. One combatant is disappointed because he receives a broken head and overhears someone say that Kate probably will not marry him. Tom Short plays so well in a football match that most people think he'll be married within a year. Nearby, a country girl contorts her body while watching her sweetheart wrestle a larger man. A young man of the country watches his sweetheart, Betty Welsh, engage in games for women. Mr. Spectator comments by comparing such games with the Greek Olympics; he is delighted that love is the end and design of these meetings.

Spectator 162. NF. Wednesday, September 5, 1711. Addison.

Mr. Spectator presents a lengthy discourse on the subject of Inconstancy, with quotations from Horace and Dryden.

Spectator 163. Thursday, September 6, 1711. Addison.

While discussing the subject of happiness and man's pursuit of it, Mr. Spectator receives a letter from Leonora, who writes of the tragic death of her beloved. Mr. Spectator tries to comfort Leonora by assuring her that others share in her loss. He then declares that he will narrate a story about two lovers, told him by a priest in a stage-coach in France, in the next issue.

Spectator 164. Friday, September 7, 1711. Addison.

Mr. Spectator tells the story of Constantia and Theodosius, who love each other but whose relationship is broken up because Constantia's father insists on marrying her to a man of his choosing. Constantia, afraid that Theodosius has killed himself, enters the convent; Theodosius, however, has also taken religious vows and become known as Father Francis. Later, Father Francis (Theodosius) becomes Constantia's confessor; when she learns that he is still alive, she decides that she may die in peace; the two are buried in the same tomb.

Spectator 165. Saturday, September 8, 1711. Addison.

Mr. Spectator laments the intrusion into the English language of many French words as a result of recent wars in Europe. To illustrate this point, Mr. Spectator presents a letter from a young soldier to his father which contains so many French words that the boy's father cannot understand it.

Spectator 166. Monday, September 10, 1711. Addison.

Mr. Spectator discusses that quality of writing which makes it the most permanent and enduring of the arts. To illustrate his point, Mr. Spectator tells the story of a man who had written atheistical tracts only to discover that he was worried about the state of his soul in a period of sickness. A young Curate tried to reassure him that his works would have no more impact after his death than they had had before his death; this approach made the author so angry that he recovered to write more such tracts.

Spectator 167. Tuesday, September 11, 1711. Steele.

Mr. Spectator, having discussed the Prating Liar in *Spectator* 136, here presents a letter from Vitruvius, whom Mr. Spectator calls a Silent Liar and who calls himself a Castle-Builder. The correspondent who does all of his building in fancy rather than on the ground, seeks a method to settle his head and cool his fevered brain.

Spectator 168. Wednesday, September 12, 1711. Steele.

Mr. Spectator presents a series of letters, the first one of which agrees with Mr. Spectator that flogging is not the best method of education. The second letter is from a boy of 14 who writes to praise his teacher, a Dr. Divinity, who teaches effectively with tenderness rather than with pain. The third letter is from a correspondent who adds to Mr. Spectator's list of Impertinents groups of obnoxious people including a Set of Whisperers, and a Set of Laughters. The correspondent urges that such people be forced to pay double for attendance in public assemblies. The final correspondent, Isaac Hedgeditch, declares that he is a Poacher; he writes for Mr. Spectator's advice on the number of dogs he may have, the number of hares he may kill in a day, and the number of pots of ale he may drink.

Spectator 169. NF. Thursday, September 13, 1711. Addison.

Mr. Spectator presents, with references to Xenophon, Sallust, and Cato, an extensive discussion of the miseries which men bring upon themselves.

Spectator 170. Friday, September 14, 1711. Addison.

Mr. Spectator presents an extensive discussion of the varieties and causes of jealousy in men and women, particularly in the jealous husband.

Spectator 171. Saturday, September 15, 1711. Addison.

Mr. Spectator, with reference to Horace, presents a discussion of how to live with a jealous husband. The essay concludes with a story of Herod and Mariamne, from Josephus. Herod, deeply jealous of Mariamne, has her brother and her father put to death. Summoned by Marc Antony, he put Mariamne in the care of his Uncle Joseph, who also fell in love with her. Upon his return, Herod had Joseph put to death. In a second journey to Egypt, he left Mariamne in charge of Sohemus, with the predictable result that Herod put both Sohemus and Mariamne to death. Herod later regretted his rage at Mariamne and for a time felt despair at not having her with him.

Spectator 172. Monday, September 17, 1711. Steele.

Mr. Spectator says that there is no greater injury to human society than for talent to be valued without regard to how it is applied. When this occurs, Omniamante, a woman of vice, will be valued as highly as virgins or discreet matrons.

Spectator 173. Tuesday, September 18, 1711. Addison.

Having reported on a project to offer prizes for British artisans (Spectator 161), Mr. Spectator is surprised to hear of a grinning contest, to be sponsored along with a race among horses and a race among asses. Mr. Spectator offers an account of a Grinning Match which took place after the English victory at Namur. Although a Frenchman tries for the prize, he is only capable of the Merry Grin. Another is master of the Angry Grin. The prize is won by Giles Gorgon, who also gets to marry a country wench for his success.

Spectator 174. Wednesday, September 19, 1711. Steele.

Mr. Spectator says nothing is more common than disagreement among people who depend on each other. He gives an example of this in an exchange between Sir Roger de Coverley and Sir Andrew Freeport over the subject of the qualities of the Carthaginians. Sir Andrew comments that the Carthaginians are known for breaking treaties; Sir Roger says that this is to be understood because that since they are a trading people, their only goal is money. Captain Sentry enters the discussion and broadens it to include all mankind. Sir Andrew lectures Sir Roger and the Captain on the ethics of the merchant and concludes that they are the same as the standards of conduct for a gentleman.

Spectator 175. Thursday, September 20, 1711. Budgell.

Mr. Spectator presents a group of letters the first of which is from a young gentleman who categorizes a new type of Woman known as the Jezebel. Such a creature spends all of her time in her house window attracting public attention. A second writer, having read Mr. Spectator's comment on "Butts," says that he decided to take one of these creatures with him on a visit to his beloved to show off his wit. The Butt, unfortunately, was able to make the correspondent the butt of any number of jokes and as a result put the correspondent in danger of losing his pretensions to wit and his mistress all at once. A third letter, from Jack Modish, says that people in the country not only wear clothes that are out of fashion in the city, but also have clothes offered to them as London fashions which have never been seen in the city. Two examples are ribbons for the hair and silver hasps for gentlemen's coats instead of buttons. Modish proposes the creation of a society in London for the inspection of modes and fashions.

Spectator 176. Friday, September 21, 1711. Steele.

Mr. Spectator receives a letter from Nathaniel Henroost in which the correspondent wishes to commend to Mr. Spectator a good sort of person known by many with scorn as "Hen-peckt." The hen-pecked man actually is a good natured man who is ruled by the best of wives. Nathaniel describes the hen-pecked man as one who is really performing a delicate act to keep his wife in good humor.

Spectator 177. Saturday, September 22, 1711. Addison.

Mr. Spectator gives a lengthy character of Eugenius as a Man of a Universal Good-Nature. This gentleman lives well within his income and thus can be charitable without impoverishing himself. Mr. Spectator concludes with lengthy quotations from the Book of Job presenting a biblical view of the charitable man.

Spectator 178. Monday, September 24, 1711. Steele.

Mr. Spectator presents a letter from Celinda, who writes to comment upon Mr. Spectator's essay on jealousy (*Spectator* 171). She feels Mr. Spectator has not completed his task because he has not presented the nature of jealousy in women. She describes her own situation, which is to be married to a man who dresses well and is good natured everywhere but at home. Mr. Spectator says he plans to discuss marriage further, but must observe some examples before he does so. He does know of a man who was very untidy before he married but now is a model of good habits because of his respect for his wife. Mr. Spectator concludes with a brief letter from Martha Housewife to her husband. Martha urges her spouse to stay more at home; she knows where he was at seven on Thursday. She warns him that the Colonel whom he told her to stay away from is now in town.

Spectator 179. Tuesday, September 25, 1711. Addison.

Mr. Spectator says that his readers are of two sorts, the Mercurial and the Saturnine. He must write papers

264

for both sorts or lose part of his audience. Mr. Spectator presents a letter from a correspondent who, having heard of the Grinning Match (*Spectator* 173), reports on a Whistling Match at Bath. The prize is for the man who can whistle without laughing, and is finally won by a Footman who whistles a variety of tunes with a straight face. The same correspondent reports of a Yawning contest which he has observed in the home of a wealthy gentleman, the prize being a Cheshire Cheese.

Spectator 180. Wednesday, September 26, 1711. Martyn.

Mr. Spectator presents a letter from Philarithmus, in which the correspondent discusses the subject of the Vanity of Conquests and the French King, who is the greatest conquerer of the age. Philarithmus adds up the total of all the things conquered by the French King and finds them not to be worth the effort.

Spectator 181. Thursday, September 27, 1711. Addison.

Mr. Spectator receives a letter telling of the problems of marrying without parental consent. He says that there is no hardness of the heart so despicable as that of parents towards their children. He continutes the discussion by telling the story of Eginhart and his beloved, a lady of great beauty who is the daughter of the emperor. The man, having visited the Princess Imma during a snowfall, has her carry him on her shoulders to escape detection by the emperor. Unfortunately, the emperor discovers the deception and decides that the only honorable solution is to insist that the two be married.

Spectator 182. Friday, September 28, 1711. Steele.

Mr. Spectator presents a letter from Alice Threadneedle, in which she finds Wenching despicable, especially since she is a victim of a Rascal. She describes her efforts to prevent a girl apprenticed to her from being seduced by Strephon. She succeeds in having the young Irishman locked up as a thief. Mr. Spectator also presents a letter from a correspondent who complains about his being imprisoned for theft when he only intended fornication.

Spectator 183. Saturday, September 29, 1711. Addison.

Declaring that fables were the first pieces of wit to make their appearance in the world, Mr. Spectator praises tellers of fables from classical antiquity as well as from English literature. He then tells, from Plato, the story of Socrates and his behavior on the day of his death. He also tells a story of two families who represent the inhabitants of Heaven and Hell. The family of Heaven consists of Virtue and Happiness with

their daughter Pleasure. The family of Hell is Pain,
the Son of Misery, the Child of Vice. **Jupiter** sends
Pleasure and Pain to earth, where they are married, thus
accounting for the close connection between the two in
this world.

Spectator 184. Monday, October 1, 1711. Addison.

Mr. Spectator presents a letter from a correspondent
who, in following up on the discussion of Grinning
(*Spectators* 173 and 179), tells the story of Nicholas
Hart, who sleeps from the fifth to the 11th of August
every year. The correspondent suggests that Hart is
only an example of a number of Englishmen who spend
most of their time Yelling, Nodding, Stretching, Turning, Sleeping, Drinking, and the like. Nicholas has be-
become so celebrated for his performance that he earns
his living from it.

Spectator 185. NF. Tuesday, October 2, 1711. Addison.

Mr. Spectator gives an extensive discussion on the subject of Zeal.

Spectator 186. Wednesday, October 3, 1711. Addison.

Mr. Spectator presents a letter from his friend the
Clergyman, who speaks on the relationship between the
Believer and the Atheist. He concludes with the story
of Socrates' giving a cot to Aesculapius in his last
moments of life and a story from Xenophon, of a prince
who offered sacrifices to Jupiter as his death approached.

Spectator 187. Thursday, October 4, 1711. Steele.

Mr. Spectator presents a letter from Charles Yellow, who
writes to describe the Jilt. She is worse than the
coquette because she takes "Delight in being a Torment
to others." Corinna, unfortunately, has found that her
reputation as a Jilt proceeds her so that she must disguise herself to practice her craft. Charles describes
his own jilting by Kitty; he also describes Hyaena and
Bilbis a pair of specially capable Jilts. Charles' current pleasure and torment is one Chloe, who attracted
him and then told him that she was in love with another.
The paper ends with an advertisement for Mr. Sly, a
Haberdasher.

Spectator 188. Friday, October 5, 1711. Steele.

Mr. Spectator describes at length the mistakes made by
those men who set their hearts on being admired by the
multitude of people. A wise man, Phocian, feels that
he must have made a mistake when he receives the adula-
tion of the multitude. Mr. Spectator ends with a letter
from a gentleman to a lady thanking her for pleasing
him.

Spectator 189. Saturday, October 6, 1711. Addison.

Mr. Spectator presents a letter, written to Mr. Buckley, his bookseller, praising Mr. Spectator for commenting on the cruelty of parents to their children. The correspondent encloses a letter from a father to his son in which the father reprimands the son unmercifully. While stating that he generally favors parents in parent-child controversies, Mr. Spectator laments the cruelty of some parents. Mr. Spectator concludes by describing Le Comte on the Chinese custom of killing the entire family of a child who kills his father, and Herodotus, on Persian customs of dealing with undutiful children.

Spectator 190. Monday, October 8, 1711. Steele.

Mr. Spectator receives a letter from Rebecca Nettletop, in which the correspondent describes her progress from being a credulous young woman to being a prostitute. Having been debauched by the owner of the estate on which she lived, she was then taken up by Sir Jeoffrey Foible, but soon had all mankind as her customer. E. Afterday writes to urge Mr. Spectator to free her from the man who keeps her at the moment and hopes that Mr. Spectator will keep her himself. He also receives a letter from a correspondent who complains that many of the men who visit her in the house of prostitution in which she works are impertinent Coxcombs who come only to observe.

Spectator 191. Tuesday, October 9, 1711. Addison.

Mr. Spectator tells the fable of the Ass caught between two bundles of hay who cannot decide which way to proceed. He feels that men who purchase tickets in the Lottery are in a similar situation, because they do not know which number to choose. He presents a letter from George Gossling, who announces his willingness to pay ten shillings more than the current price for ticket #132.

Spectator 192. Wednesday, October 10, 1711. Steele.

Mr. Spectator describes a happy family in a tribute to the disposition of the father. Ruricola's family, however, is not so happy because he is distant and aloof in his relationship with his eldest son. Another happy family is that of Cornelli, in which the father is really an eldest brother to his sons. Mr. Spectator concludes with a letter praising a young man for his grief over the death of his father.

Spectator 193. Thursday, October 11, 1711. Steele.

Mr. Spectator reports on the pleasure one can have over trying to guess the occupations and concerns of people one meets in the streets. He finds particularly diverting the manner of the good Courtier. He then tells the reasons for the success of the famous Doctor in Moor-fields. The man has a signal system whereby he can learn of a patient's complaints before he sees the patient. Mr. Spectator is particularly interested in the relationship between great men and those who work very hard at being in their good graces. Such men give up their own freedom and take away their patron's under-standing in the process.

Spectator 194. Friday, October 12, 1711. Steele.

Mr. Spectator describes a variety of faults in love and friendship which are easily cured. The first concerns Corinna, who behaves like a maid, even though she is married. Her husband is concerned because, although he knows she does not dishonor him, she will not avoid the appearance of dishonor. He then presents a letter from a man who cannot convince himself of his wife's love and a letter from a correspondent who finds himself taken advantage of by a friend.

Spectator 195. Saturday, October 13, 1711. Addison.

Mr. Spectator retells a fable from the *Arabian Nights*, in which a king is cured of a malady by playing with a Ball containing medicine. This enables Mr. Spectator to move into a lengthy discussion of the rewards of taking care of the body. (Sequel to *Spectator* 115.)

Spectator 196. Monday, October 15, 1711. Steele.

Mr. Spectator presents a letter from a correspondent who says that men delude themselves if they feel that they can be happy in this life. He feels that the great lesson is equanimity, a regularity of spirit, which he feels is exemplified by a couple of men of his acquaintance who spend their old age in tranquillity and devotion to each other. Mr. Spectator also pre-sents a letter from Biddy Loveless, who says that she is the Mistress of the Fan referred to in *Spectator* 134. She discusses her two lovers, Tom the handsome and Will the rich. She delights in Tom, but will take Will for his money.

Spectator 197. Tuesday, October 16, 1711. Budgell.

Mr. Spectator describes the imperfections which come to men as a result of the professions they pursue. After noting a number of these, he describes a conversation with Captain Sentry on the subject of lawyers. Sentry tells our narrator the story of a young lawyer who argues a case even if he knows nothing about it. This leads to a lengthy presentation advising young people to avoid arguments and keep their tempers.

Spectator 198. Wednesday, October 17, 1711. Addison.

Mr. Spectator devotes this paper to the presentation of the species of women known as Salamanders, who constantly run into the risk of losing their chastity but always seem to preserve it. For other sorts of women, Mr. Spectator warns of the danger a woman incurs by being too familiar with men. To illustrate this he tells a story, set in Spain, of a man and his wife who were forced into slavery. While in slavery, the wife falls in love with a Frenchman who eventually takes her away with him.

Spectator 199. Thursday, October 18, 1711. Steele.

Mr. Spectator receives a letter from Statira, who asks him to publish a letter from her to Oroondates, in which she tells him she wishes to marry him even if their fortunes are not equal.

Spectator 200. Friday, October 19, 1711. Steele.

Following Philarithmus and his Political Arithmetick, Mr. Spectator presents a lengthy discussion of the danger of princely ambition.

Spectator 201. NF. Saturday, October 20, 1711. Addison.

Mr. Spectator presents a lengthy discussion on the necessity to temper the passions of childhood with a discipline of devotion.

Spectator 202. Monday, October 22, 1711. Steele.

Having observed a fight in the street between an apprentice and a hackney-coachman, Mr. Spectator discusses with Tacitus the advantage of having good friends. This leads to a discussion of the folly of trying to get people to behave well on the coersive effects of fear. He also receives a letter from Susan Civil, asking him to comment on Mrs. Taberty, an eternal flirt and disturber of families. Another letter, from Thomas Smoaky, complains of the treatment he receives as footman to a cruel master. The issue concludes with a petition from John Steward, Robert Butler, Harry Cook, Abigail Chambers who complain that their masters hire people to spy on them.

Spectator 203. Tuesday, October 23, 1711. Addison.

Mr. Spectator has harsh words for men who seduce unfortunate females and have illegitimate children. He tells the story of an Impudent Libertine who created a family tree for his illegitimate children. The Rake, Will Maple, is married to Mary Maple, but has children by Kate Cole, among others. Mr. Spectator proposes that such men be transported to the American colonies. He concludes by presenting a letter from a correspondent who describes how he has suffered because of his bastard birth.

Spectator 204. Wednesday, October 24, 1711. Steele.

Mr. Spectator presents a series of letters describing various types of distress in love. Bellinda writes to Sothades and in the manner of Statira (*Spectator* 199), offers herself in marriage. A second letter describes its correspondent's love for his lady, including her faults. Another letter from Phillis says that she now knows that her lover knows of her affection for him; she cannot understand, however, why he took up the fan of a flippant creature. A final letter is from a dying lady to her husband, in which she praises him for being the best of men and a fine husband.

Spectator 205. Thursday, October 25, 1711. Addison.

Mr. Spectator receives a letter from Belvedira praising him for his discussion of the failings and foibles of women. Unfortunately, says this correspondent, he has not yet touched on vicious women, especially prostitutes, who prey upon men for money. Mr. Spectator also receives a letter from a country clergyman who writes to protest a woman of his congregation who sings the Psalms as though they were from Italian operas. Unfortunately, Squire Squeekum seems to be taking up the habit. A third letter, from Robin Goodfellow, proposes that Mr. Spectator meant bottle instead of glass when he said that four was enough for a man.

Spectator 206. Friday, October 26, 1711. Steele.

Mr. Spectator says that men are called to value those men who are modest about their marriage. Cinna, unfortunately, wishes more applause than he can ever receive. Of the same sort are Gloriana, Martilla, Chloe, Corinna, and Roxana. Mr. Spectator praises Shakespeare for having Macbeth fear the moderation of his prince. He ends the paper praising Lucceius for his good qualities, among them lack of ambition.

Spectator 207. NF. Saturday, October 27, 1711. Addison.

To explore the topic of Prayer, Mr. Spectator presents a dialogue on the subject of Plato's' dialogue *Alcibiades II*, in which Socrates and Alcibades discuss the subject; having led Alcibades to understand that what seemed to be blessings may not be so at all, he helps him see that one should pray for those things which God knows are truly good for the suppliant. After recounting other rules of prayer, Mr. Spectator concludes that Jesus exemplified them.

Spectator 208. Monday, October 29, 1711. Steele.

Mr. Spectator laments the sad state of the theater; it has devoted itself too much with show rather than the presentation of worthwhile drama. He proceeds to offer a letter from Mary Meanwell, who asks that women advertise their presence in town in the *Spectator*. A second letter praises Mr. Spectator's paper on the dangers which young girls face in the town (*Spectator* 182). A final correspondent asks that a poem to a stray heart be included in an issue of the paper.

Spectator 209. Tuesday, October 30, 1711. Addison.

Mr. Spectator retells a satiric fable of Simonides which describes the origins of ten animal types of women. He concludes that a man cannot possess anything better than a good woman or anything worse than a bad one.

Spectator 210. NF. Wednesday, October 31, 1711. Hughes.

Mr. Spectator presents a letter from a correspondent who discusses at length the value of contemplating the immortality of the soul. As an example he quotes Shakespeare's *Henry VI, Part II*, the deathbed speech of Cardinal Beaufort.

Spectator 211. Thursday, November 1, 1711. Addison.

Having decided to describe the characteristics of men, after the fashion of Simonides (*Spectator* 209), Mr. Spectator concludes that men are so various in their compositions that such characterization is impossible. He then discusses transmigration of souls, with references to Plato's vision of Erus. A letter from Melissa says that she must be a Bee, because of her behavior in her shop. Barnaby Brittle writes that he is married to a woman who may be described in terms of a horse (*Spectator* 209). Josiah Henpeck writes to say that he is married to a Cat. Martha Tempest writes that her husband believes she is an ocean, because she alternates between being stormy and sunshiny.

Spectator 212. Friday, November 2, 1711. Steele.

Mr. Spectator presents a long letter from Antony Freeman, in which he praises Mr. Spectator for showing to Sir Roger de Coverley the cruelty and perverseness of his mistress. Freeman says that he is like Nathaniel Henroost in being a henpecked husband, because his wife tyrannizes over his good nature. In addition, his wife enjoys the company of Tom Meggot because of his pretty singing. Freeman plans to have Tom read this letter to the *Spectator* aloud; on the basis of his wife's response, Freeman believes he will know the truth about that relationship and plans to act accordingly.

Spectator 213. NF. Saturday, November 3, 1711. Addison.

Mr. Spectator presents a lengthy discussion of the importance of living one's life as a Christian in light of the final judgement of one's conduct. He concludes the essay by describing Socrates' speech on the day of his execution, as given by Erasmus, to the effect that the condemned man has sought to live all of his life so as to please God.

Spectator 214. NF. Monday, November 5, 1711. Steele.

Mr. Spectator describes at length the relationship between debtors and creditors.

Spectator 215. Tuesday, November 6, 1711. Addison.

Mr. Spectator stresses the importance of education for controlling the passions. He gives as an example the suicides of uneducated Negroes upon the death of their masters. Another example is the tragedy of a beautiful Negro slave woman in the West Indies who was loved by two fellow slaves. Since neither could have her, they both took her into the woods and murdered her.

Spectator 216. Wednesday, November 7, 1711. Steele.

In a sequel to *Spectator* 212, Mr. Spectator receives a letter from A. Noewill, informing him that Mr. Freeman's wife had an attack of the vapors on his departure. A second letter, from Tom Meggot, describes the scene; he read the issue of the *Spectator* aloud, Mrs. Freeman flew into a rage, and Mr. Freeman departed. Tom asks Mr. Spectator's advice as to how he might manipulate the situation to his own benefit. He promises to obey Mr. Spectator's counsel, as Captain Sentry can testify.

Spectator 217. Thursday, November 8, 1711. Budgell.

Mr. Spectator receives a letter from Kitty Termagant, in which she describes her participation in a Club of She-Romps, a group of women who meet weekly to throw off societal conventions and behave as men do. They also demolish a Prude once a month. They invite Mr. Spectator to attend, which offer he turns down. Mr. Spectator also receives a letter from a gentleman who is distressed at the thoughts of his beloved. Suzanna Frost writes to praise the state of being an Old Maid. A final correspondent, the wife of a clergyman, decides that she is the tenth type of woman (*Spectator* 191).

Spectator 218. Friday, November 9, 1711. Steele.

Mr. Spectator describes overhearing a group of people discussing him and his seeming ability to spend large sums of money. This provokes Mr. Spectator into a discussion of the nature of Reputation; Mr. Spectator finds merchants, such as Mr. Cash and Mr. Sea room, especially subject to the whims of public opinion.

Spectator 219. NF. Saturday, November 10, 1711. Addison.

Mr. Spectator offers a lengthy discourse on the subject of Ambition.

Spectator 220. Monday, November 12, 1711. Steele.

Mr. Spectator presents a letter from Henrietta, in which the correspondent protests a suitor's applying to her father for her hand when she does not love him. A second correspondent discourses on the subject of False Wit, with special reference to a poet who writes quickly, a poet who never publishes anything he writes, and a mathematician who has tried to prepare a method of writing poetry by numbers. Another correspondent informs Mr. Spectator that he is not in love with either of two ladies who believe that he is in love with one of them. A fourth correspondent says that he considers it good breeding to take off his hat in the presence of women, a gesture which some of them feel is impertinent.

Spectator 221. Tuesday, November 13, 1711. Addison.

Mr. Spectator describes the process by which he chooses mottos for his Speculations. He knows that his mottos will not be of service to those who do not understand Latin. He tells a story of two competing preachers. The first used Latin in his sermons; when the second noticed that this seemed to please a congregation, he did likewise. Even though his quotations were not from the Church Fathers, but from rhetorical handbooks, he still was capable of increasing the size of his congregation. Mr. Spectator describes the meaning of the capital letters at the end of each *Spectator* issue and the signs' authors among his club for each of the capital letters in use. To explain why he uses these letters, he tells the story of a philosopher who carried something hidden under his clothes. Upon being asked by an acquaintance why he did this, he replied that he did it for the purpose of preventing his acquaintance from knowing what was under there. Mr. Spectator concludes by describing the elaborate explanation given by an Elizabethan clergyman of the first three words in the first verse of the first chapter of the first book of *Chronicles*.

Spectator 222. Wednesday, November 14, 1711. Steele.

Mr. Spectator receives a letter from a correspondent who notices that many men of good education fail in the management and conduct of their lives. The correspondent admits that he knows of no explanation for the inconsistent man. Mr. Spectator notes that this observation has been made by others including Horace and Dryden in his character of Zimri. Mr. Spectator concludes that everyone should learn the lesson of being able to enjoy ordinary life without having to gratify some appetite.

Spectator 223. Thursday, November 15, 1711. Addison.

Mr. Spectator tells the story of how Sappho cured, or tried to cure, a passion for Phaon by jumping from the top of a precipice into the sea, but perished in the experiment. With this as background, he presents a translation of her poem "An Hymn to Venus."

Spectator 224. NF. Friday, November 16, 1711. Anonymous.

Mr. Spectator writes a lengthy discussion on the role of ambition in the affairs of men.

Spectator 225. NF. Saturday, November 17, 1711. Addison.

Mr. Spectator presents a lengthy discussion of the role of Discretion in the conduct of human life.

Spectator 226. NF. Monday, November 19, 1711. Steele.

Mr. Spectator presents a lengthy discussion of the role of the art of painting in improving the manners of mankind. He concludes with a comment on an advertisement by a painter, newly arrived from Italy, who acknowledges himself the greatest painter of his age. Mr. Spectator notes "the Doctor paints the Poor for nothing."

Spectator 227. Tuesday, November 20, 1711. Addison.

Mr. Spectator gives a lengthy description of the Lovers' Leap described in *Spectator* 223. He quotes from Theocritus the address of a shepherd to his mistress as he prepares to jump from the leap. Esculapius writes that he believes the Lovers' Leap to be an effective cure not only for love but for all other evils. He praises immersion in water for a variety of ills. Athenais writes Mr. Spectator to declare that a gentleman who courted her for three years has just married another; she wants to know the location of the Lovers' Leap. Another correspondent, Davyth ap Shenkyn, writes to protest that Mrs. Gwinifrid has rejected his love-suit; he too wishes to partake advantage of the Lovers' Leap. Mr. Spectator promises to translate a Greek manuscript giving more details of the effectiveness of the Lovers' Leap.

Spectator 228. Wednesday, November 21, 1711. Steele.

Mr. Spectator gives a lengthy character sketch of the empty-headed Inquisitive Man. He reports on overhearing a conversation between a Talker and an Inquisitive Man, which resulted in the satisfaction of both. Mr.

Spectator also describes two gossipy gentlemen who discuss the pedigree of a man who enters a Public House he
is sitting in. When curiosity is without malice, Mr.
Spectator believes a man can be a pleasant conversationalist. He receives a letter from a correspondent
who describes, from Plutarch, the servant of Caius
Gracchus, one Lucinius, who used a pitch pipe to control his master's voice and prevent it from going to
any extremes.

Spectator 229. NF. Thursday, November 22, 1711. Addison.

Mr. Spectator presents three translations of a poem by
Sappho. The first, by Catullus, is in Latin; the second,
by Boileau, is in French; and the third by the transla-
tor of the poem in *Spectator* 223, is in English.

Spectator 230. NF. Friday, November 23, 1711. Steele.

Mr. Spectator says that men may appear beastly or god-
like depending on the way in which they are observed.
He presents a letter of Pliny to Maximus, in which he
praises his friend in the best manner. Mr. Spectator
also presents a letter from a correspondent who outlines a program of education designed to develop good
taste among Englishmen, especially as concerns the· reading of classical authors.

Spectator 231. Saturday, November 24, 1711. Addison.

Mr. Spectator presents a letter from a correspondent
who describes the difficulty in speaking in public, and
the anxiety which doing so raises in some people. This
leads Mr. Spectator to a lengthy discussion of the role
of modesty in public life, with references to Cicero,
Virgil, and Homer. He describes how a rash of suicides
among Greek women was stopped because public officials
declared that all women who attempted suicide would be
dragged naked through the streets. Finally, Mr. Spectator contrasts virtuous modesty with vicious modesty
which makes a man ashamed of his background.

Spectator 232. Monday, November 26, 1711. Anonymous.

Mr. Spectator describes a conversation with his friend
Sir Andrew Freeport on the subject of beggars. He
argues that the best way to treat begging is to put
people to work; he believes that this can be done
through a division of labor.

Spectator 233. Tuesday, November 27, 1711. Addison.

Mr. Spectator, in this paper, presents what he says is
a translation of a Greek manuscript describing those
who have availed themselves of the Lovers' Leap. The
list consists of the names of 18 Greek men and women
who have tried to cure their passions by leaping from

this high promontory; some perished in the fall, while
others were injured to a greater or lesser degree. A
final table claims that 250 had leaped in that Olympiad;
124 were males, 126 were females. Of this group, 120
were cured; 51 were males, while 69 were females.

Spectator 234. Wednesday, November 28, 1711. Steele.

Mr. Spectator compares the man who would tell the
truth even at the cost of humor with the man who would
lie to bring people pleasure. He tells the story of an
Athenian who told the people of that city they had won
a victory when they had in fact been defeated; this man
defended himself by saying he had brought the Athenians
two days of joy. Mr. Spectator describes an acquaintance
who, in the name of bringing estranged people together,
has been known to tell falsehoods for the purpose.
Philonous writes Mr. Spectator to describe the visit to
the countryside of a man from London who claims to be a
free-thinker. Upon examination, the free-thinker turns
out to be a mere heathen. Philonous wishes that those
who claim to be free-thinkers know the meaning of the
term.

Spectator 235. Thursday, November 29, 1711. Addison.

Mr. Spectator describes the strange habits of the thea-
tergoer who shows his appreciation of events on stage
by giving a loud knock on whatever is handy; he is
known as the *Trunk-maker in the Upper-Gallery*. This
gentleman is valued in theater because he signals the
audience when to applaud good performances or good
plays. His enemies claim that he can be bribed, but
Mr. Spectator believes he is a man of judgement and
discretion.

Spectator 236. Friday, November 30, 1711. Steele.

Mr. Spectator presents a letter from a correspondent
who says that he has not given marriage the full consideration it deserves. The correspondent objects to
those who tease married people; he also objects to
husbands who feel they must show their domination of
their wives in public. The correspondent urges Mr.
Spectator to help convince people of the importance of
generosity and benevolence in marriage. Tristissa
writes to warn women not to marry a fool simply for
wealth, as she has done. A third correspondent writes
to complain of those who disturb public worship by
repeating prayers after the minister.

Spectator 237. Saturday, December 1, 1711. Addison.

Mr. Spectator suggests that one of the rewards of a
virtuous life might well be an increase in understanding the divine wisdom, while one of the punishments of

an immoral life might be an increase in one's appetite
for knowledge without chance of having it satisfied.
He retells Milton's description of the fallen angels in
hell from *Paradise Lost*. He also quotes Plato and Seneca on the value of both good and evil events for
the development of character in the individual. He also
retells a story of Moses from Jewish tradition, in which
Moses sees a young boy find a purse of gold dropped by
a soldier at a spring. The soldier returning to look
for his purse, murders an old man in the belief that the
man has stolen the purse. Moses is horrified at what
he believes is a terrible injustice only to learn that
the old man was in fact the murderer of the child's
father.

Spectator 238. Monday, December 3, 1711. Steele.

Mr. Spectator presents a discussion of the subject of
the Love of Flattery. On the other hand, Mr. Spectator
can imagine nothing more desirable than to be praised
without being flattered. He retells, from Tacitus, the
story of Germanicus, who gets to overhear soldiers
praise him on the night before a battle. Another sort
of man is Malvolio, who though a witty, learned, and
discerning man, is upset when the attention of those
he is with is not fixed on him. Mr. Spectator also
presents a letter from a correspondent who presents a
translation of a letter of Aristaenetus, in which Phil-
opinax writes Chromation that he has fallen in love with
her although she is not a real woman, but only a woman
whose picture he has painted.

Spectator 239. NF. Tuesday, December 4, 1711. Addison.

Mr. Spectator presents a lengthy discourse on the subject of methods of conducting disputes. He draws his
examples from Socrates, Aristotle, and the universities.
He also includes arguing by torture, which can be very
effective in dealing with certain types of people.

Spectator 240. Wednesday, December 5, 1711. Steele.

Mr. Spectator receives a letter from a correspondent
who praises a wealthy man who supported him when he fell
into loose conduct after a disagreement with his parents.
In light of such treatment, the correspondent wishes Mr.
Spectator to devote an issue to Heroick Virtue in common Life. A second correspondent, Rustick Sprightly, a
country gentleman, describes the effect that courtier
has had on those who live around him. The courtier, because he bows to everyone he meets, has set a fashion
for all the young people in the neighborhood. Another
correspondent, Charles Easy, says that the theater-
goer of *Spectator* 235 was not at the theater recently,
but another man, a Beau, drew attention to himself by
wandering about on stage before the performance.

Spectator 241. Thursday, December 6, 1711. Addison.

Mr. Spectator presents a letter from Asteria, in which she asks for help on how to support herself during the absence of her husband. Although she works harder, looks at his picture, and spends time in familiar places, she misses him more with each passing day. Mr. Spectator presents a series of narratives which show possible ways to alleviate this anguish. The first, from a Romance by Scudery details how two lovers set aside one half-hour each day to think of the other. A second suggestion involves two lovers who agree to pray for each other every day. Another account, from Strada, concerns two friends who try to communicate over a great distance by use of sympathetic lodestones. Such devices should be given to all lovers who must spend time apart.

Spectator 242. Friday, December 7, 1711. Steele.

Mr. Spectator presents a letter from Rebecca Ridinghood describing the bad manners displayed by a rude man during a stagecoach journey. A second correspondent tells the story of a drunken weaver, whose wife bought a lottery ticket. The weaver stole the ticket and sold it, only to find out that it was a prize-winning ticket. A final letter, from Abraham Thrifty, complains that his nieces are Female Virtuosoes who discuss philosophy instead of subjects appropriate to women. One, Kitty, assures him that many great philosophers believe that pleasure and pain are imaginary, while the other, Molly, claims that snow is really black instead of white. He urges Mr. Spectator to produce a guide for female reading.

Spectator 243. NF. Saturday, December 8, 1711. Addison.

Mr. Spectator presents an essay considering the topic of whether virtue is a duty only or whether it can be delightful in itself.

Spectator 244. Monday, December 10, 1711. Steele.

Mr. Spectator receives a letter from a correspondent who praises Mr. Spectator for his helping the correspondent come to love the paintings of Raphael. He proceeds to give a lengthy description of the virtues of Raphael's painting. In a second letter, Constantia Feild agrees with Simonides (*Spectator* 209) that some women can be categorized as Apes, women who are both ugly and ill-natured. A particular group of these Apes lives near Constantia during the summer and were content to enjoy life in the country until they were ready to return to London, at which point they began to ridicule the plainness and sincerity of country women.

Spectator 245. Tuesday, December 11, 1711. Addison.

Mr. Spectator says he regards innocence coupled with folly with some amusement. St. Francis, a person of this sort, once mistook a lover's kiss for an expression of Christian charity. In light of this discussion, Mr. Spectator presents a letter from Timothy Doodle who asks Mr. Spectator for comment on some innocent diversions. He suggests some children's games and says that he wishes to play them with his wife and with a Colonel, who comes to call on them on long winter evenings. Another letter describes remedies for the pain of lovers' absences; these remedies include dividing a coin between the two lovers and contemplating the figure of a heart stuck with darts or held in the hand of a Cupid. The correspondent has himself found great benefit from a lovers' knot woven from his mistress's hair. Troilus writes to report on a Society of Trojans at the university who are opposed to the study of anything Greek.

Spectator 246. NF. Wednesday, December 12, 1711. Steele.

Mr. Spectator receives a letter from a correspondent who laments that intelligent women can give up their children to the care of women who are unsound in mind and body and who only care about the money they earn and not the children they care for. The author gives classical examples of the danger of doing this, including the story of Caligula, that his nurse moistened the nipples of her breasts with blood to make him a more effective nurser, with the effect of making him bloodthirsty and cruel later in life. The correspondent argues that nursing benefits the mother as well as the child.

Spectator 247. Thursday, December 13, 1711. Addison.

Mr. Spectator praises the ability of women in the field of oratory and categorizes a number of types of Female Orators. The first type is the woman who stirs up the passions. The second type is those who deal in Invectives and is known as the Censorious. The third type is the Worried Gossips. Mrs. Fiddle Faddle is an example; she knows everything that is going on in her neighborhood. The fourth is the Coquette, who has false quarrels with men and spends much of her time talking to her lap dog or parrot. Mr. Spectator wonders at the capacities of women in using their powers of speech; a friend promises to dissect a woman's tongue and to report on any special qualities it might have. Mr. Spectator ends with an assertion that he is wonderfully charmed with the music of the female tongue.

Spectator 248. Friday, December 14, 1711. Steele.

Mr. Spectator stresses the importance of being of benefit to one's society. An example of such a person is

Lepirius, who inherits a great estate because his older
brother leads a dissolute life. The brother reforms,
and Lepirius restores to him the ancestral estate.
Generosity also occurs within families, as a correspondent showed in a letter to a friend with a gift of fifty
thousand pounds. This paper ends with a story, heard
from a Bencher of the Temple about their choice of a
man as "King for a Season" who was so praised by the
company for giving a poor man the sum of ten pounds.

Spectator 249. NF. Saturday, December 15, 1711. Addison.

Mr. Spectator offers a lengthy discussion on the subject of Laughter and Ridicule.

Spectator 250. Monday, December 17, 1711. Anonymous.

Mr. Spectator receives a letter from a correspondent
on the subject of Eyes. The correspondent says that
the first significant Eye is the Sun; the second, Argus;
and the third, Janus. The essay goes on to describe
the colors of eyes, their qualities, and various ways
of moving them. Abraham Spy writes a letter describing the virtues of Perspective-Glasses.

Spectator 251. Tuesday, December 18, 1711. Addison.

Mr. Spectator discusses the Cries of London; Sir Roger
finds that they disturb his sleep while he is in the
city, while Will Honeycomb prefers them to the songs of
birds. Ralph Crotchett writes a letter in which he
proposes that he become Comptroller General of the London Cries; he offers a description of them. Dividing
them into Vocal and Instrumental Cries, he describes
their place and function in the city.

Spectator 252. Wednesday, December 19, 1711. Steele.

Mary Heartfree writes to comment on the discussion of
the Eye in *Spectator* 250. She says that love affects
the eye; Leonora's eye is watchful while it appears
negligent. Many come to see at the theater while
others come to be seen. Barbara Crabtree writes to
learn if she, as a Female Orator, may use a figure of
speech called a Cudgell against her sot of a husband.
Another correspondent, a lawyer, agrees with Mr. Spectator that women are successful orators. To their
powers of persuasion by means of the tongue, he adds
their use of tears, fainting fits, and the like. The
wife of this correspondent is so great an orator that
she can get money from him to buy anything she wants;
the house is filled with evidence of her persuasiveness.

Spectator 253. NF. Thursday, December 20, 1711. Addison.

Mr. Spectator produces a lengthy essay on the nature of
bad poetry, while praising Pope's *Essay on Criticism* as

a masterpiece. Mr. Spectator especially notes Pope's use of the critical principles of Longinus in his critical poem.

Spectator 254. Friday, December 21, 1711. Steele.

Mr. Spectator says he is concerned by levity of thought among young women of quality. To illustrate the point he presents a letter from Lydia to Harriot, in which the correspondent laments the horribleness of the marriage-state in which Harriot now finds herself. Lydia urges her friend to return from the country to the city and resume the life of fashion. She cautions Harriot, however, not to appear in the town in any place that would be inappropriate for a married woman. Mary Home writes a letter in response which illustrates good sense; it expresses content with the married state as one of lasting satisfaction as opposed to the transitory pleasures of life of fashion and Mrs. Modish's teatable. Mr. Spectator also receives a letter from a correspondent who asks Mr. Spectator whether he should give up his reputation for discretion by marrying a beautiful woman with no fortune. Mr. Spectator replies by asking him would he marry to please other people or himself.

Spectator 255. NF. Saturday, December 22, 1711. Addison.

Mr. Spectator presents a lengthy discussion of the purpose of passions and the desire for fame.

Spectator 256. NF. Monday, December 24, 1711. Addison.

Mr. Spectator continues his discourse on man's desire for fame.

Spectator 257. NF. Tuesday, December 25, 1711. Addison.

Mr. Spectator concludes his lengthy discussion of man's desire for fame, and its proper ends.

Spectator 258. Wednesday, December 26, 1711. Steele.

Mr. Spectator praises the need all men share for some form of recreation in their lives. He especially approves of diversions of poetry and music. Ralph Crotchet writes Mr. Spectator in appreciation for being published in *Spectator* 251, and says that he hopes he will be named Comptroller of the Cries. If this falls through, he proposes another Project, the establishment of a second theater, to be established in another part of town and run by Kitt Crotchet. Ralph hopes that the new theater will have more action as well as speaking on its stage. He is assured that the Trunk-maker will attend the new theater. Mr. Spectator also receives a letter from Thomas Clayton, Nicolino Haymn, and Charles Dieupart, in which the correspondents urge that more music be offered in the town and offer their services to this end.

Spectator 259. Thursday, December 27, 1711. Steele.

Mr. Spectator discusses those instances when common sense and courtesy come into conflict. He regrets that religion and formal conduct are so intertwined that many people are or feel barred from the services of the Established Church because they do not feel they are cultured enough to attend it. He narrates several examples.

Spectator 260. Friday, December 28, 1711. Steele.

Mr. Spectator presents a letter from Jack Afterday in which he writes of the decay of his powers and the increase of his appetite for beautiful women. He also laments the fact that he has done nothing for his country, and has lived as a bachelor all of his days. He hopes that his old friend Jack Tawdry will buy a cane and not try to act younger than he really is. His one comfort is that he will soon be worth fifty thousand pounds. Mr. Spectator also receives a letter in which the correspondent notes that his beloved has found herself subject to cold fits. He encloses a letter to his beloved in which he assures her of his love and hopes that she does not delay their marriage through such strategems. Another correspondent wonders if a gentlewoman who is constantly accusing him of things he has not done is perhaps really in love with him. A final correspondent, a footman in love with the housemaid, wonders if she is in love with him, because she hit him over the head with her shoe.

Spectator 261. Saturday, December 29, 1711. Addison.

Mr. Spectator tells us of his early life, and his father's advice on the subject of marriage. He once courted a young woman who finally decided that he was a silly fellow and married a Captain of Dragoons instead. As a result, Mr. Spectator has always had an aversion to Pretty Fellows, and has been discouraged in his fortunes with women. This leads him to a lengthy discussion of the joys of courtship.

Spectator 262. Monday, December 31, 1711. Addison.

Mr. Spectator describes his pleasure in the reception which has been accorded *The Spectator*. He describes the care with which he prepares his paper, anticipating affronts which it may cause. Because he has quoted Milton more than any other English poet, he promises a series of critical essays on *Paradise Lost*.

Spectator 263. Tuesday, January 1, 1712. Steele.

Mr. Spectator presents a lengthy letter from a correspondent who delights in fatherhood, yet is aware of the agonies a parent may feel when he is afraid his child will do something unworthy. The best parent-child relationship is one in which the father showers blessings on the son and the son tries to be worthy of having such a father. Camillus and his son are examples of this sort of relationship. The correspondent notices that prejudices and hatreds of mankind are passed on from generation to generation; he hopes that if fathers remember what being a son was like, they will break this process by being more humane with their children. To show the other side of the picture, he presents a letter from a mother to her son Frank that she is disturbed at his conduct in town, and his saying to Mr. Letacre that she could easily live on half of her income in the country, allowing him the rest. The son writes in response that he will come to beg his mother's forgiveness.

Spectator 264. Wednesday, January 2, 1712. Steele.

Mr. Spectator prepares a discourse on the subject of man's affectation for loving the pleasures of solitude, whether he is suited for such a life or not. As an example, he relates the story of Irus and others who are solitary creatures. Irus concludes that if he keeps his poverty a secret, it will not be as great a burden to him. As a result, he is able to pass in the world for a different sort of person than he really is. Mr. Spectator then gives an exchange of letters between Sir Richard Estcourt and Sir Roger de Coverley on the subject of the quality of some wine. Sir Roger describes, in his letter, the current state of life in the country, detailing the condition of the sexton's gout and the fact that old John recently has died.

Spectator 265. Thursday, January 3, 1712. Addison.

Mr. Spectator discusses the habit some women have of wearing elaborate head-dresses. He continues the discussion with Will Honeycomb; they find this sort of female adornment peculiar, especially when women display their emotions or their political affiliations through the shape, color, or makeup of their head-dresses. They especially note Melesinda, who communicates to her lover through the color of her head-dress, and Cornelia, who wears a black hood when her husband is out of town. Mr. Spectator and Will conclude by comparing Ovid's precepts with those of Will for appropriate colors of head-dress for different complexions of women.

Spectator 266. Friday, January 4, 1712. Steele.

Mr. Spectator describes Will Honeycomb's category of over-offended ladies, the outrageously virtuous. He describes a girl he met near Covent Garden, who was to him quite beautiful, but was "newly come upon the Town" from the country, dishonored, and left upon the streets. Mr. Spectator abhors such a practice. Mr. Spectator describes the process through reference to Fletcher's play, *The Humorous Lieutenant*. Lucippe, an agent for the king's lust, is seen in the process of procuring Chloe for 350 Crowns for her services to the king. Mr. Spectator laments this practice, and reports on over-hearing the process of recruitment, as a young country woman is taken from her brother and deluded into expecting a life of domestic service in the city instead of the life of prostitution which she will inevitably fall into.

Spectator 267. NF. Saturday, January 5, 1712. Addison.

Mr. Spectator offers his first paper on the subject of Milton's *Paradise Lost*; here, he discusses the relationship between the poem and the formal definition of epic.

Spectator 268. Monday, January 7, 1712. Steele.

Mr. Spectator presents a letter from James Easy, in which the correspondent objects to the practice of bullies in the theater who ring other people's noses. He also presents a letter from a correspondent who adds to Mr. Spectator's discussion of marriage by pointing out that too many men and women look for characteristics in a prospective mate, such as having money, which have much less to do with a successful marriage than the possession of virtue. Mr. Spectator receives a letter from Anthony Gape who reports that he walked into a post because he was watching a woman on the other side of the street. Another correspondent wonders if all the women of the town are wearing their hoods in different colors so that they may play the game of *the Parson has lost his Cloak*. Another correspondent reports that the Toast of Oxford at the moment is Patetia; he reports that he is being outdone in his courtship of her by another who flatters her more than he can. He hopes for Mr. Spectator's counsel. A final correspondent reports that he said to his mistress she should not use makeup because she "cannot place a Patch where it does not hide a Beauty."

Spectator 269. Tuesday, January 8, 1712. Addison.

Mr. Spectator is aroused early by Sir Roger de Coverley's coachman, who announces that the worthy squire is in town to get a sight of Prince Eugene. Mr. Spectator describes their meeting; Sir Roger reports on his chaplain's latest sermon and the welfare of Will Wimble. Will is now in trouble with Tom Touchy; Moll White is now dead. Sir Roger then proceeds to describe in detail the events of Christmastime in the country. He then asks about Sir Andrew Freeport; the two spend a delightful day in each other's company.

Spectator 270. Wednesday, January 9, 1712. Steele.

Mr. Spectator reports on his delight at the assembly in
the theater for a performance of Beaumont and Fletcher's
play *The Scornful Lady*. He finds the audience decorous
and beautiful, and is pleased that so many ladies attended a play in which the heroine exemplifies the vanity of the female sex in tormenting their admirers. Mr.
Spectator, however, does object to the part of Sir Roger
the chaplain, whom he finds not to be realistic.

Spectator 271. Thursday, January 10, 1712. Addison.

Mr. Spectator reports on the delight he takes in letters
from his correspondents. He presents a letter from Tom
Trippet, who describes the response of 13 ladies wearing
13 different colored hoods to the *Spectator* on that subject. The women are pleased that the moral is in Greek,
so that they do not have to understand it. Another letter reports the joy felt by frequenters of coffee-houses
that Sir Roger has come to town. A third letter reports
on a curiosity in the correspondent's possession--a box
in which he is able to keep a midget man, a midget woman,
and a midget horse. He describes briefly the show which
the three midgets put on under his direction.

Spectator 272. Friday, January 11, 1712. Steele.

Mr. Spectator presents a letter from Cleanthes, who
writes that he is in love with Bellinda, but is falsely
accused of caring for another by a busybody named Mrs.
Jane. Cleanthes hopes that by presenting the circumstances in the *Spectator*, the truth can be known and
his relationship with Bellinda prosper. Another correspondent asks Mr. Spectator's opinion on a woman who
turned her cheek to him for a kiss. Mr. Spectator
responds by asking which cheek she turned. The paper
concludes with an advertisement asking all ladies who
wear Hoods to church to be there before the beginning
of the service so as not to divert the attention of the
congregation.

Spectator 273. NF. Saturday, January 12, 1712. Addison.

Mr. Spectator presents his second essay on *Paradise
Lost*, this time concerning himself with the actors in
the poem.

Spectator 274. Monday, January 14, 1712. Steele.

Mr. Spectator continues his discussion of immoral sexual
practices, this time dealing with those "impotent Wen-
chers and industrious Haggs" who supply new "Sacrifices
to the Devil of Lust." He describes the method of Hags
who assure a man that the women they will be taking advantage of are inexperienced. To further the point, he
presents a letter from a correspondent who says that it

is necessary to expose the practices of Bawds; to this end, he presents a letter from a Bawd to a nobleman, describing a girl of less than sixteen years, whom she offers to the lord for his pleasure.

Spectator 275. Tuesday, January 15, 1712. Addison.

Mr. Spectator reports on a visit to the Assembly of Virtuosos, where the topic of conversation turns to the anatomy of the human body. He then dreams of the Beau's Head and the Coquette's Heart, both of which are dissected before the assembled throng. The Beau's Head is found to be filled with ribbons, lace, embroidery, love letters, and the like. A full discussion of the Coquette's heart is promised for another day.

Spectator 276. Wednesday, January 16, 1712. Steele.

Mr. Spectator presents a letter from Francis Courtly, in which the correspondent accuses Mr. Spectator of being indelicate in his writings. Mr. Spectator should remember that his writings go to the tea-table, and temper his portrayal of vice with that in mind. A letter from Celia notes that she was approached by a man who used the words "Lusty Fellow" in her presence. Pucella writes to tell of her life as a kept woman. The man who keeps her, a Bencher of one of the Inns of Court, is jealous and never lets her out of the house or allows her to see anyone except in his company. Hezekiah Broadbrim accuses the Spectator of corrupting his daughter Tabitha and his wife Susanna by talking about the fashion of head covering among women. His daughter has now come to "lust after these foolish Vanities."

Spectator 277. Thursday, January 17, 1712. Budgell.

Mr. Spectator reports on the dependence of people of fashion on clothing from France. They even arranged for a ship loaded with French fashions to come to England during the late war with France. He presents two letters on this subject. First, from Teraminta, declares her love of all things French. She describes her eagerness to see the latest French fashions and hopes that the English women of fashion will soon adopt the new ones from France. A second letter, from Betty Cross-stitch, asks Mr. Spectator to view the latest French fashions and give his opinion. Mr. Spectator reports on a visit to Betty's shop, where he observed the fashion, and finds it generally to his liking. Mr. Spectator is also told by Betty that she has created a Puppet, through the help of Mr. Powell, (see *Spectator* 14), whom she is sending to Paris to learn the appropriate ways of moving. Mr. Spectator says that he has checked things out with Will Honeycomb, as he does before making any comments public on matters such as these.

Spectator 278. Friday, January 18, 1712. Steele.

Mr. Spectator receives a letter from a merchant who says
that his business is having difficulties because his
wife, on whom he greatly depends, has begun to study
Greek and use it at odd moments. Florinda writes to say
that she is in love with a man who is perfectly suited
to be a husband, except that he is not wealthy. She
asks Mr. Spectator's advice. In a postscript, she says
that she is already married, but hopes Mr. Spectator
will give her something to help justify her actions.
Mr. Spectator also receives a letter from Thomas Clayton,
Nicolino Haym, and Charles Dieupart, in which they ask
his support for some musical entertainments they propose,
which they hope will destroy the Opera.

Spectator 279. NF. Saturday, January 19, 1712. Addison.

Mr. Spectator offers his third essay on Milton's *Paradise Lost*, this time dealing with the subject of the
sentiments of the poem.

Spectator 280. Monday, January 21, 1712. Steele.

Mr. Spectator offers a long discussion of man's Desire
of Pleasing; in the process, he describes the figure of
Polycarpus who pleases because he is "graceful in Mirth,
important in Business, and regarded with Love." He
describes Augustus as one who lived among his friends
as though he had to prove his worthiness to them. After
drawing some suggestions from Horace, Mr. Spectator describes a man, a counterpart of Irus (*Spectator* 264),
who maintains his air of dignity in the midst of poverty,
and therefore preserves his credit.

Spectator 281. Tuesday, January 22, 1712. Addison.

Mr. Spectator reports on his dream of the Assembly of
Virtuosos, and their discussion of the anatomy of a
Coquette's Heart. A Weather-Glass containing a liquid
from the heart of a Coquette rises and falls depending
on whether the person standing near it wears fashionable
clothes or those ill-fitting or out of fashion. The
heart contains a number of other characteristics appropriate to the character of the Coquette.

Spectator 282. Wednesday, January 23, 1712. Steele.

Mr. Spectator laments the fact that many people rail
against fortune when they themselves are responsible
for their misfortunes. Will Honeycomb tells of three
ladies' distresses, caused by their early refusal to
marry anyone with less estate than their own. They lose
their estate, however, and are forced to live as poor
old maids as a result of their childhood pride. This
Spectator ends with a letter from Jenny Simper, in which
the correspondent complains of conditions in her church.

The place is so over-decorated for Christmas that she
cannot be seen to make conquests. She is especially
concerned that Sir Anthony Love's pew is so heavily
surrounded by ivy, holly, and rosemary, that nothing
she can do will penetrate it.

Spectator 283. Thursday, January 24, 1712. Budgell.

Mr. Spectator offers a discourse on the subject of the
Art of Growing Rich. He lists three techniques: Thrift,
Method in Business, and Diligence. He quotes DeWit as
saying that the way to succeed in conducting a multitude
of affairs is by doing one thing at a time. Although
hard work is the customary means of growing rich, there
are other means. Mr. Spectator tells the story of Scar-
amouch, an Italian actor, who makes his living in hard
times by stealing snuff from wealthy passers-by. He
concludes by telling the story of Rabelais, who pretended that brick dust was poisoned for the royal family. Upon being apprehended, he was able to demonstrate
that the whole thing was in jest.

Spectator 284. Friday, January 25, 1712. Steele.

Mr. Spectator praises an unaffected behavior, but condemns carelessness. He presents a letter from Stephen
Courier, in which the correspondent asserts that he
never has time for what he wants to do in the present.
Another letter, from Bridget Eitherdown, says that in
spite of what some may believe she does not love the
silly fellow some link her with. A final letter, from
Francis Sternhold, says that he is the clerk of the
parish mentioned by Mrs. Simper (*Spectator* 282). He
describes Mrs. Simper's outrageous behavior in church,
and denies that he arranged the greenery to keep her
from having contact with Sir Anthony.

Spectator 285. NF. Saturday, January 26, 1712. Addison.

Mr. Spectator offers an essay on the subject of the
language of Milton's *Paradise Lost*.

Spectator 286. Monday, January 28, 1712. Anonymous.

Mr. Spectator presents a letter in which the correspondent argues that the standard of delicacy is truth and
virtue. He opposes the notions of Francis Courtly
(*Spectator* 276), and argues that Mr. Spectator should
use every instrument at his disposal to promote virtue
among women. Philobrum writes Mr. Spectator to tell
of his "Chamber Fellow" with whom he agrees about everything except women.

Spectator 287. NF. Tuesday, January 29, 1712. Addison.

Mr. Spectator praises the religion and government of England, with special notice to the nature of liberty.

Spectator 288. Wednesday, January 30, 1712. Steele.

Melania writes to protest the species of mankind known as Male Jilts. Mr. Spectator agrees with her that such characters are reprehensible, and entitles them Friblers. Mr. Spectator urges Strephon to explain in seven days a riddle he presented to Eudamia, while Chloris has an hour only to declare whether she will accept Philotas. Mr. Spectator receives a letter from Peter Motteux, in which the correspondent describes the cloth and other items he has for sale, now that he is a merchant and no longer a writer.

Spectator 289. Thursday, January 31, 1712. Addison.

Mr. Spectator describes how, when he takes his seat in a coffee-house, he draws the curious eyes of all who are present. He moves to a discussion of the virtues of contemplating death. He concludes with the story, from Sir John Chardin's travels in Persia, in which a man goes to sleep in the royal palace in the belief that it is a hotel. When confronted by the king, he concludes that the palace, because it changes its inhabitants with the generations, is not a palace but a public house.

Spectator 290. Friday, February 1, 1712. Steele.

Will Honeycomb brings the *Spectator* word of a new play, Philip's *The Distressed Mother*. Mr. Spectator praises the age for being interested in tragedy. He cites Roman examples of the importance of valuing tragedy. George Powell writes of his reaction to performing a role in this tragedy. Sophia writes to find out if she saw Mr. Spectator in the park. Mr. Spectator responds that it was not he.

Spectator 291. Saturday, February 2, 1712. Addison.

Mr. Spectator offers an essay on the subject of literary criticism, its practitioners and the marks of excellence in criticism. He concludes the paper with a story of Boccalini, of a critic who presented all the faults of an eminent poet to Apollo, who presented him with a sack of wheat to be divided into the chaff and the corn. Having done this, the critic is rewarded for his pains with a present of the chaff.

Spectator 292. Monday, February 4, 1712. Anonymous.

Mr. Spectator says that virtue is usually accompanied by the ability to excel in some particular action. To illustrate the point, he presents a letter of Pliny to Quintillian, in which the author pays a sum of money so that Quintillian's daughter may marry in an appropriate fashion. The paper concludes with a letter from Jezebell, in which the correspondent, who has complained about the rich, writes that she does so only because she is not rich herself.

Spectator 293. Tuesday, February 5, 1712. Addison.

Mr. Spectator advises those who would be successful to associate with the fortunate and not with the unfortunate. He gives numerous classical and other precedents to demonstrate the point that one should not presume to give one's self credit for one's successes. A famous Greek general, who refused to give fortune credit for his success, never prospered again in anything that he undertook. He concludes by retelling a Persian fable of a drop of water, which lamented its becoming a part of the ocean until it entered the shell of an oyster and, with time, became a pearl.

Spectator 294. NF. Wednesday, February 6, 1712. Steele.

Mr. Spectator offers a lengthy discussion on the subject of putting too great a value upon the gifts of fortune.

Spectator 295. Thursday, February 7, 1712. Addison.

Josiah Fribble writes Mr. Spectator to complain that his wife demands that he pay her four hundred pounds a year for Pin-money; he wonders if there is any precedent for this. Mr. Spectator discusses a length this tradition; he tells the story from Plato's *Alcibiades*, of Socrates' description of some lands in Persia as being the queen of Persia's pin-money. Sir Roger once told Mr. Spectator, in this connection, about the lands that he had sold to buy presents for his Perverse Widow.

Spectator 296. Friday, February 8, 1712. Steele.

Mr. Spectator receives a letter from a correspondent who hopes that the fashion for Greek among women can be replaced with the traditional Latin. Aurelia Careless writes to say how a young officer of her acquaintance attributes a lady's appearance in her window to his success in conquering her. Aurelia wishes to know how many times she may look out the window at the same man. Mr. Spectator responds, twice. Euphues writes that a lady of his acquaintance has lately shunned him; he asks Mr. Spectator's advice and is told to leave her alone for ten days. Susanna Lovebane writes to protest those coxcombs who write lampoons of people, especially one who has written a poem on Mrs. Judith Lovebane. Charity Frost writes to describe a civil company of her acquaintance who read the *Spectator* aloud to each other. John Trott writes to say that he loves dancing, yet cannot to it so well. Mr. Spectator responds that he has a right to dance if he is not awkward in it.

Spectator 297. NF. Saturday, February 9, 1712. Addison.

Mr. Spectator describes the failings of Milton's *Paradise Lost*.

Spectator 298. Monday, February 11, 1712. Steele.

Mr. Spectator receives a letter from Chastity Loveworth, in which the correspondent says that she is a virgin and will remain so. She urges Mr. Spectator to redouble his efforts at reforming licentious males and females. She describes her suitors, including a Captain and a merchant who try to seduce her by telling her of Venus' kindness toward Mars. A tradesman urges her to be more agreeable in the business of love, while a clergyman has tried to court her, but she has heard that he has been too free with a member of his congregation.

Spectator 299. Tuesday, February 12, 1712. Addison.

Mr. Spectator says that it is important to hear how men of prudence and virtue live, but also how weak men suffer from "ill-concerted Schemes of Life"; to this end be presents a letter from John Enville on his marriage to a woman named Mary Oddly, who changed his name from John Anvil to Envil. His wife makes constant changes in the conduct of their family life; her husband sees no way out of this difficulty. He was happier when poor and Anvil; his troubles have increased with his wealth and marriage.

Spectator 300. Wednesday, February 13, 1712. Steele.

Mr. Spectator receives a letter from Suzanna Decent, who urges Mr. Spectator to comment upon all the faults of the married state. She is distressed that Mr. Hotspur and his wife argue in public. At the other extreme is Tom Faddle and his wife, who make public display of their affection. Lucina has the fault of feeling that there is no subject which she cannot discuss with virgins. Philanthropos writes to protest that those people whom Mr. Spectator calls Male Coquettes are merely harmless flatterers. Mr. Strephon, a client of Philanthropos, says that he will respond as ordered in *Spectator* 288, if only given a little more time. Miranda writes to protest the strange behavior of a friend. A final correspondent praises Mr. Spectator's essays in criticism.

Spectator 301. Thursday, February 14, 1712. Budgell.

Mr. Spectator says that mankind tends to believe that time cannot rob men of the ability to do those things for which they have received praise. Thus, Clodius, who was a celebrated dancer at 25, still tries to dance when he is over 60. Of this sort is Canidia, a woman who remains proud even after her beauty has faded. Will Honeycomb offers a letter to Chloe written by a wit in the reign of Charles II. The correspondent in this letter tells Chloe of a dream in which he found himself in an allegorical valley containing a temple to Saturn

attended by two figures named Youth and Love. He also
sees Chloe lying by the river. Youth and Love are
finally dispatched by Old-Age, who embraces Chloe.

Spectator 302. Friday, February 15, 1712. Hughes.

Mr. Spectator presents a letter in which the correspondent draws a character of Emilia, who is presented as
being an almost ideal woman. For Emilia, religion is a
principle founded in reason and livened with hope, which
affects all of her actions. Honoria is of a different
sort; she is concerned only with conquest and arbitrary
power. Emilia, who is married to Bromius, has won him
from vice and folly to an ordered life based on reason.

Spectator 303. NF. Saturday, February 16, 1712. Addison.

Mr. Spectator offers a paper describing the beauties of
Milton's *Paradise Lost*.

Spectator 304. Monday, February 18, 1712. Steele.

Mr. Spectator presents a letter from Clytander, in which
the correspondent proclaims his love for a woman of
greater fortune than he possesses; he hopes that the
description of their relationship in the paper will cause
her to encourage him in the relationship. Mr. Spectator
also presents a petition from Anthony Title-Page, a
stationer, who says that he has been in this profession
since his ancestor Crouchback Title-Page was the first
of that vocation in Britain. He appeals for business.
Mr. Spectator also presents a petition from Bartholomew
Ladylove, in which the petitioner says that he and his
friends have achieved the status of Fawners; they are
now disturbed by more aggressive businessmen called the
Worriers, whose high pressure salesmanship is objectionable.

Spectator 305. Tuesday, February 19, 1712. Addison.

Mr. Spectator describes the establishment of a Political
Academy in France in which young Frenchmen will be taught
such delicate arts of statesmanship as shrugging their
shoulders properly, nodding their heads judiciously, and
conniving with either eye. They will also be taught how
to write Treaty-Latin and to open letters without being
detected.

Spectator 306. Wednesday, February 20, 1712. Steele.

Mr. Spectator receives a letter from Parthenissa, in
which the correspondent describes how she has lost her
admirers because she had smallpox. She asks for advice
on how now to behave; the ugliest man who ever paid
court to her was and is her favorite, although he now
treats her unreasonably. In response to this, Mr. Spectator presents an exchange of letters between Corinna

and Amilcar in which Amilcar tells Corinna that he admires the way in which she accepts this misfortune so deeply that he wishes to marry her. Mr. Spectator points out that many beauties are the most disagreeable of people, and he concludes by congratulating Parthenissa on her change. He says that Bellinda and Martha are beauties who are totally disagreeable, while Miss Liddy is much more agreeable, though better looking.

Spectator 307. Thursday, February 21, 1712. Budgell.

Mr. Spectator presents a letter from a correspondent who discusses mistakes which he feels are being made in the education of children. He remembers Pericles' remark that the loss of children is the most severe which a commonwealth can suffer. He tells a story of Cicero, who in educating his son Marcus, put him under the care of Cratippus; Marcus still proved to be a blockhead, therefore suggesting that there should be a universal Board of Examiners to determine the particular talents of individuals. He remembers a story of Socrates from one of Plato's Dialogues, in which Socrates points out that he cannot teach someone incapable of learning. He also tells a story of Clavius, who was thought to be a blockhead until his talents in geometry were discovered. He supplies other examples to demonstrate that education should fit the talents of the individual.

Spectator 308. Friday, February 22, 1712. Steele.

Mr. Spectator receives a letter from Mules Palfrey, in which the correspondent laments the way in which marriages are arranged and offers his services to insure better suited couples. Mr. Spectator receives another letter from a correspondent, married to a Woman of Quality, who devotes all of her time to changing the furniture in the house and the clothing of the family. He also laments the fact that he must eat fashionably as well. Reader Gentle writes to recommend a new paper called *The Historian*. Eliz. Sweepstakes writes to protest the privilege Mr. Spectator allowed John Trott, who has now brought in a whole company of minuet dancers. Mr. Spectator responds by limiting Mr. Trott's privilege to Country-Dances.

Spectator 309. NF. Saturday, February 23, 1712. Addison.

Mr. Spectator presents a lengthy discussion of Milton's characterizations in *Paradise Lost*.

Spectator 310. Monday, February 25, 1712. Steele.

Biddy Bobake writes that, though she is in love with a young man, her parents are urging her to do better; she asks Mr. Spectator's advice. Dick Lovesick writes Mr. Spectator to ask his help in marrying a lady whom he has not been allowed to see for much of the last year and a half. Clitophon says that he is a discarded lover. He presents the letter from Lydia in which the relationship is broken and offers his reply. Philanthropos writes to describe a person of the neighborhood who is given to bearing tales. A final letter protests Mr. Spectator's habit of printing letters without comment.

Spectator 311. Tuesday, February 26, 1712. Addison.

Mr. Spectator presents a letter from Tim Watchwell, in which the correspondent protests a group of young fellows known as Fortune-Stealers. He is the father of a marriageable Heiress, and is much disturbed at those who pay court to her. He has kept the girl a virtual prisoner behind barred windows for a number of years. Mr. Spectator objects to men of this sort, but distinguishes them from Fortune-Hunters. Suffenus and Cottilus are this sort; both have grown old in pursuit of women of great fortunes. A similar story is told by Will Honeycomb. The object of most of these is the rich widow, who usually is subtle enough to avoid such creatures.

Spectator 312. Wednesday, February 27, 1712. Steele.

Mr. Spectator laments that many people need to know pain in order to put a true value on life. He tells the story, from Cicero, of Pompey, who lamented the sickness of Possidonius. The philosopher declares, however, that pain is not evil. Mr. Spectator receives a letter from a correspondent who discusses those clergymen whom he feels use inappropriate expressions in their sermons.

Spectator 313. Thursday, February 28, 1712. Budgell.

Mr. Spectator receives a letter from the correspondent of *Spectator* 307 continuing the discussion of education. The issue here is the merit of education by private tutor versus education in a public school. He concludes that a private education is best for forming the virtuous man, while a public education produces the best man of business. To demonstrate the merits of public education, he tells a story of two friends in public school, one of whom took the blame for the misbehavior of the other. Later in life, they found themselves on opposite sides of the Civil War. During the war, the friend who had been helped was able to save the life of his helper.

Spectator 314. Friday, February 29, 1712. Steele.

Mr. Spectator receives a letter from Bob Harmless, in which the correspondent laments that he is never able to see his beloved alone. Mr. Spectator urges the young lady in question to stay close to her mother. John Trott writes that, because of his dancing, the father

of his beloved has denied him access to her. Another
correspondent asks Mr. Spectator what are the chief
qualifications of a good poet, to which Mr. Spectator
responds "to be a very well-read Man." Toby Rentfree
writes Mr. Spectator of his delight in battles presented on stage. He says that he enjoyed a battle between a Lion and the hero of an opera and wished to
hear the part again but was denied this privilege.
Another correspondent writes requesting Mr. Spectator's
advice on the education of young women. Mr. Spectator
concludes by announcing that he has taken upon the role
of Visitant of all Boarding-Schools where young women
are educated.

Spectator 315. NF. Saturday, March 1, 1712. Addison.

Mr. Spectator discusses at length the presentation of
the universe in Milton's *Paradise Lost*.

Spectator 316. Monday, March 3, 1712. Anonymous.

Mr. Spectator presents a letter from Samuel Slack in
which Slack discusses the distemper called idleness,
noting that the Turks wore a piece of the bones of
their prince Scanderbeg in hopes of being fired with
vigor and force. Slack offers his bones for the purpose of controlling excessive vigor among his countrymen. He hopes that fox hunters, John Trott, and Mrs.
Figet would by this means overcome their excessive
motion. Mr. Spectator also presents a letter from
Clytander to Cleone, in which he asks permission to
love her.

Spectator 317. Tuesday, March 4, 1712. Addison.

Mr. Spectator wishes that more men, like Augustus, would
ask themselves how well they play the parts in which they
find themselves. Sir Andrew Freeport offers a journal
from a sober citizen describing his daily routine over a
number of days. The gentleman is presented as an example
of one who took great care of his life, although it was
filled with trivial occurrences.

Spectator 318. Wednesday, March 5, 1712. Steele.

Mr. Spectator presents a letter from a correspondent
who tells the story of Escalus, an old man who tries to
keep up the appearance of gallantry. Isabella enjoyed
his attentions over a number of years as a diversion
from her daily life. Eventually, she expresses her love
of him, only to receive a letter from him saying that
her expression of affection, by describing her abandonment of her virtue, has destroyed his love of her. Isabella, with the help of her husband, responds with a
letter in which she offers her appreciation of his attention and reminds him of his age.

Spectator 319. Thursday, March 6, 1712. Budgell.

Mr. Spectator presents a letter from Dorinda, in which the correspondent says that she has accepted Mr. Spectator's comments on women's fashions with humor, but wishes his comments on the extravagant wigs which some gentlemen are now wearing. In reply, Mr. Spectator offers a letter from Will Sprightly, in which the correspondent describes his advocacy of fashion, including the Long Pocket, the Frosted Button, and the Scollop Flap. He describes the Cherry-colored Hat which he plans to wear this spring. Mr. Spectator says he will have Will Honeycomb's comment in the near future.

Spectator 320. Friday, March 7, 1712. Steele.

Mr. Spectator offers a letter from a correspondent who describes the practice of many women in plotting to get a husband and discusses those women who try to arrange their marriages between those whom they please to unite. He offers a letter from Corinna, instructing a woman of her acquaintance that she will marry a particular Beau. Mr. Spectator, noting that the female sex wholly governs domestic life, agrees that there is a network of women who spend their time trying to arrange marriages. Mr. Spectator also receives a letter from a correspondent on the subject of Idleness; he declares that he is a student who now regrets the time he has lost from his studies.

Spectator 321. NF. Saturday, March 8, 1712. Addison.

Mr. Spectator discusses in detail Book Four of Milton's *Paradise Lost*.

Spectator 322. Monday, March 10, 1712. Steele.

Mr. Spectator receives a letter from Octavia, in which she tells her story of life in a gentleman's household. She married the man's son in a private ceremony but soon found herself without proof of the wedding and cast out into the world.

Spectator 323. Tuesday, March 11, 1712. Addison.

Mr. Spectator says that his presentation of a journal in *Spectator* 317 produced a number of similar journals, including one from Clarinda in which she presents her diary of a number of days spent in the company of people such as Mr. Froth, Lady Blithe, Lady Betty Modely, and Mr. Veny.

Spectator 324. Wednesday, March 12, 1712. Steele.

Mr. Spectator receives a letter from Philanthropos, in which he describes a masculine fraternity called The Mohock Club, whose avowed design is doing mischief to

their fellow creatures. Mr. Spectator presents another
letter, addressed to Mrs. Margaret Clark, in which the
correspondent, an honest country gentleman, expresses
in a simple, artless fashion his love for his lady.

Spectator 325. Thursday, March 13, 1712. Budgell.

Mr. Spectator presents a story, told by Will Honeycomb,
of a young fellow's first telling his lady of his love
for her. He does so by showing her that he has his
beloved's picture in his snuff box; she discovers that
it is a looking glass. Mr. Spectator receives a letter
from a correspondent praising his essays on Milton.

Spectator 326. Friday, March 14, 1712. Steele.

A correspondent, a country gentleman, writes to describe
his experiences with fortune-hunting women. Mary Comfitt writes that a young man, who has passed her window
several times, is welcome to come in and sit by the fire.
Another correspondent writes to request a description of
the causes of longing in women, especially those with
child. The woman's fancies, in six pregnancies, have
included changing the furniture, changing the china,
and changing their diet.

Spectator 327. NF. Saturday, March 15, 1712. Addison.

Mr. Spectator presents a lengthy description of the fine
qualities of Book Five of Milton's *Paradise Lost*.

Spectator 328. Monday, March 17, 1712. Steele.

Mr. Spectator receives a letter from a correspondent
who complains that the one blemish on an otherwise happy
life is his wife's immoderate fondness for music and
foreign languages. She spends all of her time and money
on such activities, and leaves her children in a single
large room with bolts on the doors and bars on the windows.

Spectator 328*. Monday, March 17, 1712. Steele.

Mr. Spectator presents a letter identifying the author
of the letter to Mrs. Margaret Clark in *Spectator* 324
as Gabriel Bullock. More of the letter from Mr. Bullock
is printed. A letter from George Nillson to Sir William
describes Nillson's love for a lady named Mary Norton.
Two other letters from Nillson to Mary Norton are printed
which declare his love for her and declare the difficulty
he has had in courting her.

Spectator 329. Tuesday, March 18, 1712. Addison.

Mr. Spectator and his friend Sir Roger de Coverley go
together to Westminster Abbey. Sir Roger praises Mrs.
Trueby's Water. Sir Roger interrupts the journey to

buy tobacco; when they finally arrive they tour the
Abbey, noticing Sir Cloudesley Shovell and and his tomb. The
two gentlemen also discuss the other tombs, the coronation chairs, the sword of Edward III, and other things
that they see in the Abbey.

Spectator 330. Wednesday, March 19, 1712. Steele.

Mr. Spectator receives a letter from a correspondent,
the son of a merchant in London, whose father died
leaving him an estate of 200 pounds a year with no one
to counsel him in managing it. After a short time he
wound up in jail. Fortunately, he was put under the
care of a relative who took him to the country and provided him the kind of stability he needed to grow up to
be the gentleman he was capable of being. He recommends
such a process of education for others. A second letter,
from James Discipilus, a lad of 14, describes the young
man's study of Latin. He studies it so diligently that
he dreams in Latin. Unfortunately, his father does not
believe in his education and does not provide him the
money he needs for books. Mr. Spectator believes that
both letters illustrate the need of fitting education
to the talents of those people undergoing it.

Spectator 331. Thursday, March 20, 1712. Budgell.

While in Westminster Abbey, Sir Roger and Mr. Spectator discuss the relative wisdom of their ancestors who
wore beards in comparison with men of the present day
who do not. Mr. Spectator gives numerous examples from
classical antiquity which suggest the linkage between
wisdom and beards. He also finds indications of the
value of wearing beards at other times in English history.

Spectator 332. Friday, March 21, 1712. Steele.

Mr. Spectator receives a letter from Jack Lightfoot, in
which the correspondent discusses the Mohock Club.
Lightfoot describes one custom of this club, which is
to surround one of its victims with the members holding swords, the object being to stick the victim in the
middle of this circle in the behind with swords. Those
involved in this activity are called the Sweaters.
Lightfoot describes encountering a group of these characters and escaping from them. In a postscript, Lightfoot expresses his opinion of Mr. Sprightly, of *Spectator* 319. Mr. Spectator also receives a letter from
Martha Busie, Deborah Thrifty, and Alice Early, in which
the correspondents, who live in the country, describe
the value to them of reading *The Spectator*.

Spectator 333. NF. Saturday, March 22, 1712. Addison.

Mr. Spectator presents a lengthy discussion of Book Six
of Milton's *Paradise Lost*.

Spectator 334. NF. Monday, March 24, 1712. Steele.

Mr. Spectator presents a discussion of the subject of
Dancing. He presents a letter from a correspondent who
discusses the history of Dancing and the low state into
which it has now fallen. The significance of dancing
is discussed through a retelling of Macrobius' story of
Pythagoras, who when passing a blacksmith's shop, discovered the proportions of music.

Spectator 335. Tuesday, March 25, 1712. Addison.

Mr. Spectator, Sir Roger de Coverley, and Captain Sentry, attend a performance of Ambrose Phillips' *The
Distrest Mother*. Sir Roger worries about falling into
the hands of the Mohocks, but Captain Sentry protects
them. Sir Roger comments upon the action of the play,
relating it to his experience, especially that of dealing with a Widow. Mr. Spectator delights in the fact
that Sir Roger enjoys the play.

Spectator 336. Wednesday, March 26, 1712. Steele.

Mr. Spectator receives a letter on the subject of what
might promote or prejudice learning. The correspondent
asserts that repression of useful thinking is a major
hindrance to education. To prove his point, he tells
the story of Elihu, who, though young, advised Job.
Rebecca the distress'd writes to describe the club of
Female Rakes. The correspondent, who runs a tea shop,
says that such women are idle Ladies of Fashion who
force owners of tea shops to suffer from their attacks
of the Vapors.

Spectator 337. NF. Thursday, March 27, 1712. Budgell.

Mr. Spectator receives a letter from a correspondent
who urges, with classical examples, that school boys
not learn by memory only, but also understand what they
learn. He especially notes stories of the education of
Alexander the Great. He also praises Horace's way of
using contemporary examples of honor or infamy.

Spectator 338. Friday, March 28, 1712. Anonymous.

Physibulus describes his visit to the theater on the
night Mr. Spectator and Sir Roger were in attendance.
He describes his response to the play and praises the
abilities of poets.

Spectator 339. NF. Saturday, March 29, 1712. Addison.

Mr. Spectator describes at length Book Seven of Milton's
Paradise Lost.

Spectator 340. NF. Monday, March 31, 1712. Steele.
Mr. Spectator gives an extensive character-sketch of
Prince Eugene of Savoy, at a friend's request.

Spectator 341. Tuesday, April 1, 1712. Budgell.

Philomeides writes a letter in which he defends an epi-
logue found attacked in Physibulus' letter in *Spectator*
338. Philomeides uses this occasion to defend tragi-
comedy.

Spectator 342. Wednesday, April 2, 1712. Steele.

Mr. Spectator receives a letter from a correspondent
who, remembering with pleasure the story of Asteria in
Spectator 241, tells an unfortunately different story
of Hortensius and his wife Sylvana. Hortensius is a
soldier; his wife squanders his estate entertaining
other men while he is away from home. Mr. Spectator
praises women who make faithful and loving wives.

Spectator 343. Thursday, April 3, 1712. Addison.

Will Honeycomb describes a joke which was played on a
lady by Jack Freelove and the lady's monkey. He arranges to write the lady a letter of praise from Pugg
the monkey in which the monkey claims to contain the
soul of an Indian philosopher which has trans-
migrated into the form of the monkey. He describes his
adventures in different forms and shapes, and his affection for his new mistress. The Spectator notes that
the lady was never sure of the source of this letter of
praise.

Spectator 344. Friday, April 4, 1712. Steele.

Mr. Spectator receives a letter from Epicure Mammon, in
which the correspondent describes those men who value
others in terms of the quantity of food they are capable of eating. Another correspondent writes to object
to the habit some coquettes have fallen into of taking
snuff. Mr. Saunter and Flavilla are both so given to
this habit that they render themselves unbecoming because of it.

Spectator 345. NF. Saturday, April 5, 1712. Addison.

Mr. Spectator describes at length the beauties of Book
Eight of Milton's *Paradise Lost*.

Spectator 346. Monday, April 7, 1712. Steele.

Mr. Spectator praises Generosity, especially that of
Tom the Bounteous. Tom, although a Tory, is generous
in helping those less fortunate than himself.

Spectator 347. Tuesday, April 8, 1712. Budgell.

Mr. Spectator describes in more detail The Mohock Club,
including a manifesto from Taw Waw Eben Zan Kaladar,
Emperor of the Mohocks. The Emperor argues that their
activities are for the good of mankind; he offers to

defend all those who have been injured by outrageous attacks. Members of the club are ordered not to act until after eleven and never to perform the Sweat until between the hours of one and two; the Tumblers must confine themselves to the area of Drury Lane and the Temple.

Spectator 348. Wednesday, April 9, 1712. Steele.

Mr. Spectator receives a letter from Mary, in which the correspondent objects to gossiping. She describes a visit of Jack Triplett to her Lady Airye at eight o'clock. She describes the reaction to this visit as proof that both sexes enjoy passing around defaming whisperings.

Spectator 349. Thursday, April 10, 1712. Addison.

Mr. Spectator summarizes a consolatory letter of Phalaris to a man who has lost a son. The loss is made greater because the young man was of such great merit. Mr. Spectator concludes this episode with a description of the death of Thomas More and the story of the death of Moluc, during the invasion of Don Sebastian, King of Portugal. Moluc, knowing he was dying, used his last strength to rally his troops to defeat the enemy.

Spectator 350. Friday, April 11, 1712. Steele.

Mr. Spectator tells Captain Sentry's story of a letter describing warfare at sea between the French privateer and an English merchant ship. Goodwin, the captain of the English ship, is treated so badly by Pottiere, the captain of the French ship, that the French crew mutinies and causes the freeing of the Englishman and the disgrace of the Frenchman.

Spectator 351. NF. Saturday, April 12, 1712. Addison.

Mr. Spectator compares at length the stories used by Homer, Virgil, and Milton as the basis for their epics.

Spectator 352. Monday, April 14, 1712. Steele.

Will Honeycomb complains to Mr. Spectator of the decline in the state of conversations in the town, which he finds to be greatly altered for the worse in recent years. He then offers a lengthy discussion of the nature of Truth and Reality, as they are involved in the notion of Sincerity.

Spectator 353. NF. Tuesday, April 15, 1712. Budgell.

The author of letters in *Spectators* 307, 313, and 337 offers another letter on the subject of the education of youth. In this letter, the correspondent argues that the education should either render a man an agreeable companion to himself or provide him with means to make money.

Spectator 354. Wednesday, April 16, 1712. Steele.

Mr. Spectator receives a letter from Hotspur, in which
the correspondent gives the character of the woman
known as the Devotée. Such a woman constantly reminds
everyone of how religious she is and as a result reflects no good on religion. Sophrosonius writes to compare, unfavorably, the young men of London with those of
Sparta.

Spectator 355. Thursday, April 17, 1712. Addison.

At the conclusion of a lengthy discussion of his restraint in answering those who find fault with his work,
Mr. Spectator tells the fable, from Boccalini, of a
traveler, so bothered with the sound of grasshoppers,
that he stopped to kill them. The moral of the story
is that he was wasting his time because, if he had only
waited a few weeks, they would have all died naturally
anyway.

Spectator 356. NF. Friday, April 18, 1712. Steele.

In a meditation on Good Friday, Mr. Spectator notes that
most men act from self interest, and therefore are hypo-
crites when they say they are Christian. He retells the
story of the humility and the good works of Jesus and
the envy of the authorities, which resulted in His death.

Spectator 357. NF. Saturday, April 19, 1712. Addison.

Mr. Spectator discusses at length the qualities of Book
Ten of Milton's *Paradise Lost*.

Spectator 358. Monday, April 21, 1712. Steele.

Mr. Spectator describes Charles Lillie's description of
the Roman mosaics recently found in England. Mr. Spectator compares the delights of that age with those of
the present, in which groups of people on dares, have
pulled their teeth, burned their cravats, and run naked
in the streets. Mr. Spectator praises Estcourt for his
good humor appropriate to all men.

Spectator 359. Tuesday, April 22, 1712. Budgell.

At the Club, Sir Roger is unusually quiet, and Sir
Andrew Freeport comforts him. As it turns out, Sir
Roger is worried that Sir David Dundrum has been paying
court to his Widow. Will Honeycomb, in response, discusses his own adventures in love. He describes his
courting of a young woman of the country, a young widow,
Miss Jenny, a young lady of good family, another widow,
and a number of heiresses. None of these, or other
courtships, was successful. Sir Roger finally finds
consolation in Will's reading from Milton's *Paradise
Lost*, Book Ten.

Spectator 360. Wednesday, April 23, 1712. Steele.

Mr. Spectator presents a letter from a correspondent who objects to the censoring of many men of small fortune because they try to overcome the disadvantages of their limited means by dressing better than their station in life might entitle them to. He notes that Eutrapelus describes a man as a Mohock if he wears laced and embroidered suits. Describing himself as one who has studied hard, both in pursuit of a classical education and in pursuit of the Law, the correspondent notes that gentlemen of fortune pride themselves too much on their dress and notice too much the dress of others.

Spectator 361. Thursday, April 24, 1712. Addison.

John Shallow writes a letter in which he asks for a discussion of cat-calls in the theater. Mr. Spectator offers the discussion, having purchased this item. He traces the history of instruments which make the noise of birds from classical antiquity to the present. Mr. Spectator describes its use in the theater, especially as an accompaniment to Nonsense. He concludes by discussing a man who teaches the use of the cat-call, with different notes for different kinds of plays.

Spectator 362. Friday, April 25, 1712. Steele.

Tom Pottle writes Mr. Spectator to urge him to praise those who import good wine and prevent it from being adulterated. He laments that since the death of Cully Mully Puff, very few people sell wine in an unadulterated state. Will Cymon writes a letter in which he describes how his studies made him unpleasant in conversation. He describes how his love for Bellinda improved him and made him capable of gentlemanly conduct. He praises Bellinda at great length.

Spectator 363. NF. Saturday, April 26, 1712. Addison.

Mr. Spectator presents a lengthy discussion of Book Eleven of Milton's *Paradise Lost*.

Spectator 364. Monday, April 28, 1712. Steele.

Philip Homebred writes to describe the story of a widow of his acquaintance. Her son, a forward youth, enjoys displaying his learning; she thinks him a great scholar. The correspondent especially objects to the fact that the woman spends so much time with her son, especially carrying him with her on her travels. He finds no particular benefit in the child's seeing such a variety of strange things which he cannot understand. Robin Bridegroom writes to complain of drums disturbing his wedding night. Altamira writes to advertise a performance of Betterton's *The Amorous Widow*.

Spectator 365. Tuesday, April 29, 1712. Budgell.

Describing a woman's claim that because of the weather, she could not guarantee her virtue in the month of May, Mr. Spectator offers some advice on the subject of dealing discreetly with the rites of May. He tells the story of a Yorkshire gentleman who will make a special effort in his courtship of Celinda during the month of May.

Spectator 366. Wednesday, April 30, 1712. Steele.

Mr. Spectator presents a letter containing a translation of a love song from Lapland. He quotes a letter from Constantia Combbrush describing her life as a chambermaid. She is especially concerned that her mistress does not give her any cast-off clothes, as she should.

Spectator 367. Thursday, May 1, 1712. Addison.

Mr. Spectator discusses at length the relationsip between the Material and the Formal. He notes the large number of people who are required to turn paper into published works. He admits that he has lit his pipe from his own works in the last twelve months.

Spectator 368. Friday, May 2, 1712. Steele.

Mr. Spectator presents a letter from Paul Regnaud, which tells of the death of Madame de Villacerfe. Mr. Spectator finds the paper an example of an expression of the Heroick Mind.

Spectator 369. NF. Saturday, May 3, 1712. Addison.

Mr. Spectator presents a lengthy discussion of Book Twelve of Milton's *Paradise Lost*.

Spectator 370. NF. Monday, May 5, 1712. Steele.

Mr. Spectator presents a lengthy discussion of his high opinion of the theatre.

Spectator 371. Tuesday, May 6, 1712. Addison.

Mr. Spectator receives a letter from a correspondent who praises England for having the best "Whims" and "Humorists" in the world. Among them he includes the Chins, the Oglers, the Stammerers, those given to using redundant phrases, and Swearers. Each of these demonstrates his technique because a friend, once a year, organizes a banquet for each of these so that they may display their talents.

Spectator 372. Wednesday, May 7, 1712. Steele.

Mr. Spectator receives a letter from Ralph Bellfry, sexton of the parish of Covent-Garden, who writes to

proclaim that Mr. Powell will do a benefit performance
of his puppet shows for the poor children of the parish.
The correspondent concludes by noting that he believes
all insinuations made against Mr. Powell by another
writer were false. Mr. Spectator also includes a letter
from Humphry Transfer who protests a roving band of
parish-clerks. A third correspondent writes to describe
a Lawyers' Club which meets for the purpose of discussing
the cases confronting its members. All of these proceedings are recorded by its clerk Will Goosequill.

Spectator 373. Thursday, May 8, 1712. Budgell.

Mr. Spectator presents an essay on the subject of Modesty and Assurance. He tells a story of a young prince
who went to Rome to defend his father, only to find that
the charges were true. A lengthy character of the Modest Man is presented.

Spectator 374. NF. Friday, May 9, 1712. Steele.

Mr. Spectator laments the time that men lose in thinking over their past achievements. He gives an example
of Caesar's sense of the need to work regardless of his
accomplishments.

Spectator 375. Saturday, May 10, 1712. Hughes.

Mr. Spectator tells the story of an eminent citizen reduced to low condition to illustrate the nobility of a
virtuous person rising above circumstance. The gentleman and his wife were forced to live on very limited
income; they sent their daughter Amanda into the country,
where she found herself the object of a proposition by
the lord of the manor. In a letter, the lord offers her
father four hundred pounds a year for her. Her mother's
letter, insisting she refuse this offer, moves the lord
to compassion, and he agrees to marry her. He expresses
his reformation in a letter to Amanda's mother.

Spectator 376. Monday, May 12, 1712. Steele.

Michael Gander writes Mr. Spectator concerning the curious behavior of the Criers in the street. He especially
notices a crier, calling out the hours, who was followed
about the town by an old goose who quacked in response
to his calls. Mr. Spectator also receives a letter from
Rachel Watchfull, describing her experiences as a teacher
of young ladies. She now wishes to instruct her charges
in dancing, and wonders if Colonel Jumper's wife's recommendation of Mr. Trott is a useful one.

Spectator 377. Tuesday, May 13, 1712. Addison.

Mr. Spectator gives a long list, with details, of those
who have died for love. This list includes Lysander,
slain at a puppet show; Thyrsis, shot from a casement

in Picadilly; T. S. wounded by Zelinda's scarlet stocking; Will Simple, smitten at the opera by the glance of an eye; Thomas Vainlove, who died at a ball; Tim Tattle, killed by the tap of Coquetilla's fan; Sir Simon Softly; Philander, wounded by Cleora; Ralph Gapely, killed by a random shot; Sir Christopher Crazy, Sylvius, Thomas Trusty, Francis Goosequill, William Meanwell, Edward Callow all felled by an ogle of the widow Trapland; Tom Rattle; Dick Tastewell; Samuel Felt, wounded by Susanna Crosstitch; Musidorus, slain by Belinda; Ned Courtly, by Flavia; Strephon, killed by Clarinda; Charles Careless; Jack Freelove, by Melissa; William Wiseaker, by Moll Common; John Pleadwell, by Kitty Sly; and others.

Spectator 378. NF. Wednesday, May 14, 1712. Steele and Pope.

Mr. Spectator prints Pope's "Messiah."

Spectator 379. Thursday, May 15, 1712. Budgell.

Mr. Spectator prepares a dissertation, with classical examples, to illustrate the unfortunateness of the position that a man's knowledge is worth nothing if he communicates it to anyone. He concludes the paper with a story of Rosicrusius's Sepulcher. A man, digging near the tomb, found a door; upon entering, he found the statue of a man with a lamp before him. The statue stood up suddenly and destroyed the light. Upon investigation, people in the area found that the statue was simply a piece of clockwork which operated when anyone stepped inside.

Spectator 380. Friday, May 16, 1712. Steele.

Mirtilla writes Mr. Spectator of a gentleman, her lover, who is refusing marriage after meeting another woman. Another correspondent writes that a friend of Will Honeycomb is impolite in church. Another correspondent writes that a milkmaid of his acquaintance delights in the attention she gets as much as any coquette. Betty Lemon writes of how she dealt with a man who propositioned her. The Sexton writes asking Mr. Spectator's support of a charity school.

Spectator 381. NF. Saturday, May 17, 1712. Addison.

Mr. Spectator offers a lengthy discussion of the relationship between cheerfulness and mirth.

Spectator 382. Monday, May 19, 1712. Steele.

Mr. Spectator praises those men who can accept criticism; he offers as an example a correspondent who sent him a bottle of wine to drink the health of a gentleman who had pointed out inappropriate behavior on his part. Mr. Spectator illustrates this further with the story of a

Dauphin of France, who, upon giving an incorrect order
to a troop of men, was reproved by his father, the King.
The Dauphin had to ask the officer's pardon, whereupon
the officer threw himself on the earth and kissed the
Dauphin's feet.

Spectator 383. Tuesday, May 20, 1712. Addison.

Mr. Spectator goes with Sir Roger to Spring-Garden. Sir
Roger employs men who have lost an arm or a leg to carry
them in boats, greets everyone pleasantly, and generally
acts in a gracious and benevolent manner.

Spectator 384. NF. Wednesday, May 21, 1712. Steele and
Fleetwood.

Mr. Spectator rebukes another newspaper for its attitude
toward the sick heir to the French throne, and presents
an excerpt from some sermons of Bishop Fleetwood.

Spectator 385. NF. Thursday, May 22, 1712. Budgell.

Mr. Spectator presents an essay on Friendship, choosing
as examples Achilles and his friend Patroclus; and
Aeneas and his friend Achates. Atticus is an example of
the prudent friend.

Spectator 386. Friday, May 23, 1712. Steele.

Mr. Spectator gives the character of his friend Acasto,
who is witty but who is also welcome among men because
he tempers his wit with good sense and thus illustrates
the art of agreeable behavior.

Spectator 387. NF. Saturday, May 24, 1712. Addison.

Mr. Spectator offers a lengthy discussion of Cheerfulness.

Spectator 388. NF. Monday, May 26, 1712. Steele.

Mr. Spectator receives a letter from a correspondent
who presents a paraphrase of certain sections of the
Song of Solomon.

Spectator 389. Tuesday, May 27, 1712. Budgell.

Mr. Spectator retells a story of Jupiter from a book
entitled *Spacciodella Bestia triomfante* by Jordanus
Brunus. According to the story, Jupiter once cast all
of the dieties out of heaven, calling the stars by the
names of moral virtues instead.

Spectator 390. Wednesday, May 28, 1712. Steele.

Mr. Spectator laments those people who enjoy defaming
their neighbors. He gives a sketch of Orbicilla, who
has retained her sense of shame but lost her sense of
innocence.

Spectator 391. Thursday, May 29, 1712. Addison.

Mr. Spectator retells, from Book Nine of the *Iliad*, a fable in which prayers are described as daughters of Jupiter, who have faces full of cares, are crippled by frequent kneeling, and have their eyes all cast toward Heaven. Mr. Spectator also tells the fable of Menippus, in which the philosopher discovers the prayers of earthlings in a cave underneath the throne of Jupiter. The great variety of prayers is noted, including prayers both for the life and death of a tyrant-ruler. An old man, who had prayed over and over again for long life, provokes Jupiter's anger and concludes the fable.

Spectator 392. Friday, May 30, 1712. Steele.

Mr. Spectator presents a letter of a correspondent who describes The Transformation of Fidelio into a Looking-Glass. The correspondent reports that in a conversation the point arose that men should be found who spend as much time adorning their minds as women spend adorning their bodies. This gives rise to a dream of the correspondent in which Fidelio is transformed into a looking-glass because he doted on himself. The mirror into which he was transformed tells how he has seen Flavia coloring her hair, Celia showing off her teeth, Panthea heaving her bosom, Cleora brandishing her diamond, Chloe showing off her foot, and Rhodope displaying her garters. The mirror finds that women, such as Narcissa come to love the mirror to the extent to which they love themselves. The transformation into a mirror took place because Fidelio told Narcissa how ugly she looked after having smallpox.

Spectator 393. NF. Saturday, May 31, 1712. Addison.

Mr. Spectator receives a letter from a correspondent who praises the beauty of a Danish springtime. This provokes Mr. Spectator to a long discussion of the beauties of the different seasons in different countries.

Spectator 394. Monday, June 2, 1712. Steele.

Mr. Spectator presents a discussion of how little things frequently affect serious issues. Mr. Spectator describes one gentleman who took more delight in playing backgammon than he did in conducting his business.

Spectator 395. Tuesday, June 3, 1712. Budgell.

Mr. Spectator quotes Sir Roger and Will Honeycomb on the joys of springtime; he is especially led to note that the *Spectator* has had some effect on moral values. One gentleman, having been promised by his beloved that she would commit herself in May, has been put off until June after she read the *Spectator*. Thyrsis reports that Silvia has refused to walk in the fields with him after

reading the *Spectator*. Matt Meager reports that his
mistress now serves him green tea instead of chocolate.

Spectator 396. Wednesday, June 4, 1712. Steele.

Peter de Quir reports to Mr. Spectator on the state of
punning at Cambridge. This has been the privilege of
the Johnians; unfortunately, the intruder Philobrune
appears succeeding with the fair sex as well as with
puns.

Spectator 397. NF. Thursday, June 5, 1712. Addison.

Mr. Spectator admires the emotions expressed in a letter
of Ann Boleyn to King Henry VIII just before her death.

Spectator 398. Friday, June 6, 1712. Steele.

Mr. Spectator tells the story of Cynthio and Flavia,
persons of distinction in the town, who have been
lovers for ten months and who have written letters to
each other under false names for "Gallantry's Sake."
Cynthio now gives his attention to Cecilia and Laetitia,
but unfortunately, he has not informed Flavia of his
change of heart. Cynthio tries to tell Flavia, through
letters, delivered by Robin of Will's Coffee-House.
After a brisk exchange of letters, which exhausts Robin,
the relationship is broken off.

Spectator 399. NF. Saturday, June 7, 1712. Addison.

Mr. Spectator presents a lengthy discussion on the subject of hypocrisy.

Spectator 400. Monday, June 9, 1712. Steele.

Mr. Spectator discusses the relationship between Modesty
and Desire. To illustrate his point, Mr. Spectator tells
a history of Marinet the Agreeable and her suitors Lord
Welford and Colonel Hardy. Marinet was friends to them
both, but they both caused her suffering.

Spectator 401. Tuesday, June 10, 1712. Budgell.

Mr. Spectator presents a letter from Amoret, in which
the correspondent says that she is sorry she jilted
Philander and asks Mr. Spectator's assistance in getting
him back. She characterizes herself as being a member
of the Company of Jilts. She promises Mr. Spectator
gloves and favors, as well as having him and Sir Roger
be godfathers to their first boy, if Mr. Spectator will
help reunite the two. Mr. Spectator presents a letter
from Philander to Amoret, in which Amoret is said to
have preferred Antenor to Philander because Antenor
would provide her with the largest settlement. Philander
says that he hopes eventually to be able to make the
larger bequest to her. Amoret offers her apologies to

Philander, saying that she now looks upon Antenor's estate with contempt. The paper concludes with a brief note to Mr. Spectator from Amoret in which she says do not do anything to let Philander know that she has heard of the death of his rich uncle in Gloucestershire.

Spectator 402. Wednesday, June 11, 1712. Steele.

Mr. Spectator receives a letter from Sylvia, in which she laments the fact that her husband's best friend is trying to seduce her without the husband's knowing about it. Canniball writes that he is married, but has fallen in love with Emilia, a woman of strict virtue. Emilia is to be married, but Canniball finds ways of causing delays in the wedding. Mr. Spectator also receives a letter from Dorinda, in which she tells how a man who had courted her for five years finally proposed that she become his mistress. She rejects him in rage and finds a husband and wife to be good friends. Cornelius Nepos writes that nieces and nephews close to his own age do not give him the respect that he deserves.

Spectator 403. Thursday, June 12, 1712. Addison.

Mr. Spectator describes how he enjoys walking in the streets to hear the opinions of his countrymen. He remarks on the comments he heard in various taverns shortly after the announcement of the death of the King of France. The best conversation at St. James's coffee-house is found in the inner sanctum. He finds Frenchmen lamenting the death of their monarch at Giles's, while at Jenny Mans's he finds rude reflections on the monarch's demise. In the Fish-Street, Mr. Spectator finds the state of the fishing related to the death of the King. Reactions in various places in town are equally varied.

Spectator 404. Friday, June 13, 1712. Anonymous.

Mr. Spectator discusses his opinion that there is nothing in nature which does not have its purpose. Unfortunately, however, many men destroy their natural talents or do not put them to their appropriate use. Cleanthes, a man capable of any activity, and being good at it, uses these considerable talents to be a coxcomb. Valerio is skilled in almost every kind of human activity except the writing of poetry; he, of course, tries to be a poet. Caelia and Iras have a similar problem. Caelia, who has an ill voice, talks all the time. Iras has wit, but is unattractive; she, of course, never says anything.

Spectator 405. NF. Saturday, June 14, 1712. Addison.

Mr. Spectator discusses at length the relative qualities about European languages.

Spectator 406. Monday, June 16, 1712. Steele.

Mr. Spectator presents a group of letters which praise the joys of the private life. The first correspondent praises life in the country, while the second contains a translation of another Laplander poem.

Spectator 407. Tuesday, June 17, 1712. Addison.

Mr. Spectator discusses the use of gestures in oratory and describes a lawyer who always argued his cases while twisting thread on his fingers. A client one day stole the lawyer's thread, with the result that the client lost his case.

Spectator 408. NF. Wednesday, June 18, 1712. Anonymous.

Mr. Spectator presents a lengthy discussion, in a letter, of the passions, with references to Socrates and other classical figures.

Spectator 409. NF. Thursday, June 19, 1712. Addison.

Mr. Spectator presents a lengthy discussion on the subject of taste, with special reference to a man who could distinguish ten different kinds of tea at one time.

Spectator 410. Friday, June 20, 1712. Steele.

Will Honeycomb tells the club how he and Sir Roger de Coverley encountered a prostitute named Sukey in the street. Sir Roger, always the gentleman, fed the lady and invited her to visit him in the country. To avoid Sir Roger's being made a fool of, Mr. Spectator offers a translation of some of the Proverbs describing the behavior of Harlots.

Spectator 411. NF. Saturday, June 21, 1712. Addison.

Mr. Spectator offers an extensive discussion of the sense of sight. This essay begins the series on the Pleasures of Imagination, which concludes with no. 421.

Spectator 412. NF. Monday, June 23, 1712. Addison.

Mr. Spectator offers a lengthy discussion on the subject of Greatness, Novelty, and Beauty.

Spectator 413. NF. Tuesday, June 24, 1712. Addison.

Mr. Spectator discusses Final Causes at length.

Spectator 414. NF. Wednesday, June 25, 1712. Addison.

Mr. Spectator discusses works of nature and art.

Spectator 415. NF. Thursday, June 26, 1712. Addison.

Mr. Spectator offers a discussion of architecture.

Spectator 416. NF. Friday, June 27, 1712. Addison.

Mr. Spectator discusses the subject of statuary.

Spectator 417. NF. Saturday, June 28, 1712. Addison.

Mr. Spectator discusses the human power of imagining.

Spectator 418. NF. Monday, June 30, 1712. Addison.

Mr. Spectator describes man's reaction to disagreeable things.

Spectator 419. NF. Tuesday, July 1, 1712. Addison.

Mr. Spectator discusses the artistic portrayal of the horrible.

Spectator 420. NF. Wednesday, July 2, 1712. Addison.

Mr. Spectator discusses the function of the historian.

Spectator 421. NF. Thursday, July 3, 1712. Addison.

Mr. Spectator discusses the role of an artist in choosing pleasing allusions.

Spectator 422. Friday, July 4, 1712. Steele.

Mr. Spectator discusses the role of Wit and Raillery in conversation. He describes Callisthenes, who has wit and sound judgment; when he engages in Raillery, he does it harmlessly and with good nature. Acetus, who has wit but lacks judgment, rails without mercy and thus divides the company. Minutius combines wit with love and thus always implies that he shares in the folly he points out in another. Fortius has the quality of seeking perfection in others so that his own faults are overlooked in gratitude.

Spectator 423. Saturday, July 5, 1712. Steele.

Mr. Spectator offers a letter that he has written to Gloriana, a rich, witty, beautiful and young woman who is in danger of being taken advantage of by two of her suitors. The letter warns Gloriana of the artfulness of Strephon and Damon in their approach to her. The two men work together so that one may appear agreeable to her when the other one appears disagreeable.

Spectator 424. Monday, July 7, 1712. Steele.

Mr. Spectator prints a letter from a correspondent on the subject of choosing one's own company. He praises the life lived in the country and says that Sir Roger is a model of the benevolent host. The correspondent describes the plans made by a company of people living in the country who set about to make life as pleasant for all as possible; this includes setting up a wing of the house for those people who at the moment are discontented or in ill humor.

Spectator 425. Tuesday, July 8, 1712. Anonymous.

Mr. Spectator presents a letter from a correspondent who describes a dream, inspired by reading Milton's *Il Penseroso*, in which he sees the seasons and their characteristics personified. Mars and Venus are there, attended by Flora and the various months of the year. Comus and Necessity, the mother of Fate, carry on their revels in the presence of Saturn and Vestal.

Spectator 426. Wednesday, July 9, 1712. Steele.

Mr. Spectator reports on a conversation with a friend on the subject of the relationship between parents and children which stresses the need for mutual confidence and understanding between generations. The friend tells a story of the family of Valentines. Basilius and his son Alexandrinus were both involved in occult studies; Basilius, on his deathbed, instructed Alexandrinus how to apply medicine which he thought would bring him back to life. Alexandrinus of course does nothing of the sort. Many years later, his son Renatus, is tricked by Alexandrinus into applying the same medication on the promise that it will turn his body to gold. Unfortunately for Alexandrinus, his body stirs during the application of the medicine and the container of the life-giving elixir is broken.

Spectator 427. Thursday, July 10, 1712. Steele.

Mr. Spectator presents a paper on the subject of those who defame the character of others. He tells, in this context, a story of Lady Bluemantle, who has outdone all of the women in the inventiveness and malice of her gossip.

Spectator 428. Friday, July 11, 1712. Steele.

Mr. Spectator announces that, in response to criticism, he is enlarging the scope of his papers and invites correspondents to write to him of any and all of their interests.

Spectator 429. Saturday, July 12, 1712. Steele.

Mr. Spectator receives a letter from a correspondent who reports on the establishment of an infirmary for those out of humor (see *Spectator* 424). A number of memorials are offered of those who voluntarily withdrew to this infirmary. Among them are Mrs. Mary Dainty, spinster, who retired because of her vanity; Lady Lydia Loller, who withdrew because her husband was a clown; Thomas Sudden, who withdrew because of his contentiousness; Frank Jolly, who withdrew because of his rustic sense of humor; John Rhubarb, who withdrew because he complained of sickness even when he was well; and Jeoffry Hotspur, who withdrew but begged to be restored to the company because he promised to overcome his disagreeable disposition.

Spectator 430. Monday, July 14, 1712. Steele.

Mr. Spectator receives a letter from a correspondent who requests a discourse on beggars and the lamentable state of the poor in England. Another correspondent writes to urge charity for the poor. T. Meanwell writes to urge modesty in public on the part of married people. He gives an example of inappropriate behavior of that of Lucinda who bored the company with a discussion of how the date expected for her childbirth was determined.

Spectator 431. Tuesday, July 15, 1712. Steele.

Mr. Spectator receives a letter from Richard Rentfree, who describes the rigorous and poverty-stricken childhood which his father subjected him to to keep him out of vice. A second letter is from Sabina Green, now married to Rentfree, who describes her upbringing and her habit of eating pipes and chalk. She describes her meeting with Rentfree and their marriage, and asks Mr. Spectator if he knows a meaning for her former folly of eating strange things. The letters are offered by Mr. Spectator as evidence that the calamities of children are due to the misconduct of their parents.

Spectator 432. Wednesday, July 16, 1712. Steele.

Mr. Spectator receives a letter from a correspondent who urges that men learn to give up their prejudices and rivalries, which always work to the diminishing of civic life. Ralph Thimbleton writes that his wife for some reason has not spoken to him or anyone in the family for a week. Olivia offers a letter to her from Nicodemuncio, in which the man declares himself Olivia's "Fool Elect," and tells her that if she cares enough about him to make a fool of him, she must care enough to marry him someday.

Spectator 433. Thursday, July 17, 1712. Addison.

Mr. Spectator discusses the value for society of mankind's being divided into two sexes. To illustrate his point, he tells a story, supposedly from a manuscript, "The History of the Male Commonwealth," which contains no women but which is closely allied with the Republic of Amazons. The men pursue strange habits such as never shaving or cutting their nails. Mr. Spectator promises a discussion of the female counterpart of this commonwealth in the future.

Spectator 434. Friday, July 18, 1712. Addison.

Mr. Spectator gives a short account of the "Republick of Women," who fight so much that those whose faces are scarred are considered to be the most beautiful. The army of the Amazons loses a battle either because the Secretary of State had the Vapours, or because the first Minister was great with child. When this commonwealth and the male commonwealth work together, the men of the male commonwealth shave their beards, cut their nails, and make themselves agreeable in their appearance to the women.

Spectator 435. Saturday, July 19, 1712. Addison.

Mr. Spectator discusses his role in controlling excesses in women's apparel. He remembers a discussion with Sir Roger de Coverley about ladies who dress in men's riding gear. The fashion is blamed on France, a country which Mr. Spectator says has infected all of the nations of Europe with its levity.

Spectator 436. Monday, July 21, 1712. Steele.

Mr. Spectator describes a duel between James Miller and Timothy Buck. Both men consider themselves masters of the art of self-defense, but Buck wins. Mr. Spectator thinks that the battle would have been much more intelligible if it had been over whether Elizabeth Preston was as attractive as Susanna Page.

Spectator 437. Tuesday, July 22, 1712. Steele.

Mr. Spectator tells the story of Favilla, who is married to a beast of a man because Sempronia arranged the marriage. Mr. Spectator describes Sempronia as a wicked woman, but not so wicked as those parents who would force their children into unfortunate marriages. Philanthus writes Mr. Spectator to agree with his attitude towards women who ride in men's attire (see *Spectator* 435), and to object to those women who display all their charms in public, such as Gatty.

Spectator 438. Wednesday, July 23, 1712. Steele.

Mr. Spectator describes the Passionate Man, beginning with the character of Syncropius, a man who lives a ridiculous life because he is always offending and begging pardon. Another such disagreeable person is the Peevish Fellow. After him is the Snarler; such a person is a man in a French bookshop who refused to pay for a book he had lost.

Spectator 439. Thursday, July 24, 1712. Addison.

Mr. Spectator, noting Ovid's description of the Palace of Fame, compares all Courts to this place. Mr. Spectator objects to the use of spies in court; he also objects to the account of Dionysius and his Ear, which allowed him to overhear plots of his enemies. Mr. Spectator concludes this paper with part of a character of the man with too great a curiosity.

Spectator 440. Friday, July 25, 1712. Addison.

Mr. Spectator prints a letter from a correspondent which describes the life of a group of married fellows who spend their summer together in the country. The correspondent describes a week of their delight in wine, conversation, and deciding who needs to spend time in the Infirmary. One man is sent for punning, another because of a letter he received from a woman, and still others for being disagreeable.

Spectator 441. NF. Saturday, July 26, 1712. Addison.

Mr. Spectator discusses the value of living with a faith that God can be relied upon for the blessings of this life and deliverance from its dangers. He presents a translation of the Twenty-Third Psalm to illustrate this state of mind.

Spectator 442. Monday, July 28, 1712. Steele.

Mr. Spectator describes how he uses letters which are sent to the *Spectator*, including altering them in various ways. He lists those whom he would like to contribute to the paper and describes the kind of topics that he would like for them to write about.

Spectator 443. Tuesday, July 29, 1712. Steele.

Mr. Spectator presents a letter from Camilla who describes to Mr. Spectator her reception as an opera singer in Italy. Mr. Spectator also receives a letter from a correspondent who discusses the role of trading, especially Honestus and Fortunatus, who represent opposite approaches to commerce. A third correspondent attacks those who deliberately shock other people.

Spectator 444. Wednesday, July 30, 1712. Steele.

Mr. Spectator examines a lengthy advertisement for a cure for venereal disease. He describes a quack doctor who charms his customers with a crude barometer. Another doctor, of Mouse-Alley, cures cataracts by putting people's eyes out. Charles Ingoltson claims to cure childrens' diseases because both his father and his grandfather had them.

Spectator 445. NF. Thursday, July 31, 1712. Addison.

Mr. Spectator discusses the impact of the Stamp Tax on his work.

Spectator 446. NF. Friday, August 1, 1712. Addison.

Mr. Spectator compares the English stage with the Greek and Roman stage. He notes that the presence of Cato at a Roman play once prevented its performance because the audience refused to see the indecent parts of the play while Cato was present.

Spectator 447. Saturday, August 2, 1712. Addison.

Mr. Spectator, while discussing custom, retells a story, from Dr. Plot, of an idiot and a clock. The idiot is in the habit of counting and striking the hour with the clock, and when the clock stops, he continues to perform in this fashion.

Spectator 448. Monday, August 4, 1712. Steele.

Mr. Spectator discusses the subject of punctuality, and gives the character of Jack Snippet, who is always late and should be detested more than he is. Mr. Spectator says that he is severe on the subject of tardiness because Sir Andrew Freeport testifies that he is guilty of the crime. Mr. Spectator says that a similar vice is the opening of another's mail. Will Trap and Jack Stint once fell in love with the same woman. Trap pursued her directly, while Stint wrote her letters. Trap, suspecting that Stint was reading his mail, accused him in a letter of losing a faithful friend to obtain an inconstant mistress.

Spectator 449. Tuesday, August 5, 1712. Steele.

Mr. Spectator begins a series of characters of women who deserve imitation by others. The first of these is Fidelia, who gives up a busy social life to nurse her sick father. Scabbard Rusty writes Mr. Spectator of the fraternity of Basket-Hilts, who arrange and conduct duels.

Spectator 450. Wednesday, August 6, 1712. Steele.

Mr. Spectator receives a letter from Ephraim Weed, in which the correspondent gives a history of his family's problems with money. They are beset with one calamity after another, yet Ephraim still loves money.

Spectator 451. NF. Thursday, August 7, 1712. Addison.

Mr. Spectator offers an essay on the subject of Defamatory Papers and Pamphlets.

Spectator 452. Friday, August 8, 1712. Addison and Pope.

Mr. Spectator notes the widespread hunger in his countrymen for news even of the most trivial sort. He presents a letter from a correspondent who writes to propose a daily paper which will contain only the most

trivial news. Some examples which the correspondent
offers include the putting of a horse in the pound in
Knights-bridge, the death of William Squeak, the Sow-
gelder, among others.

Spectator 453. NF. Saturday, August 9, 1712. Addison.

Mr. Spectator presents an extensive discussion on the
subject of Gratitude, including a poem on the subject
of man's gratitude toward God.

Spectator 454. Monday, August 11, 1712. Steele.

Mr. Spectator describes his yielding to an urge to rove
the countryside for 24 hours; so he goes by land and sea
from Richmond to London. He describes people he sees,
a ride in his coach alongside a Coach-Woman, and the
performance of the People of Fashion.

Spectator 455. Tuesday, August 12, 1712. Steele.

Mr. Spectator receives a letter from a correspondent in
which he presents an allegory of education in which the
different stages are compared to the growth of plants
and flowers. Infants are seeds, who soon put forth
leaves in the form of words and flowers in the form of
fancy and imagination. Eventually, with maturity,
these man-plants can produce fruit in the form of wisdom. Another correspondent praises Mr. Spectator for
his essay on Custom (*Spectator* 447). He comments upon
the fact that he is married to a Scold, which runs in
her family. Phil Garlick writes that he is neither
master of money or his wife. A final correspondent
writes on the subject of those who do not understand
how to use similes; last Sunday, he noted that elephants
have no knees, which they do.

Spectator 456. Wednesday, August 13, 1712. Steele.

Mr. Spectator offers an essay on the subject of bank-
ruptcy, which leads to a letter in which the correspondent, who has lost his wealth, asks another, more wealthy
man, to help him. A second letter from the still-wealthy
man, declares his willingness to help in any way possible.

Spectator 457. Thursday, August 14, 1712. Addison and Pope.

Mr. Spectator receives another letter from the Projector
of *Spectator* 452, this time proposing a "News-Letter of
Whispers." This paper, to include all those things
which are told as secrets, will be done by Peter Hush
and Lady Blast, who together know all the secrets of
men of the town and women of the Crimp Table. In response to a book entitled *An Account of the Works of the
Learned*, the correspondent says he will publish every
month *An Account of the Works of the Unlearned*.

Spectator 458. Friday, August 15, 1712. Addison.

Mr. Spectator gives a narrative of a young man who cannot refuse the delights of the bottle. As a result, he thoroughly embarrasses himself. This gives rise to a discussion of the relationship between true and false modesty. Mr. Spectator notes a special modesty in England on the subject of religion.

Spectator 459. NF. Saturday, August 16, 1712. Addison.

Mr. Spectator discusses religion under two categories, what we are to believe, and what we are to practice.

Spectator 460. Monday, August 18, 1712. Steele and Parnell.

Mr. Spectator presents a vision of the "Paradise of Fools," in which he meets Error, Opinion, Flattery, Affectation, Vanity, and other such inhabitants of this World of Vanity. At the center of the dream is the Palace of Vanity, which Mr. Spectator tours, noting the personification of human vices. Mr. Spectator receives a letter from a correspondent who writes on the customs of some otherwise well-bred people who take up time in church by ceremoniously addressing one another.

Spectator 461. Tuesday, August 19, 1712. Steele and Watts.

Mr. Spectator presents a letter from a correspondent who praises the *Spectator* for its promotion of virtue and includes a paraphrase of Psalm 114. A second correspondent promises to tell tales on those who complain of the *Spectator*'s increase in price.

Spectator 462. Wednesday, August 20, 1712. Steele.

Mr. Spectator describes the power of Pleasantry in company, with special reference to Dacinthus, who pleases all because he is a very pleasant fellow. Mr. Spectator goes on to present a letter from a correspondent who tells of his feelings about pride and tells a story of Sir Robert Viner, Mayor of London, who so thoroughly enjoyed entertaining King Charles II that he did not notice the King had left the company.

Spectator 463. Thursday, August 21, 1712. Addison.

Mr. Spectator describes a dream, brought on by thinking about the image of the balance in Homer, Virgil, and Milton, in which he sees a pair of golden scales that show the value of everything that is in esteem among men.

Spectator 464. Fiiday, August 22, 1712. Addison.

Mr. Spectator describes how Poverty and Wealth, compare in their ability to produce virtues or vices in men. He tells an allegory, from Aristophanes, of Cremylus who asks Apollo for advice on giving his riches to his son. Told to follow the first person he meets, he winds up with Plutus, the God of Riches. As a result, all good men are caused to grow rich; these newly fortunate put Plutus in the place of Jupiter in the temple.

Spectator 465. NF. Saturday, August 23, 1712. Addison.

Mr. Spectator discusses how faith can be instilled and nourished in the mind of man. The paper concludes with a poem on the subject of God's glory.

Spectator 466. Monday, August 25, 1712. Steele.

Mr. Spectator retells briefly an episode of Virgil's encounter in a wood with a woman of great charm and movement. This moves Mr. Spectator to a praise of dancing. He also offers a letter from Philipater, in which the correspondent describes how he tried to educate his daughter after his wife's death. He delights especially in her dancing. Mr. Spectator describes Marianne who is a skilled dancer, and Chloe who reveals in her dancing that she is a simpleton.

Spectator 467. Tuesday, August 26, 1712. Anonymous.

Mr. Spectator gives a character of Manilius, who is not only among the greatest of men, but who also does not seek praise.

Spectator 468. Wednesday, August 27, 1712. Steele.

Mr. Spectator presents an obituary for Richard Estcourt, his former companion.

Spectator 469. NF. Thursday, August 28, 1712. Addison.

Mr. Spectator claims that to an honest mind the advantages of power are the opportunities that arise for doing good.

Spectator 470. Friday, August 29, 1712. Addison.

Mr. Spectator objects to the proliferation of variant readings in editions of the classics. He parodies this practice in a mock edition of a traditional English song.

Spectator 471. Saturday, August 30, 1712. Addison.

Mr. Spectator presents an essay on the subject of human Memory, and, in the process, retells the story of Pandora's Box. From this, Mr. Spectator moves to a discussion of the fact that happy life is a life filled with hope, especially religious hope.

Spectator 472. Monday, September 1, 1712. Steele.

Mr. Spectator notes that he received a proposal from a correspondent who noted that the rich who have certain

diseases should look with special pity on the poor who
have the same diseases. He presents a letter from
Lazarus Hopeful to Mr. Basil Plenty, asking some money
in light of the fact that both have the gout. Philan-
thropus writes Mr. Spectator a letter describing the
pleasures of sight. He relates his enjoyment of looking
at the stars and other pleasant objects of sight. He
concludes with a quotation of some lines from Milton on
sight.

Spectator 473. Tuesday, September 2, 1712. Steele.

A correspondent writes to tell Mr. Spectator of life in
the country. He especially notes the delight that some
men seem to take in their imperfections; a man known to
be forgetful may have to forget things, while others
may be unable to learn foreign languages or to dance.
Timothy Stanza writes Mr. Spectator to say how he
snatched a kiss from Bellinda and writes her a poem to
explain why. Bob Short writes a short epistle about
his letter being a short epistle.

Spectator 474. Wednesday, September 3, 1712. Steele.

Mr. Spectator receives a letter from a correspondent
who, having retired from commerce, now delights in solitude and regrets the time he must spend with other
people. He is especially concerned about toasting and
discussions of horse-back riding, which he sees as a
waste of his time. He describes an ideal scheme of
country life, in which he would delight in the close
companionship of three or four agreeable friends. Dul-
cibella Thankley writes Mr. Spectator of a fortune
teller who is dumb like the Spectator but who predicted
accurately her present happiness. Mr. Spectator instructs his inspectors to investigate and report on
this Mr. Campbell.

Spectator 475. Thursday, September 4, 1712. Addison.

Mr. Spectator writes that politicians would rather in-
gratiate themselves with their sovereign than do him
real service. The same is true of lovers, and those
who give them advice. Hipparchus, having asked Philander to comment on his choice of a wife, was told
the truth and thus challenged Philander to a duel.
Celia asked Leonilla to express her opinion of a young
man, whereby Leonilla told her that the man was worth-
less. Celia forced her to stop, because she had been
married to the man for two weeks. Melissa asks everyone in town whether she should marry Tom Townly, only
to have an occasion to declare her doubts and get over
them in public. Will Honeycomb asks Mr. Spectator
whether he should marry Betty Single, to be told that
Mr. Spectator approves if the lady does as well. A
correspondent writes to ask about Mr. Shapely, who is

in every way attractive, except that he has no estate. She asks Mr. Spectator if she should marry him in spite of his poverty.

Spectator 476. Friday, September 5, 1712. Addison.

Mr. Spectator describes the way he writes the *Spectator* papers, pointing out that some are carefully prepared while others are jotted off as thoughts come to their author. He praises the use of Method, and illustrates his point by telling a story of Tom Puzzle and Will Dry. Tom has six topics which he can discuss, and Will knows this. Will is thus able to turn any conversation against Tom.

Spectator 477. Saturday, September 6, 1712. Addison.

Mr. Spectator presents a letter from a correspondent who delights in the humor and confusion of his strange garden. It is a "Confusion of Kitchen and Parterre, Orchard and Flower Garden," which are all mixed together in a pleasing diversity.

Spectator 478. Monday, September 8, 1712. Steele.

Mr. Spectator receives a letter from a correspondent who describes a walk to the shops with a friend. He notices the varieties and differences in dress and conversation, and proposes a Repository for Old Fashions. Mr. Spectator agrees with the value of this proposal and urges his correspondents to nominate those qualified to serve on the board of directors of this Fashionable Society.

Spectator 479. Tuesday, September 9, 1712. Steele.

Mr. Spectator says he receives many complaints from husbands about their wives, but discovers that most of the problems lie within themselves. Men who join reason to their passions make suitable husbands, while those who let passions rule are unhappy. Tom Trusty finds that the noises of family life help him do his work, while Will Sparkish abandons the family for the tavern. Mr. Spectator visits another couple who lavish attention on their four-year-old child. Mr. Spectator concludes by quoting Socrates on the subject of henpecked husbands; the philosopher concludes that the wise man can make the best of any situation.

Spectator 480. Wednesday, September 10, 1712. Steele.

Mr. Spectator presents a letter from Jean Chezluy to Pharamond, in which the correspondent refuses Eucrate's invitation to join the court. The correspondent says that in being chosen for the position, he has received all the true honor which a man can have, and therefore turns down the chance to gain the applause of the people. Mr. Spectator also presents a letter from a

correspondent who describes the disadvantages faced by
men of small fortunes; he is a man with fluency in both
ancient and modern languages, but sees no chance of
gaining his fortune.

Spectator 481. Thursday, September 11, 1712. Addison.

Mr. Spectator comments on the fact that people of different stations in life value the same things in different ways. To illustrate this, he tells a story of overhearing a conversation of a circle of Inferior Politicians, who talk very heatedly about things of which they
know nothing. The subject is the current state of affairs in political Europe; although the debate is heated,
Mr. Spectator concludes it is above their own heads.

Spectator 482. Friday, September 12, 1712. Addison.

Mr. Spectator describes how his paper on henpecked husbands (*Spectator* 479) has produced a great deal of response. Benjamin Bamboo, coupled with a Shrew, says
that he is trying to deal with her in lawful ways; Tom
Dapperwit says that he finds marriage to be a Purgatory.
Xantippe says that she must take care of the affairs of
the home because her husband, a bookish man, has no
knowledge of the world. A final correspondent is a
woman who claims that her husband is a Cott-Queen, more
of a woman than she. A good cook, he is always quarreling with the cook they have hired. His wife wishes he
were a man of rougher temper.

Spectator 483. Saturday, September 13, 1712. Addison.

Mr. Spectator says that it is uncharitable to interpret
the afflictions of one's neighbors as being punishments
or judgments. He tells the story of Nemesis, who is a
woman and a "discoverer of Judgments." To her, everyone's misfortune is appropriate reward for crimes, flaws,
and sins. When Dihuras, an atheist, was on a ship in a
storm, he was accused of being responsible. He pointed
out that all the other ships around them were in the
same storm and he was on no ship but this one. Biton
and Cleobis once came to pick up their mother at Juno's
temple; she asked Juno that they be given the greatest
gift that can be bestowed on men, and as a result they
died.

Spectator 484. Monday, September 15, 1712. Steele.

Mr. Spectator receives a letter from a correspondent
who praises the Modest Man, and gives a lengthy character sketch of him. Mr. Spectator disagrees somewhat
with the correspondent because he says that such a
fellow often is only spiritlessly sheepish. He must
admit, however, that the age is overstocked with blusterers, such as Charles Frankair, who can run off twenty
bashful people of ten times his sense.

Spectator 485. Tuesday, September 16, 1712. Steele.

Mr. Spectator receives a letter from a correspondent who discusses, at length, the grave error of concluding that some men are incapable of doing injury to others. He receives a letter from another correspondent, who addresses his attention to his neighbor Prettyman, who spent the month of May devoting himself to the services of women by posturing before an open window in a splendid nightgown. Robin Shorter writes a shorter letter than Mr. Short's letter in *Spectator* 473. This issue concludes with an advertisement for information as to the name of the woman seen riding in men's attire.

Spectator 486. Wednesday, September 17, 1712. Steele.

Mr. Spectator produces a letter from a correspondent who describes the kinds of women who tyrannize men. Just as serious as the wife who has a henpecked husband is the unmarried woman, who tyrannizes her suitors. The correspondent knows one woman who so dominates her lovers that she has been able to keep three at the same time. A particularly infamous woman is Betty Duall, who is the wife of a sailor and the mistress of a man of quality at the same time.

Spectator 487. NF. Thursday, September 18, 1712. Addison.

Mr. Spectator offers a lengthy discussion of the subject of dreams.

Spectator 488. Friday, September 19, 1712. Addison.

Mr. Spectator offers a series of observations by his correspondents on a rise in the price of the *Spectator*. One correspondent says that the price increase has deprived him of his breakfast, while Eugenius finds that the more expensive *Spectator* is too expensive. Philomedes, on the other hand, offers to pay a higher price. Laetitia, one of a large family of daughters, tells how her sisters have agreed to give up bread and butter if they are allowed to continue to take the *Spectator*. Mr. Spectator also declares that a new collected volume of his papers will soon be available. He concludes with an epigram for the paper recently written by Nahum Tate, Poet Laureate.

Spectator 489. NF. Saturday, September 20, 1712. Addison.

A correspondent writes Mr. Spectator of his sea voyage and says that he is always inspired to be in awe of greatness when he sees the ocean. He concludes his letter with a poem on the greatness of God, as revealed in His creation.

Spectator 490. Monday, September 22, 1712. Steele.

Mr. Spectator describes his ambition of making the word
"wife" the most agreeable name in nature. He praises
married love, and describes its joys. Uxander and Vira-
mira are offered as examples of a couple who are happily
married, while Dictamnus and Moria are a couple who are
always squabbling and impatient with each other. Mr.
Spectator offers Will Honeycomb's translation of an
epigram by Martial, which describes the delight which a
husband might have in his wife upon seeing her bathing.

Spectator 491. Tuesday, September 23, 1712. Steele.

Mr. Spectator, to illustrate man's love of justice,
tells a story of Claudius Rhynsault, appointed governor
in Zealand by Charles Duke of Burgandy. Rhynsault, upon
assuming office, observed Sapphira, wife of Paul Danvelt,
and decided to have his way with her. To achieve his end,
Rhynsault offered Sapphira a choice of being unfaithful
to her husband or having him killed. Upon yielding, she
discovered that her husband had been killed as well.
Charles, upon being informed of this, instructed Rhynsault to marry the woman and give her his estate. At
this point, he had Rhynsault executed.

Spectator 492. Wednesday, September 24, 1712. Steele.

Mr. Spectator receives a letter from Matilda Mohair, in
which she says that women who are freer with their
charms are more noticed by men than she is. She points
out Glycera and her dancing walk, Chloe and her run,
Dulcissa and her pretty shiver, and Dulceorella and her
indolent manner.

Spectator 493. Thursday, September 25, 1712. Steele.

In a discussion of the letters of recommendation which
pass around London, Mr. Spectator tells a story of Jack
Toper, a rake, who turns away a servant who wishes to
work for him because the servant is too good for him.
He offers a letter of recommendation to this effect,
which should get the man, very quickly, a new position.
Mr. Spectator concludes with a letter from Horace, to
Claudius Nero, in praise of Septimius, in which the
correspondent carefully and subtly recommends the person in question.

Spectator 494. Friday, September 26, 1712. Addison.

Mr. Spectator describes the fashion of appearing sorrowful so as to be thought religious. Mr. Spectator retells the story, told him by a learned gentleman, of a
visit to the home of an Independent Minister, in which
he was greeted by a gloomy-looking servant, conducted
down a long dark gallery, and ushered into a chamber
hung in black. Sombrius is another Son of Sorrow, who

considers it a duty to be sad and scandalized. Mr.
Spectator argues that true religion is cheerful.

Spectator 495. NF. Saturday, September 27, 1712. Addison.

Mr. Spectator offers a lengthy discussion of Jews. Mr.
Spectator finds three unique features of these people,
their Numbers, their Dispersion, and their Adherence to
their Religion.

Spectator 496. Monday, September 29, 1712. Steele.

Mr. Spectator receives a letter from a correspondent who
praises the ancients for their understanding of the different stages of man. He is drawn to this reflection by
noting Paulino, an old man who behaves like a young one,
while his son is prohibited from all diversions. The
other extreme is the young man Antonio, who has natural
talents but, being the son of a coxcomb, wastes them.
Mr. Spectator also receives a letter from Rachel Shoestring, in which she criticizes Matilda Mohair's description of frolics in the country. Sarah Trice writes that
Mohair is a crooked-legged minx. Alice Bluegarter and
another correspondent also claim that Matilda has
crooked legs.

Spectator 497. Tuesday, September 30, 1712. Steele.

Mr. Spectator describes the need for a sense of justice
in men of position; he tells the story of a minister of
Don Sebastian of Portugal, who would let no one come
near him who did not show wisdom in his face. The opposite extreme is Pope Leo X, who delighted in having
buffoons in his company. Mr. Spectator presents a letter to the Pope from a priest and former acquaintance
who points out the danger of having such characters
around.

Spectator 498. Wednesday, October 1, 1712. Steele.

Mr. Spectator receives a letter from Moses Greenbag,
who writes of the young men in the Inns of Court, who,
in their spare time, drive hackney-coaches. One of
these drivers forced the correspondent to undergo the
fate of his brother Phaeton, of being thrown on his head
in the coach. Another of these drivers was forced to
yield his seat to a passenger who wished to drive himself.

Spectator 499. Thursday, October 2, 1712. Addison.

Mr. Spectator offers a letter from Will Honeycomb which
tells of a discussion on the subject of whether there
are more bad husbands than bad wives. Will tells the
story of a seige of a city by the emperor Conrade; when
the seige was clearly going to fail, the women of the
city, upon receiving permission to carry out on their

backs whatever they wished, all carried out their husbands. Tom Dapperwit says that men should certainly be willing to do the same thing for their wives, since the load would be lighter. Will says that after this conversation, he had a dream in which he saw women leaving an English city with burdens on their backs which turned out not to be their husbands, but china, a lover, a monkey, a lapdog, and gold. At the conclusion of the dream, Will says that he saw twelve women carrying off one man, who turned out to be Mr. Spectator.

Spectator 500. Friday, October 3, 1712. Addison.

Mr. Spectator presents a letter from Philogamus, in which he tells of the advantages of marriage and the pleasures he gets being king of his household and looking at his additions to the kingdom.

Spectator 501. Saturday, October 4, 1712. Addison and Parnell.

Mr. Spectator allows a gentleman to relate a dream allegory of a trip to the Grotto of Grief, along the river of Tears, in a boat steered by Misfortune. Patience persuades some not to take the journey, but the narrator and others do, in a boat whose sail is filled with Sighs. The inhabitants of the land include Dejection, Paleness, Care, Anguish, and Troubles. At the end of the journey, the party is joined by Patience, who delivers them finally into the hands of Comfort.

Spectator 502. Monday, October 6, 1712. Steele.

Mr. Spectator says that when men read, they read and notice what accords with their own inclinations. The paper at hand is drawn from a comedy of Terrence, the Self-Tormentor. Mr. Spectator describes the evening at the theater in which this play was performed; an old woman was carried off the stage; he tells the story of this woman, who has that negligence of person which is exhibited by so many who are careful of their minds. The audience of the play, Mr. Spectator notes, is composed of those who enjoy the pleasures of the body and those who enjoy the pleasures of the mind. He himself delights in the play the Country-Wake, a play which is delightful to watch, although it is not especially didactic.

Spectator 503. Tuesday, October 7, 1712. Steele.

Mr. Spectator receives a letter from Ralph Wonder, in which the correspondent describes the misbehavior of people in church. He notes especially a very attractive young lady who upset an entire parish last Sunday by acting with such ease and grace that all admired her, although she disturbed the rustic churchgoers with her sophisticated ways.

Spectator 504. Wednesday, October 8, 1712. Steele.

Mr. Spectator describes word games which pass for conversation among those who lack wit. Others who try to
overcome for lack of wit are Biters, who think those
with whom they converse are fools though they do not
think of them as knaves. After describing such characters, Mr. Spectator tells the story of a surgeon at
Newgate who is duped by a condemned prisoner whose body
the surgeon was trying to buy. The prisoner, after ex-
tracting absolutely as much as he could for his body,
declared that he was to be executed in such a way as to
render his body useless for the physician.

Spectator 505. Thursday, October 9, 1712. Addison.

Mr. Spectator discusses the number of wizards and fortune tellers to be found in the community, and prints a
letter from Titus Trophonius, who writes to set himself
up as interpreter of dreams.

Spectator 506. Friday, October 10, 1712. Budgell.

Mr. Spectator receives a correspondent who tells a fable
in which Wealth is the father of Love. He discusses
what can make a marriage happy, and says that too great
a familiarity after marriage can banish love very quickly. Keeping love alive after marriage requires effort,
and so the narrator tells a history of Laetitia and
Erastus. Their marriage is a happy one because they
pay great attention to pleasing each other. Flavilla
and Tom Tawdry are described as a couple who have a bad
marriage because they take each other for granted.

Spectator 507. NF. Saturday, October 11, 1712. Addison.

Mr. Spectator offers a lengthy discussion on the subject
of Lying.

Spectator 508. Monday, October 13, 1712. Steele.

Mr. Spectator presents a letter from a correspondent who
protests the misuse of power in clubs. He names one
such tyrant Dionysius, and describes how he served minor
offices in the club in such a way that club members
thought he was working for the good of all rather than
to satisfy his own desires. Now made head of the club,
he tyrannizes over lesser members. A second correspondent writes Mr. Spectator to describe men who act in-
appropriately in courtship. A gentleman whom she meets
while staying at a country house tries to imitate, in
his relationships with her, those better than he.

Spectator 509. Tuesday, October 14, 1712. Steele.

Mr. Spectator receives a letter from Hezekiah Thrift,
who writes on matters of money, which he says Mr. Spectator has neglected. He laments the proliferation of

beggars and street-vendors at the Royal Exchange, and argues that "one should Keep your Shop, and your Shop will keep you." He praises the merchant Mr. Gumley, as well as Mr. Tobias Hobson, a Carrier, who served his customers well.

Spectator 510. Wednesday, October 15, 1712. Steele.

Mr. Spectator relates and reflects on an incident which happened while he was driving in a Hack. He saw a girl who had made herself part of the landscape by putting her chin on a window sash. He wonders out loud at the force of beauty and at the powers that women have over men.

Spectator 511. Thursday, October 16, 1712. Addison.

Mr. Spectator presents another letter from Will Honeycomb on the subject of women. He tells a story from Herodotus of Persian Fairs in which all the unmarried women of society were put on display to be sold to the highest bidder. As a result, the rich married the beautiful women, while those of lesser means married the Agreeable. Honeycomb recommends a Fair of this sort for England, in which noblemen would be matched with poor girls and noblewomen with poor men. He tells another story in which a General of the Tartars, having conquered a town in China, put all the women of the town up for sale in sacks with their value marked on the outside. A man who bought an expensive sack discovered that it contained an old woman; he was enraged until he learned that she was the sister of a rich man who would share his wealth with his brother-in-law. Honeycomb hypothesizes a dream vision, in which he finds the women of London for sale in sacks, with allowances of the price taken for those who are Scolds, Prudes, and Coquettes.

Spectator 512. Friday, October 17, 1712. Addison.

Mr. Spectator writes an essay on the receiving of advice. He encourages the giving of advice obliquely, so as to overcome the resistance of the person who receives the advice. To illustrate this, he tells an oriental fable of two owls in a tree who exchange villages which a Sultan has destroyed as the dowry for marriage between the son of one owl and the daughter of the other. The Sultan, learning what they were saying, ordered the villages rebuilt and began to be concerned for what was good for his people.

Spectator 513. Saturday, October 18, 1712. Addison.

Mr. Spectator presents a letter from the Clergyman, who writes on the subject of man and sickness. He urges that we think of sickness and death only as something necessary to reach the Throne of God. He concludes with a hymn, composed during his own sickness, in which he describes hope for the future state of his soul.

Spectator 514. Monday, October 20, 1712. Steele.

Mr. Spectator presents a letter from a correspondent who describes a dream, inspired by reading Virgil, of Solitude, Silence, and Contemplation, who were discovered by the dreamer in a wood. Solitude directs him to go up to Mt. Parnassus where he finds the dwelling-place of the muses. On the way, he discovers the Troop of Vanity, nymphs named Fancy and Judgment, and Wit enthroned on the top of the mountain.

Spectator 515. Tuesday, October 21, 1712. Steele.

Mr. Spectator presents a letter from the correspondent who wrote of the coquette in church in *Spectator* 503. He describes following her to learn that her business is winning hearts and then throwing them away, enjoying only the triumph. He offers a letter, to his friend Jenny, which presents the lady as a happy, self-loving woman, who takes all the admiration she can get and returns none of it. He describes her encounter with Mr. Fanfly, whom she delights in causing to perform for her. The correspondent also offers his friend's reply to Gatty, in which she describes Gatty's delights as barren, superficial pleasures.

Spectator 516. NF. Wednesday, October 22, 1712. Steele.

Mr. Spectator presents a lengthy discussion of the despicable fact that many Christians fight each other in the name of the God of Peace. He presents an excerpt from Steele's *The Christian Hero* on this subject.

Spectator 517. Thursday, October 23, 1712. Addison.

Mr. Spectator reports with sadness the death of Sir Roger de Coverley at his house in the country. Sir Andrew Freeport has received a letter describing the old man's final sickness. Mr. Spectator presents a letter from Edward Biscuit, describing the death itself. Sir Roger found that he was unable to eat roast beef, that he received a kind letter from his Widow Lady; he took leave of his servants, and breathed his last. The news is received with sadness at the Club. Sir Andrew bursts into tears upon seeing a book which Sir Roger sent to him concerning their last debate.

Spectator 518. Friday, October 24, 1712. Anonymous.

Mr. Spectator receives a letter from a correspondent who laments the death of Sir Roger and offers a choice of epitaphs. Tom Tweer writes a letter on the subject of Phisiognomy, and says that since the inner man and the outer man are related, inner talents are reflected in outer action. Thus, theologians, scholars of literature and language, and poets, can be described in terms of their gait, their dress, the look on their face, and the size of their noses.

Spectator 519. NF. Saturday, October 25, 1712. Addison.

Mr. Spectator describes the pleasures of contemplating the varieties of life in the universe.

Spectator 520. Monday, October 27, 1712. Steele.

Mr. Spectator receives a letter from a correspondent who describes his grief at the loss of his wife and asks for a discussion by Mr. Spectator of the subject of male widowhood.

Spectator 521. Tuesday, October 28, 1712. Steele.

Mr. Spectator presents a letter from a correspondent who tells how he has been forced to perfect his inattention to all that men say because he has learned by experience that he can believe none of it. He describes how he has learned to draw people out in their telling of stories so that they move easily from the probable to the marvelous and then to the impossible. He describes a gentleman of his acquaintance who enjoyed telling a lie at eight o'clock in the morning and then following it through town until eight o'clock at night. He delights in the reaction to his lie at different clubs and public houses throughout the town.

Spectator 522. Wednesday, October 29, 1712. Steele.

Mr. Spectator stresses the importance of married life and says that he would be a happy man if he could contribute in some way to helping his readers improve their choice of a marriage partner. To illustrate his point, Mr. Spectator gives histories of Lysander and Will Thrash to suggest the kind of person who is successful in marriage. Lysander is a good choice for marriage because of his wit and understanding, but Will is unhappy because both he and his wife are very dull people. To conclude his discussion, Mr. Spectator presents two letters from suitors to the Lady Fair. The first, from a man of great estate, suggests that he is only concerned about the financial aspects of the match, while the second, from a man of lesser estate, suggests that he is concerned with making her happy. Mr. Spectator says that the lady's uncle Edward, who is also concerned only with money, is insistent that she marry the first gentleman; Mr. Spectator hopes that she will make use of the first light night to show the second gentleman that she understands marriage is not a common bargain.

Spectator 523. NF. Thursday, October 30, 1712. Addison.

Mr. Spectator discusses the proper manner of writing a poem to celebrate a Great Man. He praises the recent work of Alexander Pope. He offers an Edict on the subject of heroic poetry, urging that poets follow certain rules to avoid "that Effusion of Nonsense, which we have good Cause to apprehend."

Spectator 524. Friday, October 31, 1712. Anonymous.

Mr. Spectator discusses the popularity of dream visions among his correspondents; one of them tells a dream in which men who drink of the river of worldly wisdom are led astray, while those who drink from the waters of heavenly wisdom escape danger.

Spectator 525. Saturday, November 1, 1712. Hughes.

Mr. Spectator says that he takes every opportunity to discover the success of his writings; he is delighted to learn that a number of Pretty Fellows have decided to become Heads of Families. He regrets that much of the literature of an earlier age made fun of marriage. He argues that Conjugal Love is a higher state of the affection than love felt by unmarried people. He finds that love also affects the writing style of those who feel it. As an example, he notes the absurdity of the love letters which Narcissa gets and praises the good sense found in those which Benevolus writes to his wife. He concludes with a letter of Pliny to Hispulla, the aunt of his wife. The content of the letter is a recitation of the virtues of Pliny's wife.

Spectator 526. Monday, November 3, 1712. Steele.

Mr. Spectator presents a letter from Moses Greenbag, describing the behavior of Hackney-Coachmen. Mr. Spectator turns the problem of correcting the behavior over to his friend John Sly for immediate handling of these Enormities. Greenbag addresses Mr. Spectator as "Dear Dumb" and points out that a number of students are still spending their time driving coaches. Mr. Spectator instructs John Sly to notice carefully the behavior of those who drive coaches and those who ride in them.

Spectator 527. Tuesday, November 4, 1712. Anonymous.

Mr. Spectator presents a letter from Philagnotes, in which the correspondent describes how a husband became jealous of his conversations with the man's wife. The writer hopes that this letter will prevent an innocent conversation from being turned into something else and causing a splendid lady to be unhappy as a wife. A second correspondent tells of Cephalus, who became suspicious of her husband and followed him into the woods, only to be killed accidentally by his javelin.

Spectator 528. Wednesday, November 5, 1712. Steele.

Mr. Spectator receives a letter from Rachael Welladay, in which the correspondent writes of her misfortunes at the hands of men. She finds that the libertinism of young men infects all of society, and laments the number of men who go through life without marrying.

Spectator 529. NF. Thursday, November 6, 1712. Addison.

Mr. Spectator discusses Rules of Precedence, noting that authors of larger books, such as folios, feel themselves superior to authors of quartos and smaller books. He is especially interested in the Rules of Precedency in the learned professions, noting that tragic actors are considered superior to comic actors.

Spectator 530. Friday, November 7, 1712. Addison.

Mr. Spectator notes that many who have ridiculed marriage find themselves married and as the object of their own ridicule. Will Honeycomb, who has been witty on the subject of women, has now married a Farmer's Daughter and in a letter presents a picture of a converted Rake. He addresses Mr. Spectator as "My Worthy Friend" and describes how delighted he is with the country life now that he is married. He hopes that Mr. Spectator can get his friend Tom Dapperwitt to take his place in the club.

Spectator 531. NF. Saturday, November 8, 1712. Addison.

Mr. Spectator discusses at length man's concept of God.

Spectator 532. Monday, November 10, 1712. Steele.

Mr. Spectator says that he is pleased with the help that he has been able to give others, especially writers. He presents a letter from a correspondent who describes a conversation on the subject of the verses of the emperor Adrian, composed on his deathbed. He concludes with a poem, by Tickell, on the subject of Mr. Spectator's success in promoting virtue. Mr. John Sly reports that all those he observed riding in hackney-coaches behaved decorously.

Spectator 533. Tuesday, November 11, 1712. Steele.

Deuterrerastus writes to describe his parents' cruel treatment of him. They are especially concerned that he marry, and urge him to observe Katherine, Betty, Dorothy, and Fidelia. Unfortunately, he is in love with Miranda and has urged his parents to agree to his marrying her. Penance Cruel writes to describe her mistreatment in a recent journey by coach. Two men, seemingly gentlemen, take the opportunity of the coach-ride to talk to her in indecent terms.

333

Spectator 534. Wednesday, November 12, 1712. Steele.

Sharlot Wealthy writes Mr. Spectator to describe the problems she has in being wealthy, beautiful, and young. She regrets that her intelligence is overlooked in favor of her appearance. Abraham Dapperwit asks if the poem in *Spectator* 378 is by Alexander Pope. Mr. Spectator confirms that it is. Jeremy Comfitt writes on the problems of mixing business and pleasure. Lucinda Parly writes on the indecent addresses she receives from a gentleman while serving as a barkeeper. Mr. Spectator instructs Mr. Sly to consider the behavior of people in a larger area than he has previously done.

Spectator 535. Thursday, November 13, 1712. Addison.

Mr. Spectator discusses the nature of vain and foolish hope. Mr. Spectator, to illustrate his point, tells an Arabian Fable of Alnaschar, an idle fellow who lost his fortune dreaming of how he was to increase it. Having invested in glass, he contemplates how he will spend his wealth; unfortunately, he accidentally kicks the basket containing his glassware and breaks it all.

Spectator 536. Friday, November 14, 1712. Addison.

Mr. Spectator describes how a young girl passed him a letter while he was in a bookshop, in which the correspondent suggests that Rakes should take up knitting. This would give them something constructive to do and would still allow them to show off their hands. A letter from a second correspondent describes the use of men as Whiflers or Shoeing-Horns. Such men serve as suitors for women until they have found the person, or Shoe, whom they wish to marry. The correspondent speculates that Will Honeycomb served as such a Shoeing-Horn; he says that he has served as such a person for 20 years.

Spectator 537. NF. Saturday, November 15, 1712. Hughes.

Mr. Spectator receives a letter from a correspondent who discusses mixtures of beauty and deformity in the human form. He says that whatever imperfections men may have, they are called upon to rectify them in the name of religion and virtue. It is some consolation for men to be reminded that, due to the common mortality, all imperfections will eventually be put off. This leads him to a discussion of old age, with a citation from Xenophon of Cyrus' attitude towards his death as a reminder to be concerned with the soul and not with the body.

Spectator 538. Monday, November 17, 1712. Addison.

Mr. Spectator notes that although surprise is the soul of humor, those who surprise by outraging nature produce only stares and not laughter. He discovers this in the process of a conversation with a group in which the subject of discussion is various dislikes held by members of the group. The conversation is stopped by a man who says that he is so disturbed by cats that he nearly faints after passing under a sign with a picture of a cat on it. Mr. Spectator says that the way of dealing with this situation is either to treat it with silence or to try to say even more surprising things. A correspondent offers Mr. Spectator another epitaph.

Spectator 539. Tuesday, November 18, 1712. Anonymous.

Mr. Spectator receives a letter from Relicta Lovely, who writes of the trials she faces as a rich young widow. She finds herself surrounded by suitors, some of whom are dying with hope, while others are dying of fear. Eustace writes of his problems in addressing a young lady because her parents feel she is too young to marry. A third correspondent, upon hearing a young clergyman, hopes that he is one of Sir Roger's chaplains, but discovers to his dismay that the clergyman is confusing instead of enlightening.

Spectator 540. NF. Wednesday, November 19, 1712. Steele.

Mr. Spectator receives a letter in which the correspondent discusses the poetry of Edmund Spenser.

Spectator 541. Thursday, November 20, 1712. Hughes.

Mr. Spectator offers a farewell essay from the Templar on the subject of punctuation and action, the rules being drawn from Cicero and the examples from great works of English literature, including Shakespeare.

Spectator 542. Friday, November 21, 1712. Addison.

Mr. Spectator is pleased to hear that the letters printed in the *Spectator* are among its most popular features. He especially notes the letter from the Valetudinarian (*Spectator* 25), a discussion of the Fan Exercise and the Hooped Petticoat (*Spectator* 28 and 102), among others. Mr. Spectator hopes that his audience can distinguish truth from falsehood in these letters. He concludes with a letter from Philo-Spec, in which the correspondent laments Sir Roger's death, Captain Sentry's move to the country, Will Honeycomb's marriage, and the Templar's taking up of the practice of law.

Spectator 543. NF. Saturday, November 22, 1712. Addison.

Mr. Spectator discusses the human body as evidence for the existence of a transcendentally wise and powerful being.

Spectator 544. Monday, November 24, 1712. Steele.

Mr. Spectator receives a letter from Captain Sentry describing his taking over the estate of Sir Roger de Coverley. He praises Sir Roger as a man of a warm and well-disposed heart, who though having a small capacity, is superior to men with great talents but cold hearts. He says that he has tried to follow Sir Roger's example in his treatment of the servants and those who live on or near the estate. He hopes to encourage former army officers to visit him in the country, especially Colonel Camperfelt.

Spectator 545. Tuesday, November 25, 1712. Steele and Gigli.

Mr. Spectator presents a letter from the Emperor of China to the Pope in Rome. This letter proposes a union of the Chinese and Roman churches. He concludes with a note from John Sly reporting that many large French hats have recently been seen.

Spectator 546. Wednesday, November 26, 1712. Steele.

Mr. Spectator reports on a visit to the theater to watch a play by Colley Cibber, part of which was translated from French. This description is to illustrate the problem of knowing the difference between what is real --i.e. what is Cibber's own--and what is borrowed--what he translated from the French. Mr. Spectator concludes the paper with a letter from a correspondent who expresses his gratitude to a friend for lending him money in such a generous way.

Spectator 547. Thursday, November 27, 1712. Addison.

Mr. Spectator presents a letter from a correspondent who has found a way to compliment the editor without embarrassing him. The method is to prepare an advertisement for the *Spectator* as though it were an advertisement for a physician. The paper is presented as a remedy for all problems, unequalled in the universe. Will Crazy testifies that the paper has cured him of his anxieties over his wife Mary, a younger woman. Charles Easy finds it a sure cure for hypochondria. Christopher Query says it has cured him of a distemper of his tongue. Martha Gloworm finds it a natural friend to the complexion, while Samuel Self found it a sweetner of the blood, Elizabeth Rainbow was cured of a distemper in the head, and George Gloom was cured of an illness of the spleen. Others who have found it useful include Nathaniel Henroost, Alice Threadneedle, Rebecca Nettletop, Tom Loveless, Mary Meanwell, Thomas Smokey, Anthony Freeman, Tom Meggot, and Rustick Sprightly.

Spectator 548. Friday, November 28, 1712. Anonymous.

Mr. Spectator presents a letter from a correspondent who praises Mr. Spectator's critical essays as excellent "Cleansers of the Brain." He himself offers a continuation of Mr. Spectator's discussion of Poetical Justice.

Spectator 549. Saturday, November 29, 1712. Addison.

Mr. Spectator describes a meeting with Sir Andrew Freeport in which Sir Andrew tells why he is retiring from active business life. He offers a letter from Sir Andrew in which the businessman discusses more at length his reasons for taking this step. Mr. Spectator declares the club to be entirely dispersed and promises to consult the reader about the formation of a new one.

Spectator 550. Monday, December 1, 1712. Addison.

Mr. Spectator says that there has been great public interest in replacements for the various members of the club. Some have offered, with bribes, to take the place of various members. Mr. Spectator proposes a new club which will be "the very Flower and Quintescence of Clubs." He also plans to talk in his new club, contrary to his former habits.

Spectator 551. Tuesday, December 2, 1712. Anonymous.

Mr. Spectator offers a letter from a correspondent who offers a choice of epigrams from classical literature, a letter from a correspondent who offers another epigram in praise of Homer, and a letter from Philonicus, in which the correspondent describes his success in legal proceedings. This third correspondent reports on a trip to the low courts in which he discovers that those who participate in legal proceedings use unusual language, when they owe their clients good English.

Spectator 552. Wednesday, December 3, 1712. Steele.

Mr. Spectator laments his not speaking enough of the "industrious Part of Mankind." He praises the richly filled warehouses of Peter Matteux and declares his support of a proposal of Renatus Harris to build an organ over the West Door at St. Paul's Cathedral. He also prints an advertisement by John Rowley for contributions toward the building of a pair of Globes, one of the Heavens and one of the Earth.

Spectator 553. Thursday, December 4, 1712. Addison.

Mr. Spectator describes the letters he has received in response to his proposal in *Spectator* 550 to start a new club in which he will open his mouth. A bookseller wishes to print the speech while others seek members of a new club to be formed around Mr. Spectator. Other correspondents point to the number of problems which need Mr. Spectator's attention. Four correspondents join in a letter in which they urge him to live forever and wonder if Mr. Philo-Spec's guess that Mr. Spectator himself is about to take leave could possibly be true. They accept the loss of Will Honeycomb, the Templar, and Sir Roger, but they promise to read earlier papers with pleasure.

Spectator 554. NF. Friday, December 5, 1712. Hughes.

Mr. Spectator offers an essay on the subject of the wonders which the human mind is capable of achieving.

Spectator 555. Saturday, December 6, 1712. Steele.

Mr. Spectator, under the name of Richard Steele, declares that he must make his farewell. He expresses his appreciation to the two men who have helped him most, and says that with Sir Andrew Freeport, he has balanced his accounts with all his "Creditors for Wit and Learning." He promises a collected edition and takes, with pain and sorrow, his farewell. He concludes with a letter from a correspondent who describes the Academy of Painting, of which Mr. Spectator has been a member. The correspondent describes the nature of painting and praises England for producing the best Face-Painters.

Spectator 556. Friday, June 18, 1714. Addison.

Mr. Spectator tells of his activities in the interim period since the end of the first series of the *Spectator*. They include joining clubs in which he talks; after making his first speech, of 6 sentences, he was so hoarse that he could not talk for three days. He has now found a variety of other ways to express himself vocally, including learning about the current state of political and social affairs in the country. He proclaims his intention to resume his old habit of offering speculations on useful subjects.

Spectator 557. Monday, June 21, 1714. Addison.

Mr. Spectator describes the value of all conversations held by the Man of Integrity. To illustrate this, he tells the story of Cato, from Plutarch, in which a judge refuses to accept one witness in place of two, and declares that he cannot do it even if the one witness were Cato himself. Mr. Spectator concludes with a letter from the Ambassador of Bantam to his King upon his arrival in London. He notes to his master that the strange inhabitants of London speak hyperbolically. One man, who told the Ambassador that he was to consider his house as the Ambassador's own, was dismayed when the Ambassador started to knock down one of the walls and carry away some of the goods. After other such incidents,

the Ambassador wishes that he were dealing with more
sincere people.

Spectator 558. Wednesday, June 23, 1714. Addison.

Noting that Socrates and Horace say that a man's troubles
are always less difficult for him to handle than someone
else's might be, Mr. Spectator describes a dream in
which Jupiter proclaims that all mortals should bring
all their griefs and calamities and throw them in a heap.
The mortals who do this are aided by a figure of Fancy,
who leads mortals to the place where they deposit their
troubles. Mr. Spectator notes that some of the cargo
includes deformities and the affects of aging, diseases,
and the burdens of Lovers, which they refuse to put down.
At the end of the dream, Fancy reveals to Mr. Spectator
the true appearance of his face.

Spectator 559. Friday, June 25, 1714. Addison.

Mr. Spectator continues his dream of *Spectator* 558, in
which Jupiter, with the help of Fancy, decrees that
mortals might exchange their misfortunes with each
other. A man who put down the Colick and took up an
ungrateful son, quickly was ready to give the son back.
A slave exchanged his chains for the gout, one man ·
swapped one blemish for another, and Mr. Spectator himself exchanges his short face for a long one. The result of this exchange is further lamentation, and the
resumption of each old burden by the person who used to
carry it. Fancy's place is taken by Patience, who helps
men bear their particular burden.

Spectator 560. Monday, June 28, 1714. Budgell.

Mr. Spectator receives a letter from Cornelius Agrippa,
who writes to tell of his being a silent conjurer who
has decided, after Mr. Spectator's example, to use his
voice. Another correspondent writes to tell Mr. Spectator of the Chit-Chat Club; she also congratulates Mr.
Spectator on the use of his tongue. She says that the
members of the Club would like to speak with Mr. Spectator; he will find them at Lady Betty Clack's, where
he will be given one minute in ten to speak, without
interruption. Two correspondents from Oxford also
write to congratulate Mr. Spectator on opening his
mouth; they look forward to his future observations.
Frank Townly writes to note that since Mr. Spectator
has begun to speak, he is now talking in his sleep.

Spectator 561. Wednesday, June 30, 1714. Addison.

Mr. Spectator receives a letter from a correspondent who
describes the Widow Club, whose function is to tell of
the pleasures of single life and persuade other women
not to marry so that the members of the club may have

all the men to themselves, to marry, bury, and marry
again. The members of the club include Mrs. Snapp, Mrs.
Medlar, the Widow Quick, Lady Catharine Swallow, the
Lady Waddle, widow of Sir Simon Waddle and James Spindle,
Deborah Conquest, widow of Sir Samson Conquest, the Widow
Wildfire, courted by John Felt, and Mrs. Runnet.

Spectator 562. Friday, July 2, 1714. Addison.

Mr. Spectator presents an essay on the Tribe of Egotists.
He concludes by telling how he cured a young man who
tried to present himself as a witty fellow by updating
old jokes; Mr. Spectator showed him a copy of old joke
books which contained all of his jests.

Spectator 563. Monday, July 5, 1714. Anonymous.

Mr. Spectator presents a letter from Blank, who describes
his protean nature. Mr. Spectator also presents a letter
from a correspondent, a wife who describes the peculiarities of her husband. The husband's chief vice is that
when he is angry he breaks the china; he has broken an
enormous amount of the stuff since their marriage.

Spectator 564. Wednesday, July 7, 1714. Budgell.

Mr. Spectator presents an essay on those who, blinded by
prejudice and inclination, readily pronounce their verdict on the characters of others. To illustrate his
point, he tells the story, from Xenophon, of Cyrus
the Great. The ruler, upon confronting Araspas with
charges that he tried to seduce Cyrus' wife Panthea,
discovered that the man feels he is possessed of a good
soul and a bad soul. He acts according to which soul
is dominant at the moment. Mr. Spectator concludes
with a story of Isadas, a Spartan, who was so zealous
for the defense of his city that he fought in the nude
against a sudden attack of the Thebans. The young man
was first praised by the Spartans, and then fined for
going into battle unarmed.

Spectator 565. Friday, July 9, 1714. Addison.

Mr. Spectator describes a walk in the country and tells
of his wonder at the varieties of color he sees in the
open fields and in the sky as night falls. He reflects
on his situation as a creature of a God who made such a
universe.

Spectator 566. Monday, July 12, 1714. Budgell.

Mr. Spectator devotes a paper to letters from soldiers.
The first, from Will Warly, describes the value of
a military education for producing an excellent lover.
Another correspondent writes requesting Mr. Spectator's
help in knowing the best way to approach a widow. Peter
Push writes of his pursuit of a young lady, which he describes in military terms.

Spectator 567. Wednesday, July 14, 1714. Addison.

Mr. Spectator says that he has been advised to spice up
his papers with scandal. He sets out to imitate writers
of scandal papers in a use of initials and dashes instead
of names. He then proceeds to use this technique in
telling proverbs and saying things which no one will
have any trouble understanding.

Spectator 568. Friday, July 16, 1714. Addison.

Mr. Spectator describes a conversation he overheard in
a coffee-house on the subject of the *Spectator*. The
men having the conversation note that the paper is more
witty than wise, and that it cannot stay out of politics.
One of the correspondents is very upset with Mr. Spectator's experiment with dashes in words; Mr. Spectator
dubs this group of people the Over-Wise.

Spectator 569. Monday, July 19, 1714. Addison.

Mr. Spectator describes how difficult drunkenness is to
cure. He tells a tale of Anacharsis, who demanded the
prize in a drinking bout because he was drunk when he
arrived. Mr. Spectator also tells of Will Funnell, who
is proud of the vast quantity of alcohol he has consumed during his life. The bottle had a fatal effect
on Bonosus, and can easily bring out hidden faults in a
man.

Spectator 570. Wednesday, July 21, 1714. Budgell.

Mr. Spectator describes the odd situation in which people grow famous for unusual and trivial accomplishments;
such a man is a tavern-keeper who can play tunes with
tobacco pipes. Another man of the company could imitate
with amazing accuracy the songs of birds.

Spectator 571. NF. Friday, July 23, 1714. Addison.

Mr. Spectator presents a letter from a correspondent
describing the problems which an intellectual being can
have with religion. Such a person needs to be aware of
God's presence, mercy, and goodness.

Spectator 572. Monday, July 26, 1714. Pearce.

Mr. Spectator presents an essay from a correspondent on
the subject of Quacks, who claim that their medicines
cure all things, although they are for sale in coffee-
houses. This reminds the correspondent of a story of
a man who told another that he had a sure cure for the
gout. The man with the gout rejected the claim on the
grounds that if the cure were infallible it would have
already made the man rich. The correspondent concludes
the essay by retelling a story, from Virgil's *Aeneid*,
of the curing of Aeneas's wound by Japis.

Spectator 573. Wednesday, July 28, 1714. Lady Mary Wortley Montagu.

Mr. Spectator receives a letter from the President of the Widows' Club which tells of the great troubles she had with her numerous husbands. Married at 14, she has since been married to Sir Nicholas Fribble, John Sturdy, Lord Friday, all the while being courted by Edward Waitfort. She goes through the difficulty of having her necklace stolen by Jenny Wheadle and numerous confrontations with Dr. Gruel. She is given advice by Cousin Wishwell. The correspondent debates whether she will marry her 7th husband or not.

Spectator 574. Friday, July 30, 1714. Addison.

Mr. Spectator describes a conversation with a Rosicrusian; Mr. Spectator finds the man's enthusiasm about the Great Secret to be amusing. Mr. Spectator goes on to discuss the true virtue and power residing in the ability to regulate one's life. Mr. Spectator describes with approval Pittacus, who rejected the fortune because he said he already had more money than he knew what to do with. Mr. Spectator notes that everyone should consider how much more unhappy he might be than he really is; to illustrate this point, he tells the story of a Dutchman who broke his leg but was thankful he had not broken his neck. Mr. Spectator praises the contented mind as the greatest blessing of this life.

Spectator 575. Monday, August 2, 1714. Addison.

Mr. Spectator describes an encounter between a hermit and a young man. The young man suggests that the old man is in a miserable condition if there is not an afterlife, but the hermit says that the young man is even in worse shape if there is one. This leads Mr. Spectator into a discussion of the need of all men to devote their lives to the happiness of others.

Spectator 576. Wednesday, August 4, 1714. Addison.

Mr. Spectator gives a character of a young man who desires to appear fashionable. After working hard by keeping late hours, joining clubs, and spending all of his time carousing, he died of old age at 25. Men should therefore live according to the dictates of reason, although this can also be taken too far. The other extreme is a man who desires to act wholly on the basis of natural appetites, and therefore does nothing at regular times. As a result, a man who tried to live entirely by reason was thought to be insane.

Spectator 577. Friday, August 6, 1714. Budgell.

Mr. Spectator receives a letter from a correspondent who describes his peculiarities. People think he is mentally deranged because he paces around and makes noise while he is reading Milton's *Paradise Lost*. John à Notes and John à Styles submit a petition to Mr. Spectator to help them get the courts to work faster on their legal concerns.

Spectator 578. Monday, August 9, 1714. Budgell.

Speculating on personal identity, Mr. Spectator retells a story from *The Persian Tales*. This story concerns Fadlallah, who became enchanted by a young man in his court who was able to reanimate the recently dead body of an animal. Fadlallah tried this activity but discovered to his horror that the magician was treacherous and tried to take over his kingdom while Fadlallah was in the body of a deer.

Spectator 579. Wednesday, August 11, 1714. Addison.

In a paper on the subject of adultery, Mr. Spectator gives a history of the dogs of Vulcan. While guarding the temple of this god, they could tell whether a visitor to the temple was chaste or not by using their extraordinary sensitive noses. Venus was especially upset about this because she found her husband's attitude toward her shaped by the reaction she got from the dogs upon returning home. One of these dogs was used by the Prince of Syracuse, to great effect. The dogs were finally killed when they revealed the adultery of a priest.

Spectator 580. NF. Friday, August 13, 1714. Addison.

Mr. Spectator receives a letter from a correspondent who continues the discussion of the nature of God.

Spectator 581. Monday, August 16, 1714. Budgell.

Mr. Spectator quickly responds to letters from Phyladelphus, Miss Kitty, Tom Nimble, Fill Bumper, Grace Grumble, Sarah Loveit, Tom Turnover, Philanthropos, Celia, and others, including Sampson Bentstaff. He presents a letter from Constantio Spec, in which the correspondent praises his beloved. He also receives a letter from Amanda Lovelength, who questions why Mr. Spectator only appears on Mondays, Wednesdays, and Fridays, when he used to appear more frequently.

Spectator 582. Wednesday, August 18, 1714. Addison.

Mr. Spectator tells an allegory of England's Itch of Writing, in which this interest is seen as a disease.

Spectator 583. NF. Friday, August 20, 1714. Addison.

Mr. Spectator describes the need for men to accept the duties of life as it presents itself to them.

Spectator 584. Monday, August 23, 1714. Addison.

Mr. Spectator tells the story of Hilpa, who was loved
by Harpath and married by him in the time before Noah's
Flood. When he died at the age of 250, Hilpa was wooed
by Shalum, a man who had loved her before her first
marriage. Shalum had planted a beautiful garden which
attracted Hilpa's attention as he once again tried to
marry her.

Spectator 585. Wednesday, August 25, 1714. Addison.

Mr. Spectator continues the story of Hilpa and Shalum.
Shalum persisted in his pursuit of Hilpa, only to discover he had a rival in Mishpach. Fortunately for
Shalum, Mishpach's city was destroyed by fire so that
he had to purchase wood from Shalum to rebuild. Shalum
became so much richer than Mishpach that he finally
attracted the attention of Hilpa, who consented to
marry him.

Spectator 586. Friday, August 27, 1714. Byrom.

Mr. Spectator receives a letter from John Shadow, who
writes a letter on dreams and urges that all who go to
bed free of passion and clear of intemperance will avoid
bad dreams. Mr. Shadow promises to share with Mr. Spectator some of his own dreams and visions.

Spectator 587. Monday, August 30, 1714. Anonymous.

Mr. Spectator receives a letter from a correspondent who
describes a dream vision he had inspired by reading
the Life of Mahomet. According to the source, Mahomet
was santched up by the angel Gabriel at the age of four
to have the cause of sinfulness in man removed from him.
This provokes in the correspondent a dream vision in
which he sees the hearts of various sorts of people in
transparent Phials. The conditions of the hearts reflect the temperament and character of their owner's
inner spirit. A fiery red heart belongs to the soldier
Tom Dread-nought. A black heart belongs to Dick Gloomy,
while a shiny heart belongs to Will Worthy. Freelove
has a charitable heart, while the heart of Coquetilla
is constantly changing. Melissa's heart increases with
size as it receives attention, while the heart of
Seraphina is without blemish.

Spectator 588. NF. Wednesday, September 1, 1714. Grove.

Mr. Spectator offers an essay on the relationship between self-love and benevolence.

Spectator 589. Friday, September 3, 1714. Budgell.

Mr. Spectator receives a letter from a correspondent
who writes of trees and the joys they bring to mankind.
He tells the story, from Virgil's *Aeneid*, of the ships

which Aeneas made from the trees on Mount Ida which were
turned into sea goddesses. The author tells another
story, from Apollonius, of a man named Rahaecus, who
saved an old oak tree which was about to blow over. The
Nymph who lived in the tree offered herself to Rahaecus
as his lover. She sent a bee to summon Rahaecus, who
happened to be gambling at the time, and was not interested. As a result, the Nymph took away the use of
Rahaecus's limbs. He got his revenge by cutting down
her tree.

Spectator 590. NF. Monday, September 6, 1714. Addison.

Mr. Spectator offers his reflections on the subject of
eternity.

Spectator 591. Wednesday, September 8, 1714. Budgell.

Mr. Spectator reports on a letter he has received from
a man who writes to offer his services in the capacity
of a "Love Casuist." He promises to describe exactly
what constitutes a squeeze of the hand, what is an ab-
solute denial from a maid and from a widow, how much
one can caress the maid to succeed with the mistress,
and other such significant questions in the matter of
love. He offers some maxims on the subject, such as
"There are more Calamities in the World arising from
Love than from Hatred." The paper concludes with a
poem written by the correspondent in which he describes
his despair over his relationship with Corinna.

Spectator 592. NF. Friday, September 10, 1714. Addison.

Mr. Spectator discusses criticism of the theatre.

Spectator 593. Monday, September 13, 1714. Byrom.

Mr. Spectator receives a second letter from Mr. Shadow,
on the subject of dreams. He urges that we examine
dreams with care because we spend so much of our lives
asleep. Mr. Shadow praises sleep, noting that we are
in control of our thoughts while we are awake but not
in control of them while we are sleeping.

Spectator 594. NF. Wednesday, September 15, 1714. Addison.

Mr. Spectator discusses the very human habit of spreading scandal about other people.

Spectator 595. Friday, September 17, 1714. Tickell.

Mr. Spectator publishes an essay on the subject of the
mixing of metaphors. He concludes with a letter from
a correspondent containing an extreme number of metaphors.

Spectator 596. Monday, September 20, 1714. Budgell.

Mr. Spectator receives a letter from Jeremy Lovemore, in which the correspondent writes of the impertinence of an importunate lover. The correspondent, prevented from marrying until the age of twenty-six by his father, has spent his life pursuing women of no fortune. His relationship with Parthenipe was cut short when he was forced to leave Oxford University. After a series of such relationships he is finally expelled from the University. At the moment he has courted both the older and younger of a pair of sisters, and is threatened by his father with being sent to the South Seas.

Spectator 597. Wednesday, September 22, 1714. Anonymous.

Mr. Spectator reports on the dreams of a number of his correspondents. One, Gladio, says that his beloved will not pay attention to him until he has done valorous deeds, such as defeat knights and slay dragons. Another, whose dreams have him convicted of stealing horses, hopes that he may wake up before his execution. Another dreamed of the city of London being on fire, while still another dreamed of eating a cake, only to wake up and discover that he had in fact done so. Some dreamers would like Mr. Spectator to devise a means of silencing those who make noises in the street and wake dreamers. Others, however, have been awakened from bad dreams by such early risers and are grateful. Mr. Spectator says that he will not comment upon dreams that take place during the day, such as Fritilla's dream in church last Sunday.

Spectator 598. Friday, September 24, 1714. Addison.

Mr. Spectator writes an essay on the Serious Man and the Merry Man.

Spectator 599. Monday, September 27, 1714. Anonymous.

Mr. Spectator reports on a dream, he had while taking his afternoon nap, in which he found himself in possession of the cave of Trophonius. Having sent out a call for those who wish to become more serious for the rest of their lives, he found himself swamped by a Merry-Andrew, conquettes, comedians, and others, all of whom wished to be more responsible and sober men and women. One woman, who laughed at Mr. Spectator's short face, was so high-spirited, that her visit to the cave only made her a pretty prude.

Spectator 600. NF. Wednesday, September 29, 1714. Addison.

Mr. Spectator discusses various opinions on the subject of the Immortality of the Soul.

Spectator 601. NF. Friday, October 1, 1714. Grove.

Mr. Spectator presents an essay from a correspondent who discusses the causes of a certain narrowness and lack of benevolence in men.

Spectator 602. Monday, October 4, 1714. Anonymous.

Mr. Spectator presents a letter from the Love-Casuist, in which the correspondent notes the kinds of men who seem to be successful with women. He discovers that these include the Man of Importance and the Man of Intrigue. One particularly successful gentleman makes a point of bowing to all the right people, knowing all the right people, and being agreeable with others of importance. Mr. Spectator concludes with an excerpt from Ovid, the *Art of Love*, translated by Dryden, on the subject of love in the theatre.

Spectator 603. NF. Wednesday, October 6, 1714. Byrom.

Mr. Spectator presents a poem from a correspondent, in which the speaker proclaims his love of Phoebe and his sorrow of being separated from her.

Spectator 604. Friday, October 8, 1714. Tickell.

Mr. Spectator discusses man's desire to know future events, and claims that this desire is founded on self love. Mr. Spectator notes that to the degree to which the liberal arts are practiced, such superstitious practices are diminished. He describes a trip to Grand Cairo, in which he met a good-natured Musselman who believed on the basis of a fortune teller's prediction, that he would become Prime Minister. Mr. Spectator was taken to visit the fortune teller but fell asleep before the interview could take place. His dream reminds him of the inevitability of old age and death with all their attendant miseries. He sees Sir Roger, Will Honeycomb, and other members of his club, as well as their fates. As a result of the dream, Mr. Spectator refuses to meet with the fortune teller.

Spectator 605. Monday, October 11, 1714. Tickell.

Mr. Spectator presents a letter from Fanny Fickle, in which the correspondent asks for advice as to whether she should marry a man who is pleasing to women or one who is pleasing to men. Mr. Spectator presents, as well, the reply of the Learned Casuist, who urges that she marry the man of honor, in the belief that if she marries such a man love for him will follow the wedding day. He provides a test of love; a woman is in love with a man when she uses his expressions, tells his stories, or imitates his manner. The Casuist concludes his discussion with the story of King Edgar, an ancient British king, who fell in love with the daughter of a

duke and insisted that he sleep with her that night.
The mother of the daughter provided him, as a bed partner, a young maid, one of her attendants, who was such
good company for the king that he refused to part with
her and made her his first Minister of State.

Spectator 606. Wednesday, October 13, 1714. Tickell.

Mr. Spectator presents a letter from a correspondent
who is having trouble keeping control of her nieces.
She wishes that Mr. Spectator instruct them on the value
of needlework so that they will have something to do besides practice the arts of flirtation. Mr. Spectator
complies, praising the value of needlework, and agrees
that it is useful to take away opportunities for idle
mischief. He encourages all young women to undertake
it. He tells a story of a custom of Grecian ladies,
of not remarrying until they had woven a shroud for
their deceased husbands. He reminds us that this ruse
saved Penelope while Ulysses was still away from home
at the Trojan Wars.

Spectator 607. Friday, October 15, 1714. Tickell.

Mr. Spectator presents a letter from the Love-Casuist
who writes to show, with numerous examples, that matrimony often produces love rather than the other way
around. The correspondent says that the virtues necessary for happy marriages are discretion, virtue, and
good nature. He concludes with a story from Dr. Plot
about Sir Philip de Somerville, who offered to all of
those living in his domains a Flitch of Bacon if they
were still happily married one year and one day after
the day of their marriage.

Spectator 608. Monday, October 18, 1714. Tickell.

The writer of the letter in *Spectator* 607 lists a number
of people who have requested the Flitch of Bacon from
Sir Philip de Somerville. Aubry de Falstaff, having
bribed two of his father's friends to swear falsely,
was the first to claim the bacon. Allison, wife of
Stephen Freckle, appealed for the bacon and hit her
husband in the ear when he answered the questions in-
correctly. Philip de Waverland and Richard de Loveless
are also among those rejected. Joceline Jolly and his
wife are the only ones to receive the bacon. Numerous
others apply and are also rejected.

Spectator 609. Wednesday, October 20, 1714. Anonymous.

Mr. Spectator receives a letter from a correspondent
who objects to the pretensions of young clergy who feel
they must wear the richest sort of scarf, even though
it is a piece of foppery which they do not deserve to
wear. Tom Nimble writes a letter on the subject of the

imagination, in which he describes a rational China cup,
an egg that walks on two legs, a talking shoulder of
veal which squawks at the sight of a knife, and a cat
who has helped him in his courting of his beloved Mrs.
Lucy. Cleora writes to protest Mr. Spectator's urging
of needlepoint on young ladies; she hopes to kill a hundred lovers before the best housewife in England can
stitch a picture of her first battle.

Spectator 610. NF. Friday, October 22, 1714. Tickell.

Mr. Spectator presents an essay on the subject of greatness versus the appearance of greatness.

Spectator 611. Monday, October 25, 1714. Anonymous.

Mr. Spectator presents a letter from Lesbia, which describes her seduction at the age of sixteen. Although
another man soon after marries her, he is a tyrant who
will let her do nothing without his permission. Mr.
Spectator concludes with a story of revenge; an English
gentleman, while in Madrid, saw a strange sight of a
woman who cut the heart from the body of her false lover
and, having torn it to pieces, trampled it under her
feet.

Spectator 612. Wednesday, October 27, 1714. Tickell.

Mr. Spectator presents a letter from a correspondent who
discusses the folly of pursuing the background of one's
family. He reports on a visit with a country relative
in which the two men spend most of that time perusing
their family's history. Although there are notables in
the family tree, it also contains a large number of
black sheep. Margery the Milk-maid and others of her
branch of the family are thrown from the family tree so
that it will be more presentable.

Spectator 613. Friday, October 29, 1714. Anonymous.

Mr. Spectator says that since it is ill breeding for
one man to talk to himself all the time, he occasionally
allows his readers to talk. He presents a letter from
Will Hopeless, in which the correspondent protests that
he seeks action though he is chained in obscurity. A
second correspondent writes on the eloquence possessed
by the beggars of the city. Monimia writes to describe
her loss of her suitors because of a case of the smallpox. She considers herself well rid of many of the
suitors, but wishes to get one back who only contacted
her by writing letters.

Spectator 614. Monday, November 1, 1714. Tickell.

Mr. Spectator presents a letter from the Love-Casuist,
who deals with questions of widowhood. Amoret wonders
if she should be bound to a promise of marriage made to

Philander while her husband was still alive. Sempronia
wonders about promises she made during the illness of
her husband. Cleora wonders if a vow she made to her
husband not to remarry is still valid. Sophronia, a
woman of great estate, wonders if she should marry
Camillus, an idle man of no estate. The Love-Casuist
says that a widow should possess the love of her deceased husband, the care of her children, and prudent
conduct. He concludes by telling the story of a custom
in Berkshire of forcing widows who do not live chastely
to ride a black ram backwards and proclaim themselves
publicly to be whores.

Spectator 615. NF. Wednesday, November 3, 1714. Tickell.

Mr. Spectator presents a discussion of the subject of
fear.

Spectator 616. Friday, November 5, 1714. Tickell.

Mr. Spectator describes a practice among those who think
they are wits of using language in curious ways. As an
example, he presents a letter to Jack from a Country Wit
in which he describes, in affected style, country cele-
brations on the occasion of the coronation of George I.
The fireworks caused great distress to Tom Tyler, among
others.

Spectator 617. Monday, November 8, 1714. Tickell.

Mr. Spectator presents another letter, to Chum, written
in a pedantic style derivative of the university, to
contrast to the letter presented in *Spectator* 616. The
events described in both letters are the same; only the
style is different. Since one subject of both letters
is fireworks, Mr. Spectator concludes with a translation
of an Italian poem describing a display of fireworks in
Rome.

Spectator 618. NF. Wednesday, November 10, 1714. Philips
and Tickell.

Mr. Spectator presents a letter from a correspondent who
writes on the subject of epistolary verse. He proposes
Ovid as a model for mirth and Horace as a model for humor.

Spectator 619. Friday, November 12, 17.14. Tickell.

Mr. Spectator offers brief replies to a large number of
letters which he has received from correspondents on
various subjects. Charissa's letter is referred to the
Dumb Man for an answer. Other letters are referred to
the Love-Casuist, while another is sent to Society of
Reformers. A treatise on the art of fencing is returned to the author, while Tom Truelove is asked to
remember that it has been some time since Mr. Spectator
was in love. Monimia's lover is revealed as Castalio,

while the petitions of Mr. Dapperwit and Charles Cocksure are rejected. The memorial of Philander is postponed.

Spectator 620. NF. Monday, November 15, 1714. Tickell.

Mr. Spectator presents a poem by Tickell, as an example of the true sublime. The poem is entitled "The Royal Progress" and celebrates the coronation of George I.

Spectator 621. NF. Wednesday, November 17, 1714. Tickell.

Mr. Spectator receives a letter from a correspondent who writes on the subject of false or misguided pride. He urges that mankind value only what superior beings think is important.

Spectator 622. Friday, November 19, 1714. Tickell.

Mr. Spectator receives a letter from a correspondent who, to illustrate the point that true greatness does not consist of pomp and show, presents the memoirs of "an honest country-Gentleman," who lived well in obscurity. The memoirs reveal that he travelled rather than run the risk of an affair with his cousin's wife, that he gave up the chance of an estate so as not to anger another relative, that he generously contributed from his own funds to prevent a dispute within the family, and that he was good to his tenants and encouraged them to live up to his own high standards of conduct.

Spectator 623. Monday, November 22, 1714. Tickell.

Mr. Spectator receives a letter from the Love-Casuist who describes to him those widows who have had to ride a black ram in public admitting their sexual improprieties. The widow Frontly buys a ram because she expects to need it annually. Mrs. Sarah Dainty, widow of John Dainty, the Widow Ogle, Mrs. Sable, Mrs. Quick, the Widow Fidget, the Widow Maskwell, and other widows of the neighborhood were forced to ride the ram. The Widow Maskwell, having fired her old chambermaid, was forced by that revengeful woman to ride the ram nine times in one day.

Spectator 624. NF. Wednesday, November 24, 1714. Tickell.

Mr. Spectator offers a meditation on the consideration that all of mankind is divided into two parts--the busy and the idle.

Spectator 625. Friday, November 26, 1714. Tickell.

Mr. Spectator offers, from the Love-Casuist, a series of questions and his answers. The correspondent who poses the questions is concerned about what she must do about Mr. Fondle, who is a handsome fellow and is forbidden access to the house. All of the lady's questions

351

turn on whether or not she should marry Fondle, and to all of them the Love-Casuist responds, "No." Thomas Quid-nunc writes Mr. Spectator to describe his means of getting the news by going from coffee-house to coffee-house and catching it while it is still warm. He believes that a piece of news loses its flavor when it has been in the air for over an hour, and therefore he spends much of his time in pursuit of warm news.

Spectator 626. NF. Monday, November 29, 1714. Grove.

Mr. Spectator receives a letter from a correspondent whose subject is the effects of novelty on the young. The most trivial occurrences of life provide this correspondent with the material of his essay. The subject is, naturally, mankind's inclination for novelty.

Spectator 627. Wednesday, December 1, 1714. Tickell.

Mr. Spectator presents a letter from a correspondent who describes a friend, recently deceased, as a gentleman and a lover of gardens. Because he had always been uneasy in the company of women, his friends were interested to learn, upon his death, that he had once been in love with one Zelinda. The correspondent presents a letter from the friend to Zelinda in which he describes to her his efforts in creating a beautiful garden on his estate for her to delight in. In addition, the letter notes that Zelinda married the man's rival.

Spectator 628. NF. Friday, December 3, 1714. Tickell.

Mr. Spectator presents a letter from a correspondent who expands on the subject of "Infinity and Eternity," which he finds to be his favorite subjects among the *Spectator*. He concludes his essay with Latin and English versions of a speech by Cato from the play by Addison.

Spectator 629. Monday, December 6, 1714. Tickell.

During a discussion of man's desire for position, Mr. Spectator presents a series of petitions which were put forward by Roundheads at the time of the Restoration of King Charles II. One is quoted at length, in which the petitioner describes the trouble he has gotten into because of his drinking, a result of his support of the royalist cause.

Spectator 630. Wednesday, December 8, 1714. Anonymous.

Mr. Spectator presents a letter from a correspondent who praises the virtues of music. A second correspondent describes the Rattling Club, which now has invaded the churches and, with its constant noise of rattling pews, disrupts services.

Spectator 631. Friday, December 10, 1714. Tickell.

Mr. Spectator comments on a ride out of town in a stage-coach on which he observes a "dirty Beau" and a "pretty young Quaker woman." The slovenliness of the gentleman is in sharp contrast to the elegant simplicity of the woman's dress. This leads Mr. Spectator to a lengthy discussion of the virtues of cleanliness. He concludes with a story of an Oriental religious leader who, on the morning he forgot to wash his hands, broke a crystal cup, had his son break an arm, and received a kick from a sacred cow.

Spectator 632. Monday, December 13, 1714. Tickell.

Mr. Spectator discusses the love of Symmetry and Order, and says that the *Spectator* is soon to come to a close. The essay concludes with a letter from a correspondent who describes the "Case of the Poetical Ladies," who cannot resist making grottoes. The paper concludes with a poem on the subject of the grottoes fancied by some women.

Spectator 633. NF. Wednesday, December 15, 1714. Pearce.

Mr. Spectator offers an essay from a Cambridge correspondent on the subject of why there are so few truly fine orators. The correspondent says that St. Paul's sermons provide examples of good Christian oratory.

Spectator 634. Friday, December 17, 1714. Tickell.

Mr. Spectator discusses the various notions of the truly happy man, as presented by a variety of classical philosophies in contrast with Christian notions. He concludes with a story, out of Julian, in which the great rulers of Rome are asked by the gods what their highest aspirations are. Marcus Aurelius is awarded the favorite of the gods because he answers that his goal has been to imitate the gods.

Spectator 635. NF. Monday, December 20, 1714. Grove.

Mr. Spectator presents an essay in which the writer discusses the nature of the world and concludes it is the part of a divine mind which man should enjoy as his highest, wisest, and noblest end.

INDEX TO *SPECTATOR* CATALOGUE

Flavia S79, S91, S392, S398
Flavilla S344
Flirt S202
Florio S149
Florinda S278
Foible, Sir Jeoffrey S190
Fortius S422
Fortunatus S443
Frankair, Charles S484
Freeman, Antony S212, S216
Freeport, Sir Andrew S2, S34, S69, S82, S109, S118, S126, S131, S174, S232, S317, S359, S448, S517, S549, S555
Frost, Charity S296
Froth, Abraham S43
G--Gander, Michael S376
Gape, Anthony S268
Gapely, Ralph S377
Garlick, Phil S455
Gatty, Mrs. S437, S515
Gentle, Reader S308
Germanicus S238
Giddy, Patience S137
Gladio S597
Glaphyra S110
Gloom, George S547
Gloomy, Dick S587
Gloriana S206, S423
Gloworm, Martha S547
Glycera S492
Goodfellow, Robin S205
Goodwin S350
Goosequill, Francis S377
    Will S372
Gorgon, Giles S173
Gospel-Gossip S46
Gossling, George S191
Green, Sabina S431
Greenbag, Moses S498, S526
Gruel, Dr. S573
Grumble, Grace S581
Gumley, Mr. S509
Gwinifrid, Mrs. S227
H--Hardy, Colonel S400
Harmless, Bob S314
Harpath S584
Harriot S254
Hart, Nicholas S184
Haymn, Nicolino S258, S278
Heartfree, Mary S252
Hecatissa S48, S52, S79, S87
Hedgeditch, Isaac S168
Henpeck, Josiah S211

Henrietta S220
Henroost, Nathaniel S176, S211, S547
Hilpa S584, S585
Hinton, Moll S77
Hipparchus S475
Hobson, Tobias S509
Holliday, Susan S118
Home, Mary S254
Homebred, Philip S364
Honestus S443
Honeycomb, Will S2, S4, S11, S34, S41, S45, S57, S67, S77, S79, S105, S131, S151, S156, S251, S265, S266, S277, S282, S290, S301, S311, S319, S325, S343, S352, S359, S380, S395, S410, S475, S490, S499, S511, S530, S536, S542, S553, S604
    Simon S154
Honoria, Lady S91, S302
Hopeful, Lazarus S472
Hopeless, Will S613
Hopewell, Sam S89
Hortensius S342
Hotspur, Jeoffry S300, S354, S429
Housewife, Martha S178
Hush, Peter S457
I--Ignotus S75
Imma S181
Inkle S11
Iras S404
Irus S114, S264, S280
Isabella S318
Isadas S564
J--James S71
Jane, Mrs. S272
Jenny, Miss S359, S515
Jett-well, Elizabeth S377
Jezebel S292
Jolly, Frank S429
Joceline S608
Jumper, Colonel S376
K--Katherine, Mrs. S533
Kidney S24
Kimbow, Thomas S24
Kitty S187, S242, S581
L--Ladylove, Bartholomew S304
Laertes S114
Laetitia S33, S398, S488, S506
Lath, Squire S32
Latinus S53
Lemon, Betty S380
Leonilla S123, S475

Narrative Forms

Narrative Techniques

362

S25, S28, S30, S32, S33, S35, S43, S47, S48, S51, S52, S53, S54, S66, S71, S73, S75, S76, S80, S84, S86, S87, S90, S91, S92, S94, S95, S97, S98, S100, S101, S102, S124, S128, S129, S134, S137, S140, S141, S143, S144, S148, S153, S155, S157, S159, S160, S161, S164, S165, S166, S167, S171, S172, S173, S175, S177, S178, S179, S181, S182, S183, S184, S188, S189, S191, S192, S195, S198, S203, S204, S205, S206, S208, S209, S211, S215, S217, S221, S222, S227, S233, S235, S237, S238, S241, S245, S247, S254, S258, S259, S262, S264, S268, S271, S274, S280, S283, S284, S291, S292, S293, S299, S302, S304, S305, S306, S312, S314, S320, S323, S330, S338, S342, S346, S347, S355, S361, S365, S366, S373, S375, S377, S379, S382, S386, S389, S390, S391, S394, S396, S398, S400, S402, S404, S406, S407, S422, S423, S428, S431, S433, S434, S437, S438, S439, S440, S444, S447, S449, S452, S456, S457, S458, S461, S462, S464, S466, S467, S470, S471, S472, S475, S478, S480, S483, S484, S491, S493, S497, S504, S505, S508, S509, S512, S522, S524, S527, S532, S535, S542, S545, S550, S552, S557, S560, S563, S566, S567, S575, S576, S578, S579, S582, S584, S585, S586, S587, S591, S593, S595, S598, S606, S611, S612, S613, S616, S617, S619, S623, S629, S630, S632, S634

As transmitter or eyewitness:
S2, S3, S5, S6, S10, S13, S15, S20, S27, S31, S38, S41, S49, S50, S55, S57, S58, S64, S67, S72, S81, S82, S88, S99, S103, S105, S111, S120, S121, S125, S127, S138, S150, S151, S156, S163, S174, S176, S186, S192, S197, S200, S218, S228, S231, S234, S251, S265, S270, S275, S281, S282, S289, S295, S301, S311, S317, S319, S325, S343, S350, S352, S395, S403, S426, S435, S436, S448, S481, S482, S488, S490, S494, S499, S501, S502, S506, S525, S526, S530, S538, S541, S544, S546, S569, S574, S581, S605

As actor: S1, S4, S7, S11, S12, S26, S34, S37, S45, S46, S63, S69, S75, S77, S83, S85, S106, S107, S108, S109, S110, S112, S113,

S114, S115, S116, S117, S118, S119, S122, S123, S126, S130, S131, S132, S133, S152, S202, S232, S261, S266, S269, S277, S290, S308, S329, S331, S335, S358, S359, S367, S383, S410, S454, S460, S463, S468, S475, S479, S510, S517, S536, S549, S556, S558, S559, S562, S565, S568, S570, S599, S604, S631

The Spectator Club:
Sir Roger de Coverley: S2, S6, S34, S37, S100, S101, S106, S107, S108, S109, S110, S111, S112, S113, S114, S115, S116, S117, S118, S119, S120, S121, S122, S123, S125, S126, S127, S128, S130, S131, S137, S141, S161, S174, S211, S251, S264, S269, S271, S295, S329, S331, S335, S338, S359, S383, S395, S410, S424, S435, S517, S518, S539, S542, S544, S553, S604

Will Honeycomb: S2, S4, S11, S34, S41, S45, S57, S67, S77, S79, S105, S131, S151, S156, S251, S265, S266, S277, S282, S290, S301, S311, S319, S325, S343, S352, S359, S380, S395, S410, S475, S490, S499, S511, S530, S536, S542, S553, S604

Sir Andrew Freeport: S2, S34, S69, S82, S118, S126, S131, S174, S232, S317, S359, S448, S517, S549, S555

Captain Sentry: S2, S34, S152, S174, S197, S216, S335, S350, S517, S542, S544

the Templar: S2, S22, S34, S105, S530, S541, S542, S553

the Clergyman: S2, S27, S34, S103, S186, S513

Letters:

To Mr. Spectator: S8, S14, S16, S17, S20, S22, S24, S25, S28, S30, S32, S36, S41, S43, S46, S48, S51, S52, S53, S54, S66, S67, S78, S79, S87, S88, S89, S92, S95, S96, S102, S104, S127, S129, S131, S134, S136, S137, S140, S141, S142, S145, S147, S154, S155, S158, S161, S163, S167, S168, S175, S176, S178, S179, S180, S181, S182, S184, S187, S190, S191, S194, S196, S199, S202, S203, S205, S208, S211, S212, S216, S217, S220,

S222, S227, S228, S231, S234, S236, S238, S240, S241, S242, S244, S245, S250, S251, S252, S254, S258, S260, S263, S264, S268, S271, S272, S274, S276, S277, S278, S282, S284, S286, S288, S290, S292, S295, S296, S298, S299, S300, S302, S304, S306, S308, S310, S311, S312, S313, S314, S316, S318, S319, S320, S322, S323, S324, S325, S326, S328, S328*, S330, S331, S336, S338, S341, S342, S344, S347, S348, S354, S360, S361, S362, S364, S366, S368, S371, S372, S376, S380, S392, S396, S401, S402, S406, S410, S424, S425, S429, S430, S431, S432, S437, S440, S443, S449, S450, S452, S455, S456, S457, S460, S461, S462, S466, S472, S473, S474, S477, S478, S480, S482, S484, S485, S486, S488, S492, S496, S498, S499, S500, S503, S505, S508, S509, S511, S513, S515, S517, S518, S520, S521, S524, S526, S527, S528, S530, S532, S533, S534, S536, S538, S539, S542, S544, S545, S546, S547, S548, S549, S551, S553, S555, S560, S561, S563, S566, S572, S573, S577, S581, S586, S587, S589, S593, S595, S596, S602, S605, S606, S607, S608, S609, S611, S612, S613, S614, S622, S623, S625, S627, S630, S632

Issues containing 2 letters: S8, S24, S28, S36, S46, S52, S66, S67, S78, S79, S87, S95, S134, S137, S155, S182, S194, S196, S202, S216, S244, S250, S258, S272, S277, S286, S288, S290, S319, S320, S330, S331, S336, S344, S354, S362, S366, S376, S406, S431, S461, S474, S508, S518, S527, S532, S533, S536, S581, S630

Issues containing 3 or more letters: S14, S22, S48, S53, S140, S145, S158, S168, S175, S190, S205, S208, S211, S217, S220, S227, S236, S240, S242, S245, S252, S260, S268, S271, S276, S278, S284, S296, S300, S308, S310, S314, S326, S364, S372, S380, S430, S432, S443, S455, S473, S485, S496, S534, S539, S551, S560, S566, S609, S613

Of praise or blame: S14, S53, S88, S92, S95, S96, S134, S140, S145, S158, S205, S208, S236, S252, S276, S300, S308, S310, S325, S455,

S461, S509, S548, S553, S560, S581, S609

Seeking advice or assistance: S8, S14, S24, S36, S46, S48, S51, S52, S53, S66, S95, S134, S140, S145, S149, S158, S168, S190, S191, S202, S208, S227, S236, S241, S242, S245, S252, S254, S260, S268, S277, S278, S290, S292, S295, S296, S310, S314, S326, S361, S380, S401, S402, S430, S475, S520, S566, S605, S606

Of narration or description: S8, S14, S17, S20, S22, S24, S25, S28, S30, S32, S36, S41, S43, S46, S52, S53, S54, S67, S78, S79, S87, S89, S96, S102, S104, S127, S129, S136, S137, S140, S141, S142, S145, S147, S154, S155, S158, S161, S163, S167, S168, S175, S176, S178, S179, S180, S181, S182, S184, S187, S190, S194, S196, S202, S203, S205, S211, S212, S216, S217, S220, S222, S227, S228, S231, S234, S236, S240, S241, S242, S244, S245, S250, S251, S252, S258, S260, S263, S268, S271, S276, S277, S278, S282, S284, S286, S288, S290, S295, S296, S298, S300, S304, S306, S308, S310, S312, S313, S314, S316, S318, S319, S320, S322, S323, S324, S326, S328, S330, S331, S336, S338, S341, S342, S344, S347, S354, S360, S362, S364, S366, S368, S371, S372, S376, S380, S392, S396, S401, S402, S406, S424, S425, S429, S430, S431, S432, S437, S440, S443, S449, S450, S452, S455, S456, S457, S460, S461, S462, S466, S473, S474, S475, S477, S478, S480, S482, S484, S485, S486, S492, S496, S499, S500, S503, S505, S508, S509, S511, S513, S154, S517, S518, S520, S521, S524, S526, S527, S528, S530, S532, S533, S534, S536, S539, S544, S546, S549, S551, S560, S561, S563, S566, S572, S573, S577, S586, S587, S589, S593, S596, S602, S607, S608, S609, S611, S612, S613, S614, S622, S623, S625, S627, S630

From Mr. Spectator: S38, S48, S52, S148, S149, S192, S254, S290, S296, S306, S308, S423, S526, S534

Between characters: S24, S27, S71, S91, S108, S142, S164, S165, S178, S188, S189, S199, S204, S220, S248, S254, S260, S263, S264, S274,

S301, S306, S316, S318, S320, S324, S328*, S343, S368, S375, S398, S401, S410, S423, S432, S448, S456, S472, S480, S493, S511, S522, S545, S616, S617, S627

As alleged source: S59, S148, S350, S365, S395, S472, S482, S488, S525, S553, S581, S591, S597, S619

Mock Petitions: S36, S78, S80, S134, S202, S304, S310, S577, S619, S629

Issues containing no fiction: S18, S29, S39, S40, S42, S44, S59, S61, S62, S65, S68, S70, S74, S93, S135, S139, S146, S162, S169, S185, S201, S207, S210, S213, S214, S219, S224, S225, S226, S229, S230, S239, S243, S246, S249, S253, S255, S256, S257, S262, S267, S273, S279, S285, S287, S294, S297, S303, S309, S315, S321, S327, S333, S334, S337, S339, S340, S345, S351, S353, S356, S357, S363, S369, S370, S374, S378, S381, S384, S385, S387, S388, S393, S397, S399, S405, S406, S408, S409, S411, S412, S413, S414, S415, S416, S417, S418, S419, S420, S421, S441, S445, S446, S451, S453, S459, S465, S469, S487, S489, S495, S507, S516, S519, S523, S529, S531, S537, S540, S543, S554, S571, S580, S583, S588, S590, S592, S594, S600, S601, S610, S615, S618, S620, S621, S624, S626, S628, S633, S635

Subjects frequently discussed:

Church, Clergy, conduct in: S112, S125, S133, S186, S205, S207, S236, S237, S272, S284, S312, S317, S343, S349, S354, S460, S489, S494, S503, S539, S545, S571, S575, S580, S609, S630

Conduct of men, young and old: S6, S9, S11, S13, S17, S21, S24, S38, S46, S49, S52, S55, S57, S67, S69, S75, S86, S90, S93, S94, S99, S101, S105, S116, S138, S141, S143, S145, S148, S151, S153, S158, S168, S173, S174, S177, S179, S184, S190, S192, S193, S211, S220, S231, S232, S233, S236, S240, S242, S260, S275, S284, S288, S300, S301, S330, S331, S341, S360, S361, S362, S365, S375,

S385, S386, S394, S430, S434, S438, S454, S455, S458, S460, S463, S467, S479, S486, S498, S502, S508, S513, S521, S526, S528, S532, S533, S536, S537, S569, S574, S598, S602, S611, S613, S631, S634

Conduct of women, young and old: S4, S8, S11, S13, S32, S33, S37, S41, S43, S45, S52, S53, S57, S58, S73, S79, S80, S89, S90, S91, S98, S99, S102, S104, S138, S144, S145, S148, S155, S158, S168, S187, S190, S194, S196, S208, S209, S211, S216, S220, S236, S238, S242, S244, S247, S250, S252, S254, S260, S265, S266, S268, S270, S271, S274, S275, S276, S281, S298, S300, S302, S306, S320, S326, S336, S342, S344, S361, S365, S375, S410, S430, S434, S435, S437, S444, S449, S454, S460, S462, S466, S478, S485, S486, S492, S499, S502, S503, S510, S511, S515, S536, S538, S539, S542, S545, S606, S609

Country life and standards of conduct: S6, S15, S57, S66, S106, S108, S109, S112, S114, S115, S116, S117, S119, S120, S121, S122, S125, S127, S130, S131, S168, S175, S240, S324, S326, S332, S380, S406, S424, S429, S473, S477, S473, S496, S622

Courtship: S4, S15, S20, S30, S73, S89, S90, S91, S113, S123, S128, S141, S148, S154, S156, S180, S182, S187, S199, S203, S204, S208, S215, S217, S223, S261, S268, S272, S280, S282, S284, S288, S296, S298, S304, S306, S310, S311, S314, S315, S318, S320, S325, S326, S328, S359, S362, S364, S375, S380, S396, S398, S400, S401, S402, S423, S432, S436, S437, S440, S448, S473, S475, S508, S511, S515, S522, S539, S566, S581, S591, S596, S602, S605, S613, S619, S622, S625, S631

Dress, especially fashionable, of men and women: S16, S20, S41, S45, S48, S53, S57, S64, S81, S87, S96, S98, S102, S127, S134, S138, S140, S145, S150, S175, S204, S238, S240, S265, S266, S268, S271, S272, S277, S319, S344, S360, S435, S437, S454, S478, S485, S542, S545, S609

Education: S64, S66, S79, S95, S140, S157, S168, S189, S222, S230,

S307, S313, S314, S330, S336, S337,
S353, S376, S379, S380, S455, S466,
S502, S576, S626

Language, its uses and abuses:
S23, S35, S45, S58, S63, S70, S71,
S78, S80, S83, S103, S140, S132,
S165, S166, S183, S220, S221, S230,
S247, S251, S296, S314, S330, S352,
S366, S388, S389, S394, S396, S406,
S407, S422, S427, S440, S452, S455,
S457, S474, S481, S518, S551, S557,
S595, S616, S617, S618, S633, S677

Marriage and the family: S7,
S10, S89, S100, S110, S128, S149,
S154, S167, S176, S178, S181, S192,
S194, S199, S204, S206, S211, S216,
S220, S236, S241, S245, S246, S248,
S263, S276, S278, S282, S295, S299,
S300, S302, S304, S308, S322, S328,
S342, S402, S430, S432, S440, S455,
S475, S479, S482, S486, S490, S491,
S499, S500, S506, S522, S525, S527,
S530, S533, S539, S563, S564, S566,
S573, S579, S584, S585, S607, S608,
S611, S614, S623

Mr. Spectator and his newspaper:
S1, S2, S10, S12, S34, S46, S52,
S85, S87, S88, S124, S131, S179,
S261, S262, S286, S325, S367, S395,
S428, S442, S476, S488, S518, S524,
S532, S537, S547, S548, S549, S550,
S553, S555, S556, S567, S628

Peace and war: S152, S166, S350,
S366, S544, S566, S629

Politics: S50, S57, S81, S126,
S305, S475

Servants and masters: S88, S96,
S107, S118, S137, S202, S260, S322,
S348, S366, S375, S493, S623

Theater: S5, S13, S14, S18, S22,
S29, S31, S36, S45, S51, S65, S75,
S141, S208, S235, S240, S258, S268,
S270, S278, S290, S314, S335, S341,
S361, S443, S446, S502, S529, S546

CRITICAL STUDIES OF PROSE FICTION IN THE *TATLER* AND
THE *SPECTATOR* FROM THE AGE OF JOHNSON TO THE PRESENT:
AN ANNOTATED BIBLIOGRAPHY

Achurch, Robert Waller. "Richard Steele, Gazetteer and
Bickerstaff." *Studies in the Early English Periodical.*
Ed. Richmond P. Bond. Chapel Hill: Univ. of North
Carolina Press, 1957. Pp. 49-72.

Though primarily describing the declining frequency and
quantity of news in the *Tatler*, Achurch suggests that
the news correspondent Humphrey Kidney is a disguise
for the Gazetteer editing the St. James department.

Aiken, J[ohn]. "On the Humour of Addison and the Character of Sir Roger de Coverley." *The Monthly Magazine*, 9
(1800), 1-3.

Aiken, suggesting that Samuel Johnson's view of Addison's humor is too limited, believes that he rejected
no promising source of laughter, including caricature
and "agreeable extravagance." He lists Aiddison's
humorous pieces which please through more fanciful
qualities. Aiken judges Sir Roger an inconsistent character, treated more kindly by Steele than by Addison,
who used him for "covert" satire of the Tory foxhunter.

Aikin, Lucy. *The Life of Joseph Addison.* 2 vols. London:
Longmans, 1843.

Aikin suggests that the *Tatler* revived prose fiction
with Steele's brief narratives of domestic adventures
and Addison's humorous pictures. The *Spectator* expanded
these tendencies, especially in the sketches of Sir
Roger de Coverley, which she judges an Addisonian improvement of Steele's conception.

Aitken, George A. *The Life of Richard Steele.* 2 vols.
London: Wm. Isbiter, 1889. Rpt. New York: Greenwood,
1968.

In chapters on the *Tatler* and the *Spectator*, Aitken
argues that Steele originated each innovation in the
periodicals, excelled in his varied portraits and stories of pathos, and had a larger share in drawing Sir
Roger de Coverley than Addison's apologists have
granted him.

Aldridge, Alfred Owen. "Addison's 'The Visions of Mirzah.'"
The Explicator, 6 (1948), item 37.

Aldridge cites three possible sources.

Allen, Robert J. *The Clubs of Augustan London*. *Harvard
Studies in English*, Vol. 7. Cambridge, Mass.: Harvard
Univ. Press, 1933.

After a chapter on "The Rise of the Club," Allen assesses and categorizes actual clubs in "The Club and the
Town," and describes several types represented in the
Tatler and the *Spectator*, like clubs of rakes or quid-
nuncs. In a chapter on "The Fictitious Club," Allen
uses both periodicals often to exemplify satiric portraits of fictitious clubmen and to present pictures of
club life. The society at the Trumpet and the Spectator Club are prominent in the fourth chapter, "The Club
Framework and the Essay Periodicals." Allen praises
Steele's creation of authentic clubmen in the *Tatler*
but judges the club device to be completely sustained
first in the *Spectator*, where he seldom finds six consecutive issues in which the club does not figure.
Allen also describes the various uses, exemplary and
satiric, the club members serve. He concludes with a
chapter on "The Club and the Author."

_____. "Contemporary Allusions in *The Tatler*." *Mod-
ern Language Notes*, 55 (1940), 292-94.

Allen identifies "expected" references to actual persons
in two issues.

_____. "Steele and the Molesworth Family." *Review of
English Studies*, 12 (1936), 449-54.

Allen discusses the family used as the basis of a fictional illustration in *Tatler* no. 189.

Aubin, Robert A. "Behind Steele's Satire on Undertakers."
PMLA, 64 (1949), 1008-26.

Aubin details the background of Steele's ridicule of
this profession in his play *The Funeral* and of his use
of the upholders themselves as a means of satire in the
Tatler.

Backman, Sven. *This Singular Tale: A Study of the Vicar
of Wakefield and its Literary Background*. Lund Studies
in English, 40. Berlingska Boktryckeriet: Lund, 1971.

In relating the *Vicar of Wakefield* to the periodical
essay tradition in Part Two of this study, Backman finds
the work of Addison and Steele especially important. He
discusses their realistic narrative sketches, the con-
tinuity provided by framework characters, narrative
economy, the essay and the chapter, the eidolon,

sentimental exemplary tales, and Sir Roger de Coverley, often citing analogues with Goldsmith's novel.

Baldwin, Edward Chauncey. "La Bruyère's Influence upon Addison." *PMLA*, 19 (1904), 479-95.

Baldwin shows how *Les Caractères* individualized the method of the character through the use of names, personal details, and other devices. He demonstrates Addison's familiarity with La Bruyère, citing borrowed or parallel passages and general stylistic similarities.

_____. "Marivaux's Place in the Development of Character Portrayal." *PMLA*, 27 (1912), 168-87.

In relating Marivaux to delineators of character preceding and following him, Baldwin shows how *Le Spectateur Francais* augments Addison's purpose and style with sentimental analysis.

_____. "The Relation of the Seventeenth-Century Character to the Periodical Essay." *PMLA*, 19 (1904), 75-114.

To show why the character became increasingly individualized and why the periodical rather than the purer form influenced the novel, Baldwin surveys the characters of Joseph Hall, Thomas Overbury, John Earle, Thomas Fuller, and the *Spectator*. He compares Sir Roger de Coverley with Overbury's "Country Gentleman."

Bateson, F. W. "Addison, Steele and the Periodical Essay." *Dryden to Johnson*. Ed. Roger Lonsdale. *History of Literature in the English Language*, Vol. 4. London: Barrie & Jenkins, 1971.

Bateson suggests that Addison rescued English humor from obscenity, but judges his major achievement to be his style, often manifested in the juxtaposition of brilliant rhetoric with homely objects. He comments on Addison's fiction—its romanticism and amiable humor. Though allowing Steele to be an innovator, Bateson believes that he has been overrated and that Swift had a major role in beginning the *Tatler*, a mock-newspaper. He finds Steele's treatment of Sir Roger de Coverley heavy-handed.

Beachcroft, T. O. *The English Short Story*. London: Longmans, 1967.

In this "Writers and Their Work" pamphlet Beachcroft judges the moral stories enclosed in the essays of Steele and Addison to be on the verge of true short stories because they present individual people with ordinary modern names.

_____. *The Modest Art: A Survey of the Short Story in English*. London: Oxford Univ. Press, 1968.

In chapter vii, "The Character Books, and the Story Emerging from the Essay," Beachcroft finds the art of the apologue in the fiction of Addison and Steele to be tempered by the invention of individual people rather than characters. These authors vouch for the truth of their fiction and present some stories deliberately as stories.

Beattie, James. "On Laughter, and Ludicrous Composition." *Essays*. Edinburgh: William Creech, 1776. Rpt. New York: Garland, 1971.

Beattie discusses the comic display of "singular" characters, the seriousness of humor, the laughter arising from incongruity, and the liberty of English humor, using examples from the *Tatler* and *Spectator*. He praises the juxtaposition of dignity with insignificance in the Journal of the Court of Honor and the pleasantry of Isaac Bickerstaff.

Beljame, Alexander. *Le Public et les Hommes de Lettres en Angleterre au dix-huitieme Siecle 1600-1744 (Dryden--Addison--Pope)*. Paris: Hachette, 1881. Trans. E. O. Lorimer, ed. Bonamy Dobree. London: Keegan Paul, 1948.

In chapter 3, "Joseph Addison 1688-1721," Beljame declares that Addison's influence made Steele's tentative *Tatler* into an important journal of manners and that it dominated the *Spectator*, especially in the shaping of the detached and impartial Mr. Spectator.

Béranger, Jean. *Les Hommes de Lettres et la Politique en Angleterre de la Revolution de 1688 a la mort de George I er: Essai d'exposé et d'interprétation des attitudes et des idées dans l'action politique de De Foe, Swift, Addison, Steele, Arbuthnot et Pope*. Bordeaux: Faculté des Lettres et Sciences humaines de l'Université de Bordeaux, 1968.

Béranger provides useful background and interpretation of political fiction, by Addison and Steele, mostly from the *Tatler*, about "la politique religieuse" and monarchy. Notable among his discussions are their essays on waxwork religions, the ecclesiastical thermometer, and Felicia.

Bissell, Benjamin. *The American Indian in English Literature of the Eighteenth Century*. *Yale Studies in English*, no. 68. New Haven: Yale Univ. Press, 1925.

In chapter iii, "Civilization as Seen by the Savage," and chapter iv, "The Indian in Fiction," Bissell discusses *Tatler* no. 171 and *Spectator* no. 50 and no. 11.

Blanchard, Rae. "Richard Steele and the Status of Women." *Studies in Philology*, 26 (1929), 325-55.

Blanchard evaluates Steele's views in the context of contemporary thought about four topics: the nature of women, their education, their status in marriage, their social roles. She discusses many characters and tales from the *Tatler* and the *Spectator* which exemplify Steele's ideas.

Bloom, Edward A. and Lillian D. *Joseph Addison's Sociable Animal: In the Market-Place, on the Hustings, in the Pulpit.* Providence, R. I.: Brown Univ. Press, 1971.

The Blooms' book, not primarily about Addison's fiction, describes its economic, social, and religious context in detail. But in Chapter 1, "The Squire and the Merchant," they evaluate the "genial fiction" of the Spectator Club as an argument for accord between the middle class and the gentry and as a satiric antidote to class rigidity. Sir Roger de Coverley, Sir Andrew Freeport, and Will Wimble are discussed in this context. In Chapter 2, "The Social Virtues," the Blooms call the exemplum Addison's means of teaching the "joys of productive life" and provide illustrations. In Chapter 3, "The Mercantilist Principle," they explicate two pieces of economic fiction, *Spectator* no. 3 and no. 69. Later chapters contain fewer references to fictional examples.

Blunden, Edmund. *Votive Tablets: Studies Chiefly Appreciative of English Authors and Books.* London: Cobden-Sanderson, 1931.

In an essay originally printed in the *Times Literary Supplement* for August 29, 1929, Blunden describes Bickerstaff's aptness as an observer and commentator and calls the *Tatler* a microcosm. He notes Steele's invention of the Spectator Club and other figures and clubs.

Bolton, J. H. *A Commentary and Questionnaire on the Coverley Papers (Addison and Steele).* London: Sir Isaac Pitman & Sons, 1927.

Bolton's guide to the appreciation of these papers includes a brief sketch of England during the period, comments on the styles of Addison and Steele, summaries of thirty-three papers about Sir Roger and the Spectator Club, and a description of Addison's humor, irony, and politics. Brief notes and one hundred questions on the papers conclude the pamphlet.

Bond, Donald F. "Introduction." *The Spectator.* Oxford: Clarendon Press, 1965. I, xiii-cix.

In describing the contents and dramatis personae of the periodical Bond evaluates Mr. Spectator's unifying function and the illustrative qualities of the Spectator

371

Club. He assesses the authorship and diverse uses of
letters from correspondents. In determining the relative contributions of Addison and Steele, Bond describes
their shared ethical purpose, expressed more seriously
and straightforwardly by the latter and more variously
and comically by the former. As he surveys the characters and tales of each, Bond judges both responsible
for vivid pictures of ordinary life, with many of
Steele's best papers in the manner of La Bruyère and
many of Addison's best devoted to Sir Roger de Coverley.

Bond, Richmond P. "Introduction." *New Letters to the*
Tatler *and* Spectator. Austin: Univ. of Texas Press,
1959. Pp. 3-29.

In presenting his edition of 96 unpublished letters
from correspondents, Bond shows the proportionately
greater role of letters in the *Spectator* and the increasing use of several letters in single issues. Confident that Addison and Steele wrote many letters
wholly or partly, revised many, and utilized ideas from
others, Bond believes the major functions of the letters
to be dramatizing the persona and his circle and advancing satire or social reform. The viewpoints provided
by letters contributed to the sense of dramatic interplay in the periodicals.

_____. "Isaac Bickerstaff, Esq." *Restoration and*
Eighteenth-Century Literature: Essays in Honor of Alan
Dugald McKillop. Ed. Carroll Camden. Chicago: Univ.
of Chicago Press, 1963. Printed for Rice Univ. Pp.
103-24.

Bond presents the context in which Swift created the
mock astrologer to satirize false learning and false
religion. He then assesses the emergence of the "second" Bickerstaff in the *Tatler*, which Steele made the
first essay journal to sustain the device of an imaginary author-editor. Bond constructs a composite portrait of this Bickerstaff from the autobiographical
materials scattered throughout the *Tatler* and illustrates the authors' skilled use of him to describe and
narrate.

_____. "Mr. Bickerstaff and Mr. Wortley." *Classical*
Medieval and Renaissance Studies in Honor of Berthold
Louis Ullman. Ed. Charles Henderson, Jr. Rome:
Edizioni di Storia e Letteratura, 1964. II, 491-504.

Bond cites Edward Wortley's influence on the portrayal
of marriage settlements in *Tatler* no. 199 and no. 223.

_____. *Queen Anne's American Kings*. Oxford: Clarendon
Press, 1952.

In Chapter III Bond describes literary portrayals of
the visit of four Iroquois chiefs to London in 1710;
these include *Tatler* no. 171 and *Spectator* no. 50 and
no. 56.

_____. *The* Tatler: *The Making of a Literary Journal.*
Cambridge, Mass.: Harvard Univ. Press, 1971.

In Chapter I, "The Men behind the Mask," Bond discusses
the editor and other authors of the *Tatler.* In Chapter
II, "The Business of Publication," he describes the
periodical project, its format, its advertising, and
its finances. In Chapter III, "Current Affairs," he
surveys topics of the town, news, and politics. In
Chapter IV, "The Social Substance," Bond assesses the
reforming purpose behind the portrayal of morals and
manners in the *Tatler;* this discussion provides the
context for numerous character types, such as the rake
and the coquette, and for tales about love, marriage,
and education. In Chapter V, "Arts and Sciences," Bond
finds Bickerstaff to be an Enlightenment figure in his
attitude toward the stage, literature, criticism, language, philosophy, religion, and science. In Chapter
VI, "The Formal Structure," after explaining the "en-
veloping process" of the informal essay, Bond evaluates
the other forms it encloses. He reviews the letters
found in the *Tatler*--their authorship and revision,
their suggestive names, varied purposes, timeliness,
and sources. The character in the *Tatler,* influenced
most by La Bruyère, is never "a thing apart in a rigid
mold" but presents an individual in believable circumstances. Bond also evaluates the episode, the tale,
the allegory (dream vision, exemplum, fable, apologue),
and other minor forms. Although most stories are contained in a single issue, Bond discusses the "cumulative
episode" and the serialized narrative. He finds the
point of view in this fiction to be predominantly that
of Bickerstaff, who provides unity and authority for it.
In Chapter VII, "The Words and Ways of Bickerstaff,"
Bond describes the style, the editorial devices (Bickerstaff himself, Jenny Distaff, Pacolet, the Upholders),
and the departments of the *Tatler.* After Chapters VIII,
"The End of the Tatler," and IX, "The Table of Fame"
(contemporaries, imitations, reprints, continuations),
Bond concludes that the *Tatler* was the "first great
socio-literary journal" and the "first true organ of
the English Enlightenment."

Boyce, Benjamin. "English Short Fiction in the Eighteenth
Century." *Studies in Short Fiction,* 5 (1968), 95-112.

Boyce discusses the conventions that the *Tatler* and the
Spectator established for later short fiction regarding
length, kinds (character sketch, oriental tale, allegory,
tales of passion, social criticism), purpose, mode

(realism), and technique, including the formal, economical style.

_____. "News from Hell: Satiric Communications with
the Nether World in English Writing of the Seventeenth
and Eighteenth Centuries." *PMLA*, 58 (1943), 402-37.

Boyce lists *Tatler* no. 26 and no. 118 as examples of
this genre.

_____. "Two Debits for Tom Brown, with a Credit from
Joseph Addison." *Philological Quarterly*, 14 (1935),
263-69.

Boyce documents Brown's influence on portrayals of
visits to Westminster Abbey in *Spectator* no. 26 and no.
329.

Brauer, George C., Jr. *The Education of a Gentleman:
Theories of Gentlemanly Education in England 1660-1775.*
New York: Bookman Associates, 1959.

In this survey Brauer discusses various idealized and
satirical characters from the *Spectator* to illustrate
theoretical positions.

Butt, John. *The Augustan Age.* 3rd ed. New York: Norton,
1965.

After praising the character sketch, the letter device,
and the grouping of characters as attractive devices in
the *Tatler* and the *Spectator*, Butt discusses the oblique
social criticism in the de Coverley papers.

Canby, Henry Seidel. *The Short Story in English.* New
York: Holt, 1909.

In Chapter IX Canby assesses the "miniature fictions"
of Addison and Steele, finding little narrative written
for its own sake rather than for what lies behind it,
but judging few pieces "mere pendents" to essays. He
discovers the strength of this fiction in delightful
characters rather than plot, in which the authors show
little interest. He describes the objective social
criticism and the truthful representation of reality as
seen by the authors.

Cardwell, Guy A., Jr. "The Influence of Addison on
Charleston Periodicals, 1795-1860." *Studies in Philology*, 35 (1938), 456-70.

Cardwell describes three fictional devices used by
Addisonian imitators.

Cazamian, Louis. *The Development of English Humor*, Part
II. Durham, N. C.: Duke Univ. Press, 1952.

In this survey Cazamian describes the yoking of sympathy with humor in the *Spectator*, where a "better tone of jesting" was identified with social decency.

_____. "Le Classicisme (1702-1740)." Book 7 of Émile Legouis and Cazamian, *Histoire de la Littérature Anglaise*. Paris: Hachette, 1924. Trans. W. D. MacInness and Cazamian. New York: Macmillan, 1927.

Cazamian describes the comic figure of Bickerstaff, his imaginary portraits, and the "composite" Spectator, who makes vice and affectation look ridiculous. He calls Steele's fiction, with its portrayal of tender sentiment and family affection, the germ of the Richardsonian novel and finds the *Spectator* a forerunner of the novel of moral observation. Cazamian remarks on the indulgent irony of Sir Roger's portrayal and the idyllic qualities of the Spectator Club.

Chambers, Robert D. "Addison at Work on the *Spectator*." *Modern Philology*, 56 (1959), 145-53.

Chambers describes Addison's use of some previously unpublished essays in the *Spectator*: most frequently the "I" of the manuscript became Mr. Spectator, but six of the essays were given more fictional contexts.

Chandler, Frank Wadleigh. *The Literature of Roguery*. 2 vols. Boston: Houghton, 1907.

Chandler mentions the satiric devices in *Tatler* no. 249 and *Spectator* no. 343.

Churchill, R. C. *English Literature of the Eighteenth Century*. London: University Tutorial Press, 1953.

In comments on the *Spectator* Churchill finds the Spectator Club typical of the upper middle class, notes the effective use of the country setting, and calls the de Coverley papers intermediate between the essay and the novel.

Clark, Priscilla P. "Newspapers and Novels: Some Common Functions and Themes." *Studies in the Novel*, 7 (1975), 166-80.

Clark argues that these two forms in the eighteenth century were oriented toward social exploration, "acculturation" through social and moral guidance, and the reinforcement of social and cultural norms. Judging the *Spectator* to be the archetype of the "social journal," where role models abound, she finds the formal point of view, Mr. Spectator, inseparable from the moral perspective.

Conant, Martha Pike. *The Oriental Tale in England in the Eighteenth Century.* New York: Columbia Univ. Press, 1908. Rpt. New York: Octagon, 1966.

Conant groups these tales in four categories: imaginative, moralistic, philosophic, and satiric. Addison's tales figure prominently in her survey, particularly in the last two categories. She finds the morality of his tales, despite its oriental disguise, to be either English or universal. She praises his restraint in the use of oriental ornament and imagery, his generally "light" touch in comparison with other authors. Conant discusses fifteen tales from the *Spectator.*

Courthope, W. J. *Addison.* London: Macmillan, 1884.

In this English Men of Letters volume, Courthope discusses the advocacy of virtue in the fiction of the *Tatler* and judges Addison's contribution to be the introduction of ironical commendation in character portrayal. Courthope traces the connections between the *Tatler* departments and eidolon and the club of the *Spectator* and suggests that Addison and Steele transcended the example of La Bruyère in their characters.

Crawley-Boevey, Arthur W. *"The Perverse Widow": Being Passages from the Life of Catharina, Wife of William Boevey, Esq., of Flaxley Abbey, in the County of Gloucester.* London: Longmans, 1898.

Crawley-Boevey reviews the essays about Sir Roger de Coverley relating to the beloved widow and identifies her with Catherine Boevey, a personal acquaintance of Steele, who wrote most of the pertinent issues.

Cross, Wilbur L. *The Development of the English Novel.* New York: Macmillan, 1899.

Cross finds the character sketches of the *Tatler* and the *Spectator*, in their use of representative details, to be among the forms that contributed to the novel.

Davis, N. Darnell. *The "Spectator's" Essays Relating to the West Indies.* Demerara [British Guiana]: Argosy Press, 1885.

Davis reviews the contents and sources for Steele's stories in *Spectator* nos. 11, 80, and 493, suggesting what he invented or embellished. He also comments on the "wild tragedy" depicted by Addison in *Spectator* no. 215.

Day, Robert Adams. *Told in Letters: Epistolary Fiction Before Richardson.* Ann Arbor: Univ. of Michigan Press, 1966.

Though he deals mostly with letter fiction which appeared in books, Day notes that periodicals cultivated readers' taste for this kind of fiction by presenting everything from clearly fictional letters to the editor to miniature letter novels. Addison and Steele, in addition to exploiting the letter to particularize character and make discourse life-like, discovered its pathetic possibilities. Day includes an appendix, "A List of Letter Fiction in Periodicals," in which he describes two examples from the *Tatler* and thirteen from the *Spectator*.

Dobrée, Bonamy. *English Literature in the Early Eighteenth Century, 1700-1740*. *Oxford History of English Literature*, Vol. 7. Oxford: Clarendon Press, 1959.

In a chapter on "Essayists and Controversialists" Dobrée praises the character sketches and various adumbrations of the novel, finding in the *Tatler* the reality of middle-class life; he contrasts the sympathy of Steele with the morality of Addison.

_____. "The First Victorian." *Essays in Biography 1680-1726*. London: Oxford Univ. Press, 1925. Pp. 197-345.

Though mostly concerned with dethroning Addison from his Victorian eminence, Dobrée cites his mastery of gentle humor and his way of appealing to everyone in visions dealing with exalted themes. Dobrée sees Addison's mask slipping in the satire of *Tatler* nos. 100 and 102.

_____. *Variety of Ways: Discussions on Six Authors*. Oxford: Clarendon Press, 1932.

In the fifth essay of this book, responding to Macaulay, Dobrée prefers Steele to Addison. He describes Steele's capacity for acute feeling and his originality; Steele began the *Tatler*, wrote the first sketch of the Spectator Club, and composed the first letters, anecdotes, and allegories.

Dobson, Austin. *Miscellanies (Second Series)*. New York: Dodd, Mead, 1901.

In "The Story of the 'Spectator'" Dobson praises Addison's fiction in the *Tatler* but reminds us that Steele was the originator, and Addison, the elaborator in both periodicals. Dobson finds Sir Roger de Coverley a "lucky accident" of invention instead of a preconceived figure because he does not become important until *Spectator* no. 106. He notes the scarce use of the remaining characters in the Spectator Club.

377

_____. *Richard Steele*. London: Longmans, 1886.

In chapters on the *Tatler* and the *Spectator* Dobson discusses Steele's realistic portrayals of domestic life,
while recognizing Addison's skill with irony. He
judges Steele's depiction of Sir Roger's love for the
perverse widow as his best contribution to that character but finds Steele's fiction in the *Tatler* better.

Drake, Nathan. *Essays Biographical, Critical and Historical Illustrative of the* Tatler, Spectator *and* Guardian.
3 vols. London: John Sharpe, 1805. Rpt. New York:
Johnson Reprint, 1968.

In three essays on the style, invention, imagery, pathos,
humor and character delineation of Steele, Drake suggests that he seldom departs from ordinary life in his
fiction, aims for the pleasures of compassion and sympathy, and shows astonishing fertility in his portraits.
In three essays on Addison's style, humor, comic painting, fable, imagery, and allegory, Drake finds the
essence of his humor to be a sharp focus on aspects of
character or incident most susceptible to laughable
associations. He suggests how Addison renders more
fanciful narratives subservient to the purest morality.
He finds an "inviolable integrity" in the design of Sir
Roger's character, adhered to by Steele and Budgell. He
includes a brief essay on the latter, demonstrating his
humor and wit.

Duke, R. E. H. *Reflections on the Character and Doings
of Sir Roger de Coverley of Addison*. London: Elliot
Stock, 1900.

Duke speculates that Addison drew on images of the
country from his childhood in portraying Sir Roger, a
grateful remembrance of Richard Duke, a neighboring
squire in Bulford. He reviews Addison's essays about
Sir Roger to adduce internal evidence.

Dunham, W. H. "Some Forerunners of the *Tatler* and the
Spectator." *Modern Language Notes*, 33 (1918), 95-101.

Dunham connects these two periodicals to character writing in the first eight years of the eighteenth century,
reprints of Theophrastus and La Bruyère and original
works. These sources showed Steele how the character
could become part of the essay.

Eleanore, Sister M. *The Literary Essay in English*. Boston: Ginn, 1923.

Sister Eleanore briefly describes the fiction of Addison and Steele as the "short-story essay." She judges
their tales to be without plot, permitting digressions,
illustrations, and ornaments.

Elioseff, Lee Andrew. "Joseph Addison's Political Animal: Middle Class Idealism in Crisis." *Eighteenth-Century Studies*, 6 (1973), 372-81.

In this review essay of *Joseph Addison's Sociable Animal*, by Edward A. and Lillian D. Bloom, Elioseff notes that Addison did not argue the central myth of Whig ideology so often as he represented it in allegory, story, or lyrical effusion. He states that Sir Roger de Coverley was a delightful, warmly condescending portrait not mistaken for a real picture of a shrewd Tory opponent.

Elkin, P. K. *The Augustan Defense of Satire*. Oxford: Clarendon Press, 1973.

In Chapter 7, "Personal Reference," Elkin points out that both the *Tatler* and the *Spectator* contain a considerable amount of personal reference, despite the editors' opposition to libel and slander and despite their claims to avoid individual satire. In Chapter 8, "Smiling versus Savage Satire," Elkin documents their preference for the former. He finds the overall effect of the *Tatler* and the *Spectator* to be the "purifying" of contemporary satire.

Fairchild, Hoxie Neale. *The Noble Savage: A Study in Romantic Naturalism*. New York: Columbia Univ. Press, 1928.

In Chapter II, "The Noble Savage in the Pseudo-Classic Period," Fairchild describes *Tatler* no. 171 and *Spectator* no. 50.

Foà, Giovanna. *Two Essayists (Richard Steele and Joseph Addison)*. Milan: La Goliardica, [1957].

Foà describes the settings of the *Tatler* and the *Spectator* and finds their characters pseudonyms for real persons, who are often envisioned as types. He discusses Mr. Spectator's relationship with the reader and calls Sir Roger de Coverley an idealized portrait of a landowner.

Forster, John. *Historical and Biographical Essays*. 2 vols. London: John Murray, 1858.

In an essay reprinted, with additions, from the *Quarterly Review* (1855), Forster responds to Macaulay's opinion that the *Tatler* lacked distinction until Addison began to contribute. He cites the originality of the first eighty issues. He then shows, with abundant illustration, Steele's mastery of the character and his skill in recreating "actual life." He notes Steele's invention of Sir Roger de Coverley and Will Honeycomb in the *Spectator*.

Frazer, Sir James George. *Sir Roger de Coverley and Other Literary Pieces*. London: Macmillan, 1920.

These five impressionistic essays, often extrapolating additional action from hints provided in the *Spectator*, stress the childlike frankness and innocence of the character, along with his pure heart. The essays are "A Visit to Coverley Hall," "The Spectator in the Country," "Sir Roger in Cambridge," "Sir Roger in Covent Garden," and "Sir Roger in the Temple."

Freeman, Phyllis. "Who Was Sir Roger de Coverley?" *The Quarterly Review*, 285 (1947), 592-604.

Freeman argues that William Walsh of Abberley Lodge in Worcestershire, the close friend of Addison and unsuccessful suitor of Mrs. Catherine Bovey, was the source for Sir Roger. She suggests that Addison made Steele's original sketch "peculiarly his own."

Gally, Henry. *A Critical Essay on Characteristic-Writing from his Translation of the Moral Characters of Theophrastus (1725)*. Ed. Alexander H. Chorney. Augustan Reprint Society no. 33. Los Angeles: Clark Library, 1952.

Gally praises the *Tatler* and the *Spectator* for interspersing characters and manners, admires the humorous eccentricities of Sir Roger de Coverley, and insists that these characters are types.

Godshalk, William L. "Artist and Spectator." *Kalki: Studies in James Branch Cabell*, 3 (1969), 109.

Godshalk sees a possible reminiscence of the Spectator Club in Cabell's *The Cream of the Jest*.

Graham, Walter. "Defoe's *Review* and Steele's *Tatler*--the Question of Influence." *Journal of English and Germanic Philology*, 33 (1934), 250-54.

Although he notes the influence of other periodicals published between 1700 and 1709, Graham judges the *Review* to be the "progenitor" of the *Tatler*. Like Defoe, Steele vivified his character sketches by using real people as models. Defoe's suggestions about the value of entertainment led Steele to treat topics of reform through narrative devices like the court or the dream.

_____. *English Literary Periodicals*. New York: Thomas Nelson, 1930.

In this survey Graham states that the five viewpoints were the only original feature of the *Tatler*; he cites precedents for various narrative strategies. Graham believes that the Bickerstaff family provided the continuing narrative interest that unified the periodical.

_____. "Some Predecessors of the *Tatler*." *Journal of English and Germanic Philology*, 24 (1925), 548-54.

Graham finds analogues for various narrative devices in the *Tatler*--dating essays from familiar places, using letters, the club idea, and the character, and employing the single essay form--in English periodicals published between 1690 and 1709.

_____. *The Beginnings of English Literary Periodicals: A Study of Periodical Literature, 1665-1715*. New York: Oxford Univ. Press, 1926.

In Chapter IV, "The *Tatler*, *Spectator* & *Guardian*," Graham sketches precedents for characters, letters, and the club device in earlier periodicals. He describes briefly the importance of Isaac Bickerstaff and Mr. Spectator.

Halsband, Robert. "Lady Mary Wortley Montagu and Eighteenth-Century Fiction." *Philological Quarterly*, 45 (1966), 145-56.

Halsband examines her contribution to *Spectator* no. 573 and other pieces.

Hazlitt, William. *Lectures on the English Comic Writers*. London: Oxford Univ. Press, 1907.

In the fifth lecture of this series, originally published in 1818, Hazlitt discusses the periodical essayists as moral historians and praises Addison and Steele for their use of dramatic contrast and ironical viewpoints. Though he believes the *Spectator* records manners better, Hazlitt finds the characters and humor of the *Tatler* to be "truer," less like a lecture, with more left to the reader. He judges Steele a less artificial, more original writer and describes his use of pathos.

Hendrix, W. S. "Quevedo, Guevara, Le Sage, and the *Tatler*." *Modern Philology*, 19 (1921), 177-86.

Hendrix cites parallels between several narrative devices in the *Tatler*--Pacolet, the court device, the magic ring, and certain dream visions--and techniques in *Sueños*, *Diablo Cojuelo*, and *Diable Boiteux*.

Hooker, Edward N. "Humour in the Age of Pope." *Huntington Library Quarterly*, 11 (1948), 361-85.

In charting the changes in humor between Swift and Sterne, Hooker mentions the Spectator Club and discusses Sir Roger, whose amiable oddity lifts him out of a stereotype and reflects his abundant life.

Horne, Colin J. "Notes on Steele and the Beef-Steak
Club." *Review of English Studies*, 21 (1945), 239-44.

Horne describes Steele's relationship with Richard
Estcourt, the basis for Tom Mirrour in the *Tatler* and
the author of a letter purporting to be from Sir Roger
de Coverley in the *Spectator*.

Hughes, Helen Sard. "English Epistolary Fiction Before
Pamela." *The Manly Anniversary Studies in Language and
Literature*. Chicago: Univ. of Chicago Press, 1923.
Pp. 156-69.

Hughes discusses *Tatler* no. 30 and *Spectator* no. 375.

Humphreys, A. R. *Steele, Addison and Their Periodical
Essays*. London: Longmans, 1959.

In this "Writers and Their Work" pamphlet, Humphreys
discusses the domestic-social fiction in the *Tatler*,
which arises from interactions in the Bickerstaff's
affairs, and praises Steele's descriptions of family
life.

Hunt, Leigh. *A Book for a Corner; or, Selections in
Prose and Verse from Authors the Best Suited to that
Mode of Enjoyment: with Comments on each, and a General
Introduction*. 2 vols. London: Chapman & Hall, 1849.

In printing fourteen pieces of fiction from the *Tatler*
and *Spectator*, Hunt describes the "warmth" and pathos
of Steele's "unpremeditated" accounts and calls Sir
Roger de Coverley a truthful type, more permanent than
what he represents.

Irving, William Henry. *The Providence of Wit in the English Letter Writers*. Durham, N. C.: Duke Univ. Press,
1955.

In Chapter 5 Irving discusses "Augustan Attitudes" reflected in the letters printed in the *Tatler* and *Spectator*. The "suspicious" stylistic uniformity leads him
to conclude that Addison and Steele thoroughly revised
the letters they used. He finds the manuscript letters
much heavier, lacking the wit that gives unity to the
periodicals.

Jack, Jane H. "The Periodical Essayists." *From Dryden
to Johnson*. Ed. Boris Ford. *The Pelican Guide to English Literature*, Vol. 4. Hammondsworth: Penguin, 1957.
Pp. 217-29.

In this brief survey Jack emphasizes the "civilization
through conciliation" in the *Tatler* and the *Spectator*,
judging the latter's club an important rhetorical device
and symbol.

Johnson, Samuel. "Joseph Addison." *Lives of the English Poets.* Ed. George Birkbeck Hill. Oxford: Clarendon Press, 1905. Rpt. New York: Octagon Press, 1967.

Johnson praises the *Tatler* and the *Spectator* for their descriptions of life and manners, finding in Addison's characters originality without excessive exaggeration. He attributes Sir Roger's oddity to "rusticity" rather than deviance.

Kay, Donald. *Short Fiction in* The Spectator. Studies in the Humanities, No. 8. University: Univ. of Alabama Press, 1975.

After a brief introduction Kay surveys "The Storytelling Tradition and Periodical Antecedents to *The Spectator*" (from the *Athenian Mercury* to the *Tatler*), finding precedents for different types and uses of fiction. In Chapter 2 Kay discusses the character, describing the central tradition and the predominant social types. He divides forty examples from the *Spectator* into the "typical" (either formal, brief, and objective in the manner of Theophrastus or informal, loose, and subjective in the style of La Bruyère), and the "individual." The more informal typical characters, with increased narrative interaction and speech, possess complexity and elasticity. The individual characters, with more action and conflicts of interest, verge on the short story. Steele used this form twice as often as Addison. In Chapter 3 Kay evaluates twenty-three fables by type (oriental, animal, allegorical) and function, stressing the reader's involvement in the morality of this form. In Chapter 4 Kay describes the seventeen pieces of fiction he calls "the dream vision-cum-allegory," sketching their basic structure (introduction of the dreamer, contact with a world of personifications, and the final waking to truth) and their three major purposes—political, literary, and moral. In Chapter 5 Kay assesses eleven oriental tales which, like the visions, are mostly Addison's. When Addison uses the form for satire rather than for moral or philosophic exposition, he employs a narrator other than Mr. Spectator. Kay judges plot more important than character in this form. In Chapter 6, "Miscellaneous Forms," he discusses examples of the mock-sentimental tale, the fabliau and rogue literature, the satirical adventure story, and the domestic apologue. He finds Steele the predominant author of these types. Of the one hundred pieces of short fiction he considers, Kay concludes that the authors needed varied ways to image abstractions. Steele's fiction is more sentimental, more domestic, and more often epistolary than Addison's.

Kenney, William. "The Morality of 'The Spectator.'" *Notes and Queries*, 202 (1957), 37-38.

Kenney notes that Addison and Steele, despite their reforming aims, occasionally use anecdotes of questionable morality for illustrations or entertainment.

Kinsley, William. "Meaning and Format: Mr. Spectator and His Folio Half-Sheets." *ELH*, 34 (1967), 482-94.

Kinsley explores the *Spectator*'s medium and persona as factors in persuading readers to cooperate in social reform. Mr. Spectator's "silent didacticism" succeeded because of his periodical's mobility and easy accessibility. Kinsley argues that Addison and Steele equated their narrator's personality with its printed manifestation, creating the voice of the collaborative public silently through print. He uses nos. 212 and 216 to show the *Spectator* as both mover and actor.

Klotz, Gunther. *Das Werturteil des Erzählers: Formen der Bewertung der epischen Gestalten im "Tatler" und "Spectator."* Halle: Max Niemeyer, 1960.

Klotz, following the idea that the *Tatler* and the *Spectator* intended to effect a moral revaluation, shows how Isaac Bickerstaff and Mr. Spectator lead the reader to judgments about characters, through their choice of subject matter and means of making evaluations, both direct and indirect. The former method involves emphatic evaluative statements, names of characters, and clearly defined contrasts. The latter includes evaluating characters through other's estimates, their opinions (as in letters), actions, ridicule, sympathy, and the distribution of justice. Klotz illustrates these concepts through extensive analysis of character portrayal.

Koster, Patricia. "'Monoculus' and Party Satire." *Philological Quarterly*, 49 (1970), 259-62.

Koster discusses the unsavory James Ashburne, fictionalized in the *Tatler* as Monoculus.

Law, Frederick Houk. "Social Degeneration and the De Coverley Papers: Classics in the Light of Modern Conditions." *The Independent*, 108 (1922), 336-37.

Law urges his belief in the universality of these papers.

Leavis, Q. D. *Fiction and the Reading Public*. London: Chatto & Windus, 1939.

Leavis stresses the focus of the *Tatler* and the *Spectator* on *moeurs* rather than morals and their use of a lucid style based on contemporary speech. She finds the *Tatler* livelier, subtler, and more risqué. She suggests that these periodicals made the modern novel possible by combining two previously separate audiences

(Aphra Behn's and John Bunyan's), by dealing with life as their readers lived it, and by finding an idiom for common standards of taste and conduct.

Legouis, Émile. "Les Deux 'Sir Roger de Coverley': Celui de Steele et celui d'Addison." *Revue Germanique*, 2 (1906), 453-71. Rpt. *Dernière Gerbe*. Paris: H. Didier, 1940.

Legouis argues that Addison's portrayal of Sir Roger is more negative than Steele's. As seen in his attitude toward Moll White, his encounter with a gipsy fortune teller, and his behavior at the assizes, Addison's Sir Roger is more naive fool and unlightened conservative than Steele's eccentric, but benevolent character.

L'Estrange, A. G. *History of English Humour, with an Introduction upon Ancient Humour*. London: Hurst & Blackett, 1877. Rpt. New York: Burt Franklin, 1970.

L'Estrange discusses both the *Tatler* and the *Spectator*, contrasting the greater precision and importance of Addison's allegories with the stranger and more daring genius of Steele's fiction.

Lewis, C. S. "Addison." *Essays on the Eighteenth Century Presented to David Nichol Smith in Honour of His Seventieth Birthday*. Oxford: Clarendon Press, 1945. Pp. 1-14.

In discussing this "comfortable" writer, Lewis comments on the cheerfulness of Mr. Spectator and describes Addison's success in making Sir Roger de Coverley, the political "enemy," into a lovable old man, neither dangerous nor to be taken seriously.

Lockwood, Thomas. "The Augustan Author-Audience Relationship: Satiric vs. Comic Forms." *ELH*, 36 (1969), 648-58.

Lockwood contrasts the attitudes of the Tory satirists Swift and Pope, writing for an elite minority, with those of Addison and Steele, for whom the audience and the world were interchangeable. Characters satirized by the former as deviants from moral norms are replaced in the latter's writings by lovable social eccentrics. Lockwood contrasts Pope's Sporus with Sir Roger de Coverley, the satiric scapegoat with the humorous reminder of our humanity. The ridicule of Addison and Steele embodies the integrating tendencies of comedy and suggests the hope of reunion between the humorist and the society. The point of the Court of Honor trials in the *Tatler*, Lockwood states, is likewise social rather than moral, presentational rather than persuasive.

Lovett, Robert W. "Mr. Spectator in *Bleak House*." *The Dickensian*, 59 (1963), 124.

Lovett finds *Spectator* nos. 440 and 450 sources for Mr. Jarndyce's Growlery and the Smallweed family.

Macaulay, Thomas Babington. "The Life and Writings of Addison." *Edinburgh Review*, 78 (1843), 102-37.

In praising Addison as an acute observer of human life and a great satirist, Macaulay compares his portraiture and humor favorably with that of Shakespeare, Cervantes, Swift, and Voltaire. Addison's ridicule in the *Tatler* is tempered with good nature and good breeding. Macaulay allows Addison primary responsibility for the *Spectator*, calling him the inventor of the persona and the real creator of Sir Roger de Coverley and Will Honeycomb from the "rude" hints of Steele. He believes the *Spectator* papers form a "whole" with the compelling interest of a novel.

McCutcheon, Roger P. *Eighteenth-Century English Literature*. New York: Oxford Univ. Press, 1949.

In chapter 3 McCutcheon discusses the *Tatler*, the *Spectator*, and the *Guardian* and contrasts Steele's intimate warmth with Addison's more objective approach to characterization. He finds Bickerstaff an effective censor because he is never so tactless or rigorous that he is disliked; Mr. Spectator's usefulness and charm stems from his being an observer rather than a censor. Of Sir Roger de Coverley, McCutcheon says that the reader must balance friendly affection with awareness of weaknesses.

McIntosh, Carey. *The Choice of Life: Samuel Johnson and the World of Fiction*. New Haven: Yale Univ. Press, 1973.

In Chapter 5, "Three Voices: Periodical-Essay Fiction before 1750," McIntosh describes first the Addisonian Humourist, whose whimsical, genteel, intimate tone controls much fiction in the *Spectator*--fantasies inflating minor foibles to absurd dimensions, letters to the "public uncle," and narratives about eccentric characters. Though the Catonist is found in the *Guardian*, McIntosh identifies the Man of Sentiment primarily with Steele in the *Tatler*, the *Spectator*, and the *Lover*. This narrative voice presides over more serious amorous difficulties and pathos.

McKillop, Alan Dugald. *English Literature from Dryden to Burns*. New York: Appleton, 1948.

McKillop notes how the *Tatler* and the *Spectator* combined previous uses of the club as a board of editors and as a group portrayed satirically.

Marr, George S. *The Periodical Essayists of the Eighteenth Century.* New York: Appleton, 1924.

In Chapter 2, "The *Tatler* and *Spectator*, and Other Periodical Essay Work of Addison and Steele," Marr praises Addison's genius for tale telling, Steele's characters of women, and the advantages of the club framework in the *Spectator*.

Mayo, Robert D. *The English Novel in the Magazines 1740-1815.* Evanston, Ill.: Northwestern Univ. Press, 1962.

In Chapter 1, "The Magazine Tradition in Prose Fiction," Mayo points out the "pivotal" importance of the *Tatler* in magazine fiction because of the quantity and ethical appeal of its narratives. Discourse and narrative were intertwined in stories with mostly contemporary settings and familiar characters, mostly from genteel society just below the highest classes. Mayo surveys various types of narrative in the *Tatler*, calling it a courtesy book in periodical form. He finds that the *Spectator* used proportionately less fiction and calls the oriental tale the only major formal addition. Mayo also discusses serial fiction in both periodicals.

Minto, William. *The Literature of the Georgian Era.* Ed. William Knight. Edinburgh: Blackwood, 1894.

Minto finds the beginnings of the novel in the *Tatler* and the *Spectator* with their abundant portrayal of manners and characters (especially in letters) but notes the absence of a story to unify the detached studies.

_____. *A Manual of English Prose Literature, Biographical and Critical, Designed Mainly to Show Characteristics of Style.* Edinburgh: Blackwood, 1872.

Minto contrasts the styles of Addison and Steele, finding in the former's polite ridicule more delicacy and elaboration than in the more genial and hearty humor of the latter. Minto sees malice in the midst of amiability in Addison's portrait of Sir Roger de Coverley, who is treated more kindly by Steele.

Montgomery, Henry R. *Memoirs of the Life and Writings of Sir Richard Steele, Soldier, Dramatist, Essayist, and Patriot.* 2 vols. Edinburgh: William P. Nimmo, 1865.

In chapter 5, "The Periodical Essayist and Delineator of Character 1709-10," Montgomery shows how the *Tatler*'s dramatic framework unified the techniques of Montaigne and La Bruyère. He praises Steele's characterization of Isaac Bickerstaff and discusses how the censor insinuated morality in sketches of characters thought real by his contemporaries. In chapter 7, "The Periodical Essayist--Spectator 1711, 1712," Montgomery suggests that the club enhanced the periodical's drama, praising especially Steele's invention of Sir Roger de Coverley and his analysis of the sentimental cause of the knight's oddities.

Morgan, Charlotte E. *The Rise of the Novel of Manners: A Study of English Prose Fiction between 1600 and 1740.* New York: Columbia Univ. Press, 1911.

Morgan, relating the *Tatler* and the *Spectator* to Renaissance conduct books, judges their illustrative stories and didactic characters a "perfect" expression of the ideas of the age. She suggests that the papers relating to Sir Roger de Coverley verge on a novel of manners. She discusses briefly characters, oriental tales, and apologues.

[Morris, Corbyn.] *An Essay towards Fixing the True Standards of Wit, Humour, Raillery, Satire, and Ridicule to which Is Added, an Analysis of the Characters of an Humourist, Sir John Falstaff, Sir Roger De Coverley, and Don Quixote (1744).* Ed. James L. Clifford. Augustan Reprint Society No. 10. Los Angeles: Clark Library, 1947.

Morris finds humor most delightful when it arises from generous instincts and benevolence; accordingly he insists that the reader love and esteem Sir Roger for his oddities.

Newlin, Claude M. "The English Periodicals and the Novel, 1709-40." *Papers of the Michigan Academy of Science Arts and Letters,* 16 (1931), 467-76.

Newlin describes how the writers of periodicals, especially Addison and Steele, "moralized" and "sentimentalized" English fiction, both through criticism of other prose fiction and through the publication of stories. Isaac Bickerstaff and Mr. Spectator saw the potential for a moral type of novel based on real life; they were true to their critical doctrine in the stories they presented.

Noel, Thomas. *Theories of the Fable in the Eighteenth Century.* New York: Columbia Univ. Press, 1975.

Noel includes Addison's use of this form as a moral story giving the reader the impression of self-guidance.

Oliphant, Margaret Oliphant. *Historical Characters of the Reign of Queen Anne.* New York: Century, 1894.

In a chapter on Addison, "The Humourist," Mrs. Oliphant discusses the indulgent humor exemplified in the harmless vanity of Ned Softly and the endearing rusticity of Sir Roger de Coverley. She suggests that Mr. Spectator is objective but never detached from the society in which he finds models, subjects, and readers.

Papenheim, Wilhelm. *Die Charakterschilderungen im "Tatler," "Spectator," und "Guardian": Ihr Verhältnis zu Theophrast, La Bruyère und den Englischen Character-Writers des 17. Jahrhunderts.* Beiträge zur Englischen Philologie, 15. Leipzig: Bernhard Tauchnitz, 1930.

Papenheim, after assessing the Theophrastan tradition and the French and English character writers of the seventeenth century, analyzes the formal methods of the character in these periodicals. He describes the flexibility of the essay, its concessions to other literary forms, the problems of generality versus particularity and objectivity versus subjectivity in the character, and two methods of characterization (one direct and descriptive and the other indirect and representational). In dividing the basic subject matter of the character into thirteen categories (such as pedantry or foppishness), Papenheim uses parallel quotations from La Bruyère to show his dominant influence, though he finds Addison and Steele more optimistic.

Paulson, Ronald. *The Fictions of Satire.* Baltimore: Johns Hopkins Press, 1967.

In "The Fiction of Whig Satire," a brief conclusion to the third chapter, Paulson discusses the Spectator Club as a social microcosm, analyzes the Horatian structure of *Spectator* no. 2, and explores the denials by Addison and Steele that they wrote satire. He suggests why their ridicule lacked the representative element of Tory satire.

_____. *Satire and the Novel in Eighteenth-Century England.* New Haven: Yale Univ. Press, 1967.

While describing their genial satire, Paulson relates the *Tatler* and the *Spectator* to the rise of the novel in three ways: the equality of viewpoints among humorous characters; the projections of major character types; and the creation of a limited milieu, in the family and the club.

Perry, Thomas Sergeant. *English Literature in the Eighteenth Century.* New York: Harper, 1883.

Perry suggests that Addison's sketches aided the rise of the novel in two ways: by drawing numerous scenes of real life and by uplifting the middle class.

Pitcher, Edward W. "On the Conventions of Eighteenth-Century British Short Fiction: Part I, 1700-1760." *Studies in Short Fiction,* 12 (1975), 199-212.

Pitcher finds the "marriage" of realism to didacticism in this fiction to be distinctive. He isolates tendencies to use plot, character, and scene to illustrate a moral thesis, to state the thesis in a preface or

intrusion, to affect direct communication between narrator and reader, and to use contemporary, familiar
situations. He emphasizes the "presentational realism"
of fiction like that in the *Tatler* and the *Spectator*,
in which the relationship between the narrator and the
reader is more important than that between the narrator
and the story. Pitcher suggests that the fictional
letter's potential to authenticate realistic narrative
was not fully developed because authors preferred to
stress the common, not the distinctive. Their preoc-
cupation with telling rather than showing produced few
and poor descriptive passages.

Price, Lawrence Marsden. *Inkle and Yarico Album*.
Berkeley: Univ. of California Press, 1937.

Introducing an anthology of later versions of the story
in *Spectator* no. 11, poems and plays published in England and three other countries, Price discusses the
simple elegance of Steele's tale. He contrasts its use
to prove the fidelity of women with later emphasis
the juxtaposition of the faithless Christian with the
faithful Indian.

Proper, C. B. A. *Social Elements in English Prose Fiction
between 1700 and 1832*. Amsterdam: H. J. Paris, 1929.

Proper suggests that the fiction of Addison and Steele
led to the novel of "moral purpose." He finds their
introduction of a respectable merchant, Sir Andrew
Freeport, significant and discusses their attention to
social problems, especially in the married life of the
middle classes. Proper believes Steele's solution to
social difficulties to be the sympathetic, Christian
heart.

Ramsey, Roger. "The Ambivalent Spectator." *Papers on
Language and Literature*, 9 (1973), 81-84.

After a detailed analysis of *Spectator* no. 1, Ramsey
judges Mr. Spectator to be neither Addison nor a complete character, but a narrative vehicle who is more
complex than generally accepted.

Rawson, C. J. "Frozen Words: A Note to 'Idler,' No. 46."
Notes and Queries, 215 (1970), 300.

Rawson cites an analogue in *Tatler* no. 254 and common
sources for Johnson and Steele in Butler, Plutarch,
Rabelais, and Castiglione.

Ricken, Wilhelm. *Bemerkungen über Anlage und Erfolg der
wichtigsten Zeitschriften Steele's und den Einfluss
Addison's auf die Entwicklung derselben*. Elberfeld: A.
Martini & Grüttefien [1885].

Ricken comments briefly on the comic mask of Isaac Bickerstaff, its origin and uses, on the initial framework of the *Tatler*, and its best-known characters; then he assesses Mr. Spectator and his club. Disagreeing with Macaulay, he judges Steele's best performances equal to Addison's.

Routh, Harold. "Steele and Addison." *The Cambridge History of English Literature*. Ed. A. W. Ward and A. R. Waller. New York: Macmillan, 1917. IX, 29-72.

Routh praises Steele for discovering the modern short story and being on the verge of the serial domestic novel in the *Tatler*. He discusses satires of high and low life and papers in which Steele shows how an ordinary character is inextricably woven into the social fabric. Routh describes Steele's use of the fictional letter in the *Spectator*.

Saintsbury, George. *The Peace of the Augustans: A Survey of Eighteenth Century Literature as a Place of Rest and Retirement*. London: G. Bell, 1916.

In Chapter 1, "The Heritage of Dryden," Saintsbury judges the characters of the *Spectator*, whether or not they had originals, to be as lively as diary portraits. He believes that the papers about Sir Roger lose their special quality by being read together. He praises Steele for his sentiment and invention and Addison for his temperament, taste, and style.

Shawcross, I. "Addison as a Social Reformer." *The Contemporary Review*, 153 (1938), 585-91.

Shawcross states that Addison wrote with the sole object of entertaining, confident that such entertainment would be morally profitable. Because the intellect was important in Addison's analysis of aesthetic pleasure, he mastered allegory.

Sherburn, George and Donald F. Bond. "Addison, Steele, and the Periodical Essay." *A Literary History of England*. Ed. Albert C. Baugh. 2nd ed. New York: Appleton-Century-Crofts, 1967. Pp. 870-82.

Sherburn and Bond describe Addison's mastery of good-natured satire and Steele's interest. in domestic fiction in the *Tatler*. They discuss the diverse social criticism and sobering narratives in the *Spectator*. Many of the best essays rely for their appeal on descriptions of everyday life.

Singer, Godfrey Frank. *The Epistolary Novel: Its Origin, Development, Decline, and Residuary Influence*. Philadelphia: Univ. of Pennsylvania Press, 1933.

Singer relates *Spectator* no. 375 to *Pamela*.

Smithers, Peter. *The Life of Joseph Addison*. 2nd ed.
Oxford: Clarendon Press, 1968.

In writing about the *Tatler* in Chapter V, Smithers describes Addison's grave humor, his predilection for
allegory and fable, and his belief that example is more
persuasive than precept. In Chapter VI, "A Spectator
in the Wilderness," he argues for Addison's dominant
role in the *Spectator* and sees Sir Roger de Coverley as
his skillful filling out of Steele's original. Smithers
also explores the device of letters written by the
authors.

Snyder, Henry L. "The Identity of Monoculus in *The
Tatler*." *Philological Quarterly*, 48 (1969), 20-26.

Snyder finds the original for this character to be James
Ashburne, a well known, one-eyed gambler.

Stephens, John C., Jr. "Addison as Social Critic." *Emory
University Quarterly*, 21 (1965), 157-72.

Stephens argues that Addison had to instruct by indirection and thus used satire, raillery, and fiction to
express his social assumptions about human interdependence, the gentleman, women, and marriage. Stephens
discusses individual examples.

Stevick, Philip. "Familiarity in the Addisonian Familiar
Essay." *College Composition and Communication*, 16
(1965), 169-73.

Stevick describes the rhetorical means Addison and
Steele used to make Mr. Spectator the spokesman for men
of taste, moderation, and good will. He shows how the
"pseudo-I" of the *Spectator* came to represent the shared
reasonableness of authors and audience, "we," while
fictional characters, "they," assumed dubious positions.
The fictional letter to the editor further broke down
the "one way communication" from Mr. Spectator to the
general reader to induce his participation.

Taine, H. A. *History of English Literature*. Trans. H.
Van Laun. Edinburgh: Edmonston & Douglas, 1871.

Taine identifies Addison with Mr. Spectator and believes
his narrative technique uses too much telling instead
of showing. He suggests how Addison transformed his
morality into sketches and stories and calls him the
unwitting inventor of the novel.

Tave, Stuart M. *The Amiable Humorist: A Study in the
Comic Theory and Criticism of the Eighteenth and Early
Nineteenth Centuries*. Chicago: Univ. of Chicago Press,
1960.

Although Tave refers often to the theories of Addison and Steele in developing his concept of amiable humor, his only extended discussion of their work appears in Chapter 5, "True Humor and English Liberty." There he analyzes the character of Sir Roger de Coverley, whose essential quality is not one folly but a "diffuse delightfulness and innocence." This comic character is an expression of good nature, not a satiric victim. Tave argues that Sir Roger is instructive as well as amusing and that he possesses important virtues.

Thackeray, William Makepeace. *The English Humourists of the Eighteenth Century. A Series of Lectures.* Ed. C. B. Wheeler. Oxford: Clarendon Press, 1913.

In this series, originally published in 1853, Addison is the subject of half of the second lecture; Steele, of the third. Thackeray calls the former a gentle satirist and kind judge and praises Sir Roger de Coverley as delightfully ridiculous. In describing the "naturalness" of Steele, Thackeray states that the fiction of the *Spectator* is its "truest" part.

Thompson, Elbert N. S. "Tom Brown and Eighteenth-Century Satirists." *Modern Language Notes,* 32 (1917), 90-94.

Thompson finds antecedents for fictional techniques and scenes in the *Spectator* in Brown's works.

Turner, Margaret. "The Influence of La Bruyère on the 'Tatler' and the 'Spectator.'" *Modern Language Review,* 48 (1953), 10-16.

Through analysis of various characters Turner shows how the example of La Bruyère led Addison, Steele, and Budgell to create portraits which are more personal than typical, yet also illustrative of social or moral categories.

Upham, Alfred H. *The Typical Forms of English Literature.* New York: Oxford Univ. Press, 1917.

In a chapter on the personal essay Upham describes briefly the forms found in the *Tatler* and the *Spectator* --the detached observer, the moral tale, the key novel, the comedy of manners, character satire, and imaginary letters.

Walker, Hugh. *The English Essay and Essayists.* London: Dent, 1915.

In Chapter 5, "The Queen Anne Essayists," Walker makes appreciative comments about the club framework in the *Spectator,* praises Sir Roger de Coverley as Addison's major achievement, and defends Steele from previous detractors.

Watson, Melvin. *Magazine Serials and the Essay Tradition 1746-1820*. Humanities Series, No. 6. Baton Rouge: Louisiana State Univ. Press, 1956.

In Chapter 1, "The Tradition Established," Watson judges Addison's fiction more effective in satirizing foibles and Steele's better in matters of practical morality linked to manners. He discusses their use of the persona and framework, the letter, the character sketch, the vision, the fable, the oriental tale, and other minor devices, like the courts. He concludes that Steele could subordinate his morality to his storytelling more effectively than Addison.

_____. "The *Spectator* Tradition and the Development of the Familiar Essay." *ELH*, 13 (1946), 189-215.

Watson argues that the fictitious character of the speaker in the *Tatler* and the *Spectator* was antithetical to the nature of the familiar essay and inhibited its development.

Weitzman, Arthur J. "The Oriental Tale in the Eighteenth Century: A Reconsideration." *Studies on Voltaire and the Eighteenth Century*, 58 (1967), 1839-1855.

Finding moralizing and sententious features intrinsic to the first translation of the *Arabian Nights* (by Antoine Galland), Weitzman discusses how European authors used the oriental tale as a "painless" means of teaching. His analysis of *Spectator* no. 159 shows a fusion of Christian allegory and oriental myth. Weitzman believes that the vague oriental milieu of fiction by Addison, Johnson, and Voltaire emphasized the generality of their truths.

_____. "Pseudonymous Publication as a Mode of Satire." *Satire Newsletter*, 6 (1968), 12-19.

Weitzman discusses the advantages of the device of an ironic observer in the *Tatler* and the *Spectator*.

Welker, John J. "The Spectator's Notable Jew." *Studies in Philology*, 28 (1931), 519-21.

Welker identifies a political reference in *Spectator* no. 380, in a fictional letter from Betty Lemon.

Wheatley, Katherine E. "Addison's Portrait of the Neo-Classical Critic (The *Tatler*, No. 165)." *Review of English Studies*, n.s. 1 (1950), 245-47.

Wheatley identifies a source for this character in Molière's *Critique de l'École des Femmes*.

Wiatt, William H. "A Note on Addison's Upholsterer." *Notes and Queries*, 197 (1952), 236.

Wiatt points out some absurdities in the newsmonger of
the *Tatler*.

Winter, Albert. "Joseph Addison als Humorist in seinem
Einfluss auf Dickens Jugendwerke." *Anglia*, 21 (1899),
453-508.

Winter establishes Dickens's familiarity with the
Tatler and the *Spectator* and shows their influence on
Sketches by Boz, *The Pickwick Papers*, and *Master Humphrey's Clock*, especially in character delineation and
the use of comic and pathetic situations. He finds
analogues in the *Sketches* for Mr. Spectator, Sir Roger
de Coverley, and Will Honeycomb, for example, and cites
more than fifty parallel passages in Addison's fiction
and Dickens's.

Winton, Calhoun. *Captain Steele: The Early Career of
Richard Steele*. Baltimore: Johns Hopkins Press, 1964.

In Chapter V, "Isaac Bickerstaff's *Tatler*," Winton
states that Bickerstaff's good humor was a departure
from the prevailing tone of pamphlets and periodicals.
He provides useful information for reconstructing the
context of some of the more topical fiction, especially
political allegories. In Chapter VI, "The Years of the
Spectator," Winton discusses the sympathetic representation of trading interests and suggests how the reader's
respect for Sir Roger de Coverley was diminished by the
"formidable" Sir Andrew Freeport.

_____. "Steele, The Junto, and *The Tatler* No. 4."
Modern Language Notes, 72 (1957), 178-82.

Winton analyzes this political allegory, judging it to
be Whig propoganda.

Addendum: Item appearing too late for alphabetical listing.

Furtwangler, Albert. "The Making of Mr. Spectator."
Modern Language Quarterly, 38 (1977), 21-39.

While suggesting that Addison and Steele created the
fictional editor of the *Tatler* and the *Spectator* chiefly
for self-protection, Furtwangler argues the results were
full-blown characters who provided a new way of giving
voice to the interests, hopes, restraints, and ideals of
their age. He traces the development of this eidolon,
from Steele's beginnings with Isaac Bickerstaff in 1708
to Addison's presentation of Mr. Spectator in 1711, as a
new method for education of the reading public. Stressing the links between the *Tatler* and contemporary newspapers, Furtwangler points out the originality of the
Spectator as a daily essay paper, a result of Addison's
going beyond the limitation of the *Tatler* format. The

character of Mr. Spectator, he argues, resulted from a
unique interaction of authors, situation, and audience.

114511